Thorana S. Nelson, PhD
Terry S. Trepper, PhD
Editors

101 More Interventions in Family Therapy

Pre-publication
REVIEWS,
COMMENTARIES,
EVALUATIONS . . .

The Haworth Press, Inc.

101 More Interventions in Family Therapy

HAWORTH Marriage and the Family
Terry S. Trepper, PhD
Executive Editor

101 More Interventions in Family Therapy

Thorana S. Nelson, PhD
Terry S. Trepper, PhD
Editors

The Haworth Press
New York • London

The Haworth Press, Inc., 10 Alice Street, Binghamton, NY 13904-1580

Cover design by Marylouise E. Doyle.

Library of Congress Cataloging-in-Publication Data

101 more interventions in family therapy / Thorana S. Nelson, Terry S. Trepper, editors.
     p. cm.
   Includes bibliographical references and index.
   ISBN 0-7890-0570-0 (alk. paper).
   1. Family psychotherapy. 2. Family psychotherapy—Case studies. I. Nelson, Thorana Strever. II. Trepper, Terry S.
RC488.5.A17 1998
616.89'156—dc21

97-51448
CIP

To Vic, Travis, Stacy, and Wendi

* * *

In memory of my father, Arthur Trepper, for the wisdom
he imparted, for the motivation to work hard he expected,
and the playfulness and creativity he inspired.

CONTENTS

ABOUT THE EDITORS

Thorana S. Nelson, PhD, is the Director of the Marriage and Family Therapy Program and Associate Professor of Family and Human Development at Utah State University in Logan, Utah. She has taught in marriage and family therapy training programs since 1986 and has been a family therapist since 1981. The experience of teaching and supervising student therapists has given her a wide perspective about the practice of family therapy.

Terry S. Trepper, PhD, is Director of the Family Studies Center, Professor of Psychology, and Professor of Marriage and Family Therapy at Purdue University-Calumet in Hammond, Indiana. He is an APA Fellow, an AAMFT Clinical member and Approved Supervisor, an AASECT Certified Sex Therapist, and a Diplomate in the American Board of Sexology. He is the Editor of the *Journal of Family Psychotherapy* and Executive Editor of The Haworth Press's Marriage and the Family book program. Dr. Trepper is the co-author (with Mary Jo Barrett) of *Systemic Treatment of Incest: A Therapeutic Handbook; Treating Incest; A Multiple Systems Perspective* (The Haworth Press, 1987); and (with Thorana Nelson) *101 Interventions in Family Therapy* (The Haworth Press, 1993).

CONTRIBUTORS

Jerome F. Adams, PhD, is Associate Professor of Family Therapy, Department of Human Development and Family Studies, University of Rhode Island, Kingston, Rhode Island.

Scot M. Allgood, PhD, is Assistant Professor in the Department of Family and Human Development, Utah State University, Logan, Utah.

Tom Andersen, MD, was the first country doctor in northern Norway, before entering psychiatry. He is currently Professor of Social Psychiatry at the University of Tromso in northern Norway.

Charles P. Barnard, EdD, is Professor and Director of Marriage and Family Therapy, University of Wisconsin-Stout, Menomonie, Wisconsin.

Linda G. Bell, PhD, is Professor of Psychology and Director of Training in Family Therapy, University of Houston-Clear Lake, Houston, Texas.

Judith Maria Bermúdez, MS, is a graduate of the Marriage and Family Therapy Program at Purdue University Calumet, Hammond, Indiana, and is currently a doctoral student in the Marriage and Family Therapy Program at Virginia Polytechnic Institute and State University, Blacksburg, Virginia.

Richard J. Bischoff, PhD, is Assistant Professor of Marriage, Family, and Child Counseling at the University of San Diego, San Diego, California.

Pasha D. Blundo, MFT, is a graduate of Pacific Lutheran University and is currently leading primary preventive programs in Essex, Connecticut.

Stephanie Brooks, MSW, LSW, is Associate Director, Graduate Programs in Couple and Family Therapy; Assistant Professor, Department of Mental Health Sciences, Allegheny University of the Health Sciences; and is in private practice with Centra, Philadelphia, Pennsylvania.

Don G. Brown, MEd, STD, is in private practice in Fort Walton Beach, Florida.

Rudy Buckman, EdD, is a therapist with the Salesmanship Club Youth and Family Centers and is a faculty member of the Reunion Institute, Dallas, Texas.

Özlem Çamli, PhD, is a clinical psychologist at Connecticut Children's Medical Center School, Newington, Connecticut.

Gabrielle Carey, MA, is an associate of the Marriage and Family Institute of San Antonio and a PhD student at St. Mary's University, San Antonio, Texas.

Thomas D. Carlson, MS, is a doctoral student in Marriage and Family Therapy and co-director of the Reauthoring Center at Iowa State University, Ames, Iowa.

Brenda Carroll, MA, is a marriage and family therapist with Crittenton Behavioral Health Center in Kansas City, Missouri.

Young Hee Chang, MS, currently resides in Chicago, Illinois.

Wanda Clark, PhD, is in private practice in Lubbock, Texas, and on the faculty of South Plains College.

Jacqueline Corcoran, PhD, is Assistant Professor and co-director of the Community Service Clinic at the School of Social Work, University of Texas at Arlington, Arlington, Texas.

Denise D. Daniels, MA, is a Clinical Psychology Intern at Boston Medical Center, Center for Multicultural Training, and is a student in the PhD program in Clinical Psychology at Loyola University, Chicago, Illinois.

Mary E. Dankoski, MS, is a doctoral student in Marriage and Family Therapy at Purdue University, West Lafayette, Indiana.

Sharon A. Deacon, MS, is a doctoral student in Marriage and Family Therapy at Purdue University, West Lafayette, Indiana.

Debra L. Del Vecchio is a family therapist in Phoenix, Arizona.

Shannon B. Dermer, MS, is a PhD candidate, Kansas State University, Manhattan, Kansas.

Gary M. Diamond, PhD, is a Post-Doctoral Fellow in the Department of Psychiatry at the University of Pennsylvania and the Child Guidance Center of the Children's Hospital of Philadelphia, Philadelphia, Pennsylvania.

Gary C. Dumbrill, CQSW, MSW, is a doctoral social work student at the University of Toronto, and is a consultant and trainer specializing in child welfare issues.

Patricia M. Dyer, BA, is an MSW candidate at the University of New England School of Social Work, Biddeford, Maine.

Mony Elkaïm, MD, is a neuropsychiatrist and family therapist. He is Professor at the Free University of Brussels, Belgium, Director of the Institute for Family and Human System Studies in Brussels, and President of the European Family Therapy Association.

Beth M. Erickson, PhD, is Founder and Clinical Director of Family Resources Institute in Santa Fe and Albuquerque, New Mexico.

Ana Ulloa Estrada, PhD, is Assistant Professor, Department of Family Resources Human Development, Arizona State University, Tempe, Arizona.

David L. Fenell, PhD, is Professor of Counselor Education and Coordinator of the Counseling and Human Services Masters Degree program at the University of Colorado at Colorado Springs. He is also the Director of the University Counseling Center and Coordinator of family therapy training.

Celia B. Ferguson, PhD, LMFT, is in private practice in Knoxville, Tennessee and is an adjunct faculty member at Carson-Newman College, Jefferson City, Tennessee.

Maria T. Flores, PhD, is in private practice at the Marriage and Family Institute of San Antonio, Texas.

Yvette G. Flores-Ortiz, PhD, is Associate Professor of Psychology and Director of the Chicana/Chicano Studies Program, University of California, Davis.

Catherine E. Ford Sori, MS, is a doctoral student in Marriage and Family Therapy at Purdue University West Lafayette, Indiana, and a staff therapist at Samaritan Counseling Center in Munster, Indiana.

Peter Fraenkel, PhD, is Director and faculty member of Research and Program Evaluation, Ackerman Institute for the Family, New York City; Clinical Assistant Professor, Department of Psychiatry, New York University Medical Center; and Director of PREP at NYU, New York City.

Cynthia Franklin, PhD, is Associate Professor in the School of Social Work at the University of Texas at Austin.

Diane R. Gehart-Brooks, PhD, is Assistant Professor of Marriage and Family Therapy, California State University, Fresno.

Donald K. Granvold, LMSW-ACP, PhD, is Professor, School of Social Work, University of Texas at Arlington, and maintains a part-time clinical practice in Arlington, Texas.

Kim Hander, MS, is a family therapist for Youthville, Garden City, Kansas.

Penny Haney, MA, is a doctoral student in Child Clinical and Family Psychology at Loyola University, Chicago.

Evan F. Hanson, MA, LMFT, is in private practice in Ogden, Utah.

Adam L. Hill, MS, is a doctoral candidate, Kent State University's Counselor Education and Supervision program, Kent, Ohio.

Peter J. Jankowski, MS, is a PhD student in Marriage and Family Therapy at Texas Tech University, Lubbock, Texas.

Lee N. Johnson, MS, is a doctoral candidate in Marriage and Family Therapy at Kansas State University, Manhattan, Kansas.

Sharon Z. Johnson is a doctoral student at Loyola University at Chicago-Lake Shore in their Clinical Psychology program.

Peter A. Kahle, PhD, is a faculty member of the Reunion Institute in Dallas, Texas.

Florence W. Kaslow, PhD, is Director of the Florida Couples and Family Institute in North Palm Beach. She is Visiting Professor of Medical Psychology in Psychology at Duke University Medical Center, Durham, North Carolina, and Visiting Professor of Psychology at the Florida Institute of Technology Graduate School, Melbourne, Florida.

Nadine J. Kaslow, PhD, ABPP, is Associate Professor, Emory University Department of Psychiatry and Behavioral Science, and Chief Psychologist at Grady Health System, Atlanta, Georgia.

David L. Kearns, PhD, is Associate Professor of Clinical Family Medicine, University of Iowa, Iowa City, Iowa.

Bruce P. Kuehl, PhD, is Associate Professor, University of Wisconsin-Stout, Menomonie, Wisconsin.

Luciano L'Abate, PhD, ABEPP, is Professor Emeritus of Psychology, Georgia State University, Atlanta, Georgia, and Director of Multicultural Services, Cross Keys Counseling Center, Conley, Georgia.

Peter Lehmann, DSW, is Assistant Professor of Social Work, University of Texas at Arlington, Arlington, Texas.

Karen G. Lewis, ACSW, EdD, is in private practice in Washington, DC.

Howard A. Liddle, EdD, is Professor of Psychiatry and Behavioral Sciences, and Deputy Director, Center for Family Studies, University of Miami School of Medicine, Miami, Florida.

Susan K. Mackey, PhD, LMFT, is Director of Postgraduate Education at the Family Institute of Northwestern University, Evanston, Illinois.

William C. Madsen, PhD, is on the faculty of the Family Institute of Cambridge, Watertown, Massachusetts.

Peter E. Maynard, PhD, is Professor and Director of the Marriage and Family Therapy Program at the University of Rhode Island, Kingston, Rhode Island.

Beverly McKee, PhD, LCSW, is in private practice in Knoxville, Tennessee.

Israela Meyerstein, LCSW, is in private practice in Baltimore, Maryland, where she directs the Family and Marriage Therapy Program of Sheppard Pratt.

Katherine J. Michelson, MS, is a doctoral candidate at Purdue University and a marriage and family therapy resident at Marriage and Family Counseling Service in Rock Island, Illinois.

Maureen L. Minarik, PhD, graduated in 1997 from American University and is currently completing postdoctoral hours in Connecticut.

Jan Nealer, PhD, is part-time Assistant Professor in the Marriage and Family Therapy Program at the University of New Hampshire and a Clinical Program Manager at Stafford Psychotherapy and Family Services in Dover, New Hampshire.

Victor H. Nelson, STM, is the director of Evergreen Family Therapy Center in Logan, Utah, and is co-founder of Innovative Management Systems, a consulting company in Ogden, Utah.

D. Kim Openshaw, PhD, LCSW, LMFT, is Associate Professor of Family and Human Development and Marriage and Family Therapy, and Adjunct Associate Professor of Clinical Psychology in the Department of Psychology at Utah State University, Logan, Utah.

Jan Osborn, PhD, is a core faculty member at the Family Institute of Northwestern University in Evanston, Illinois, and is in private practice in Chicago.

S. Carolyn Patton, EdD, is in private practice in Knoxville, Tennessee.

David Pearson, PhD, is a faculty member in the Family Therapy Training Program, Calgary Regional Heath Authority, Calgary, Alberta, Canada.

Carol L. Philpot, PsyD, is Associate Dean, Associate Director of Clinical Training, Director of Community Psychological Services of Florida Tech, and Professor of Psychology at the School of Psychology, Florida Institute of Technology, Melbourne, Florida.

Fred P. Piercy, PhD, is Director of the Marriage and Family Therapy Program, Department of Child Development and Family Studies, Purdue University, West Lafayette, Indiana.

Phoebe S. Prosky, MSW, is Director of A Center for the Awareness of Pattern in Freeport, Maine.

David W. Purcell, JD, PhD, is a Behavioral Scientist for the Centers for Disease Control and Prevention, Behavioral Intervention Research Branch, division of HIV and AIDS, Atlanta, Georgia.

Sharon G. Renter, MS, is Director of AIDS Education, Nebraska Department of Health and Human Services, Lincoln, Nebraska.

Norman H. Reuss, PhD, SCADC, is the Substance Abuse Services Treatment Coordinator for Community Health Plan/Kaiser Permanente in Burlington, Vermont.

John M. Robbins, PhD, is a family therapist at the Salesmanship Club Youth and Family Centers, Inc. in Dallas, Texas.

Janine Roberts, EdD, is Professor and family therapist at the University of Massachusetts, Amherst, Massachusetts.

Thomas W. Roberts, PhD, is Chair of the Department of Family and Consumer Sciences at California State University at Long Beach.

Kristin E. Robinson, LCSW, PhD, manages a partial day treatment program at the Children's Behavior Therapy Unit of Valley Mental Health in Salt Lake City, Utah.

Joellyn L. Ross, PhD, is in private practice in Cherry Hill, New Jersey, and is a faculty member of the PENN Council for Relationships (founded as The Marriage Council of Philadelphia).

Stephanie A. Ross, MA, is a doctoral student in Clinical Psychology at Loyola University, Chicago.

Laura M. I. Saunders, PsyD, is a staff psychologist at the Institute of Living and a coordinator of Your Turf, a gay/lesbian youth group in Hartford, Connecticut.

Catherine R. Scanlon, PhD, is Director of the Counseling and Human Development Center in Kent State University's College of Education, Kent, Ohio.

Maureen Semans is a doctoral student in Marriage and Family Therapy at Syracuse University in Syracuse, New York.

Wendy Wen-Yi Shieh, PhD, is the Deputy Director of Tanjong Pagar Family Service Centre and MacPherson Moral Family Service Centre in Singapore.

Craig W. Smith, PhD, is Associate Professor of Marriage and Family Therapy, University of Nebraska, Lincoln, Nebraska.

Debra W. Smith, MEd, LCSW, is Program Coordinator at Rutgers University School of Social Work, Continuing Education Program; is on the faculty of Warren County Community College, Washington, New Jersey; and is in private practice.

Geoffrey L. Smith, MA, MFCCI, is a therapist on the Sex Abuse Treatment team at Tulare Youth Service Bureau, Tulare, California.

Richard B. Smith, MS, is the marriage and family therapist on the Geriatric Adult and Adolescent Psychiatric Unit of East Alabama Medical Center, Opelika, Alabama.

Maryhelen Snyder, PhD, is Clinical Director of the New Mexico Relationship Enhancement Institute, and adjunct faculty at the Department of Psychiatry and Psychology at the University of New Mexico, Albuquerque, New Mexico.

Robert F. Stahmann, PhD, is Professor of Family Sciences in the Marriage and Family Graduate Programs, Brigham Young University, Provo, Utah.

Frank N. Thomas, PhD, is Associate Professor, Family Therapy Program, Texas Woman's University, Denton, and Adjunct Faculty, Brite Divinity School, Texas Christian University, Forth Worth, Texas.

Volker Thomas, PhD, is Assistant Professor of Marriage and Family Therapy, Department of Child Development and Family Studies, Purdue University, West Lafayette, Indiana.

Tina M. Timm, ACSW, LCSW, is a doctoral student in Marriage and Family Therapy, Purdue University, West Lafayette, Indiana.

Carolyn Tubbs, PhD, is Assistant Professor of Family Social Science and a member of the MFT faculty, University of Minnesota, St. Paul, Minnesota.

James Verser, MDiv, MS, EdS, is a Marriage and Family Therapist in private practice in Bloomsbury, New Jersey.

Betty Vos, PhD, LCSW, is Adjunct Associate Professor, University of Utah Graduate School of Social Work, Salt Lake City, and is also in private practice at the Salt Lake Bristlecone Center in Salt Lake City, Utah.

Ellen F. Wachtel, JD, PhD, is in private practice in New York City.

Allison Waterworth, PsyD, is currently completing her post-doctoral residency at the Center for Emotional and Behavioral Health in Vero Beach, Florida, specializing in work with children and families.

Kyle N. Weir is enrolled in a doctoral program at the University of Southern California at Los Angeles.

Joseph L. Wetchler, PhD, is Professor and Director of the Marriage and Family Therapy Program at Purdue University-Calumet, Hammond, Indiana.

Mark B. White, PhD, is Assistant Professor, Department of Human Development and Family Studies, Auburn University, Auburn, Alabama.

Daniel J. Wiener, PhD, is Associate Professor of Marriage and Family Therapy at Central Connecticut State University, New Britain, Connecticut.

G. Alan Willard, DMin, LMFT, is affiliated with the Family Place and the Pastoral Counseling Center, in Roanoke, Virginia, and is a doctoral candidate in Marriage and Family Therapy at Virginia Polytechnic University in Blacksburg, Virginia.

Jon L. Winek, PhD, is an Assistant Professor and Program Director of Marriage and Family Therapy, Department of Human Development and Psychological Counseling, Appalachian State University, Boone, North Carolina.

Toni S. Zimmerman, PhD, is Associate Professor in the Department of Human Development and Family Studies at Colorado State University, Fort Collins, Colorado. She is also the Director of the Marriage and Family Therapy Graduate Program.

Preface

Five years ago, when we published *101 Interventions in Family Therapy*, we had no way of knowing the interest it would generate. It has received wonderful reviews in professional journals across the disciplines, we have had much better than expected sales of the book from all around the world, and we received a large number of inquiries from clinicians wanting to contribute to a second book, should it ever be written. The book was not only being used by professional clinicians seeking stimulating ideas to improve their therapy, but also as a graduate text *in practica* in all clinical disciplines. People were writing things such as "Creativity just oozes from the pages . . ." and describing the book as "exciting and energizing" and "highly entertaining and enlightening."

Needless to say, we have been quite pleased with the response. Our original idea, to gather exciting and innovative interventions from *practicing* clinicians, was clearly a success. We had hoped to replicate in book form the experience of going to a conference, meeting with other therapists, and sharing our personal great clinical discoveries. From all that we have seen and heard, our original intentions have been realized.

What we also realized, however, was that there is an almost endless supply of great ideas from people in the field. Soon after we submitted our first book, we started receiving queries about a second one from people who hadn't heard about the project until the book was completed. *The Journal of Family Psychotherapy* had been running a section called Intervention Interchange, which offered short, innovative interventions in a format similar to those in *101 Interventions* and which had many more excellent submissions than could be published. And whenever we did training and workshops, participants would offer wonderful interventions that we wished we could have put in *101 Interventions in Family Therapy*. There was only one thing to do: put together a second book!

The current book is a culmination of a great deal of work by a great number of people. Certainly we want to thank the authors who have contributed their experience, ideas, and insights. Some of their names you will recognize as leaders in many disciplines loosely joined by the term "family therapy." Some of their names you will not recognize because they are therapists from around the world who, while perhaps not famous, are nonetheless brilliant in their work.

We want to thank Bill Palmer of The Haworth Press, who has had constant faith in both of these projects throughout. His support of these books, along with the entire Haworth Marriage and the Family series, has been very important to us.

Finally, we want to thank Laura Reinke, who tirelessly and carefully edited and indexed both books. She did this while working with a full caseload of clients, going to graduate school full-time, writing her thesis, and trying to have some semblance of a family life. For this extra effort, we are truly grateful.

We hope you will enjoy *101 More Interventions in Family Therapy* as much as most readers did the first book. You will find this volume full of interesting, exciting, and delightful interventions that you can use immediately in your work. Although the book has a topical index, we hope you will just read it, one chapter at a time, for pleasure. You may not know what could spark your own creativity, and reading and storing away an idea may lead to a solution with a totally different type of case down the road. However you read it, we hope that it will inspire you to try new things in your clinical work.

Thorana S. Nelson, PhD
Terry S. Trepper, PhD

Don't Just Do Something, Stand There

Mark B. White

INTRODUCTION AND THEORETICAL FOUNDATION

One of the classic interactional patterns familiar to therapists who work with couples is the emotional pursuer-distancer relationship. One member of the couple desires greater intimacy and emotional closeness and pursues his or her partner. The other member of the couple is uncomfortable with greater intimacy and, accordingly, distances. A reciprocal, vicious cycle is then created. The more one partner pursues, the more the other partner distances. When the pursuer tires of pursuing and begins to distance, the roles often reverse, with the former distancer now pursuing the former pursuer (Freeman, 1992; Karpel, 1994).

Until recently, I have not had a great deal of success assisting couples in breaking this cycle. I have tried the intervention described in this chapter several times with limited success; however, it worked quite splendidly with the last couple with which I tried it. As I have reflected on its success, I believe that several variables were associated with this couple and with the way in which the intervention was implemented that have given me a better understanding of how to use it. The essence of this intervention is to encourage the persuer to stand still, neither pursuing nor distancing. This allows the distancer to approach on his or her own terms.

The theoretical foundation for this intervention has three basic elements. First, it begins with the conceptualization of this pattern as a reflection of a basic systems property. The behavior of one person or element in a system perturbs the other persons or elements in the system, who behave in response to this perturbation. Second, to better explain the "fuel" that often drives these interactions, I have turned to Bowen Family Systems Theory (Kerr and Bowen, 1988). In this theory, anxiety is identified as the key emotional process that drives the distance-pursuit cycle. Third, I have framed this emotional process as similar to magnetism in the physical universe. When I was a boy, my father returned from a business trip with a pair of small, white dogs with magnet bases. When the dogs were face to face, an advance by one would result in a retreat by the other. If I held one firmly and advanced the other, I could feel the magnetic "tension" in the relationship. With practice, I could gingerly advance one dog until I began to feel the tension and noticed the other dog beginning to move. This is the process I hoped to translate into marital interaction. Teaching members of a couple to stand still involves teaching the pursuer to stop pursuing at the onset of the tension and then to stand still and to wait until the partner is able to tolerate increased intimacy or make his or her own overtures for increased closeness.

ASSESSMENT

Recognizing a pursuit-distance cycle tends not to be difficult; most couples come in citing it as part of the presenting problem (e.g., "She's always nagging at me when I try to watch TV and relax after work"; "He often closes up and doesn't want to talk with me after we have sex"; "After that brief fling with my co-worker I've tried everything to get close to her and she keeps pushing me away.") If not identified at intake, this cycle has a way of revealing itself the first time the therapist prescribes any sort of intimacy-enhancing intervention. The intervention described here is appropriate if the therapist and the clients are in agreement that this pattern is a problem they want to focus on. Other issues, such as sexual dysfunction, power struggles, violence, infidelity, and so on, take precedence. Once these more pressing issues are resolved or made more manageable, then work on the pursuit-distance cycle can proceed.

INTERVENTION

There are five steps to the intervention. First, the couple is asked to identify typical situations that either trigger the pattern or are associated with the pattern. Second, each member of the couple is asked to identify his or her thoughts and feelings throughout the process. Of specific importance are (1) the thoughts and beliefs associated with the anxiety that propels the pursuer and (2) the thoughts and beliefs associated with the need to distance on the part of the distancer. Third, the clients are encouraged to develop new, shared ways to communicate their internal experiences during these times. Simple phrases such as "I need connection right now," "It's getting too hot in here for me," or "I'm feeling nervous again" can be agreed upon and then used by the couple in these situations. Fourth, assuming that one partner typically initiates the pursuit pattern, the pursuer is coached in the art of standing still. Standing still involves discontinuing the pursuit, but not distancing. It involves managing the anxiety associated with the distance from the partner by engaging in other activities or seeking out friends or other family members. The critical (and difficult) aspect of standing still occurs when the former distancer makes advances. When this occurs, it is crucial that the former pursuer not pull back by refusing to engage in intimate conversation or by withholding affection or sex. Rather, he or she should cautiously accept the advances, allowing the degree of intimacy to increase gradually. Finally, it is helpful for the therapist to work with the couple in finding a positive metaphor for the process. Although this may include using the shared language discussed previously, it also includes finding ways to depathologize both the pursuer and the distancer roles and encourages the couple to see the relational nature of their "dance."

RESULTS

My most recent success with this intervention was with a young, traditional, blue-collar couple that sought marital therapy after the wife returned home from a several-month stay with some friends in order to decide the future of her marriage; I will call them Ted and Alice. Alice had left following the revelation that Ted had been unfaithful. Ted reported that he had very little need for intimacy and connection and that Alice's persistent requests for connection and for assurance that he wanted to be in the marriage had pushed him further away. Alice noted that her family of origin was quite dysfunctional and that she was frequently insecure in social relationships, especially her marriage in light of the disclosure of Ted's affair. She was willing to forgive and stay in the relationship if Ted could provide her with some sort of hope for the future. Ted replied that he was there in therapy and that was all the evidence that she ought to need.

Their pursuit-distance cycle was framed in terms of Ted's and Alice's differing intimacy needs as well as Alice taking more than her share of the responsibility for the emotional functioning of the relationship. I assured Ted and Alice that Ted would begin taking more emotional responsibility once space was created for him to do so. Encouraging Alice to stand still was an attempt to create this space. She was quite perplexed by the assignment to stand still. My prescriptions did not possess face validity in her eyes; she did not think that *not* working hard on the relationship would further its growth. Nevertheless, she complied and indicated that she was willing to try what I recommended. I encouraged her to call or visit friends at those times when she wanted further closeness with Ted and it was apparent that he was not ready. We discussed the language each could use when they needed to manage their anxiety about intimacy. She learned to ask for assurance about the future of the relationship without pursuing further if it was not exactly how she would like it. He learned to ask for time in the "meat cooler" when things were getting too hot.

As Alice stood still and took less responsibility for the relationship, Ted began to take more initiative and responsibility. We met weekly for about a month. During those four weeks, Alice and Ted made significant progress in managing the intimacy and anxiety in their relationship. Both were somewhat confused about how this occurred, but they persisted in playing out their new roles. They terminated somewhat prematurely, in my opinion, because they were moving to another part of the country. However, the last feedback I got about them was that things were going quite well. Standing still appears to have been successful.

CONTRAINDICATIONS

In my experience, a negative correlation exists between the degree of anxiety in the couple system and the potential success of this intervention. In other words, couples for which significant anxiety exists concerning the future of the relationship are not good candidates for "standing still." It is also crucial that both parties commit to working on the relationship, regardless of the outcome. As a student therapist intern, I was frustrated by my inability to intervene successfully with couples who displayed a pursuit-distance cycle, and I began to develop this intervention. I prescribed standing still for a very dependent man whose wife had recently had an affair and who was seriously considering ending the marriage. Unfortunately, it was impossible for him to stand still. Unlike the couple mentioned above, this man and woman were unable to commit to working on the marriage for a set period of time.

Pursuit-distance patterns can be very frustrating for therapists and couples alike. However, if both individuals are willing to work on the relationship, the level of anxiety is tolerable, and violence or other crises are not present, I recommend standing still as a potential intervention.

REFERENCES

Freeman, D. W. (1992). *Family therapy with couples: The family-of-origin approach.* Northvale, NJ: Jason Aronson.

Karpel, M. A. (1994). *Evaluating couples.* New York: W. W. Norton.

Kerr, M. E. and Bowen, M. (1988). *Family evaluation.* New York: W. W. Norton.

Mirroring Movement for Increasing Family Cooperation

Daniel J. Wiener

I became interested in applying theater techniques (particularly improvisation) to family therapy in 1985 and have used, modified, and devised many such games and exercises in working clinically since that time (Wiener, 1994). The main advantages of these techniques are twofold: (1) in common with other action techniques, they encourage participation from less verbally-oriented family members (particularly children) who often become bored or feel excluded in "talk-only" therapy; and (2) they create effective learning experiences that often serve as blueprints or models for desirable changes in family interaction. This article features mirroring, an elementary theater exercise that heightens the connection that actors build with one another. I have used mirroring in the form described below in working with over a hundred couples and families.

INSTRUCTIONS FOR MIRRORING

Two players stand facing one another about five feet apart, remaining *silent* while looking into each other's eyes. The therapist assigns the roles of "leader," who moves his/her body slowly and continuously, and "follower," who moves symmetrically in sync with the leader, *within* their own limitations in physical mobility and flexibility, until the therapist calls "Change!" (usually from twenty seconds to one minute later), at which point they switch roles while movement continues. Movement can be of any sort so long as eye contact is maintained. Care should be taken to instruct the leader to move slowly and in such a way that the follower can keep up and not be forced to break the mirror. After calling a few alternating turns at leading and following, the therapist calls "Mutual!" which signals the participants to give up intentionally leading or following in favor of moving simultaneously. The entire exercise usually lasts less than five minutes.

5

Mirroring is primarily dyadic but can also be done by three or more family members who face inward in a circle. Then, however, reciprocal eye contact cannot be used, and movement symmetry is no longer mirror-like for all. Another variation is to have paired family members within a multiple-family group or a couples group maintain mirroring at a much greater distance in a large room where other pairs of players may come between them, necessitating movement that maintains eye contact and an ability to remain focused on one's partner despite considerable visual distraction.

Mirroring promotes attentiveness to one's partner. Since eye contact is held throughout, players use peripheral vision to track the movement of their partners, and they gain a greater awareness of the physical movement capacities and limitations of their partners. Players also come to terms with their attitudes toward cooperation as they experience the constant need to give in, adjust, and trust their own internal impulses. Cooperation entails a willingness to give up what is often experienced as one's prerogative to define self as distinct from others—a partial surrender of freedom of choice. On the other hand, there is an increase in positive emotional energy in receiving cooperation from others. Mirroring is both a test of family members' cooperation and an opportunity for them to practice it. The turns-taking structure of this exercise, where the roles of leader and follower quickly alternate with each other, rewards both players for cooperating.

The phase of mutuality opens the players to the possibility of belonging to a "we-ness" beyond hierarchy. While players usually report a preference for either leading or following, both positions are familiar. Mutuality is an elusive experience for most dyads; some players express doubt that it is even possible to achieve it. I have these clients move their own hands symmetrically and ask which hand was leading. It seems that mutuality comes and goes, easily replaced by leading or following. Yet, the more attentive the players are to each other when a reciprocally cooperative attitude is present, the greater the likelihood for achieving and sustaining mutuality. When attained, mutuality has a transcendent, joyous quality.

PRACTICAL ASPECTS IN CLINICAL APPLICATION

As I view mirroring as a form of cooperative play, I always emphasize that participation is voluntary and support any reluctant clients to wait until they feel ready, rather than coax them to try the exercise. Also, I side with a reluctant client whose family members are pressuring him/her to play. Eventually, nearly all members participate.

Not infrequently, players violate the instructions of this exercise because they experience them as too challenging, too restrictive, or an invitation to oppositional impulses. Of course, the therapist must distinguish instruction-violating responses from those engendered by confusion or inattention. Many leaders playfully or competitively attempt to "fake out" the follower with sudden or acrobatic moves that the follower cannot keep up with, while followers often break eye contact with their partners, moving in an asymmetrical way in relation to the leader. Rather than automatically focusing on attaining compliance, the therapist is often better off "joining the resistance" by adding instructions that encompass the different response, for example, by adding the instruction that players may now break the symmetry of the mirror and move in rhythm with their partners. Should the follower's movement be not only asymmetrical but also uncoordinated with the leader's, the therapist can instruct the players to continue moving in free form. On a deep level, the therapist who modifies the instructions in such ways is verbally mirroring the players, thereby making them "look good." The frequent result is that the follower follows instructions more closely thereafter. Later, such family members often report welcoming the contrast between such treatment and the upset of being "made wrong" by others in the past.

I use mirroring in therapy with virtually all couples and families in two distinct ways: to gauge the degree of attentiveness and cooperation available to different pairs of family members and as an intervention to facilitate greater attentiveness and cooperation. As a means of assessment, mirroring is best timed to coincide with the phase following the verbal exploration of presenting problems, when clients feel assured that the therapist has enough knowledge of their case to begin treatment.

Contraindications for utilizing mirroring fall into two categories: (1) when one or more family members have made clear that their agenda is not about cooperation (as when abuse or betrayal is the main issue); and (2) when there is considerable overt conflict or ill will, since I usually want them to have a successful experience. Clients who are highly defended intellectually not infrequently insist on my elaborate justification of the exercise, which comes down to their anxious attempts to control the session. With these clients, I find it best defer introducing mirroring, rather than become drawn into lengthy disputes.

Rarely, I offer the exercise to dyads that I expect will fail to cooperate at all, when verbal denial of any problem is present; their performance failure is far more convincing to them than any remark on my part. I usually introduce the exercise as a means by which all of us might better understand family interaction, whether or not the presenting problems previously described directly concern attention or cooperation. I also stress that it doesn't matter if they do well at it, that we will all learn from whatever happens.

After all of the pairs who are willing to play have had their turns, I ask about preferences for the role of leader or of follower, whether mutuality occurred, and for comparisons of their experiences with different partners. Frequently, family members make insightful connections between what happened during Mirroring and their interactions outside of therapy. By playing this exercise myself with different family members, I can also comparatively assess the degree of alignment I experience with different family members (naturally, therapists wishing to use Mirroring clinically should first practice it themselves with a variety of nonclinical partners).

As a family therapy intervention, I always use Mirroring after the family has already identified their problems as related to insufficient attentiveness and cooperation, and usually at a later stage when exclusively verbal therapy is yielding diminishing returns and clients are receptive to something new. I usually have the least conflictual dyad present attempt the exercise once, leaving later turns for more intensive work on the more distant or problematic relationships. Here I offer Mirroring as a safe method of practicing useful skills; I have them repeat the exercise while I coach them to improve. Their improvement in doing this exercise is often a powerful antidote to the demoralization that accompanies repeated, unsuccessful interaction around the real-life relationship problem. Once introduced, Mirroring can also be used at the beginning of sessions to promote a climate of focused support for the benefit of the work during the remainder of the session, or as homework to strengthen alignment and cooperation between distant or conflictual dyads.

REFERENCE

Wiener, D. J. (1994). *Rehearsals for growth: Theater improvisation for psychotherapists.* New York: W.W. Norton.

3

Seeing the Obvious:
Data Collection in Therapy

Joellyn L. Ross

When measurement replaces discussion, then calculation replaces debate.

S. S. Stevens

Collecting data and assessing the resulting objective information can be an effective intervention facilitating positive change while circumventing resistance. This therapeutic strategy is especially helpful for patients who have difficulty acknowledging the cause-and-effect relationships between their actions and their predicaments. Cognitive therapists have a long and effective tradition of asking patients to chart their dysfunctional behaviors and thoughts in order to develop mastery and to alleviate depression (Burns, 1980, 1990).

I have identified two types of data collection that are helpful in clarifying how the patient's own behavior or mood might contribute to the problem. In one, the patient is asked to do a "science project" wherein his or her problem behaviors are analyzed in relationship to a variety of variables. In the other, the patient is assigned the job of collecting data about the environment.

There are two types of patient problems which I have found lend themselves to therapeutic data collection and analysis: (1) psychogenic illness and other physical problems, and (2) dealing with young people who are not realistic about their expectations and limitations. Clinical examples will illustrate both ways of using data to clarify problems and generate solutions.

PHYSICAL PROBLEMS

People with psychosomatic health problems often feel controlled by their symptoms. Keeping charts on which the patient tracks three or four different variables can be very helping in determining what might be contributing to physical symptoms while helping the patient identify ways to develop some control over them. Also, by collecting data on both physical and emotional variables, patients who disavow an emotional connection to their physical problems can see the mind-body connection for themselves without feeling as if their actual physical symptoms are being discredited.

The most dramatic and unusual instance in my practice in which data collection helped with a physical problem—which we found was not psychogenic—occurred with a young woman who suffered severe irritable bowel syndrome (IBS—formerly known as colitis), which her frustrated family physician believed was "all in her head" since no medical intervention had helped and all diagnostic tests had come back normal.

At the first meeting with Sheila K., we discussed her IBS and how it was interfering with her life. She said she suffered severe abdominal cramping that sometimes forced her to stay home from work or school, and sometimes kept her from going out socially. She was a twenty-three-year-old woman who lived with her parents and was working part-time and going to school part-time. She had a new boyfriend with whom she reported having a good relationship, and said that living with her parents was fine for the time that she was working toward her college degree. Sheila said that she knew her physician thought she was some sort of "head case," but she disagreed strongly with his assessment of her. "My life is fine," she said, "except for these terrible stomach cramps."

I suggested to Sheila that a way we could find out for sure what was going on would be for her to collect data about herself and her cramps. Specifically, I asked her to chart (1) her cramps and their severity (on a scale of 1 to 10) on a daily basis; (2) everything she ate (i.e., keep a food diary); (3) unusual or stressful events each day; (4) where she was in her menstrual cycle; and (5) her mood each day. I told her I thought she probably was correct that it was a physical and not an emotional problem, and that was why we would chart her food intake, but that "just to see," we would collect the data about stressful events and her moods. Given that she was reporting no other problems that needed to be addressed, we scheduled an appointment for a month later.

My experience has been that when patients are willing to do the charting, they do it very well. The challenge is to encourage reluctant and less organized people to give it a try. Sheila was willing and she came in a month later carrying her chart, which she had kept diligently. We sat together and reviewed it and, to both our surprise, the only thing that seemed to be related to her abdominal symptoms was eating potatoes. Potatoes! I'd never heard of anyone being allergic to them, but maybe she was a first. We reviewed the chart carefully again, looking to see if we could draw other conclusions, but nothing came to mind. So, I suggested that Sheila stop eating potatoes for a month and continue to keep her chart. She agreed.

One month later, Sheila came back very happy to report that staying away from potatoes had resulted in no more abdominal cramps or pains. Who would have guessed that was the cause of her problems? Sheila was pleased and we agreed she need not return to therapy unless some problem were to arise. We also agreed that I would contact her physician who, reluctantly, later acknowledged he had misdiagnosed her problem.

I have had other patients for whom these "science projects" helped to identify emotional factors that were contributing to their physical distress and have found that keeping the chart and having hard data has facilitated the discussion of emotional issues.

ADOLESCENTS

Data collection and analysis also can help in working with adolescents who tend to be unrealistic about themselves and about what is necessary to live as an independent adult. Marnie G., for example, was a young woman whom I initially saw because she was being bullied by a student at her school and also because she suffered migraines. Assertiveness skills helped her to deal with the bully; charting and analyzing variables affecting her migraines helped us to isolate some of the causes of her headaches. She used this information to make changes that reduced the number of headaches she had.

Despite these significant gains, several years after I first met with Marnie and her family, she again came to see me, this time because she was unhappy with her life. After graduating from high school, Marnie had taken a clerical job with the municipality where she lived. Initially, she had liked the job a lot because there were many procedures to learn and she enjoyed the responsibility. She also liked having her own money. Soon, however, she became bored because, once she learned her job and had been doing it awhile, she realized that there likely would be no new challenges. She also quickly realized that what had seemed like big money to a high school graduate didn't go very far when it came to buying a car, paying car insurance, and paying other expenses.

We talked about her taking some college classes or going for technical training, but she resisted these ideas, saying that she was too tired in the evenings to think about doing anything other than watching TV. Her boyfriend, Barry, was in a similar rut, in an entry-level job with no significant future opportunities.

Over the course of several meetings, we talked about life and work and education, and I encouraged Marnie to think about what she wanted for her life five to ten years down the road. She reluctantly researched several local colleges and training programs, but still resisted taking any courses or even looking for another job. She did, however, have some ideas about what she wanted for her future: a nice house, travel (including cruises), a nice car, and pretty clothes.

One meeting, as I was talking with Marnie, S.S. Stevens' saying (at the beginning of this chapter) floated into my consciousness. I pulled out my calculator and handed Marnie some paper so she could write down numbers. "Okay," I said, "Let's figure out how much money you and Barry will need to make in order for you to have the kind of life you say you want." We started with the neighborhood in which she might want to live and how much houses there cost, and then went down a long list of monthly expenses: mortgage (or rent), utilities, telephone and cable TV, car payments and insurance, food, medical expenses, entertainment, clothes, etc., estimating amounts as we went along. As you might expect, the life Marnie wanted cost much more than either she or Barry ever could make in their present jobs. "You have a lot to think about," I told her. "I'd love to see you get what you want in life, but maybe you'll need to learn to live with less."

I didn't see Marnie for several months, since it was summertime, when many people take vacations from therapy. The following September, however, she came back and reported both she and Barry had signed up for courses, hers at a technical school and his at a local junior college. Calculation had, apparently, replaced debate.

REFERENCES

Burns, D. D. (1980). *Feeling good: The new mood therapy.* New York: Avon Books.

Burns, D. D. (1990). *Feeling good handbook.* New York: Plume Books.

4

Of Clocks and Rubber Bands:
On the Use of Props in Family Therapy

Luciano L'Abate

The purpose of this chapter is to describe the use of two props that have been used by this writer as invariable prescriptions in approximately four decades of clinical practice with children, couples, and families. A search of the literature failed to find any reference to similar use in therapy except for the use of tokens in behavioral therapies. Behavioral techniques, of course, have long used incentives and tokens as reinforcements for meritorious or positive behavior. Props have no incentive nor rewarding value. They are used to correct deficits or dysfunctional pattens of relating that need more than just words to be changed.

The first prop consists of prescribing the use of an alarm clock rather than allowing adults to continue functioning as alarm clocks for their child(ren). The second prop consists of prescribing the rubber band for extremely enmeshed couples who are not able to break away from each other and who persist in using the partner's behavior to excuse their own.

THE CLOCK

In most dysfunctional families, one symptom of dysfunction is problems going to bed at night and waking in the morning. Oftentimes, one of the more involved caretakers takes responsibility for waking up the child(ren). Once the adult takes responsibility for the child's getting up, among other symptoms, the child tends to rebel against the wake-up call by continuing to sleep, avoiding the wake-up call in a passive-aggressive fashion. This oppositional reaction on the child's part, of course, provokes an escalation on the part of the adult, such as becoming angry and frustrated and ending up screaming, usually resulting in a miserable morning for the whole family. The caretaker's overinvolvement with the identified patient (IP), of course, should be considered within its historical and situational antecedents as well as its consequences for the whole family (L'Abate, 1994; L'Abate and Baggett, 1997b).

The Meaning of the Symptom

Difficulties in getting up in the morning on the child's part are one of the many symptoms of family dysfunction when adult caretakers have failed to convey clear and firm instructions to the child, indicating a failure in hierarchical and generational boundaries that can be traced to the adult caretakers' inability to establish a clear coalition between adults and appropriate boundaries between caretakers and children. Caretakers have probably failed to develop a partnership that would allow them to parent children as a couple rather than as individuals. In single-parent families, this failure may indicate a covert power struggle between parent and child that may mirror the power struggle that occurred between parents before they split. In such struggles, nobody wins.

Prescription of the Clock

The prescription consists of having caretakers buy an alarm clock with the most unpleasant sound they can find. After the purchase, the caretakers need to sit down with the IP and inform him or her that, from now on, because the child is growing up, the child needs to learn to wake up without the help of the caretaker. Of course, this information is usually ignored by the child to the point that he or she "forgets" to set the alarm before going to bed or, when the alarm sounds in the morning, turns it off and continues to "sleep."

All of these maneuvers, of course, should be predicted and discussed beforehand so that an appropriate strategy can be devised to cope with the child's predicted reluctance to take responsibility. A strategy that is most difficult for enmeshed caretakers to follow, of course, is to leave the child to suffer the natural consequences of his or her actions. This idea may be difficult if it means the child will be late for school or will miss a day. If both caretakers work away from home during the day, it may be too dangerous to leave the child home alone. Hence, different strategies and consequences need to be considered. The child may be included in these deliberations. The therapist needs to consider all realistic and practical choices with the family and form a hierarchy of choices, ranging from the most to the least realistic and practical. It would be helpful to construct such a hierarchy in writing with a copy of the instructions for the parents and one copy for the therapist's file (L'Abate, 1997a).

Parents should expect that if the new prop is used consistently, the child will resist it for at least four days in a row. Hence, it is important for the caretakers to be very firm and consistent in its use. If the prop is used inconsistently, it will help demonstrate how the family works or fails to work. Usually, the parental coalition needs to be examined in terms of how caretakers defeat each other, often along authoritarian-permissive and over-involved-underinvolved polarizations. The child may learn to defeat the caretakers in the same way that they may defeat each other.

Contraindications for the Prescription

Clocks are extremely useful with families with preschool children, where prodromal patterns of overdependency can be broken more easily than with elementary school children. The younger the child, the easier and more successful this intervention can be. Clocks are useless after elementary school age because by this time, parent-child patterns of conflict around overdependency and denial of dependency are well established. After elementary school, the child already may be out of control; it will take more than a clock to break the inevitable denial of dependency that is part of this pattern. However, clocks still are useful as an intervention if this specific pattern of dependency (one caretaker taking responsibility to wake the child instead of the child taking responsibility for getting up) is still present in the family with other children.

THE RUBBER BAND

This prop is used with highly resistant and enmeshed couples who use the pronoun "you" to talk about the partner's behavior at the expense of using the pronouns "I" or "We."

The Meaning of the Symptom

The theoretical background for this enmeshment as well as for the previous symptom (being awakened by an overinvolved caretaker) is found in a recently published relational and contextual theory of personality development (L'Abate, 1994; L'Abate and Baggett, 1997b). One can safely assume that this enmeshment is due to various intra-individual and intra-dyadic conditions, including the "can't live with you and can't live without you" pattern, among others.

Prescription

Prescription of the rubber band needs to be made after a variety of interpretations, suggestions, and recommendations have resulted in failure, including a variety of homework assignments on how to argue and fight (L'Abate, 1992; 1993). Depending upon the level of sophistication of the couple and the clinical persuasion of the therapist, the nature of the enmeshment may be explained in terms of giving up the self for the other out of love, as shown by the predominant use of the pronoun "you." This reframing of the symptom allows the therapist to conclude that each partner seems driven to prove that the other is "bad" and that the self is "good," rather than to consider that both partners are "good."

Once the context of the symptom is positively reframed, the therapist should furnish two rubber bands that allow ample circulation in the wrist. Then the following instruction should be given: "Snap the band every time you think or talk negatively about your partner. Of course, if you want to continue defeating each other, you do not have to do it." If possible, this prescription should be accompanied by the instruction to log how many times each partner has given himself or herself a snap every day.

Contraindications for this Prescription

Rubber bands should not be prescribed to physically and sexually abusive couples. This prescription is intended for symbiotically enmeshed couples who cannot live with and cannot live without each other who may be verbally abusive. They may even complete written homework assignments about arguing and fighting (L'Abate, 1993), but it is clear that these assignments are not working because both partners are still "you-ing" each other to death and are unable (and sometimes unwilling) to use the "I" or "we" pronouns. Hence, the rubber band is a concrete reminder that these two pronouns should be used instead of "you."

CONCLUSION

Both the clock and the rubber band have been found useful in family and couples therapy. Unfortunately, I have only my clinical experience to back up their use. I have not been able to think of research on how to validate their clinical usage. However, if, at the beginning of my practice, I had bought stock in a clock company, by now I would be a rich man.

REFERENCES

L'Abate, L. (1992). *Programmed writing: A self-administered approach for interventions with individuals, couples, and families.* Pacific Grove, CA: Brooks/Cole.

L'Abate, L. (1993). An application of programmed writing: Arguing and fighting. In T. S. Nelson and T. S. Trepper (Eds.), *101 interventions in family therapy* (pp. 350-354). Binghamton, NY: The Haworth Press.

L'Abate, L. (1994). *A theory of personality development.* New York: Wiley.

L'Abate, L. and Baggett, M. S. (1997a). *Manual: Distance writing and computer-assisted training in mental health.* Atlanta, GA: Institute for Life Empowerment (http://www.mentalhealthhelp.com).

L'Abate, L. and Baggett, M. S. (1997b). *The self in the family: Toward a classification of personality, criminality, and psychopathology.* New York: Wiley.

5

Know the Enemy's Strategies
and You Will Know Your Own Power

Joellyn L. Ross

Sandy G. was despairing about herself and her life with her husband, whom she described as verbally and emotionally abusive. Sandy was referred to me by a social worker who was helping her with some medical problems; the social worker knew of Sandy's husband's abusiveness and was frustrated at her inability to help Sandy.

Sandy was in her mid-forties and had been married to her husband, Frank, for twenty-six years. They had three grown children, all of whom were living outside the home. She worked as a nurse's aide at a local nursing home, and her husband was a school administrator. A deeply religious woman, Sandy valued the fact that she and her husband had been together "through thick and thin" and she said that she could never leave him due to her religious beliefs.

She was able, however, to talk about her husband's abusiveness, and what effect it had on her, that is, how she felt terrible about herself, had little self-confidence, and was isolated from friends. Furthermore, the social worker who had referred Sandy to me was worried that Frank's abusive behavior was helping to worsen Sandy's health problems, which Sandy agreed was the case.

Like many people who are overwhelmed by their situations, Sandy could see no way out and no way of coping with what was happening to her. The work of Michael White (1991) has been helpful for me in working with people like Sandy who are victims of oppression. White has studied the work of Michel Foucault, the influential French philosopher who is renowned for his analyses—called deconstructionism—of how social forces act upon individuals (e.g., Foucault, 1980).

With Sandy, therefore, I decided to deconstruct her husband's abuse by asking her to specify the "techniques of oppression" used against her, that is, the specific and recurrent things her husband said and did to her that made her feel terrible about herself. She was able to come up with the following, which we wrote down. In addition, we talked about ways she could counteract and neutralize his "techniques of oppression," which we also wrote on a piece of paper that she could carry with her at all times.

Frank's Techniques of Oppression

1. criticizing my appearance (makes me feel ugly and says that no one else ever would want me);
2. guilt trips—blaming me for everything that goes wrong;
3. sexual punishment (e.g., not having sex with me);
4. criticizing me for not working outside the home and not taking college courses, even though he knows my health problems prohibit my doing so;
5. isolating me from my friends (e.g., not giving me phone messages);
6. telling me things that just are not true (e.g., about money matters).

Ways of Counteracting Frank's Techniques of Oppression

1. know that it's OK for me to take care of myself (I don't need to worry about him);
2. know his "techniques" and practice identifying them as he uses them;
3. keep my sense of humor and use it against Frank.

I advised Sandy to review this list often, so that the next time her husband used one of these techniques, she would be able to recognize it for what it was—an attempt to control her by diminishing her—and would be able to fight against it using effective neutralizing and/or counteractive techniques of her own.

What I value about this intervention is how quickly it empowers people who have been feeling utterly defeated by circumstances they have believed to be beyond their control. Using this intervention early in therapy—even at the first visit—sets the patient's expectations that positive change is within reach and can be achieved relatively quickly.

This certainly was the case for Sandy, who was visibly delighted that we had taken her husband's seemingly uncontrollable behavior and had codified it into six specific behaviors she easily could identify and counteract. The next time I saw her, she reported she had been able to fight successfully against three of Frank's techniques. At one point, she even was able to tell him that she knew what he was doing (trying to make her believe something untrue) and she wasn't going to fall for it anymore. Furthermore, she said that several days after our first meeting she had discovered the list was missing from her handbag—she presumed Frank had taken it—and that he had been behaving more respectfully ever since. It didn't "cure" him of his abuse, but it certainly seemed to put him on notice that his abusive behavior was being identified and thus helped Sandy to see that her action could be effective.

This intervention was an effective and powerful starting point for therapy with Sandy, which is still ongoing. After working with me for eleven months, as Frank continued to escalate his abusive behavior while Sandy escalated her counterabusive techniques, she decided to leave him—a bold and affirmative choice for her. The therapeutic frame throughout our work has been numerous versions of the same message: "You are a strong and resourceful woman who can be effective against the abusive techniques of your husband. If you can identify the abusive behaviors, you can fight against them."

Because this can be a powerfully effective intervention, the therapist must be assured the patient is not at risk for physical abuse from the person whose oppression s/he is trying to counteract. Challenging Frank, for example, would have been too risky for Sandy if he had a history of being physically abusive and I would have worked with her in other ways to deal with the physical abuse.

This intervention also can result in a rather dramatic emotional disconnect of the patient from the abuser, with which the patient also must be prepared to cope. The therapist, therefore, needs to be very clear in the assessment phase that the patient is willing to cope with the consequences of this disconnection.

Postscript: One of the interns that I supervised, Pai-Ling Teng, began working with a family overwhelmed by the obstreperous, manipulative behavior of the sixteen-year-old daughter. I suggested that Ms. Teng help the parents to identify the specific behaviors the daughter used to intimidate them, and to give the parents the list of behaviors so they could fight against them. She did this and the parents were able to take control of their family situation and their daughter very quickly. The daughter was unhappy with her loss of power, but the parents considered the brief therapy very helpful.

Another intern, Gracemarie Kehoe, added the suggestion that in the process of discussing the techniques of oppression, it can be helpful to identify the patient's usual response to the oppressive technique, then formulate a new, alternative response.

REFERENCES

Foucault, M. (1980). *Power/knowledge: Selected interviews and other writings.* New York: Pantheon Books.

White, M. (1991). Deconstruction and therapy. *Dulwich Centre Newsletter, 3,* 21-40.

6

The Race Is On!
A Group Contingency Program
to Reduce Sibling Aggression

Kristin E. Robinson

"Stop that fighting!" Teasing, arguing, and physical aggression are typical among most children, especially between siblings, given the amount of time they spend together. Parents must cope with an average of eight conflicts between siblings per hour (Dunn and Munn, 1986). When sibling squabbles escalate to potentially harmful, physically abusive levels, parents are faced with a dilemma: What is the best course of action? Some have suggested that parents should ignore sibling conflicts and allow children to work it out themselves (Schacter and Stone, 1987); however, research shows that untreated aggression tends to persist (Olweus, 1979; Achenbach, 1991). Nonintervention can even promote learned helplessness in a younger, smaller, or less competent child (Bennett, 1990). On the other hand, harsh punishment (e.g., spanking) or inconsistent punishment result in increased rates of aggression (Patterson, 1977). The strongest evidence suggests that parents should intervene to promote replacement of aggression with prosocial coping skills. An effective program will include the combination of a consistent, mild discipline component (e.g., time out) with reinforcement of appropriate coping behaviors (Olson and Roberts, 1987). The intervention presented is a group contingency in which siblings participate individually and as a team to earn chosen reinforcers for their use of anger management skills to replace physical aggression in sibling conflicts.

THEORETICAL ORIENTATION

The present intervention is based on social learning theory (Bandura, 1977), which states that all behavior is learned, and thus, can be changed. Change occurs primarily by reinforcing desirable behaviors and removing reinforcement for undesirable behaviors. The present intervention accomplishes this by issuing a group contingency, in the form of a game, with all children in a family. A group contingency is a system for the delivery of a contingency to an entire group based upon the behavior of individuals in that group (Reavis et al., 1993).

Group contingencies have been widely applied in classroom settings in the form of a Good Behavior Game. Using this technique, students are assigned to groups, and each inappropriate behavior engaged in by a group member is recorded. If a group's inappropriate behaviors do not exceed a previously defined criterion, the group receives an agreed-upon reinforcement. The Good Behavior Game has been successfully applied to decreasing disruptive behavior across several diverse classroom settings (Rice, 1994; Swiezy, Matson, and Box, 1992) and has also been shown to be an acceptable intervention to the adults and children involved (Tingstrom, 1994; Kosiec, Czernicki, and McLaughlin, 1986). Taking into account the repeated success of the Good Behavior Game in school classrooms to manage behavior, it seems appropriate to bring group contingencies into the home setting to decrease disruptive and aggressive behavior.

DESCRIPTION OF INTERVENTION

The present intervention is a modification of the Good Behavior Game, in that it provides a delivery system for reinforcement contingent upon the use of anger management skills. The racetrack-shaped behavior chart (Figure 6.1) includes a fixed number of boxes for each child, each representing a day. Children are assigned a track and color a square for each day they have no incidents of physical aggression. Approximately half of the boxes are labeled with dice. Each number on the dice represents a small reinforcer. Upon landing on a box with dice, children are allowed to roll one die and be rewarded with a variable reinforcer. When all children have completed the last square, a group reinforcer is earned. The chart serves several important functions: as a stimulus to remind children of their goals, as a means of posting progress, and as a simple procedure for tracking data.

CASE EXAMPLE

The identified client, RG, is a nine-year-old boy, living with his biological parents and two brothers, CG (age seven) and HG (age five). RG was referred to an after-school social skills program at a public mental health outpatient clinic due to problems with noncompliance and aggression. Upon closer examination, it was found that sibling aggression was a core issue and included all three boys. Thus, an intervention was designed to affect all boys in the family. Family therapy over the next seven weeks

FIGURE 6.1. The Race Is On!

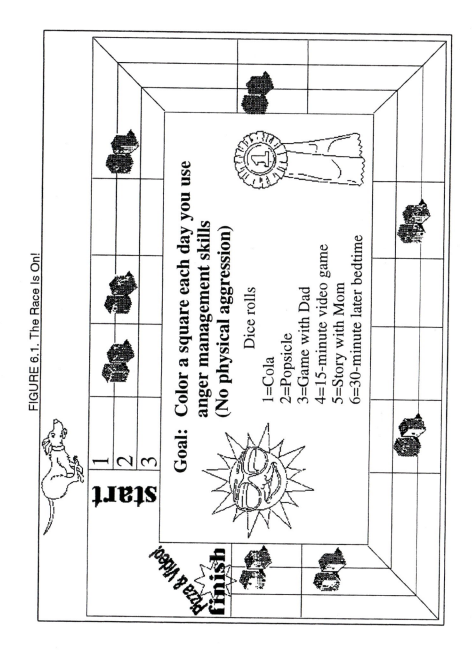

Goal: Color a square each day you use anger management skills (No physical aggression)

Dice rolls

1=Cola
2=Popsicle
3=Game with Dad
4=15-minute video game
5=Story with Mom
6=30-minute later bedtime

start

1
2
3

finish
Pizza & Video!

proceeded as follows. First, the family defined "physical aggression" to mean any physical contact with oneself, another person, or an object in anger, including hitting, kicking, biting, and throwing objects. Next, the parents began collecting baseline data on the boys' aggression rates.

During one session, the boys were asked to verbally generate appropriate behaviors to replace aggression in response to sibling conflict situations. All boys demonstrated adequate knowledge of skills, and could name several alternative coping mechanisms of impulse control and relaxation techniques (e.g., go to room, talk to parent, take a deep breath, walk away, stop and think). These skills were illustrated in a poster the boys took home. The family agreed on reinforcers to be used: several small items/activities (e.g., soda, gum, game with dad, fifteen-minute video game) and one larger group reward (e.g., rent a movie and order pizza). During the third week of therapy, the contract was implemented by the parents in the home. The parents were consistent in allowing the boys to complete contracts every night before bedtime.

Outcome

Results of the intervention are presented in Figure 6.2. Substantially reduced rates of physical aggression were noted for all children following the implementation of the contract. Overall physical aggression of all boys decreased from an average baseline level of seven per week to a treatment level of .6 per week. In addition, parents reported that cooperative behavior increased in the home among all boys. Parents reportedly found no difficulty in consistently following the procedure daily, and indicated that the intervention was easy to use. Parents indicated they would continue using the intervention as designed, and to remediate other problems. All boys were enthusiastic about the intervention, and wanted to continue the "game" at home for other behaviors.

CONTRAINDICATIONS

This intervention is suitable for clients who have at least average reading ability and good understanding of concepts presented. Parents who can objectively monitor their own behaviors, recognize positive behaviors of their children, and consistently follow the program are also more likely to experience success. Families that exhibit extreme dysfunction (e.g., marital discord, domestic violence, substance abuse) may warrant more intensive treatment than this program alone.

FIGURE 6.2. Weekly Total Physical Aggression

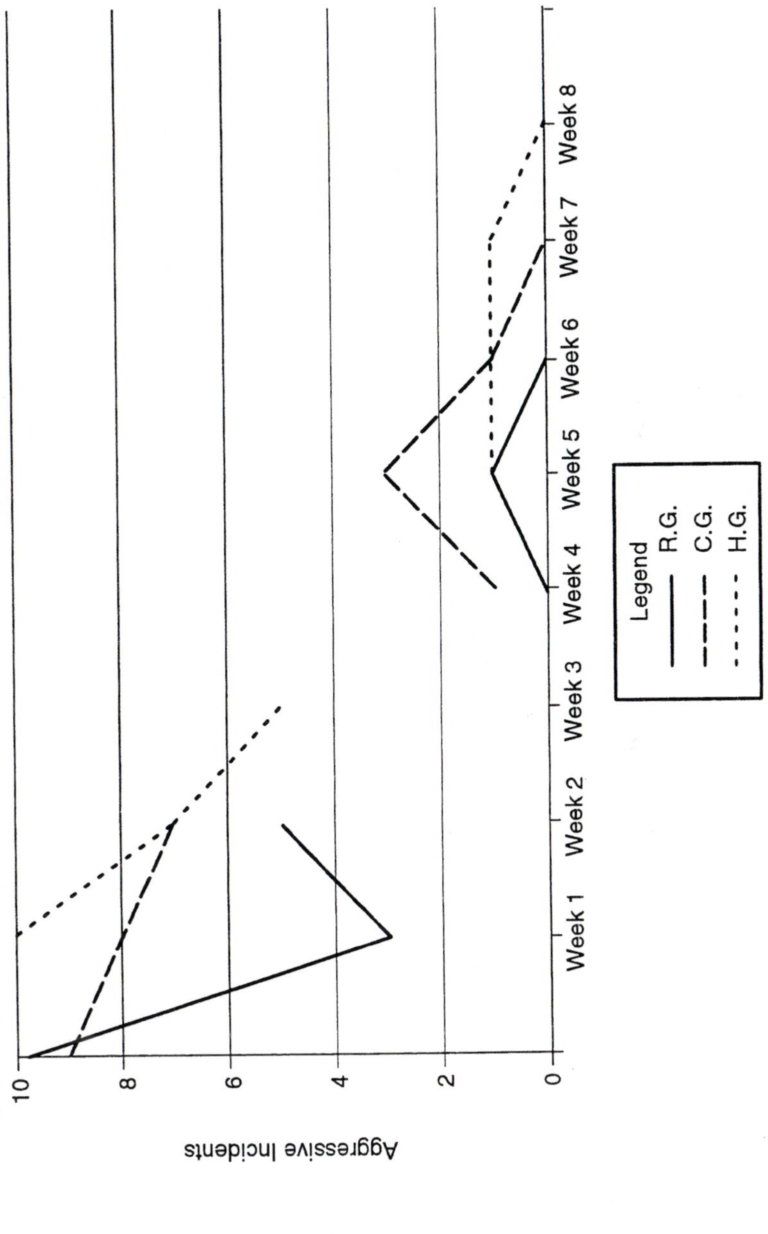

Legend
R.G.
C.G.
H.G.

Aggressive Incidents

Week 1 Week 2 Week 3 Week 4 Week 5 Week 6 Week 7 Week 8

CONCLUSIONS

Group contingency contracts have proven effective in reducing disruptive behaviors in school settings since the early 1970s. The present case study used a modified group contingency to reduce physical aggression between three male children in a parent-mediated treatment program. Given that sibling aggression is a very stable behavior over time without intervention that may negatively affect children's long-term development, it seems appropriate that group contingency models be added to the family therapist's repertoire. The intervention described engages all members of the family in reinforcement of appropriate behavior. The program has shown promising effects, and is reported by both parents and children to be an acceptable procedure.

REFERENCES

Achenbach, T. M. (1991). Child behavior checklist for ages 4-18. Burlington, VT: University of Vermont Department of Psychiatry.

Bandura, A. (1977). *Social learning theory*. Englewood Cliffs, NJ: Prentice-Hall.

Bennett, J. C. (1990). Nonintervention into siblings' fighting as a catalyst for learned helplessness. *Psychological Reports, 66*, 139-145.

Dunn, J. and Munn, P. (1986). Sibling quarrels and maternal intervention: individual differences in understanding and aggression. *Journal of Child Psychology and Psychiatry, 27*(5), 583-595.

Kosiec, L. E., Czernicki, M. R., and McLaughlin, T. F. (1986). The good behavior game: A replication with consumer satisfaction in two regular elementary school classrooms. *Techniques, 2*(1), 15-23.

Olson, R. L. and Roberts, M. W. (1987). Alternative treatments for sibling aggression. *Behavior Therapy, 18*, 243-250.

Olweus, D. (1979). Stability of aggressive reaction patterns in males: A review. *Psychological Bulletin, 86*, 852-875.

Patterson, G. R. (1977). Accelerating stimuli for two classes of coercive behaviors. *Journal of Abnormal Child Psychology, 5*, 335-350.

Reavis, H. K., Jenson, W. R., Kukic, S. J., and Morgan, D. P. (1993). *Using group contingencies to improve academic achievement*. Salt Lake City, UT: Utah State Office of Education.

Rice, M. P. (1994). *A classroom management game for middle school educators*. Unpublished master's thesis, Salt Lake City, UT: University of Utah.

Schacter, F. F. and Stone, R. K. (1987). Comparing and contrasting siblings: Defining the self. *Journal of Children in Contemporary Society, 19* (Spring/Summer), 55-75.

Swiezy, N. B., Matson, J. L., and Box, P. (1992). The good behavior game: A token reinforcement system for preshoolers. *Child and Family Behavior Therapy, 14*(3), 21-33.

Tingstrom, D. H. (1994). The good behavior game: An investigation of teachers' acceptance. *Psychology in the Schools, 31*(1), 57-65.

7

Attitude as Intervention

William C. Madsen

This chapter begins with a premise that our basic attitude toward families is our most powerful intervention. The chapter offers a series of questions to ask ourselves in an attempt to help us develop and maintain healing attitudes toward the families we designate as "difficult" and applies these ideas to a particular case.

CONTEXT OF THE INTERVENTION

I will begin with a story that contextualizes this belief about the importance of attitude. A number of years ago, I was hired by an agency providing home-based family therapy to help them develop their family therapy skills. I was greeted enthusiastically by staff who welcomed my expertise in family therapy and I entered with a certain degree of hubris. I had a lot of experience providing family therapy training and believed the agency would greatly benefit from that experience. I initially saw myself as drawing upon my "professional knowledge" to teach them, but quickly came to appreciate how much their "local knowledge" had to offer me.

Although many of the frontline staff were quite experienced in home-based therapy and very open to learning about family systems ideas, they were not technically proficient therapists. They did not have an articulated conceptual framework nor a set of techniques from which to draw. And yet, they were doing remarkable work with families that nobody had been able to engage. They were going into the homes of families typically described as "chaotic," "multiproblem," and "dysfunctional," and not only successfully engaging them, but helping them make significant changes in their lives. This was initially puzzling to me. It challenged much of what I had learned as a family therapist. They knew very little about family therapy and yet were doing great work with families. How was I to make sense of this?

As I talked to both staff members and families, I was struck by consistent themes. The staff, by and large, didn't see these families as resistant, dysfunctional, or pathological. They described them as "regular folks who were quite nice once you got to know them." While some might describe these workers as inexperienced, "in denial," or simply naive, they preferred to think of themselves as "experienced optimists." The families, in describing their experience of receiving services, repeatedly said such things as, "They were so respectful. No matter how hard we tried to convince them we were dirtbags, they just kept coming back." "They were the first therapists who really listened to me." "They treated my kid like a normal kid rather than a mental kid." "I liked talking to them because they always believed I could do better."

As I pondered the apparent paradox of staff without "adequate training" doing incredible work with families that no one else had been able to reach, I became convinced that at its core this work is first and foremost about our basic attitude toward clients. I think this is particularly true in our work with "difficult" families. Our basic attitude toward families is the foundation for our conceptual models and interventions. The ways in which we think about families (our conceptual models) and the ways in which we act with families (our interventions) can invite the enactment of this basic attitude or inadvertently constrain its expression.

I believe the elements of what I'll call a "healing attitude" are grounded in core values such as respect and curiosity, connection and persistence, and hope and possibility. It is expressed in fundamental assumptions of:

1. *Resourcefulness:* Families have many more strengths than we often recognize. (Waters and Lawrence, 1993)
2. *Empowerment:* Our job is to support family functioning, not to fix "dysfunction" and inadvertently supplant their functioning. (Durrant, 1993)
3. *Partnership:* Therapy proceeds better when based on a collaborative relationship. However, cooperation is a two-way street and therapists as well as clients can be "noncompliant." Since we as therapists are in a leadership position, a collaborative relationship begins with us finding ways to cooperate with clients rather simply expecting them to cooperate with us. (Berg, 1994)
4. *Cultural Competence:* Families and providers can be viewed as distinct cultures with particular beliefs and preferred styles of interacting. Treatment can be seen as a cross-cultural negotiation in which family actions may be more understandable through the family's lens than through the provider's lens. To fully understand the complexity of each family, it is useful to approach them as a foreign culture in order

to learn as much as possible about their culture. A useful metaphor might be to think about entering each family as an anthropologist looking to discover their meaning rather than as a missionary looking to assign our meaning to their interactions. (Epston, 1984)

I think a healing attitude begins with a full appreciation of family resources. Unfortunately, many of our conceptual models tend to invite more focus on pathology than on competence. In addition, therapy often takes place within a problem-saturated story that promotes selective attention to family dysfunction and difficulties, and selective inattention to family strengths and resources. In my work, I've often found it useful to engage families outside of the problem to gain a thorough appreciation of their resources. This can be done by initially asking a family to help you get to know them without the problem, or by helping you discover what things they are particularly proud about. This provides a solid foundation for a different relationship and the development of a healing attitude.

One way to maintain a healing attitude is by continually evaluating the degree to which our conceptual models and interventions invite the enactment of that attitude. I think it is important to consider the family's experience of their interactions with us and the degree to which they find the interactions respectful, connecting, and hopeful. The rest of this chapter describes a series of questions that we can ask ourselves or pose to each other to help maintain a healing attitude.

QUESTIONS TO PROMOTE A HEALING ATTITUDE

The following questions may be useful in entering the client's phenomenological world and developing an appreciation for their strengths and resources.

- What is this interaction like from the client's perspective?
- How would I react to this situation if I were in their shoes?
- What could I do as the therapist to make this situation worse?
- What in fact might I already be doing to make the situation worse?
- What is the positive intent behind their behavior that I find frustrating?
- How can I come to respect and appreciate that?
- What strengths and resources haven't I discovered yet about this family?
- What do I not know about this family that would change my opinion of them?
- What could I learn from this family?

CASE EXAMPLE

To clarify the usefulness of these questions, I will describe a case in which they were used. A therapist consulted me for help with a family with a single-parent mother and three children, including a hyperactive nine-year-old who was the identified client. Treatment had focused on helping the mother provide a consistent, containing environment for the boy, getting him started on Ritalin, and improving his relationships with his siblings. The mother had recently taken back her verbally abusive ex-husband, who was unemployed and described by the mother's family of origin as lazy, shiftless, and a drain on the household resources. He undercut her attempts to provide structure for the children, especially the identified client, and encouraged the boy to not take Ritalin because "he's no nut case." The therapist had fallen into believing the mother should kick the ex-husband out of the house and spent significant time discussing his negative influence on her son and the household. The client listened to and agreed with the therapist, but did nothing. The therapist was becoming more and more frustrated with the lack of progress on the case, was increasingly disparaging of the ex-husband, and was coming to view the mother as immature, codependent, and not committed to her children's well-being. Both the mother and the therapist felt stuck and the mother was thinking about discontinuing therapy.

As the therapist considered the questions listed above, she began to develop a new perspective of the situation. She came to believe that therapy from the mother's perspective was beginning to feel like a "pop quiz in which she kept coming up with the wrong answer." When asked to put herself in the client's shoes, the therapist responded that she would have reacted to her interventions by having less and less interest in therapy. The therapist decided that she could make things worse by further pushing the mother to take a particular course of action (covertly of course), and concluded with the statement, "I realize I'm not listening to what the mother *is* saying because I've become so focused on what I think she *should* be saying."

The ex-husband refused to participate in therapy sessions, but the therapist examined his experience of it by imagining him watching videotapes of the sessions. She thought the ex-husband would view the therapist as "just one more mental health hack meddling in his kid's life" and thought that he would feel judged and discounted. She came to believe that if she did not establish some connection with him, she would lose his support for therapy. She began phoning him regularly to update him on the therapy and drew on him as a consultant to help her "avoid the danger of becoming a therapist who would treat his son as a nut case."

As the therapist considered the positive intent behind the mother's unwillingness to take a particular stand with her ex-husband, her frustration with the mother eased. She saw the mother as wanting to create a more stable environment for her son and appreciated the mother's belief (though she did not agree with it) that her son needed a man around to provide that stability. That shift opened up space for the therapist to begin to respect the mother's commitment to her children and to see her as more mature and less codependent. As the therapist began to contemplate the mother's undiscovered strengths and resources, she decided to spend a session asking the mother for a consultation on what it was like being a single mother of three kids and what advice she would offer other single mothers. As the therapist further appreciated the mother's competence and ability to make decisions for her children, the mother began to show more confidence and trust her own judgment. She began to examine her belief that only a man could provide stability for her son and started expecting her ex-husband to support the rules of her house when he was in it. As the mother did this, the therapist expressed increased confidence in and respect for the mother's parenting ability. Finally, one day the mother said to the therapist, "I knew that I was going to make it when I saw the difference in your eyes."

The therapist agreed with the mother. She concluded that the shift in her basic attitude toward the mother was pivotal in "unsticking" the case. She believed that if she had not shifted her attitude, the therapy would have ended. These questions did not point out directions for the therapist to intervene with the family. What they did do was open up space for the therapist to develop a different attitude toward the family that allowed her to then intervene differently. The subsequent interventions were grounded in a healing attitude that informed more constructive interventions. While these questions were asked in a supervisory context, they could also have been used individually by the therapist as a series of questions to ask herself.

CAVEATS

I can think of two situations that provoke additional reflection about this "intervention." The first is a situation in which our own reaction to a case constrains our ability to enter the client's phenomenological world. This might include situations in which chronically stuck treatment has given rise to a pervasive atmosphere of hopelessness and negativity in which the therapist has lost hope for the possibility of change and has begun to interact in ways that protect him or her from feelings of blame and failure. In this instance, I would recommend that the therapist begin by focusing on his or her own experience of working with this family (preferably in consultation with a supervisor or colleague). One way to approach this would be to externalize some aspect of that experience (for example, frustration, hopelessness, or fear) in order to help the therapist step out of the experience and begin to develop a different relationship to it. This highlights the need for awareness of our own phenomenological world as well as the family's.

A second situation involves violence. It is very important that an attempt to view the world through the client's lens does not inadvertently collude with a minimization of violence. A respectful attitude does not mean accepting or condoning particular behaviors, but rather attempting to appreciate their internal logic. The ability to hold multiple realities is helpful here. It is possible to fully appreciate how a situation has developed and still take a stance against it. It is important for therapists to take strong stands against violence. At the same time, disrespectful situations (such as violence) do not dismiss the need for respectful, connecting, and hopeful interventions. In fact, in such situations, the need for a healing attitude of respect and curiosity, connection and persistence, and hope and possibility may be strongest.

REFERENCES

Berg, I. K. (1994). *Family-based services: A solution-focused approach.* New York: W. W. Norton.

Durrant, M. (1993). *Residential treatment: A cooperative, competency-based approach to therapy and program design.* New York: W. W. Norton.

Epston, D. (1984). Guest address. *Australian Journal of Family Therapy, 5*(1), 11-16.

Waters, D. B. and Lawrence, E. C. (1993). *Competence, courage, and change: An approach to family therapy.* New York: W. W. Norton.

8

Sculpting Stepfamily Structure

Toni S. Zimmerman

Due to their increasing numbers, stepfamilies have been the focus of a great deal of family research (Pasley and Ihinger-Tallman, 1994; Darden and Zimmerman, 1992). As therapists, we see them in our offices frequently due to the many transitions they must make when blending two families. One of the primary issues these families face is blended parenting. "Do I parent your children?" "Do I just parent my children?" "Can I discipline your children?" "Why don't your children want to be close to me; why don't they trust me?"

STEPFAMILY STRUCTURE

Therapists working with stepfamilies who are struggling with blending their parenting frequently refer to the work of Visher and Visher (1988). Many times, despite the couple's best intentions, they will initially be unable to parent following the structural model of biological families. Therefore, rather than parenting side by side, as a team, Visher and Visher suggest that parents take primary responsibility for parenting and disciplining their biological children. Furthermore, the stepparent takes on a role similar to that of a baby-sitter. This baby-sitter role encourages the stepparent to support rules set by the biological parent: "I know you would like to stay out later, but your mom set your curfew at 10:00. You must be in by 10:00." "On the job chart that your dad made, it says you need to clean your room."

In the same way that a baby-sitter reinforces rules set by the parents, the stepparent reinforces and supports rules set by the biological or primary parent. This frequently decreases resistance by the child to the stepparent, "He is just reinforcing Mom's rules; he is not bossing me around." It therefore, creates more of an opportunity for the stepchild and stepparent to bond with each other with fewer power struggles. "I don't have to follow your rules; you're not my dad!"

SCULPTING

In explaining the baby-sitter model to stepfamilies, I incorporate sculpting to aid their understanding. Sculpting is an experiential technique developed by Virginia Satir (1983). When using this technique, the family is physically positioned (or positions themselves) in ways that represent the behaviors and feelings associated with the therapeutic issue they're struggling with. For instance, a man who feels pulled between his loyalty to his wife and his loyalty to his family of origin might position himself between his wife, who would be pulling on one arm, and his family of origin, pulling on his other arm. The therapist would then discuss with the couple how this situation feels and how they would like to change it. Sculpting helps families experience the dilemma and encourages them to creatively change their behaviors.

BLENDING SCULPTING AND STEPFAMILY STRUCTURE

As I explain the baby-sitter model to stepfamilies, I position or sculpt them in the following way. I ask the child to stand and face some direction. I ask the biological parent to stand just behind the child. The parent places his or her hands on the child's shoulders, supporting the child. I then ask the stepparent to stand just behind the biological parent with his or her hands on the spouse's shoulders, thus supporting the spouse, who in turn is supporting his or her child. All family members are facing the same direction. This sculpt demonstrates that the parents are not side by side, parenting equally. There is a primary or "frontline" parent. Yet, the stepparent is not uninvolved or left out; he or she plays a key role in supporting and reinforcing the primary parent.

To further demonstrate this type of stepfamily structure, I ask the parents to stand side by side just behind the child. I then ask the child to do a "trust fall" (Glover and Midura, 1992). A trust fall is requesting someone to fall back into someone else's arms, trusting that they will be caught. Most often, the child will not fall back for fear of falling between the parents. If the child does fall back, frequently the parents are confused about who will catch the child. This demonstrates that the child needs time to build trust and the parents need time to build cohesion and communication in coparenting. I again ask the family to resume the original sculpt, one behind the other. I then ask the child to do another trust fall. Most often the child will fall back and the biological parent successfully catches him or her while the stepparent supports the parent's catch. For safety, it is important to spot these falls.

In addition to educating the families, this sculpt has been very effective with my clients who, session after session, refer back to it when describing their efforts during the week. For example, clients will report, "I found myself cutting in front of her and taking over. This made Jennifer [stepdaughter] furious at me so I got back in line!" "They [dad and daughter] have a long history together. I need to remember to observe and support from back here instead of thinking I have all of the answers." "We [stepson and mom] seem much closer now that I'm supporting Dad's rules, not setting them." "I like it when he [husband] turns and consults with me about rules even though he delivers the rules to his kids."

REFERENCES

Darden, E. and Zimmerman, T. S. (1992). Blended families: A decade review. *Family Therapy, 19*(1), 25-31.

Glover, D. and Midura, D. (1992). *Team building through physical challenges.* Chicago, IL: Human Kinetics Publisher.

Pasley, K. and Ihinger-Tallman, M. (1994). *Stepparenting: Issues in theory, research, and practice.* Westport, CT: Praeger Publishers.

Satir, V. (1983). *Conjoint family therapy.* Palo Alto, CA: Science and Behavior Books, Inc.

Visher, E. and Visher, J. (1988). *Old loyalties and new ties: Therapeutic strategies with stepfamilies.* New York: Brunner/Mazel.

—9—

Taped Supervision as a Reflecting Team

Richard J. Bischoff

The narrative (White, 1986) and languaging approaches (Andersen, 1991; Anderson and Goolishian, 1988) emphasize that change takes place when clients notice a "difference that makes a difference" (Andersen, 1991; Bateson, 1972). Consequently, therapists working from these perspectives target client meaning systems in co-creating competing explanations of a client's life and life situations. One helpful but often impractical strategy for sharing and creating competing meaning systems is the reflecting team (Andersen, 1991).

Tom Andersen's (1991) reflecting team generally consists of two or more professionals who observe a therapy session from behind a one-way mirror. At some point in the therapy session, the therapist and clients become the observers of the reflecting team as the team members discuss their observations of the clients, the clients' situation, and the treatment. The reflecting team's role is not to instruct the therapist and clients in what they should talk about, only to share their reflections on the conversation they were observing. As the clients and therapist listen to the team's discussion, the clients' meaning system is challenged with new questions and alternative meanings, leading to competing explanations and change. After the reflecting team has finished, the therapist and clients talk to one another about the ideas they had while listening to the team's discussion.

There are several goals of this strategy: (1) The clients and therapist are able to use the team's reflections to stimulate new questions that would not previously have been considered; (2) The team's reflections and the clients' reflections on these reflections stimulate the creation of new meaning. When this new meaning is very different, but not too different, from the existing meaning system, a competing explanation that is more helpful to problem resolution can be created; (3) The clients are able to hear perceptions of them and their problems from other professionals. This breaks down the secrecy barriers that often exist between the inquirer (client) and the knower (therapist). Therapy becomes more collaborative.

Although helpful, Tom Andersen's reflecting team strategy is often impractical in clinical settings where time and resources are scarce. It is difficult for many clinicians to coordinate schedules and free up time to participate in a reflecting team for a particular client. However, the benefits of the reflecting team can still be obtained through the use of other media. One of these media is the video- or audiotaping of supervision or conversations about clients with other professionals.

TAPING THE REFLECTING TEAM PROCESS FOR LATER VIEWING

Whether in supervision or not, many clinicians engage in formal discussions about clients with other professionals. The strategy to be described here is one I use in supervision, but it can easily be used in other situations.

The members of a supervision group can easily function as a reflecting team. However, the interactions within the supervision need to be different from supervision that is not being taped for this purpose. I have found that the following format facilitates the reflecting team process. The entire sequence of events described below should be videotaped.

To begin, the therapist briefly describes the clients, their problems, and the work in therapy. The team is allowed during the therapist's presentation to ask for additional detail and information about how the therapist views the situation. However, the team is not allowed to offer treatment suggestions or advice at this time. The team then watches a representative segment of videotape from a recent session or sessions with the clients. I recommend the therapist select segments of tape that best represent the clients and their description of the problem. At least fifteen minutes of videotape should be shown. The team should watch the tape without sharing observations of the clients, the problem, or the treatment. Each team member should watch with an eye toward how the clients' situation can be described differently from the presented description and the presented explanation (Andersen, 1991).

When the team is finished watching the videotaped segment, team members share with each other their reflections on the clients and the issues presented. The team does not provide advice and suggestions at this time. Rather, the team discusses their ideas about how things would be different for the clients if a different explanation of the problem existed. They also discuss what might be different if questions about the clients' situation that were not asked had been asked (Andersen, 1991). During this time the therapist quietly observes the team discussion.

When team members are finished sharing their reflections, the therapist reflects on what was heard while the team listens. When the therapist has finished making sense of the team discussion, the therapist and team can then discuss treatment recommendations, if there are any.

During the next session with the clients, the therapist informs them about which segment of tape was shown to the team. The clients and therapist then watch the videotaped team discussion. The clients are instructed to save their reflections on the team discussion until the video-taped segment is completed. Then the clients and therapist reflect on the team discussion, focusing on client reactions to the discussion. The therapist and client discussion should also focus on questions and ideas that were raised as a result of the observations.

Because the therapist has already heard the team discussion and has had an opportunity to reflect on it, the therapist should wait to share her/his perceptions until the clients have an opportunity to reflect. Having heard the team discussion before, it may be tempting for the therapist to use the reflecting team as an opportunity to "prove" something to the client, or to strategically direct the session discussion. I caution against the use of the taped reflecting team for these purposes. It is important that the clients be given the opportunity to create their own meaning of what was heard.

The therapist should plan on at least thirty minutes of the session for the videotape review and discussion. I suggest starting the videotape review at the beginning of the session so there is ample time for discussion. Informing the clients during the previous session of the possibility of a reflecting team facilitates this process.

Ethical Considerations: Obtaining Informed Consent

A therapist planning to share client and session data with colleagues and/or supervisors should inform the clients before information is shared and should receive the clients' written informed consent to do so. By signing the informed consent document, the clients should be giving per-mission to their therapist to videotape sessions and to share session data with other professionals. Also, clients should be told about the process of the reflecting team before it occurs so they are aware who will be partici-pating in the team, what information will be shared, what they can expect from the team, and how this procedure may be helpful to them and their therapist. The clients' right to not be taped and to not have identifiable session data shared with colleagues should always be honored.

CASE EXAMPLE

A therapist was treating a blended family in which a fourteen-year-old boy was experiencing poor school performance, was getting into trouble with his friends, was fighting with his stepmother's children, and was not participating positively in family activities. The father and boy had lived together, alone, for nearly ten years before the father's current marriage. Shortly before the marriage, the stepmother and her three daughters moved into the house. The family had constructed an explanation for the child's behavior that defined the boy as the problem and the source of the family difficulties. Although the therapist had attempted to restructure this family and to develop improved parenting practices, family members did not see themselves as making progress.

With the family's permission, the therapist videotaped a session with the family and showed a portion of this tape to the supervision team. The supervision team, acting as reflecting team, generated alternative explanations of this child's behavior including, among other things, the struggles associated with becoming a blended family. The team also generated questions that might have been asked of the family but were not, and hypothesized about how the outcome might be different if these questions were asked.

At the beginning of the next session the therapist showed the taped reflecting team discussion to the clients. They sat quietly while they watched and for several moments afterward. The boy's stepmother was first to speak by saying that she had never thought becoming a blended family would be so difficult. The father then began to share his ideas about not having as much time alone with his child as he had before the two families came together. This stimulated a discussion among the family about how both the father and mother could maintain their positive personal relationships with their biological children without sacrificing their commitment to the cohesiveness of the blended family and to each other's children. This was a discussion that changed the course of treatment and that probably would not have happened without the clients' and therapist's observations of the reflecting team's discussion.

The family did not agree with all of the team's reflections; in fact, they reacted negatively to some and rejected others outright. The therapist complimented them on their ability to hold onto ideas that would help them and to entertain but reject ideas that they did not see as helpful. The use of the reflecting team encouraged the creation of new possibilities and competing meaning systems for this family.

CLIENTS AND CLIENT PROBLEMS SUITED FOR THIS INTERVENTION

Using the taped conversation of colleagues as a reflecting team is appropriate for almost any client and client problem that a therapist working from a narrative framework is seeing. It has been my experience that hesitation in using procedures like this more often comes from the therapist than from the client. Clients are generally very interested in the perceptions professionals have of them and in the discussions others have about them. However, the procedure may be more appropriate for some clients than for others.

The procedure may be appropriate for clients who are having difficulty entertaining alternative explanations of their behavior and their problems. People and systems with a singular or constraining view of themselves and their problems may find that they can entertain alternative explanations more easily when they hear the reflecting team discussion. Also, people and systems who appear chaotic may benefit from the procedure. These people may have too many alternative explanations, all competing for dominance. The reflecting team can help these people select those explanations that are most useful.

Contraindications

The tape of the team discussion should not be shown to clients who come into therapy with a real crisis. The crisis should be dealt with first to ensure the clients are safe and secure, both emotionally and physically. When emotional and physical security is threatened, people will not be able to reflect appropriately on the team discussion.

Do not rush the procedure. Allow enough time for both the clients and the therapist to share their reflections.

Showing the tape to the client is contraindicated when the client does not want to observe the reflecting team discussion. It would be counterproductive if, when trying to get the client to hear other voices, the therapist shuts down the client's voice. If the client does not want to participate, the therapist still has had the opportunity to hear the team reflections and to reflect personally. This, in and of itself, can be a powerful and change-promoting experience from which the clients benefit.

REFERENCES

Andersen, T. (1991). *The reflecting team: Dialogues and dialogues about the dialogues*. New York: W.W. Norton.
Anderson, H. and Goolishian, H. (1988). Human systems as linguistic systems. *Family Process, 27,* 3-12.
Bateson, G. (1972). *Steps to an ecology of mind*. New York: Ballantine.
White, M. (1986). Negative explanation, restraint and double description: A template for family therapy. *Family Process, 25,* 169-184.

10

Becoming the "Alien" Other

Maryhelen Snyder

Each of us really understands in others only those feelings he is capable of producing himself.
—Andre Gide (in Mitchell and Black, 1995, p. 229)

Justin had been listening to Phyllis, his partner for five years, describe her experience of a conflict that they had had the previous evening. As I watched him sitting opposite her on my office couch, I saw his face become increasingly flushed, the muscles in his neck begin to protrude, and his whole body appear to tighten. For approximately half a dozen sessions, I had been teaching them Relationship Enhancement (RE) skills (Guerney, 1977) for effective expression and empathic attentiveness. I sensed that it might be extremely difficult for Justin to empathize authentically and accurately with Phyllis because of his apparent anger. Earlier in therapy, he had revealed a history of abuse and trauma originating in childhood and compounded during his experience as a soldier in the Vietnam war. He had spoken of himself as someone quick to rage.

I asked him if he felt that he could empathize with Phyllis or if he would prefer me to do it in this situation. He said that he wasn't at all sure he could do it because he felt so angry, but he thought that perhaps if he "became" her it would work. I had taught them how to do the *identification* process in the first session on empathy. Guerney recommends this as an initial step in helping clients to experience empathy as the ability to step into the lifeworld of the other person. Guerney had also been using the term "becoming" to describe a technique the therapist could use in crisis intervention situations where the clients might need the therapist's active assistance in understanding each other. In these situations, each client could speak "through" the therapist to the other person. After listening to each client, the therapist would "become" that client speaking to the other person. The therapist would deepen the communication and also "launder" it to be consistent with the RE skills of effective expression.

Until the session with Justin and Phyllis described previously, it had not occurred to me that the technique of *identification* or *becoming* might be particularly suitable for calming emotions in conflict situations. Turning to Phyllis, Justin spoke as though he were her about the perceptions, meanings, feelings, and desires evoked the previous evening. As he did so, I watched his face resume its natural color and the muscles relax. When he finished, he checked with her about the accuracy of his empathy. She had sat apparently enthralled throughout the time he was speaking as her.

In describing what this experience of *becoming* was like for him, Justin spoke of being amazed. He said that in addition to noticing that his anger was gone, he felt as though he actually understood Phyllis's perspective for the first time as though from the "inside."

Since then, I have used this technique more frequently in my work as an individual and family therapist and as a supervisor and trainer (Snyder, 1995). I am particularly inclined to use it, or recommend its use, in situations where the listener feels emotionally reactive, critical, or confused.

It has been important in this work to distinguish what this technique is from what it is not. It is not role-playing. By this I mean that one characteristic of the experience of *becoming* is that there is no subjective sense of being oneself playing the part of the other. One's "self" (its perspective, emotions, ways of organizing reality) is suspended during the experience and is missing from consciousness. For example, in a couples group that I am currently facilitating, Suzanne and Bob were having a conversation about a recent experience in which he had tried to be helpful by bringing some order to an office space that she had just acquired in their home (hanging pictures, moving boxes, etc.) while she was on an errand. She attempted in the group to share with him her feelings about this event. Bob then *became* her, expressing these feelings as though from her perspective. When I asked him how he felt while doing this, he said, "I wish she didn't feel that way." This is a clue that the person doing the *becoming* hasn't really been successful. I invited him to "suspend" that wish for a moment and let himself *really* "become" Suzanne. Somewhat to my surprise, almost everyone appears to understand this distinction with little or no further clarification.

When Bob then returned to the task, he deepened Suzanne's feelings spontaneously, beyond what she had already expressed. She was then able to take it even further herself and to remember (in her body) the strong emotions of not having space that was her own. Her grief about this was released in the context of Bob's accurate understanding. Bob's wish that she not "feel that way" completely vanished in his experience of understanding subjectively the meaning of the event for Suzanne.

Two other critical distinctions are that *becoming* is not mind reading and it is not analyzing. The person doing the *becoming* is cognizant that he/she may not be accurate, and is responsive to indications, verbal and otherwise, that something said is not felt as true by the other person. There is no room in the process for assuming that the person doing the *becoming* knows better.

The technique is very helpful when a therapist feels at an impasse in understanding a client, or when the client indicates in any way that he/she does not feel understood. Instead of thinking of resistance, defensiveness, argumentativeness, inauthenticity, etc., as characteristics of a client, the assumption here is that what is generally missing is the experience of feeling accurately understood. It is no accident that when the therapist does accurately understand a client, there is no feeling on the therapist's part that is inconsistent with compassion and interest; that is, the therapist's resistance, defensiveness, argumentativeness, and inauthenticity vanish.

To date, I have not observed any contraindications for the use of this technique. There are, however, important cautions. Although there is considerable variation in the ability or willingness of clients to use it, my experience thus far indicates that if a person is able and willing, there are no apparent adverse effects. It is essential, however, that permission be asked of the person who will be receiving this method of empathy. It is also essential that both persons involved in the process understand that the method is only an imperfect and partial tool for facilitating a deeper understanding. Whatever is spoken in the process of *becoming* another could be inaccurate and in need of correction. Furthermore, no act of *becoming* can in any way be inclusive of the immense complexity and continual movement of another person's organization of meanings. It is the responsibility of the therapist to clarify these cautions and limits.

One final comment: There is often a moment of discomfort (even fear) that occurs in the *becoming* process when one remains intent on doing it accurately and deeply. This moment is related to what Martin Buber described as "the most intensive stirring of one's being" that occurs with the "bold swinging" into the life of the other (1988, p. 71). It is vital for the therapist to allow and invite this discomfort to occur. I have noticed recurrently that when I or a client don't settle for stopping on this side of the discomfort involved in risking a deeper level of subjective joining to a person whom we are b*ecoming,* an emotional discharge is very likely to occur for *both* persons, as well as that mutually shared shift in meanings that is at the heart of dialogue and intimacy. When I, for example, unreservedly step into this level of relationship with a client, I usually experience deep emotion, and I change.

REFERENCES

Buber, M. (1988). *The knowledge of man: Selected essays* (M. S. Friedman and R. G. Smith, trans.). Atlantic Highlands, NJ: Humanities Press.

Guerney, B. (1977). *Relationship enhancement*. San Francisco: Jossey-Bass.

Mitchell, S. and Black, M. (1995). *Freud and beyond*. New York: Plenum.

Snyder, M. (1995). "Becoming": A method for expanding systemic thinking and deepening empathic accuracy. *Family Process: 34:* 241-252.

11

Playing Baby

Ellen F. Wachtel

The "Play Baby" intervention is used in the brief, integrative, child-focused family therapy that I call "child-in-family" therapy.[1] One aspect of child-in-family therapy is that it incorporates attention to the unconscious needs of the child into systemic and behavioral interventions. The therapist coaches the parents on ways to address the child's concerns.

Playing Baby is an intervention in which the parents relate, in play, to the baby that still exists under the facade of the "big" child. It is used both with excessively anxious or immature children and with youngsters whose surface adaptation is almost the opposite—children who have renounced dependency needs and seek neither affection nor approval from parents. It has also been helpful in dealing with resentments, both expressed and unexpressed, that an older child may feel for a younger sibling despite the parents' attempts to give the older child equal or more attention.

Play Baby involves asking parents to initiate pretend games and other activities whose aim is to let the child know that the parents are aware of, accept, and love the child's baby self. Play Baby is a shorthand term that covers a wide range of activities all aimed, in one way or another, at reminding the child that no matter how big he or she has become or how self-reliant he or she acts, the parent knows and accepts the unarticulated or even renounced wish to be nurtured. Parents are asked to initiate games and other activities that will let the child know that although the youngster is still expected to behave in an age-appropriate manner, in some sense "you'll always be my baby." In making a "game" of the child's needs, the parent models for the child the acceptability of regressive longings without threatening the child's growing sense of maturity and autonomy.

Play Baby activities will vary greatly depending upon the age and personality of the child and how comfortable the parents are with regressive play. For instance, some parents report having great fun wrapping their school-aged child in a "blankie," giving him a "baba," and pretending that he is a newborn infant just arrived home from the hospital. Other parents and children will be more comfortable pretending that a parent is excited to see a toddler just learning to crawl, walk or say a first word. For others, Play Baby might simply consist of the parents' reminiscing about when the child was a baby or taking out baby pictures or dearly loved transitional objects.

The Play Baby technique addresses the child's longings without the youngster having to admit openly to these wishes. This is particularly important with children who have repressed or renounced dependency needs. Rather than interpret to the child the meaning of his behavior, the therapist helps the child get in touch with and gratify largely unconscious longings through these symbolic enactments. Thus, it is the parent who suggests the game because "though I'm proud of how big you are I sometimes miss my little baby." Play Baby statements and games not only obliquely bring the child's needs to consciousness and symbolically speak to these needs but perhaps most importantly, actually change the quality of parent-child interactions. Youngsters who are receiving this kind of attention are far less likely to try to involve their parents in provocative and negative ways.

Playing baby is usually great fun for the child and thus is a strong positive reinforcer. It is important to remind parents that they should not use Play Baby at times when immature or negative behavior might be inadvertently reinforced.

CLINICAL EXAMPLE

Miranda, age seven, often seemed to be quite angry at her parents. They reported that although she complained that her younger brother was getting more attention than she was, she in fact rejected most of the overtures that her parents made to engage her. Although Miranda was open about her dependency needs (e.g., she would be upset when her parents went out for the evening), conflicted feelings about wanting nurturance from her parents was evident in the way Miranda interrupted warm and intimate interactions shortly after they began to occur. Thus, for instance, moments after joyously laughing during some playful roughhousing with her dad, Miranda would get angry that he had inadvertently "hurt" her or should have stopped the wrestling earlier when she was jokingly yelling "stop!" Similarly, shortly after cozying up with her mother for some quiet reading time, Miranda would get miffed about some annoyance (often an interruption caused by her younger brother) and would reject offers to resume even when her mother had remedied the difficulty and made herself completely available.

Miranda was intensely jealous and critical of her younger brother. She was also extremely self-critical and perfectionistic. She seemed to feel that she did not have what it takes to hold her parents' love. She vacillated between trying to get their love by demanding it (behavior that annoyed her parents and further confirmed her feelings of rejection) and renouncing any need for them. When the parents initiated Play Baby, Miranda was at first reluctant to participate. Only when they persisted in telling her stories about how cute she was as a baby and conveyed to her that it was *they* who wanted to relive through play those wonderful baby years, did she relax and enjoy the gratification of a need that she was not required to own as her own. A great deal of warmth developed between Miranda and her parents just from this simple intervention. Miranda very quickly became much less rejecting and demanding. The parents too felt much better about their interactions with her and were more able to say "no" to her when it was appropriate to do so.

It is helpful to alert parents to the fact that although a child may not show any obvious enjoyment of Play Baby and may act like he or she is putting up with something annoying, the child has heard and taken in the parents' symbolic communication regarding the child's needs.

CONTRAINDICATIONS

Most children respond quite positively to Play Baby, but some children indicate quite adamantly that they really do not like the game. Play Baby powerfully circumvents defenses and occasionally one encounters a child who seems to find this too threatening. When a child seems seriously upset by the parents' overtures at Play Baby, the parents should not force it on him or her. Instead a milder version of Play Baby should be used, such as looking at photo albums or telling anecdotes about the child as a baby.

Play Baby can be used with seriously disturbed children as long as thought disorder is not present. One would not want to suggest Play Baby when ego functioning is not strong enough to distinguish fantasy play from reality. The child must be able to understand that statements such as "you'll always be my baby" are not to be taken literally.

Some parents are very uncomfortable with the Play Baby method. Since the aim of the technique is to help the child feel more comfortable with disavowed aspects of the self, it is important that the parents do not communicate anxiety about this sort of play. If parents are still anxious about doing Play Baby after it has been explained in detail, it is best that they not do it. As trust between the therapist and the parents develops, it will become clearer why this method may be particularly difficult for the parents to accept. It is important to remember that the Play Baby method is not done in isolation. Family sessions are used to address the issues of vulnerability and regressive longings for the family as a whole. Thus "resistance" to this approach is regarded as a clue to productive directions in family sessions.

NOTE

1. This approach is described in Wachtel, E. F. (1994). *Treating troubled children and their families.* New York: Guilford.

—12—

Competing Voices:
A Narrative Intervention

Gabrielle Carey

Many of us have competing voices in our minds, flowing in a contrapuntal fashion, not unlike a Bach fugue. Yet sometimes these voices no longer sound euphonious. We may have slipped into the wrong key or missed a beat, upsetting precarious rhythms. When the dominant theme is discordant, lives can be unpleasant or even chaotic. As therapists, we can encourage our clients to listen to each of their voices and decide whether to fine-tune or tone down the melody. In realizing the role of composer, clients can become more proficient in creating the lives they want for themselves.

BACKGROUND INFORMATION

This intervention was inspired by the works of Michael White and David Epston (1990), Alan Parry and R. E. Doan (1994), and Steve de Shazer (1982). Competing Voices involves deconstructing the problem story or composition and externalizing the problem as competing voices. Access points are identified after the problem story is deconstructed and a new version of the musical piece is reconstructed.

Treatment Applicability

This is a versatile intervention that can be used with individuals, couples, families, and groups. Although its applicability can be left to the imagination of the therapist, I have found it to be of the utmost help with single women. It has been useful with a woman in her forties who was suffering from mild depression, a recently separated woman of thirty-five with four young children, a divorcée who was still attracted to her abusive ex-husband, and with teenage mothers.

Description of the Intervention

The intervention begins by introducing the concept of multiple voices. The refrains of powerlessness and frustration versus the partially hidden strains of determination and positive self-esteem are reframed as competing voices. They can be described as louder voices competing with softer voices or old voices competing with new voices. The origins of the old or loud voices are explored. "Did you hear that while you were growing up?" "Who used to say that to you?" These questions may provide insight into the sources of the themes of the problem-dominated story.

The new voices are compared to the old. The origins of these newer voices are also explored. "When did you first hear these voices?" "What effect do they have on the refrains?" "When you hear the old voice is it possible to counteract it with the new voice?" "What happens when the voices compete?" "When do the old voices become the dominant melody?" "What can you do to enhance the volume of the new voice and weaken the impact of the old voice?"

Presenting the problem story as a chorus of old voices has the effect of externalizing the problem. Voices can be changed. New words and new stories can liberate the client from the problem story. The client is encouraged to retell the story. "Every telling or retelling of a story, through its performance, is a new telling that encapsulates and expands upon the previous telling" (White and Epston, 1990, p. 13).

Once the problem story has been externalized, access points can be identified. Access points are areas of reactivity for the client. These areas can be used by the therapist to point out the places where the old story imposes on the new story (Parry and Doan, 1994). Examples of access points are periods of low energy and depression, or spells of wild, self-destructive behaviors, or seemingly uncontrollable rages. The access points are used for entry into discussion of ways the old story is still drowning out the new story. Ideas for changes in behavior are explored. The gradual process enables the client to see how her weak voice is shrinking and her strong voice is gaining confidence. The intervention is successful when the composition becomes harmonious, or the problem story disappears and the client decides she no longer needs therapy.

CASE STUDY

S is a thirty-eight-year-old woman with four children. She recently separated from her husband, J, after twenty-one years of an abusive marriage. He is a heroin addict who also drinks heavily. S put up with his addiction and physical and emotional abuse because she was unsure about how to leave the situation, and unsure of the effect on the children. During J's second hospitalization for his habit, he met a young woman with whom he began an affair. J checked himself out before he was fully recovered and went to live with his new girlfriend. S was not aware that J had even left the treatment center. When she found out about the betrayal, she created a fresh new voice. This strong voice increased in volume and she was able to say, *enough is enough!*

At this point, S sought therapy for herself. She had tried couples therapy before, but found it was not useful, due to her husband's addictions. Her weak voices sang to her to continue to love and remain committed to her husband. She struggled with bouts of depression (access points) when these old, weak refrains became the dominant themes in her mind. As S began to think of the destructive voices as external influences rather than personal weaknesses, she found it easier to resist the temptation to listen to them.

Throughout our discussions of her weak and strong voices, S was able to gain a sense of agency. She no longer felt helplessly trapped amid the discordant melodies. It became possible to sing out with new chords of personal strength and dignity. She knew she had to remain strong for her children and for herself. She began to concentrate on herself. Her physical appearance improved, she put renewed energy into her job, and her mothering skills began to take priority. S continues to come to therapy for periodic visits, but she has no doubt about her ability to survive without her destructive marriage.

CONTRAINDICATIONS

It may not be wise to use this intervention with young children or more mature people who are very literal. The use of the intervention with multiple personality disorders is also contraindicated.

REFERENCES

de Shazer, S. (1982). *Patterns of brief family therapy: An ecosystemic approach.* New York: Guilford Press.

Parry, A. and Doan, R. E. (1994). *Story re-visions: Narrative therapy in the postmodern world.* New York: Guilford Press.

White, M. and Epston, D. (1990). *Narrative means to therapeutic ends.* New York: W. W. Norton.

—13—

Start with Meditation

Linda G. Bell

Being still in order to know has been an integral and fundamental aspect of the human experience over the centuries. From the mystic to the artist, dancing or sitting, the mind seeks clarity and the heart, tranquility. Meditation is a way to make use of quiet to support therapy.

Research on meditation supports its power to reduce stress and blood pressure, increase self-esteem and mental alertness (see Carrington, 1986). Better sleep, less reactivity in relationship, and the effective management of chronic pain are all enhanced by this simple mental practice. The individual who meditates regularly gradually enjoys a subtle experiential shift in the way self is identified. Reactivity evaporates into observation, thinking into knowing. The struggle of approaching pleasure and avoiding pain evolves into a gentle holding of life-in-the-moment.

Meditation has two primary uses in therapy. The first is in the therapist's quiet as a resource going into the therapy session. A therapist's meditation practice gradually transforms and empowers his or her therapy. Maharishi Mahesh Yogi[1] says that as meditation practices progresses, Being infuses Doing. A knowledge of being becomes stronger in awareness and infuses therapeutic work—allowing it to be done more comfortably, with far less turmoil and stress, thus avoiding burnout. At the same time, the work, while easier, is also much more effective. The therapist's quiet, settled mind is more open—both to the client and to the therapist's own thinking and creative processes. Both the intuitive and the intellectual aspects of therapy are enhanced. Joseph Rosenthal (1990) describes this experience as:

> a kind of *pas de deux* between thinking and hypothesizing, on the one hand, and opening to emotional process and intuition, on the other. Usually, therapeutic approaches emphasize one or the other

ability, often in a mutually exclusive way. Strategic and cognitive therapists are known for their keen powers of analysis and conceptual detective work. Humanistic and dynamically oriented therapists emphasize the importance of the therapist's capacity for empathy and his/her ability to go with the flow and invite the client's process to unfold. Since meditation is a training that combines paying attention, opening one's heart, and remaining clearheaded even in the midst of emotional upheaval, it integrates both worlds in the therapeutic process, the ability to think and let go at the same time. Contrary to some popular misconceptions, the goal of meditation is not to destroy the intellect but to free it from the constrictions that limit the expression of its full potential.

Regular practice of meditation leads to the realization of the underlying "emptiness" out of which our moment-to-moment experience arises. No single phenomenon (including the self) can be said to exist independent of the mind's discriminating, categorizing, and labeling processes. In other words, our experienced reality is a construction, conditional and constantly changing. Buddhism shares this view of reality with some current constructivist approaches to family therapy. From the Buddhist perspective, however, in order to move beyond a mere cognitive understanding of emptiness, it is necessary to practice meditation. Even the brief experience of emptiness helps the therapist avoid locking into preconceptions and fixed ideas that can close off the new possibilities arising in the therapeutic encounter. (pp. 40-41)

Meditation empowers a wide variety of therapeutic options, from reframes to questioning to behavioral contracts. This is because the person creating the options is exceptionally clear-headed and sensitive to the client. Meditating therapists report experiencing more of themselves in the room. It is as though the "noise" is removed—so the signal is more clear. However one engages in conversation with the other, that process is enhanced. And there is a sense of the work flowing naturally. One does not control the process; the process flows. As one of my colleagues said, "If I don't run the show, it still goes." In some cases, self may be experienced, not as an individual entity, but as an aspect of a transpersonal process.

So, naturally, we come to the second way meditation can be used to support therapy. If we enjoy such fine results as meditating therapists, what about meditating clients? Many people have experienced or practiced some form of meditation or contemplation—perhaps in the course of their religious training, or through their sports or hobbies. And many, if helped to recall the experience associated with such practice, will choose to nurture that aspect of their lives. Such nurturing will support resolution and/or transformation of those experiences that led them to your office. Your work as therapist becomes even easier.

Meditation can also be brought directly into the therapeutic hour as an intervention in and of itself. One way to do this is to ask clients to arrive fifteen to twenty minutes before their appointment time. A space is provided for quiet meditation, music, or guided meditation. For others, the more effective approach is to devote the first ten to twenty minutes of the session to a meditation, clients and therapist together. Jon Kabat-Zinn (1994) has good ten- and twenty-minute tapes for this purpose.

The particular approach must be matched to the particular clients. A few people are open to the pursuit of a serious, long-term, daily practice of meditation. Couples can practice together, and parents can meditate with their children. Others are comfortable with some silence each morning, a quiet walk, or a contemplative practice structured by reading scripture or other personally meaningful material. Some are very comfortable meditating with the therapist—some definitely are not. Fortunately, as a fallback, the meditating therapist can take time to breathe, or drink a glass of water—and remind themselves when they notice they have been distracted or reactive.

I know of no contraindications for using meditation, as long as the clients are willing to try it. If for any reason it makes them uncomfortable, of course it should not be pursued. At workshops a question sometimes comes up comparing meditation and dissociation—and whether meditation would be appropriate for those without a strong, integrated sense of self. Meditation, however, supports clearer self-awareness and supports integration. In this way, it is the opposite of dissociation. Meditation helps people come *out* of trance (see Wolinsky, 1992). The only concern I would like to share is that meditation gradually relaxes or evaporates defenses at the same time that it empowers the individual to "hold" the painful experiences that emerge, to hold pain in a way that allows it to transform or heal. This experience involves knowing both pain and groundedness (centeredness, safety, mindfulness) simultaneously (see Thich Nhat Hanh, 1991, on the transformation of feelings). The therapist, then, needs to be aware that difficult memories or affective experiences may emerge unexpectedly and should prepare the client ahead of time for this possibility. When in doubt, go slow.

As a general rule, meditation at or before the beginning of therapy greatly enhances the effectiveness of the work in the remaining time. Some therapists hesitate to use valuable (expensive) time "not doing anything." But the hesitancy is easily overcome by the experience. Experiment with a little attentive quiet, and watch your work blossom. Clients become more settled and centered. The therapeutic connection is stronger, the conversation more focused. Couples and family members speak to each other more clearly; they *hear* each other more accurately. And they are more likely to talk directly about basic issues. Pain is held as an experience while it transforms itself into something else. Shifts that might have seemed difficult fall into place quite naturally.

These approaches are useful whenever they are comfortable for the therapist and clients. They support integration and a sense of wholeness—a deeper, clearer knowledge and acceptance of self.

BIBLIOGRAPHY

Bell, L. G. (1995/1996) *Meditation supported therapy,* American Association for Marriage and Family Therapy. Tapes available from the Resource Link (1-800-241-7785). 1995 is a two-hour presentation; 1996 is a one-day institute. Tapes of one-day institutes given at Texas Association for Marriage and Family Therapy in 1995, 1996, and 1997 are available from Egami A/V, 6052 Hillglen Dr., Watauga, TX 76148, (817) 577-2564.

Carrington, P. (1986). Meditation as an access to altered states of consciousness. In B. Wolman and M. Ullman, Eds., *Handbook of states of consciousness.* New York: Van Nostrand Reinhold. Reviews meditation techniques and research on their effects.

Dossey, L. (1991). *Meaning and medicine.* New York: Bantam. Summarizes medical research into the effect of prayer on healing. If you believe, on the basis of careful research, that prayer helps patients, are you obliged to pray?

Epstein, M. (1995) *Thoughts without a thinker.* New York: Basic Books. Summarizes Buddhist teaching, Buddhist psychology, and psychotherapy. Compares Buddhist psychology and Western (psychoanalytic) approaches, showing how the two complement each other and can be used together to support both healing and health.

Hanh, T. N. (1991). *Peace is every step.* New York: Bantam. Paperback, 1992. Thich Nhat Hanh is a Zen Buddhist monk who was deeply involved in peace and reconciliation work in Vietnam during the war, and with veterans and survivors on both sides after the war. He teaches meditation as a way to mindfulness (being fully awake and aware).

James, W. (1902). *The varieties of religious experience.* New York: Longmans, Green, and Co. (Mentor paperback, 1958). William James was the leading psychologist-philosopher of his day. His chapter on mysticism could have been written yesterday. He gives many examples of mystical experience from various religious traditions.

Kabat-Zinn, J. (1990). *Full catastrophe living: Using the wisdom of your body and mind to face stress, pain, and illness.* New York: Delta. Overview of

Kabat-Zinn's Stress Reduction and Relaxation Program at the University of Massachusetts Medical Center.

Kabat-Zinn, J. (1994). *Wherever you go there you are.* New York: Halcion. At the back of this book is information about ordering several helpful meditation and yoga tapes.

Kramer, S. Z. (1995). *Transforming the inner and outer family.* Binghamton, NY: The Haworth Press. Seeking to bring spirituality into the center of psychotherapeutic work, Kramer presents theory and practice using meditation, guided meditation, and guided imagery with individuals, couples, and families. The book builds on the work of Virginia Satir and includes transcripts of interviews with her about her life and work.

Rosenthal, J. (1990). The meditative therapist. *The Family Therapy Networker, 14,* 38-41, 70-71. Beautifully combines explanation and personal experience.

Wolinsky, S. (1992). *Trances people live.* Falls Village, CT: Bramble. This book, by a teacher of Ericksonian hypnosis and family therapy, is very readable. Wolinsky presents complex ideas clearly. He describes our daily "normal" life experience as a trance. The goal, through meditation and personal development, is to achieve a "no trance" state.

NOTE

1. Founder of the Transcendental Meditation Program.

—14—

Emotional Restructuring: Re-Romancing the Marital Relationship

Thomas W. Roberts

This chapter emphasizes romantic attachment in the marital relationship. While most couples get married because of romantic attachment, little is written in the marriage and family therapy literature about romantic love (Roberts, 1992). This chapter views romantic love as an emotional attachment that ebbs and flows during the marriage. In addition, because romantic love is an emotional attachment, it can change only by creating new emotional experiences. The assumption is that verbal or cognitive techniques will not effectively alter emotional attachments.

THEORETICAL BASIS OF THE TECHNIQUE

Although no major theoretical position addresses romantic love, experiential-symbolic theory is helpful in conceptualizing how love is important in the marital relationship (Whitaker and Keith, 1981). Although not developed in detail, the experiential-symbolic position on love is that love is symbolic, reflecting an emotional rather than a cognitive dimension. Others have addressed how love is similar to an emotional attachment that seems impervious to cognitive reasoning (Roberts, 1992). For example, when one "falls in love" it may be obvious in a cognitive or rational sense that the relationship is flawed, but the couple may not be able to act on this rational assessment. Instead, the emotional attachment to each other keeps them in the relationship, each hoping that the partner will change over time to meet expectations of the relationship.

Although different conceptually and theoretically, the technique described below is similar to the "re-romancing" technique developed by Hendrix

(1988). Hendrix believed that specific exercises rekindle romantic feelings in the relationship. The technique described in this article is less structured than Hendrix's technique. A highly structured exercise has little in common with the way emotional attachments are created. Emotional attachments are formed through spontaneous, a priori experiences that need not be planned.

SUITABILITY OF TECHNIQUE

Emotional restructuring of the marital relationship is suitable for long-term couples in which romantic attachment has declined. It is especially useful for couples in which one or both partners have "fallen out of love" with the other. For example, a wife may say, "I love him, but I'm not in love with him. I think I should feel more for him, but it just isn't there." This technique may be helpful also for the long-term romantic relationship in which the partners have drifted away from each other because of work or children. This kind of distance in the relationship may be a metaphor for emotional attachment that needs to be addressed.

DESCRIPTION OF THE TECHNIQUE

The technique involves five steps. First, the therapist focuses on the affective dimension of the relationship and the emotions underlying the relationship. Second, the therapist explores the childhood attachments of each spouse as forming the basis for their adult romantic attachments. Third, the therapist assigns homework that creates new emotional experiences for the couple. For example, helping couples reexperience each other in ways similar to their early relationship is considered more important than verbal exchanges that may not reduce negative behaviors between the spouses. Fourth, assuming that sexual desire and romantic attachment are generally inseparable, the therapist inquires about the couple's sexual relationship. Therapists for the most part do not explore a couple's sexual relationship unless it is presented as an issue by the couple (LoPiccolo, 1989). Ignoring the sexual dimension with couples in which romantic love is an issue is no doubt related to poor outcomes in therapy. To enhance sexual experiences of the spouses, the therapist could have them make lists of their romantic, sexual, and erotic fantasies and act them out as homework assignments. A number of books are available to guide the therapist (Kaplan, 1974; Masters and Johnson, 1966). Finally, the therapist encourages repeatable nonverbal experiences such as frequent hugs or regular dates to help the couple change perceptions of the marital relationship. This nonverbal exercise tailored for the couple may be a powerful new experience or change agent in their relationship. The couple needs new rituals to ensure that change will be lasting.

CASE EXAMPLE

Jeff and Allison came into therapy after five years of marriage. Allison complained that she no longer felt romantic passion for Jeff and did not know if she really wanted to be married. When she told Jeff this, he was very shocked and hurt. He also admitted that there should be more passion in the marriage, but still loved Allison and wanted the marriage to work. He believed they had just drifted apart. He thought a major problem was their work schedule and the limited time they had together. When they disagreed on a problem, they never had time to talk it out. At the point they sought treatment, they disagreed on almost everything.

In applying the five steps in the emotional restructuring technique, the therapist would first focus on the hurt expressed by Jeff and the disappointment underlying Allison's position. Second, the therapist would discuss with both Jeff and Allison their respective attachment histories in their families of origin and how they carry over this style of attachment in their marital relationship. Jeff had developed a somewhat avoidant style in his family of origin, which had become a similar pattern in his relationship with Allison. Allison felt her parents expressed love inconsistently and she had great difficulty knowing how she stood in relationship to her parents, especially with her father. This new insight helped them be more accepting of each other, and Allison reported new romantic feeling emerging for Jeff. Third, Jeff and Allison were given a homework assignment to have one evening during the coming week that was like their relationship when they first met. They decided to go to their old college and attend a football game on a Saturday. After the game, they went to a bar where they danced and drank until early in the morning. Not able to drive back home, they stayed in a motel. After this weekend, they came back to therapy and reported great changes. The fourth step was skipped because they were again having sexual relations and declaring how wonderful their sexual relationship was. The last step was to encourage spontaneous experiences that would generate different perceptions of each other. They agreed that attending football games at their college was a helpful ritual for them. Others included weekend sailing, which they both enjoyed but had not done since they got married. They terminated after two more visits, and a six-month follow-up found them still in love and reporting that their marriage was stronger than ever.

CONTRAINDICATIONS

For this technique to be effective in marital therapy in which love has declined, both spouses must be motivated to work on the relationship. It is more effective in an atmosphere in which the therapist and the clients have a good, trusting relationship. Since it involves new experiences and emotional expression, the couple must be open to the idea of understanding their emotional reactions and changing those reactions by new experiences.

REFERENCES

Hendrix, H. (1988). *Getting the love you want.* New York: Holt.

Kaplan, H. S. (1974). *The new sex therapy.* New York: Brunner/Mazel.

LoPiccolo, J. (1989). *The reunification of sexual and marital therapy.* Paper presented at the 51st annual meeting of the National Council on Family Relations, New Orleans, LA.

Masters, W. H. and Johnson, V. E. (1966). *Human sexual response.* Boston: Little, Brown.

Roberts, T. W. (1992). Sexual attraction and romantic love: Forgotten variable in marital therapy. *Journal of Marital and Family Therapy, 18,* 357-365.

Whitaker, C. A. and Keith, D. V. (1981). Symbolic-experiential therapy. In A. S. Gurman and D. P. Kniskern (Eds.), *Handbook of family therapy* (pp. 187-225). New York: Brunner/Mazel.

15

It's Bigger Than Both of Us

Carol L. Philpot

Although the feminist movement has done a great deal in the last several decades to improve the lives and choices of women, particularly white middle- and upper-middle-class women in the United States, there have been high prices to pay for such progress. One victim of social change has been the relationship between men and women. It has become clear that the changes in women's attitudes, roles, and behavior brought on by the feminist movement and consciousness-raising are challenging the traditional family and male-female relationships. Women are angry with men for not taking more responsibility for those tasks once designated women's work, when women have taken on the masculine task of providing a family income (Hite, 1989; Hochschild, 1989). They expect men to be as emotionally available and expressive as are their women friends. The strong, silent type who fixed the car, chased away burglars, and brought home the bacon is no longer acceptable. Women find themselves struggling under the same stresses as men, getting the same psychosomatic disorders, drinking too much, smoking too much, and having to make difficult choices between career and family. They resent the fact that men with traditional wives can seemingly have it all, and they are angered by their spouses' automatic assumption that the female's career is merely an avocation, while his is an identity. Male-bashing has become popular in the media and among yuppie females.

Meanwhile the reaction of men has ranged from an honest attempt to understand and accept the feminist perspective as valid and important to angry backlash and a yearning for the days when women were soft and submissive. The traditional middle-aged or older male feels betrayed by a wife who no longer wants to fulfill the original contract born out of the stereotypical male role of provider/protector and female role of nurturer/caretaker. He is faced with deprivation when she no longer provides for his personal needs and is both infuriated and helpless in the face of her demands which he perceives as uncharacteristically self-serving. He responds with depression and passive/aggressive maneuvers designed to thwart her efforts at independence and self-actualization. This traditional man cannot understand why anyone would want to change the former system of complementarity because it worked so well.

The younger males seem to divide into three subtypes: (1) those who are sensitive, educated, intelligent, and well-intentioned, who struggle to understand and meet the needs of the new woman, but are often criticized by impatient angry females and are left feeling confused and hurt; (2) those who are aware of what the new man should be and pay lip service to it, working the new system in a sociopathic, placating way without really seeing its value, in fact, seeing the change as very threatening; and (3) those who are blatantly angry and bitter, demanding a return to the old and venting a hatred for females in a degrading and hostile manner.

The disruption of the former complementary husband/wife relationship, which placed rigid role assignments on the sexes, has left many couples striving to redefine themselves within a relationship. In the process, both are vying for power, the women fearful of losing the ground they have gained in the past decade and the men afraid that stepping down from the dominant position necessarily will result in their being dominated. Consequently they become polarized and angry with one another, truly engaged in a battle of the sexes.

A SYSTEMIC VIEW

In spite of the fact that family ranks near the top for both sexes on surveys that ask people to prioritize the components of a satisfying life (Levinger and Moles, 1976), it appears that the couple who has successfully navigated this period of tremendous sociological change is rare indeed. As systemic thinkers who conceptualize cases in terms of circularity and neutrality, family psychologists are in a propitious position to facilitate a smoother transition. The escalation of the battle of the sexes in the wake of the feminist movement can be viewed as "schismogenesis," a polarization on issues between the sexes in which each side becomes so invested in converting the other to the "right way" that any hope for resolution is lost. A second-order change is required to release the couple from their entrenched positions and enrich their cognitive maps enough to offer a two-winner approach.

The instrument of second-order change suggested here is an expanded version of gender-sensitive psychotherapy. Although gender-sensitive psychotherapy generally refers to therapy conducted with a feminist perspective regarding the realities of different life experiences encountered by males and females, systemically-defined, gender-sensitive therapists are knowledgeable about the differing perceptions of reality for men and women growing out of biological differences, male/female developmental theory, socialization in a capitalist/patriarchal society, value systems, levels of moral development, role definitions, and real power differentials in the political, economic, and legal arenas. They understand the implications of the latest literature in women's studies, men's studies, and gender difference research. They are familiar with the theoretical bases for understanding gender differences and are aware of their uses and limitations. They impose no limits on the roles to be played by males or females and impose no limits on the potential for growth of either sex due to stereotypical expectations. They view the often predictable dichotomies of distancer/pursuer, expressive/instrumental, logic/emotion, and function/form as inevitable, but perhaps exaggerated, results of socialization, not internal pathology. And they approach therapy from as androgynous a perspective as possible, given the limitations of their own genders, maintaining an awareness of the special needs of men and women and of the techniques that will best facilitate treatment for each.

THE INTERVENTION PROCESS

The goal of therapy with a couple who has become entrenched in polarized positions over these issues is *depolarization through expansion of their cognitive maps*. Most often, both spouses are locked into a repetitive, dysfunctional mind-set in which each partner tries desperately to convince the spouse that his/her "way is the right way." They have become submerged in an either/or, right/wrong, black/white dichotomous manner of thinking, in which one perspective must defeat the other. To this end, they will attempt to triangulate the therapist as judge, each hoping to form a coalition with the expert in order to validate his/her position. It is at this point that the therapist can begin the depolarization process, which consists of four steps.

The first of these is simply *reflection* with some tentative amplification—merely restating what both husband and wife have expressed individually, sensitively restating the emotional stance and thought processes of each. When the therapist is thoroughly familiar with the issues and typical gender perspectives, he/she can follow the clients' lead and with a high degree of accuracy predict the feelings and rationale that will follow. The correct and empathic statement of positions they have not yet verbalized fully, but recognize as resonating with deeply felt emotions, has the validating, bonding effect that creates therapeutic magic. Both sexes feel heard, understood, and supported at once.

The second step is *psychoeducational* and somewhat didactic. The fact that the therapist simultaneously agrees with what the clients view as dichotomous and incompatible positions is disconcerting and stimulates curiosity. At this point the therapist can teach the clients about the construction of reality along gender lines and what attitudes and values can be expected to result from the socialization process. The educational component can be as simple or sophisticated as the client's education and intelligence can appreciate. This step has the effect of enriching cognitive maps and opening new possibilities of perception. Additionally it normalizes male/female positions and neutralizes toxic issues between the couple by clarifying their source as gender socialization and not a deliberate personal demeaning of one another's value systems.

Step three is *confrontation* with reality. It consists essentially of a short speech that points out that gender differences will exist between all men and women to some degree and must be accepted. An example might be:

Therapist: [following a discussion of Chodorow, 1978] Well, now that you understand where each other is coming from, we need to find a way to communicate so that you can meet each other's needs. Because there is one thing I can guarantee you: if either one of you imposes your perception or value system on the other, you kill the relationship. Whenever one person dominates the other, both suffer and eventually the relationship becomes bitter and unrewarding. And since you both tell me, by your very presence here, that this relationship is valuable to you, we need to start working on a two-winner approach to resolving these issues. It should also be clear by now that changing spouses (if either of you has fantasized that solution) is probably not going to help too much with a lot of these issues either, because most men and women will have been socialized in the same way. Women will be like women, and men like men, whether we like it or not. I'm reminded of Rex Harrison's lament in *My Fair Lady*, "Why can't a woman be more like a man?" But then that would probably be boring as the devil. Anyway, what I would like for you to do right now is to think of yourselves as speaking two different languages, say French and Spanish, because there are similarities in your thinking, but also differences. And for the last few sessions I've acted as an interpreter, which is okay, but I don't plan to move in with you so it would be much more efficient for me to teach you how to speak each other's language. Then you can communicate and work on solutions.

The fourth step consists of *brainstorming* for solutions. Each partner states his/her position, not with the purpose of converting the partner, but to inform his/her spouse about feelings and needs. Partners learn to listen to the experience of the other without feeling the need to defend or impose his/her own view. The therapist helps them clarify the most important underlying needs that must be met for the relationship to be satisfying to both. Creative two-winner solutions (Stuart, 1980) to problems emerge from the clients themselves. These solutions may require the therapist to do some skills training such as active listening or behavioral contracting. The therapist may need to offer a ritual prescription, use a reframe, or employ any one of the many therapeutic techniques at his/her disposal to facilitate the clients' accomplishment of their goal.

As therapy progresses, whenever such issues arise, the therapist will continue to take responsibility for interpreting them systemically, treating both male and female perspectives as equally valid, and moving from reflection to education and normalization, and from depersonalization to brainstorming for a two-winner approach. The most important element of this approach is its nonblaming viewpoint of why and how men and women think and feel differently, which unites the couple against a common enemy, gender socialization, in an effort to save their relationship. Couples develop a cooperative stance that only through understanding each other's languages and creative teamwork can they defeat this problem that is "bigger than both of them."

CONTRAINDICATIONS

Although gender socialization plays a large part in understanding the roots of domestic violence, couples therapy is not recommended in cases where abuse is present. Experts in domestic violence (Hansen and Harway, 1993) recommend group therapy for the batterer and either group or individual therapy for the victim until the violence has stopped for at least six months. Although psychoeducational material regarding the effects of gender socialization can be useful in helping both victim and batterer understand their dysfunctional patterns, this material should be introduced in the group setting first. Only after the batterer has taken responsibility for his/her behavior and the victim has been empowered will couples therapy be productive. At that time, the gender-sensitive approach described above can be useful in circumventing the feelings of shame that often drive batterers out of therapy. They will understand that they have learned dysfunctional responses to conflict through their gender socialization—responses they can unlearn. In the presence of a gender-sensitive psychotherapist, both victim and batterer can try out new ways of resolving conflict using their newfound understanding of the dysfunctional aspects of rigid gender socialization.

REFERENCES

Chodorow, N. (1978). *The reproduction of mothering.* Berkeley: University of California Press.

Hansen, M. and Harway, M. (Eds.) (1993). *Battering and family therapy: A feminist perspective.* Newbury Park, CA: Sage.

Hite, S. (1987). *Women and love: A cultural revolution in progress.* New York: Alfred A. Knopf.

Hochschild, A. (1989). *The second shift: Working parents and the revolution at home.* New York: Viking Penguin, Inc.

Levinger, G. and Moles, O. (1976). In conclusion: Threads in the fabric. *Journal of Social Issues,* (32), 193-207.

Stuart, R. (1980). *Helping couples change.* New York: Guilford Press.

16

Joining with Jenga: An Intervention for Building Trust with Stepfamilies

Wanda Clark

THEORETICAL ORIENTATION

Most initial stages of therapy involve building trust between therapist and client. Minuchin and Fishman (1981) refer to this process as "joining" with the family system and suggests it is the way the therapist lets the family know that he/she understands them and is working with them. Therapeutic systems are held together by connections formed through joining.

Structural family therapists would also attend to how family systems are aligned, who has the most power within the family system, and the presence, absence, and locations of family boundaries (Aponte and VanDeusen, 1981). When working with stepfamilies, imbalances in these alignments, boundaries, and power structures are often identified as problematic. To promote shifts or changes structurally then, it is critical that trust is built between clients and therapist early in the therapeutic process.

DESCRIPTION OF THE INTERVENTION

Jenga is a stacking game using a stack of wooden blocks, the object of which is to remove blocks from lower portions of the stack and place them on the top without knocking over the whole structure. The game does involve some hand-eye coordination and works best with children who are over six years of age. When using it as a joining technique, I generally follow the basic rules of the game but add a dimension involving asking a question with each turn. After successfully removing and placing one's block, each player may ask another player a question. If it is a first session or highly conflictual family, sometimes I place limits on the kinds of questions that can be asked, but usually the type of question is intentionally left open-ended. I offer to begin the game and start with nonthreatening questions such as, "What is your favorite food, or TV show, or kind of music?" Gradually, I try to add more depth to the kinds of questions that are circulating by shifting to questions such as, "What do you like most about (name of another family member)?" or "How is your life different since (name of stepparent) has come to live with you?" Often family members will follow my lead with similar kinds of questions and themes will emerge from the responses. These themes can then be explored later using more traditional questioning formats, or another game of Jenga can be focused on one theme in particular.

In addition to being a good way to join with stepfamilies, since having a game to focus on seems to help alleviate some of the pressure often placed on children when stepfamilies present for therapy, the game can also be useful for helping to establish therapeutic goals. Solution-focused questions such as the "miracle question" or "crystal ball" techniques (de Shazer, 1988) can be woven into the game and often produce illuminating results, especially when answered from the multiple perspectives presented by each family member.

This intervention may be contraindicated in several situations. If the therapist suspects instances of abuse, sexual or physical, or any other type of exploitative power dynamics, using a game such as this would tend to obscure accurate assessment and potentially place the victim in further danger.

Perhaps one of the most valuable outcomes of using a game such as Jenga early on in therapy with stepfamilies is that it can send the message that therapy is fun. Usually when families first come to therapy they are unsure of what to expect and rarely anticipate having a good time. Focusing some attention on a game illustrates the positive ways in which the family can function together.

CASE EXAMPLE

The initial concerns that brought the Smith family to therapy involved eight-year-old James not "getting along well" with his stepfather, Don. Don and Janice had married six months previously after a brief courtship. Janice also has a daughter, Kim, who is thirteen and by everyone's report is the straight-A student, "golden child" of the family. James is also quite gifted and shows an interest in art and theater. Recently his grades have plunged and he has been caught lying to both his mother and stepfather, events that precipitated their decision to come to family therapy.

During the initial interview, James was sullen and would not look at or speak directly to Don. He would answer questions directed at him as briefly as possible but seemed reluctant to interact with anyone except his mother. When the family came for the second session, the room was arranged with the Jenga game as the focal point on a table in the center. James immediately became curious about what it was and what we were going to do with it. After I explained the rules of the game, we began by asking each other somewhat superficial questions about favorite foods and TV shows. Initially James did not directly interact with Don but was listening to his responses to other family members.

After about three times around the circle of players, James asked Don, "Why do you and my mother want to have a baby? Do you not like me and Kim?" Fortunately, Don carefully responded that he very much liked James and Kim and that having another baby would in no way replace them but would add to their family. We then spent the rest of the session asking questions about what they wanted their new family to be like, how Kim and James might feel about a new sibling, and so on. It is quite likely that this information would have come to the foreground regardless of the type of intervention, but using the Jenga game seemed to elicit trust and safety within the session more quickly.

When the Smith family came to therapy the following week, James reported that he and Don had played a different board game at home that week, but they had asked each other questions at each turn. They seemed much more relaxed and open with each other and after a follow-up session two weeks later decided they were well on the way to building a blended family and no longer needed to come to therapy. Using a game such as Jenga to join therapists with families is useful as an intervention because it is less threatening than other forms of interviewing, it can be used as a means of assessing and gathering information about family interaction patterns, and it can build upon the positive aspects that already exist within family structures.

REFERENCES

Aponte, H. J. and VanDeusen, J. M. (1981). Structural family therapy. In A. S. Gurman and D. P. Kniskern, *Handbook of family therapy, Vol. I* (pp. 310-360). New York: Brunner/Mazel.

de Shazer, S. (1988). *Clues: Constructing solutions in brief therapy.* New York: W. W. Norton.

Minuchin, S. and Fishman, H. C. (1981). *Family therapy techniques.* Cambridge, MA: Harvard.

17

Crisis Intervention with Families:
A One-Down Position

Peter J. Jankowski

One of the most challenging aspects of working at a community agency can be doing crisis intervention with runaway adolescents and their families. Perhaps the most difficult facet of crisis intervention is establishing authority (Neuber, 1994). It is often necessary and effective to enter the room and attempt to gain control of the situation by setting rules, making good eye contact, and validating each person (Neuber, 1994). A crisis interventionist is not required to do therapy but to calm the energy level down, figure out the problem, reach a temporary solution, and make a referral for therapy (Neuber, 1994).

Despite the general effectiveness of establishing authority, there are times when it is necessary to adapt one's approach to crisis intervention. Occasionally, a crisis interventionist may need to take a "one-down position" (Fisch, Weakland, and Segal, 1982), rather than establishing him/herself in a position of authority. Taking a one-down position dictates that the interventionist give up some of the power and give it to the adolescent and/or parents. In the following case example, I illustrate that the crisis interventionist can promote change in the system by changing his or her role in the process occurring between crisis interventionist and family.

CASE ILLUSTRATION

I had been called to the sheriff's department because a fourteen-year-old male was refusing to go home with his parents. Upon my arrival, the adolescent was in a separate room from his parents. The officers felt that this was essential because they had had some previous violent encounters with the father and thought that his potential risk of becoming violent at this time was too great. I met with the adolescent, and explained what often happens in these situations. I tried to get a sense of what he was running from or to, whether or not he had a plan, and described what he needed to do to get out of the police station. He wasn't interested. In fact, for approximately forty-five minutes he sat with his head on the table and did not move or say a word.

I determined that I had better take a break since it was obvious that this approach was not working. I talked with the parents, using the same approach I had used with their son. The only information I could gather, amid the profanity and name-calling, was that the father had hit the son the previous week. The child protective agency was already involved and in the process of taking the father to court.

I attempted to reach a temporary solution by trying to find a place for the son to stay until the family could begin to receive therapy sometime within the next week. The parents wanted no part in this, demanding that the son simply come home. I explained that he could refuse to return home with them, and the law protected him. I left them with the task of thinking of a place where the son could stay. At this point, I went back to meet with the son, knowing that the situation did not seem to be changing.

I decided that when I went in with the son again I was going to abandon the notion of taking charge of the situation, and attempt to hand control over to the adolescent. I took a one-down position by declaring that I needed his help us to get out of the police station, and that at this point I didn't know what to do. I asked him what he wanted to see happen and said that it was up to him because I was running out of ideas.

After a long period of silence, he began to stir for the first time and finally looked up at me. I was relieved and encouraged. We began to talk about the episode the previous week involving his father, and as he talked it became evident that the only way he knew how to leave a violent situation was to run away. After another period of silence, I restated that I needed his help. He paused for a while, and answered that he wanted to stay with his grandmother. He then put his head back down on the table, nonverbally declaring himself finished.

On my way to meet with the parents, I figured that I would try the same one-down positioning as I had with their son. I greeted them for the second time, requesting their help in this situation. I said that I needed them to come up with an idea about how we could all get out of the police station. After a repeat of their earlier stories about children having too many rights, they proceeded to offer places for their son to stay until things could get worked out, perhaps through therapy. As soon as they listed his grandmother as a possible placement, I asked if this was a place they thought their son would be willing to stay. They both responded, "of course he would; he loves it there." They stated all the reasons why they didn't want him to stay there, then agreed to let him go.

After the grandmother had been contacted by the officer and arrived at the police station, I brought everyone together to finalize the arrangement. The arrangement, upon which all agreed, was for the son to reside at his grandmother's house and then return home two days later. I made my last plea concerning the need for therapy and said that someone from our agency would contact them in a couple of days.

Once contacted, the family stated that the son had ended up coming home the next day of his own volition. The family also refused services, claiming that they didn't need therapy. As an agency, we had no leverage to force them to come in for therapy, and thus left it as an option for them to consider. Since child protective services was involved, it meant that the family would eventually be ordered into treatment.

CONCLUSION

In the preceding case example, the family and I were engaged in a process that could be described as a power struggle. By taking a one-down position, I was able to diffuse the power struggle by changing my role in contributing to the process. As I became more collaborative with the family, they in turn began to take more of the responsibility for solving the immediate crisis.

It is important to assess the process occurring between interventionist and clients when conducting crisis intervention. Taking a one-down position would be contraindicated if the parents and/or adolescent were actively looking to the interventionist for direction. There are times when a family will respond in a way that indicates their desire to know what happens in these types of situations, and desires to know what they need to do to solve the immediate crisis.

Taking a one-down position during crisis intervention is effective because it raises clients' level of cooperation and increases their sense of personal agency in a distressing situation. The intervention is accomplished by focusing on the process occurring between interventionist and family. As a crisis interventionist changes his/her role in the process, the system will change in such a way that the immediate crisis is resolved.

REFERENCES

Fisch, R., Weakland, J. H., and Segal, L. (1982). *The tactics of change: Doing therapy briefly.* San Francisco: Jossey-Bass.

Neuber, K. (1994, April). *Basic crisis intervention skills training for direct service workers.* Workshop presented at the Illinois Collaboration on Youth Conference, DeKalb, IL.

—18—

Columbo Therapy as One-Down Positioning with Families

Peter J. Jankowski

THEORETICAL RATIONALE

The intervention described in this chapter is based on second-order cybernetic theory and the Mental Research Institute (MRI) brief therapy model. Second-order cybernetic theory (Atkinson and Heath, 1990) implies that the therapist is part of the treatment system. The therapist focuses on how he or she is contributing to the process taking place within the therapist-client system. By focusing on his or her contribution to the process, a therapist can become aware of instances in which the approach he or she is taking may need to change. A facet of a therapist's approach that may need to change is the therapeutic stance of the therapist.

One aspect of the MRI brief therapy model that contributes to the intervention described in this chapter involves the therapist taking a "one-down position" (Fisch, Weakland, and Segal, 1982). A one-down position requires that the therapist do something to remove him/herself from a stance of power and expertise, and give the client a more powerful position. Furthermore, a one-down position entails that the therapist do something that will increase the client's sense of personal agency and competence.

This chapter describes an intervention directed at the therapist's positioning during therapy. This (1993) "Columbo therapy" approach has been adapted as one way to take a one-down position with clients. Selekman's approach consists of acting confused and asking questions out of a genuine curiosity about the client's experience (Anderson and Goolishian, 1988), similar to the TV detective character's style. The case example illustrates how taking a one-down position may change the process occurring within the therapist-client system. The following case example involves a highly emotionally charged situation characterized by anger and potential violence.

CASE EXAMPLE

I had been involved in a case with a mother and her fourteen-year-old daughter for approximately four months. During this period, the stepfather had refused to come in for therapy, claiming that it was unnecessary for him to be present because the problem existed between his wife and her daughter. The family was in therapy because the daughter had repeatedly run away from home and was continuing to leave home without permission. The daughter would be gone for days at a time, only to eventually return home of her own volition.

Several attempts had been made to draw the stepfather into the therapy process. I had explained to him that he was a necessary component in the process of change. I also suggested that he act as my consultant to help me gain a clearer understanding of what was going on at home. The idea of being a consultant appealed to him, and he eventually decided to give therapy a chance.

When I met the stepfather for the first time, he immediately informed me that he was not comfortable with therapy and was reluctant to attend the session. Respectfully, I validated his feelings and let him know that I appreciated his willingness to give therapy a chance.

At some point in the conversation, the stepfather and his wife began to express that they did not know what to do anymore. They began to describe some of the things they had done to try to prevent the daughter from running away. The stepfather mentioned that he had been trying to stay out of the arguments between his wife and her daughter. I asked if he thought his efforts were making a difference in the daughter's behavior. He paused for a moment, and replied that he thought it was making some difference. In response, I commented, "I think it's important that you continue to try to stay out of their arguments." No sooner had the words come out of my mouth than he got up out of his seat and began to pace around the room. He was waving his arms and shouting, "I knew I shouldn't have come. . . . I knew he'd say it was all my fault . . . that's it, I'm leaving."

Intervention

At this point, I decided to focus on my contribution to the process occurring within the therapist-client system. I began to take a one-down position by letting him know I was genuinely confused about what had made him upset. I calmly asked him if he could help me understand what had made him angry. Silently, I waited until he stopped pacing around the room and returned to his seat. Repeating myself, I requested that he help me understand. He proceeded to explain that he was feeling guilty and experiencing a lot of self-blame concerning the daughter's running away. The rest of the session involved respectfully listening and affirming him for describing how he felt.

Outcome

Because I changed my therapeutic stance and took a one-down position by acting confused, the stepfather was able to calm down and express himself in a nondefensive and straightforward manner. While reflecting on his behavior during a later session, he explained that he had felt listened to and accepted. He stated that the reason he decided to come back was because he had not been made to feel as though he was to blame for the daughter's repeated attempts at running away. Changing my therapeutic stance not only changed the process occurring at that particular moment, but provided the basis of our therapeutic relationship in the months to come. The stepfather became engaged in the therapy process and committed to making changes necessary to keep the daughter from running away.

CONCLUSION

One of the reasons the Columbo therapy approach is successful, apart from making clients feel heard and accepted, is that it forces clients to restate information in different ways. As clients retell their stories, they begin to think about and experience the situation or problem differently. A second reason for the effectiveness of the approach is that the focus of change is on the process occurring within the therapist-client system. A change in the process is accomplished by the therapist changing his or her approach with the client.

The intervention would be contraindicated whenever a therapist is more concerned about producing a desired outcome in the client's behavior than in his or her own behavior. According to Atkinson and Heath (1990), greater systemic health is promoted by a therapist whose focus is on monitoring and changing her or his own willfulness to change a client's behavior. Rather than being excessively invested in getting the client to do what the therapist wants, a therapist can focus on the process occurring within a session and change her or his personal role in it. In the case described earlier, greater systemic health may be identified in the stepfather's willingness to participate in therapy. Greater systemic health was promoted by focusing on changing the process, as opposed to a focus on getting the stepfather to stop shouting and walking around the room.

REFERENCES

Anderson, H. and Goolishian, H. A. (1988). Human systems as linguistic systems: Preliminary and evolving ideas about the implications for clinical theory. *Family Process, 27*, 371-393.

Atkinson, B. J. and Heath, A. W. (1990). Further thoughts on second-order family therapy: This time it's personal. *Family Process, 29*, 145-155.

Fisch, R., Weakland, J. H., and Segal, L. (1982). *The tactics of change: Doing therapy briefly.* San Francisco: Jossey-Bass Incorporated.

Selekman, M. D. (1993). *Pathways to change: Brief therapy solutions with difficult adolescents.* New York: The Guilford Press.

19

Seeing Change When Clients Don't

G. Alan Willard

The intention of this intervention is for a therapist to point out change to clients at times in the therapy process when clients fail to see any change or progress. This is a general intervention that can be tailored for a variety of clients and problems.

THEORETICAL ORIENTATION

The intervention is based on both a constructivist philosophical orientation (de Shazer, 1991) and solution-focused theory (O'Hanlon and Weiner-Davis, 1989). In solution-focused therapy, scaling questions are often used in the initial session to gather baseline data where clients see themselves at the beginning of therapy using a scale from one to ten for a particular problem, behavior, or feeling. This number can be a reference point for later progress in relation to the particular problem.

Although the intervention is based on the solution-focused use of scaling questions, my idea for the intervention arose out of Friedman's use of what he calls the "arrow of progress" (Friedman, 1991). The circumstances for the use of these interventions are different, but the process going on between client and therapist is somewhat similar. Friedman uses the arrow of progress at a time when clients begin to wonder whether or not to continue in therapy. (See p. 163 of Friedman, 1991, for an elaboration of this point.) My intervention is similar in that I give my interpretation of the progress being made in therapy.

THE INTERVENTION

The following intervention can be helpful with clients who, after two to three sessions, begin to talk about ways in which they think they are not moving along fast enough in their journey toward their goals. In a sense the intervention involves the therapeutic use of a scaling technique in reverse because it is the therapist who is doing the scaling of the client's situation. This is opposite to the conventional use of scaling questions where clients are asked to state where they see themselves or their problem on a scale.

There are times when it can be valuable for therapists to point out to clients the changes the therapist has noticed. Often clients can be hard on themselves, and judge their progress (or its slowness) more harshly than outside observers.

A different way to use the scaling question is for the therapist to be mindful of how it can be incorporated into the later sessions of therapy. Such a scaling technique can be useful when clients come into sessions reporting their disappointment with themselves, their progress, or the rate of problem resolution. When this happens I have been able to use the one to ten scale as a tool for redefining or reframing where the client is at that moment, as a movement toward change.

My conversation with the client might go something like this:

> You know, when you came in here and talked about your problem the way you did a few weeks ago, I had a *mental* picture of the situation on a one-to-ten scale, with one being the worst possible scenario, and ten being the best [I draw this scale on a board]. When you came in, I thought to myself, this situation is about at a four and it is likely that the situation could be said to be better if it got to about a seven or eight on the scale, not completely perfect, but manageable. Now, the last couple of sessions, I have seen some movement in the positive direction so that I would rate it at say six. Yet to hear you speak of the situation today, it sounds as though it is like a four again for you, or maybe it has even dropped to a three. I only wanted you to know that I still see changes so that I would scale it at a six, and here are some reasons for that:
>
> 1. You have been persistent in your efforts
> 2. You have not chosen some options as an easy way out
> 3. You have done the hard work of . . .

Clients will usually respond favorably to my appraisal of them in this manner.

Instead of asking scaling questions of clients in the initial session, this use of scaling *statements* by the therapist (in later sessions) offers clients an opportunity to change their views of what they think, feel, or do. Beyond opening up conversations between client and therapist around the possibility of changing views, perhaps more important, this intervention helps the therapist to practice seeing and verbalizing change for clients. After all, if therapists are not able to look for change and comment on it, is it possible that clients will not be inclined to do so? This intervention may have the by-product of helping therapists learn to offer a more hopeful environment for themselves and for the clients with whom they work.

Possible Contraindications

For the most part this intervention is quite adaptable for diverse clients or presenting problems. However, there may be occasions when it is not useful. Some clients who are very dependent on their therapists may become even more dependent on the therapeutic evaluation of them by this technique. They may come to therapy sessions expecting the therapist to "scale them" each time, which could develop into an overreliance on the therapist's viewpoints as a barometer of progress.

Although the intervention is not intended to assume the client's motivation for change, some clients might perceive it that way. The intervention is designed to engender hope for the therapist and client. If the therapist is not very hopeful about the therapy, or if he/she cannot see progress or change, then this intervention might not be warranted.

REFERENCES

de Shazer, S. (1991). *Putting difference to work.* New York: W.W. Norton.

Friedman, E. (1991). Bowen theory and therapy. In A. Gurman and D. Kniskern, (Eds.), *Handbook of family therapy, Vol. II.* New York: Brunner/Mazel Publishers.

O'Hanlon, W. and Weiner-Davis, M. (1989). *In search of solutions.* New York: W.W. Norton.

20

Making the Genogram Solution Based

Bruce P. Kuehl
Charles P. Barnard
Thorana S. Nelson

This chapter describes how we combine narrative and solution-based interventions with genogram construction. While these approaches might appear theoretically divergent, they are in fact compatible at the level of application (Kuehl, 1995; 1996). More important, there is a subpopulation of clients for whom combining techniques from these approaches makes good sense. In the sections that follow, we orient this intervention in the current climate of family therapy theory, specify technique, and weave a clinical example throughout. For the reader who wants to learn more about genogram construction, we recommend McGoldrick and Gerson (1985).

BOWEN THEORY

The use of genograms as a clinical tool was developed primarily by Bowen therapists (Guerin, 1976). Bowen theory describes the process by which family emotionality contributes to personal and interpersonal symptoms that are transmitted across generations (Bowen, 1978). While specific symptoms might change, the key to therapy is attending to the underlying emotionality that generates them and typical responses that maintain them.

Infants and children—totally dependent on the well-being of primary caregivers—are especially vulnerable to parental dysfunction. Problems with primary caregivers can stir great anxiety in a child. Insecure children may then develop into anxious parents if the interpersonal issues are not resolved. The next generation of children, caught in the web of their parents' anxiety, are at increased vulnerability to insecurity and related symptoms, and the pattern continues. Genograms are used to diagram family membership, key events, symptoms, typical reactions to anxiety and stress, and the quality of interpersonal relationships across at least three generations (Guerin, 1976; McGoldrick and Gerson, 1985). Because symptoms are both indicative of and a response to a family's underlying emotional upset, how members relate to one another is of critical importance. Shifts in functioning often coincide with traumatic events such as job loss, divorce, natural disaster, abuse, or death in the family and emerge as patterns of typical responses. These patterns usually take the form of distance, triangling, dysfunction in one person, or conflict and often are transmitted through family roles, rules, and myths (Bowen, 1978).

With the family's help, the Bowen therapist diagrams these events and patterns and then coaches family members to alter the way they relate to one another both within the immediate family and with members of the family of origin. We place priority on making changes in interpersonal functioning that will lower anxiety in the family's emotional field to functional levels without rigidifying a particular response pattern. This often requires freeing individuals from rigid triangulations, such as children who are parentified or scapegoated as a result of parental discord (Friedman, 1991), and establishing one-on-one relationships that allow people to react differently than they do in the family's usual patterned responses to anxiety.

INDICATORS FOR GENOGRAM USE

We believe that client-theory matching occurs on a case-by-case basis and is guided by the potential for developing a shared frame of reference (Barnard and Kuehl, 1995). Employing a particular theory simply on the basis of either client diagnosis or therapist preference is inadequate. An appropriate fit between how the clients view the situation and how the therapist respects and responds to these views averts resistance and moves therapy forward. Consequently, we find constructing solution-based genograms most useful when working with clients who attribute a majority of their present difficulties to unsatisfactory family-of-origin experiences. That is, the clients are dominated by family stories that dictate particular patterned responses to anxiety to the exclusion of other, more positive responses. Difficulties that are apparent may include, but are not limited to:

- adult clients who resent being treated differently than their siblings;
- adult clients who view their parents as having betrayed them or as falling far short of their expectations;
- adult clients who believe they fell far short of their parents' expectations;
- adult clients who are afraid that they are following in the footsteps of a troubled parent or other family member;

- adult clients whose family roles include compromising their own relationship needs due to debilitating demands from members of their family of origin;
- drug abusers who recall only emotional pain and loss in their families of origin;
- parents who fear that their child is turning out (or not turning out) like someone in the family of origin;
- parents who associate a child with negative characteristics that remind them of a disliked family member;
- couples who agree that their relationship difficulties are due to the influence of extended family members;
- clients who do not implement beneficial changes in their lives for fear that family-of-origin members will respond negatively; and
- clients who seem blocked in some fashion or other from doing what seems logical to others as obvious solutions to life's dilemmas.

Fifteen-year-old Luke was ordered into therapy by the court because he threatened suicide. During the psychiatric evaluation at the hospital, he cited chronic conflict at home as his reason for threatening to kill himself. Outpatient family therapy was recommended. Therapy included Luke, his parents Kim (age thirty-eight) and Bill (age forty-two), as well as Luke's brother Jake (age eleven).

During the initial interview, Luke's parents admitted arguing frequently due to marital difficulties. Luke alleged that his mother drank abusively and had threatened to kill herself on at least two occasions. Kim and Bill, distracted by their own struggles, seemed genuinely surprised to learn how much this disturbed Luke. Jake, less obviously distressed, seemed content to let Luke take the lead in this issue. Indeed, the family admitted that Luke was often caught in his parents' struggles; more than once he attempted to stop their arguments with little success.

In a meeting with the parents as a couple, Bill described Kim's experience in her family of origin. She and a younger brother had been adopted at ages seven and four. Her adoptive father abused alcohol and was emotionally distant. Her adoptive mother was verbally abusive. Kim reported "never feeling worthy of anything." All she know about her biological parents was that they were extremely poor.

Bill described his own parents as "depressing." The only time they seemed to have fun was during such things as wedding receptions and holiday parties. He attributed this to their use of alcohol during these times. He admitted being surprised by how unpleasant

Kim became when she drank. Because he and his sister and brother were never an important part of their parents' life, he was not upset when they divorced when he was seventeen.

SOLUTION-BASED AND NARRATIVE THERAPIES

So-called solution-oriented, solution-focused, and narrative therapies share the belief that change involves helping people reinvent (O'Hanlon and Weiner-Davis, 1989; Walter and Peller, 1992) or reauthor (White and Epston, 1990) their lives. Perception is the key. Preoccupied by problems, living in "problem-saturated" stories (White and Epston, 1990), clients lose sight of their resources and what is going well. As in cognitive therapy, the job of the therapist is to help clients notice exceptions to the problems or belief systems around the problem, reframe its meaning, identify what is working, and create realistic images of what can be achieved in the future.

In these therapies, the question is the therapist's main tool (White and Epston, 1990). The therapist's and the client's curiosity are heightened as people are asked what they know about the problem, how they know what they know, and what new possibilities for solution might emerge as the problem is examined from different perspectives. Responses to these curious and respectful questions elicit images of an outcome that fits with the client's shifting view of the problem, its context, and its solution. Continued questions bring to the foreground what is already happening or what has happened in the past (including families of origin) that leads toward a preferred future, thereby providing evidence that the desired outcome is not only possible, but is indeed becoming reality.

New information casts the problem's context in new light that aids in viewing the past, present, and future in new and less problem-saturated ways. With renewed hopes and dreams, clients often initiate meaningful and rapid change.

With the agreement of each family member, a genogram was constructed. This highlighted the family-of-origin problems that Bill and Kim described and ways that some of these problems were being carried into the present. Remembering their own childhood experiences made them more sensitive to how their struggles were affecting Luke and Jake. When the topic of alcohol was broached, the therapist asked, "Did you realize how much alcohol has betrayed both of your families for three generations?" As everyone gazed in silence at the genogram, Bill remarked, "I thought it was supposed to make people happy."

This last question is an example of what White and Epston (1990) call *externalizing the problem across generations.* Externalizing involves taking a problem previously understood as part of an individual or family and framing it as apart from them. Challenging people to disconnect from the problem reminds them (and therapists) that the problem is the problem, not the family or the identified patient.

Identifying relative family influence, strengths, and exceptions is another solution-based and narrative tool (de Shazer, 1985; Walter and Peller, 1992; White and Epston, 1990) that, when used with genogram construction, highlights the family's ability to not let the problem have absolute influence across the generations and to notice exceptions to problem-based family myths. The full range of the family's responses may have been lost in the transmission of the storied beliefs; "functional" responses may have been "forgotten." Questions such as, "Who has found relief from the legacy of abuse?," "How was your aunt able to deal successfully with the abuse?," "Where has the abuse stopped?," and "Who in your family would describe this problem differently?" serve to identify areas of alternative views and relationship strengths upon which to build.

Therapists can help clients conceptualize the changes they would like to see happen in clear, concrete terms by asking questions that elicit details that might not have been noticed in the midst of the problem-saturated view of the past and of previous generations. For example, the therapist in our case might have asked Kim, "What might your adoptive mother have seen, specifically, that told her that your father was actually very interested in you and your brother; that perhaps he had been playing a role that his father had handed to him?" These questions help clients view important others as sources of strength and solution and not just weakness and problems.

Problems both worsen and improve from one generation to the next. From a solution-based perspective, noticing improvements or imagining positive difference is more helpful than revisiting what went wrong (de Shazer, 1985; O'Hanlon and Weiner-Davis, 1989; Walter and Peller, 1992). Exploring intergenerational solutions, exceptions, and successes, however small, instills in clients a sense of pride and renewed incentive. For example, the therapist might ask, "What do you notice your brother doing compared to how your parents did it?," "What does that say about you?," "What can happen next that will tell you these changes are continuing?," and "What will your son notice that tells him that you have noticed these changes?" This kind of visioning allows clients to make things different for the future, first in thought and then in deed.

The therapist said, "Bill, you said that your parents divorced from a depressing marriage. Yet, you rate your marriage as a six and theirs as only a two. How did you do this?" Bill replied, "What? Our marriage is better? Well, even though we argue a lot, we do more things as a family." Therapist: "This is impressive, because Kim said her father was distant and her mother always yelled at her. [To Kim] You seldom yell at your kids, and although you and Bill argue, I get the impression that you two are closer than your parents were. How did you do this?" After talking about these differences for awhile, the therapist said, "Pretend that the boys are grown up and have children. How would you like to see them interacting with their kids and spouses?" The therapist diagrammed an imagined fourth generation on the genogram. When asked what her adoptive mother might say about these positive changes that Kim was planning, Kim was invited to draw on previously unnoticed strengths in her relationship with her mother.

CONCLUSION

Adding a solution and future focus to an intervention that has typically focused on problems and history provides clients a more immediate link to an improved future than has been possible with prior methods of genogram construction. Spanning all three time perspectives—past, present, and future—helps clients realize what was different in previous generations that they might not have noticed, what they have already accomplished in their own lives, how the clearer image of a preferred future can be useful, and how current behaviors that are already occurring can make that future happen. The genogram becomes a tool for helping clients notice new things about themselves and important others and to generate previously not-possible solutions to their difficulties.

REFERENCES

Barnard, C. P. and Kuehl, B. P. (1995). Ongoing evaluation; In-session procedures for enhancing the working alliance and therapy effectiveness. *American Journal of Family Therapy, 23,* 161-172.

Bowen, M. (1978). *Family therapy in clinical practice.* New York: Jason Aronson.

de Shazer, S. (1985). *Keys to solution in brief therapy.* New York: W.W. Norton.

Friedman, E. H. (1991). Bowen theory and therapy. In A. S. Gurman and D. P. Kniskern (Eds.), *Handbook of family therapy* (pp. 134-170). New York: Brunner/Mazel.

Guerin, P. J. (1976). *Family therapy: Theory and practice.* New York: Gardner Press.

Kuehl, B. P. (1995). The solution-oriented genogram: A collaborative approach. *Journal of Marital and Family Therapy, 21,* 239-250.

Kuehl, B. P. (1996). The use of genograms with solution-based and narrative therapies. *The Family Journal, 4,* 5-11.

McGoldrick, M. and Gerson, R. (1985). *Genograms in family assessment.* New York: W. W. Norton.

O'Hanlon, W. H. and Weiner-Davis, M. (1989). *In search of solutions.* New York: W.W. Norton.

Walter, J. L. and Peller, J. E. (1992). *Becoming solution-focused in brief therapy.* New York: Brunner/Mazel.

White, M. and Epston, D. (1990). *Narrative means to therapeutic ends.* New York: W.W. Norton.

21

From Alienation to Collaboration: Three Techniques for Building Alliances with Adolescents in Family Therapy

Gary M. Diamond
Howard A. Liddle

Adolescents are not inclined to participate in most standard psychotherapies. Engaging teenagers in treatment is one of the greatest challenges for clinicians working with adolescents (Kazdin, 1990; Armbruster and Kazdin, 1994; Liddle, 1991; Szapocznik et al., 1988). Kazdin (1990) cites reports that between 50 and 75 percent of children referred for treatment either do not initiate treatment or terminate prematurely. Sporadic attendance and premature dropout have been identified as major obstacles to the successful treatment of children with conduct disorders (Liddle and Dakof, 1995a, 1995b; Prinz and Miller, 1994). If clinicians hope to effectively serve troubled teenagers and their families, they must find a way to increase adolescents' participation in the treatment process.

Adolescents' aversion to treatment is understandable. Most teenagers are referred or coerced into coming to therapy by their parents, school, or the juvenile justice system. They are rarely consulted about the type of treatment being used or informed about what to expect from therapy (Taylor, Adelman, and Kaser-Boyd, 1985). Furthermore, adolescents are frequently not distressed by the problem behavior that concerns the adults around them (Weisz, 1986). Teenagers are likely to feel that treatment has adopted the agenda of their parents and/or referring party and is not geared to meet their own needs or concerns. The coercive atmosphere permeating much of adolescent treatment runs counter to normative adolescent autonomy development and reduces the degree to which teenagers are motivated to participate in the therapy process (Church, 1994). Given these circum-

We thank Dana Becker, Rivi Diamond, and Cindy Rowe for their helpful comments on this chapter.

stances, it is not surprising that adolescents approach treatment reluctantly (Taylor, Adelman, and Kaser-Boyd, 1985) and with more negativity than other family members (Robbins et al., 1994).

Practitioners of Multidimensional Family Therapy (MDFT) (Liddle, 1992) place great emphasis on transforming teenagers' initial suspicion, mistrust, and disinterest into a willingness to participate in treatment. MDFT is an empirically-based, population-specific approach specializing in the treatment of adolescent problems from a family systems perspective. The model is informed by developmental knowledge and it has three main foci with respect to adolescents: understanding the adolescent's unique experience and fostering his/her cognitive and emotional development (Keating, 1990); facilitating healthy, engaged, interdependent parent-adolescent relationships (Steinberg et al., 1994; Baumrind, 1991); and helping adolescents function more effectively in extrafamilial contexts such as school and peer groups (Brown, 1990). We believe that when teenagers are motivated and agree to the goals and tasks of therapy, treatment is enhanced. When adolescents are willing to examine their thoughts, feelings, and behaviors in the contexts of familial and extrafamilial relationships, therapy can facilitate prosocial functioning.

When adolescents participate in good faith in the process of renegotiating their relationships with their parents (often framed by them as "getting my parents off my back"), parents approach the process with more receptivity, hope, and flexibility. Our research indicates that negative parenting practices can change in MDFT, and one dimension that influences improvement is a change (perception of increased cooperation) in the adolescent (Schmidt, Liddle, and Dakof, 1996). MDFT does not underestimate the adolescent's potential contribution to therapy nor the negative effects of failing to include the teenager in treatment, as our therapy process research reveals (Diamond and Liddle, 1996).

This chapter describes three developmentally based engagement techniques we use to build alliances with teenagers in the early stage of family therapy (Diamond and Liddle, 1996). These MDFT techniques are based, in part, on an understanding of how issues such as adolescent autonomy (Baumrind, 1991; Church, 1994) and contingency and control beliefs (Weisz, 1986) may affect the development of the therapist-adolescent alliance and the teenager's level of participation in the therapy process. We conceive of techniques as interdependent and sometimes sequentially applied interventions (Liddle, 1995). They represent areas of work—part of an adolescent "module" that include certain generic content matter, therapist positions, and statements that we emphasize in our work with adolescents (Liddle, Dakof, and Diamond, 1991).

ORIENTING THE ADOLESCENT
TO THE COLLABORATIVE NATURE OF THERAPY

As therapists, we immediately work to dispel the adolescent's negative expectation that therapy will be coercive and that he or she will not be heard or respected. We explain to the teenager that this therapy is going to be different from what he or she may expect. Treatment is presented as a vehicle for addressing the teenager's concerns and aspirations, not just the concerns of parents or referring agencies. We make it clear that we are interested in the adolescent's point of view and that the adolescent's perspective *will* be accounted for in therapy. We emphasize to the adolescent that we want him or her to "get something out of therapy."

Bill, a seventeen-year-old tenth grader, was on probation for stealing and was referred to treatment by his probation officer. Like many court-referred teenagers, Bill also had a history of school difficulties and periodic marijuana use. During the initial session, Bill's parents were forthcoming when asked to speak about their perceptions of each family member, family relationships, and Bill's difficulties. Bill, despite a number of invitations to join the conversation, remained silent and withdrawn. The therapist decided to spend some time alone with Bill, a common practice during MDFT sessions.

> **T:** I've heard a lot about how your parents see things, but I also know that you have your own side of the story. I would like to get to know you, your point of view, what you like, and what bothers you.
>
> **A:** I don't really like talking, especially to someone I don't even know.
>
> **T:** Yeah, it's kind of strange, this therapy thing—coming and talking to someone you've never met before. It will take a little while for us to get to know and trust one another; that's natural. I hope that the more time we spend together, though, the more comfortable you begin to feel. I want this to be a place where you can bring up things that bother you and, together, we can find a way to work them out. I want this to be a place where you can talk about things that are important to you.

Often teenagers are concerned that the therapist is only interested in getting to know them in order to pass information on to their parents, school, or probation officer. Adolescents may be reluctant to share information because they expect the therapist to respond by lecturing to them about what they should or should not be doing. We make it clear that, except in life-threatening situations, discussions between ourselves and the adolescent are confidential. We also explain that it is not our intent to *tell* the teenager what to do. Therapy is framed as a place to discuss the adolescent's aspirations, concerns, and decision-making process rather than a place to "twist the teen's arm."

> **A:** It doesn't really matter. I'm saving up money and I'm planning on moving out as soon as possible. Are you going to run to tell my parents that now?
>
> **T:** You know Bill, the stuff we talk about together in this room stays between you and me. I'm not interested in passing information on to anyone else. On the other hand, there are going to be things that you tell me that I think are important for your parents to hear from you. For instance, your plan to move out ASAP sounds like it's pretty bad for you at home. I think that it would be important for your parents to hear how miserable it is for you. Maybe we could begin to work on making things better for you at home for the remaining time you are there.
>
> **A:** Look, you can't make me decide to stay.
>
> **T:** Bill, if you decide to move out, that will be between you and your parents. I'm not going to tell you what to do or not to do. On the other hand, I would like to be able to think this through with you and help you think this through with your parents. It's a pretty big decision.

Adolescents approach therapy warily and therapists must begin work immediately to reshape the teenager's conception of and expectations from the treatment process. For adolescents to become engaged in treatment, they must be given a sense that therapy will address their concerns, aspirations, and developmental needs. Building a collaborative, noncoercive therapist-adolescent relationship is a fundamental and first step in therapy, and attention to the multiple interconnected aspects of the adolescent's present ecology is instrumental in meeting these goals (Liddle, 1994).

GOAL FORMATION

Once a collaborative set has been engendered, we move to materialize a specific and meaningful agenda with the teenager. We have not found it helpful to assume that the teenager comes to therapy to reduce drug use, to do better in school, or to stop committing violent or delinquent acts. These items may be important to parents, guardians, or involved others, but they are not necessarily important to the teenager. Instead, we listen carefully to the adolescent's comments about his or her life. As the teenager speaks about relationships, situations, concerns, and hopes, we search for a theme that might make therapy acceptable to the youngster. We look to introduce developmentally derived, generic themes including "trust," "independence," and "respect." We mark these areas as important foci of therapy and help the adolescent to shape his or her thoughts and feelings into concrete goals.

Therapy goals are dictated by the characteristics of the case and vary in their degree of specificity. Goals can range from helping a teenager speak with his mother and father about feeling uncared for to helping the adolescent negotiate a slightly later curfew. When we identify a theme that is salient for the teenager, we grab the opening, flesh out the details, help the youngster formulate a goal, and work to help him or her develop a strategy for attaining that goal.

A: I can't take it at home anymore. Every time I walk in the house, my parents are yelling at me about how I need to do this or need to do that.

T: It sounds like Mom and Dad don't trust that you can, and are going to, take care of your business by yourself.

A: Yeah! They treat me like a twelve-year-old. I get what I need to get done, even without them trying to run every second of my life.

T: Do you think life would be easier if Mom and Dad would begin to treat you like somebody your age? Is that something you would like to see happen.

A: Yeah!

T: You know, that's the type of thing we could work on in here. You and I could spend time, alone and with your parents, thinking about what it is going to take for them to begin treating you like a seventeen-year-old. Does that sound like a reasonable goal?

A: I guess so.

For many adolescents, feigned compliance is the path of least resistance. When therapists and adolescents formulate goals and tasks, it is important that the therapist check in with the adolescent to see whether the teenager has really signed on to the therapy goals or is merely complying with what he or she perceives as the therapist's wishes. Therapists should remember that a "sign-on" does not have to be a resounding and enthusiastic "yes, this is important to me." In the early stages of therapy, we are sometimes satisfied with a tentative, affirmative head shake. On the other hand, it is important to give teenagers the opportunity to say, "This is not really important to me. I am more concerned with the way my mother treats my girlfriend when she comes to visit me in the house." We make it clear that we are committed to shaping therapy's goals to meet the reasonable and developmentally appropriate concerns and aspirations of the adolescent.

GENERATING HOPE

By the time adolescents and their families arrive for treatment, they frequently have a history full of defeat and frustration. Teenagers with problems have often suffered years of failure and pain and many have given up on working things out with their family, finishing high school, or getting a well-paying job. Among poor, urban, minority teenagers, personal failure and difficult family relationships are often compounded by the tremendous obstacles of racism and a lack of resources (Franklin, 1989). When adolescents do not believe that they can do anything to make their lives better, they are less likely to participate in treatment (Weisz, 1986).

As therapists, we work to combat the hopelessness that reduces teenagers' participation in therapy. This does not mean that we minimize the difficulties teenagers and their families have had in the past, nor are we cavalier about the hard work required to effect lasting change. Each case presents real obstacles and limitations. We acknowledge adolescents' feelings of hopelessness and skepticism about their ability to change their lives, yet we take the position that things *can* be different. We clearly communicate our belief that there are things teenagers can do to influence their future.

> T: Have you talked with your parents about wanting to be treated like a seventeen-year-old?
>
> A: They don't want to hear it. It's no use. They've got their minds made up that I am irresponsible and don't care about myself or anything else. They are not going to listen.
>
> T: I can't promise you that things will change overnight and that suddenly your parents will have complete faith in you. There are probably a lot of years of mistrust on both sides of the relationship, and that won't just disappear on the spot. On the other hand, I think there are things you can do that might help your parents hear you and see you differently. It may mean sharing some feelings and thoughts with them that they haven't heard before. It might also mean letting them see those parts of your life in which you are taking responsibility—introducing them to some of your friends or showing them how you are taking care of business in school. There are things you can do that will influence the level of trust between you and your parents.

The therapist does not only challenge the adolescent; he or she offers the teen support—sometimes in very tangible ways. The therapist is presented as an ally.

> **T:** I have a lot of experience helping parents hear their teenagers. I can help your parents hear how difficult it is for you to feel like they don't trust you, and I can help them see changes that you make. I will be there in the room with you.

The therapist explains to the adolescent that having an adult on one's side can sometimes make a difference. It is not only in the family system, however, that the therapist may act as the teenager's ally. In some instances, the therapist represents the teenager vis-à-vis extrafamilial systems such as the school or juvenile justice system. The therapist may meet with a school counselor to help the teenager change a class or meet with a probation officer to advocate against placement for an adolescent who is progressing well in treatment.

Naturally, the family therapist must always be aware that he or she maintains alliances with each family member, as well as extrafamilial system members, and that family therapy is not about "child saving" but is an attempt to help all system members get some of their needs met. Therapists can maintain multiple alliances when the goals for therapy are developmentally based and offer something to all involved parties. The therapist's willingness to periodically advocate for the teen exists within the context of multiple alliances and is meant to increase the adolescent's hope and motivation for change.

The goals of a multidimensional, developmentally informed family therapy with adolescents include: addressing the teenager's intrapersonal life and coping strategies, promoting healthy, interdependent parent-adolescent relationships, and helping the teenager manage behavior and relationships in the context of extrafamilial systems. Work in each of these areas is enhanced by the adolescent's willing and active participation in the therapy process. To engage teenagers in treatment, we strive to define and deliver a therapy that is collaborative, delineates and actualizes an agenda that is personally meaningful for the adolescent, and directly addresses issues of agency, control, and hope.

REFERENCES

Armbruster, P. and Kazdin, A. E. (1994). Attrition in child psychotherapy. *Advances in Clinical Child Psychology, 16,* 81-108.

Baumrind, D. (1991). The influence of parenting styles on adolescent competence and substance abuse. *Journal of Early Adolescence, 11,* 56-95.

Brown, B. B. (1990). Peer groups and peer cultures. In S. S. Feldman and G. R. Elliott (Eds.), *At the threshold: The developing adolescent.* Cambridge, MA: Harvard University Press.

Church, E. (1994). The role of autonomy in adolescent psychotherapy. *Psychotherapy, 31*(1), 101-108.

Diamond, G. M. and Liddle, H. A. (1996). Therapist-adolescent alliance in family therapy. Poster presented at the 1996 American Association for Marriage and Family Therapy Conference. Toronto, Canada, October.

Franklin, A. J. (1989). Therapeutic interventions with urban black adolescents. In R. L. Jones (Ed.), *Black adolescents.* Berkeley, CA: Cobb and Henry.

Kazdin, A. E. (1990). Premature termination from treatment among children referred for antisocial behavior. *Journal of Child Psychology and Psychiatry and Allied Disciplines, 31*, 415-425.

Keating, D. P. (1990). Adolescent thinking. In S. S. Feldman and G. R. Elliott (Eds.), *At the threshold: The developing adolescent.* Cambridge, MA: Harvard University Press.

Liddle, H. A. (1992). A multidimensional model for the adolescent who is abusing drugs and alcohol. In W. Snyder and T. Ooms (Eds.), *Empowering families, helping adolescents: Family-centered treatment of adolescents with alcohol, drug, and other mental health problems* (U.S. Department of Health and Human Services, Office for Treatment Improvement, Alcohol, Drug Abuse, and Mental Health Administration). Washington, DC: U.S. Public Health Service, U.S. Government Printing Office.

Liddle, H. A. (1994). The anatomy of emotions in family therapy with adolescents. *Journal of Adolescent Research, 9*, 120-157. (Special issue on emotions in adolescence.)

Liddle, H. A. (1995). Conceptual and clinical dimensions of a multidimensional, multisystems engagement strategy in family-based adolescent treatment. *Psychotherapy: Theory, Research and Practice, 32*, 39-58. (Special issue on Adolescent Treatment.)

Liddle, H. A. and Dakof, G. A. (1995a). Family therapy for drug abuse: Promising but not definitive efficacy. *Journal of Marital and Family Therapy, 21*, 511-544.

Liddle, H. A. and Dakof, G. A. (1995b). Family-based treatments for adolescent drug use: State of the science. In E. Rahdert and D. Czechowicz (Eds.) *Adolescent drug abuse: Clinical assessment and therapeutic interventions* (NIDA Research Monograph No. 156, NIH Publication No. 95-3908, pp. 218-254). Rockville, MD: National Institute on Drug Abuse.

Liddle, H. A., Dakof, G., and Diamond, G. (1991). Adolescent substance abuse: Multidimensional family therapy in action. In E. Kaufman and P. Kaufmann (Eds.), *Family therapy approaches with drug and alcohol problems* (Second edition). Needham Heights, MA: Allyn and Bacon.

Prinz, R. J. and Miller, G. E. (1994). Family based treatment for childhood antisocial behavior: Experimental influences on drop out and engagement. *Journal of Consulting and Clinical Psychology, 62*, 645-650.

Robbins, M. S., Alexander, J. F., Newell, R. N., and Turner, C. W. (1994). The immediate effect of reframing on client attitude in family therapy. Paper presented at the Second Annual Meeting of North American Society for Psychotherapy Research, February, Santa Fe, NM.

Schmidt, S. E., Liddle, H. A., and Dakof, G. A. (1996). Multidimensional family therapy: Parenting practices and symptom reduction in adolescent substance abuse. *Journal of Family Psychology, 10,* 12-27.

Steinberg, L., Lamborn, S. D., Darling, N., Mounts, N. S., and Dornbusch, S. M. (1994). Over-time changes in adjustment and competence among adolescents from authoritative, authoritarian, indulgent, and neglectful families. *Child Development, 65,* 754-770.

Szapocznik, J., Perez-Vidal, A., Brickman, A. L., Foote, F. H., Santisteban, D., Hervis, O., and Kurtines, W. (1988). Engaging adolescent drug abusers and their families in treatment: a strategic structural systems approach. *Journal of Consulting and Clinical Psychology, 56,* 552-557.

Taylor, L., Adelman, H. S., and Kaser-Boyd, N. (1985). Exploring minors' reluctance and dissatisfaction with psychotherapy. *Professional Psychology: Research and Practice, 16*(3), 418-425.

Weisz, J. (1986). Contingency and control beliefs as predictors of psychotherapy outcomes among children and adolescents. *Journal of Consulting and Clinical Psychology, 34,* 789-795.

22

What I Needed versus What I Got: Giving Clients Permission to Grieve

Tina M. Timm

DESCRIPTION OF PROBLEM

As a therapist working with survivors of sexual abuse I find that my clients often struggle with what feels to them like overwhelming amounts of grief. They typically describe their childhoods as one huge loss. Below is an intervention designed to help clients gain a clearer understanding of the specific events or issues they need to grieve. This intervention validates the client and confirms what they need to grieve. It also provides a way to look at what they can do to heal, which may include grieving rituals or other ways to give themselves what they needed as a child. It is applicable for many types of clients and presenting problems. It can also be used with families and couples to facilitate empathy and understanding.

THEORY THAT INFORMS THE INTERVENTION

This intervention is based on the instrumental work of Elisabeth Kübler-Ross and the stages of grieving she established in her book *On Death and Dying* (1969). There is a gradual progression through stages of denial and isolation, anger, bargaining, depression, and finally, acceptance. However, it is not necessarily a linear process. Clients may fluctuate between stages, returning to one they had been in before, or simply progressing through them in a different order. The main purpose of the intervention described below is to move clients from the stage of denial and isolation, where they can sometimes remain stuck, unaware of what they are specifically trying to grieve. Clients in this stage may describe their childhood in neutral terms such as "uneventful" or state their parents "did the best they could." Others may be angry but not recognize the grief underneath the anger.

THE INTERVENTION

The first step is to give the client permission to grieve the things that they had but lost as well as what they wanted as a child but didn't get. This permission giving is very important because many clients don't take into account the losses that fit into the second category. For example, it is socially acceptable to grieve when one's grandparents die. However, if a client never had grandparents they still have experienced a loss—the loss of what they wanted their grandparents to be. Many clients have not taken into account these types of losses.

As a homework assignment, have clients take a piece of paper and make a list of the things they wanted and needed as a child. Then, on a separate piece of paper, make a list of what they actually got. A suggestion to give clients who don't seem to be connected to their "child side" is to write the lists with their nondominant hand. This will allow for an experience of feeling like a child when writing.

The first thing that most clients notice is the stark contrast between the lists. Some will have long lists of things they wanted and short lists of what they actually received. Others will have equal lists but find that what they got was just the opposite of what they wanted. This experience fosters greater compassion for themselves as children. This is very useful for clients who say they "didn't have it that bad," or who berate themselves for feeling sad over "nothing." Many are amazed at the simple things that they wanted as a child but did not receive.

CASE EXAMPLE

Randy was a thirty-four-year-old male who was sexually abused by his grandfather and physically and emotionally abused by his father. In his home, fear dictated that children were to be seen and not heard. There were meticulous rules about meals. He remembers being forced to sit completely still for hours every night while his dad read the paper and expected to be surrounded by his family. Playing was simply not allowed. Gum chewing prompted beatings. Here are portions of Randy's lists:

What I wanted:

- a dad who would talk to me without yelling
- to not sit up perfectly straight all the time
- to giggle or laugh without being hit
- to eat a meal without fear
- to chew bubble gum
- to fly a kite

What I got:

- a dad who ruled by fear
- a mom who never protected me
- rules that prevented me from being a kid
- locked in my room for going outside
- bruises
- sexual abuse

Response to the Intervention

His actual lists went on and on. They filled up pages. After making the lists he reported feeling as if he had a right to be sad. He also said he was mad. Before doing the assignment, he felt as if his parents had "done a good job" and he got most of what he needed as a child. After he did the assignment he felt validated that there was a lot to be sad about and recognized some things he could do to make up for what he hadn't gotten.

The next day he went out and bought the kite that he never had. When he flew his kite, he gave himself permission to chew gum, slouch, and to laugh as much as he wanted. He was learning how to reparent himself and begin the healing process.

COMMENTS

I have found this assignment helpful in validating childhood losses and as a place to begin healing from those losses. Clients can focus on specific losses instead of being overwhelmed by a global sense of grief or simply not knowing what there is to grieve. The realization that clients can parent themselves can be a double-edged sword. They feel empowered to know they can give themselves the things they always wanted but are hit with the additional sadness of having to do it themselves. It is not uncommon to have a lifelong wish to have those needs met by significant others. Finding out you can do it yourself can be exciting but anticlimactic.

This intervention has an additional benefit for clients who have children. The reminder of what they wanted as children allows them to view their own children more compassionately. They may reevaluate how much time they spend playing with and listening to their children. Behaviors that were previously viewed as naughty may now be seen as a need for attention. They have a greater awareness of the simple things children want and like to do.

CONTRAINDICATIONS

This intervention is not particularly helpful with clients who only want to "parent bash" and use the assignment as proof of what bad parents they had. It is not an assignment to be used to support one's identity as powerless victim. Instead, it should be used to support healing grief and positive action. Also, this assignment has the potential to evoke immense sadness and rage. Thus, you should not use this assignment with any client who has seriously threatened physical harm to family members.

REFERENCE

Kübler-Ross, Elisabeth. (1969). *On death and dying*. New York: Macmillan.

23

Starting with the Familiar:
Working with "Difficult" Clients

Diane R. Gehart-Brooks

THEORETICAL BACKGROUND

The idea of "starting with the familiar" can be traced back to the work of Gregory Bateson. Bateson describes learning as resulting from the "news of difference" (Bateson, 1972). News can only be interpreted as different if it is compared to the familiar, the complement of difference. A therapist who recognizes that learning occurs within the context of the familiar approaches clients from a position that honors the familiar world of the client. The therapist starts with the familiar not because it allows the therapist to join or assess the system but because it is the context for new ideas that will be meaningful to the client.

The intervention described in this chapter is more an expression of the therapist's philosophical stance than a technique that can be cut and pasted as needed. Inspired primarily by the work of Anderson and Goolishian (Anderson, 1995; Anderson and Goolishian, 1992), starting with the familiar is an important part of facilitating a therapeutic conversation. In this conversation, the therapist explores the client's everyday world, allowing new ideas to develop from the conversation. As the therapist begins to understand the client's view, "the therapist's learning process naturally shifts to a mutually puzzling process in which therapist and client become engaged in conversation with each other in co-exploring the familiar in a manner that leads to co-development of the new" (Anderson, 1995, p. 36). Curious inquiry about the client's everyday understandings provides a comfortable context that promotes the development of new ideas and insights.

Continuing the conversation about familiarity and difference, Tom Andersen (1995) adds that the therapist's comments must not be too familiar or too unusual for the client. Either extreme fails to convey news of meaningful difference. To gauge the appropriateness of their comments, therapists must first become acquainted with the familiar.

FOR USE WITH WHOM BY WHOM?

Clients

Starting with the familiar is appropriate for all clients, but it is ideal for use with "difficult" clients. Clients are experienced as difficult when the therapist is unable to engage them in meaning-generating conversation. Whether difficult is defined as "resistant," "borderline," "mandated," "nonverbal," or "psychotic," labeling a client as difficult suggests that the therapist has not explored the familiar. Until the therapist can enter the client's familiar world, the client will most likely be unable to apply therapeutic conversations to everyday life.

Therapists

Therapists who identify their work as cybernetic, systemic, or post-modern can comfortably incorporate the idea of familiarity into their work. Although implied in the work of Bateson, this idea has been over-looked or misinterpreted by many cybernetic-based approaches. The concept has been reemphasized and reinterpreted in the postmodern therapies, such as collaborative language systems (Anderson and Goolishian, 1992) and narrative therapy (White and Epston, 1990).

DESCRIPTION OF THE INTERVENTION PROCESS

The therapist facilitates conversations with clients by engaging them in discussion about their familiar stories. Some clients may talk about the familiar story with little prompting, while others may tell it in a dialogue format with a curious therapist who inquires about it. With younger children, the familiar may be a form of play, such as drawings or storytelling. Persons with diagnosed psychotic features or violent histories may tell stories that the therapist is tempted to disregard, but their stories must be explored if the client is to hear news of difference. The therapist's inexhaustible curiosity about the client's story encourages conversation about the familiar.

While discussing the client's familiar story, the therapist maintains a stance of curiosity and not knowing (Anderson and Goolishian, 1992). Questions are asked to gain a better understanding of the client's worldview rather than to confirm the therapist's hypotheses. The curious therapist freely contributes ideas when they flow naturally out of the conversation rather than a predetermined treatment plan. The therapist's ideas are used to enrich the conversation, and the client is not viewed as uncooperative or resistant for disliking an idea. Instead, as "expert" in his or her own story, the client is free to accept or reject ideas based on their perceived usefulness to the client at the time.

CASE EXAMPLE

A therapist receives a call from a single mother requesting an appointment. She says that the court has required her to attend counseling with her thirteen-year-old and eleven-year-old daughters because the school reports that the younger daughter has frequently been absent. When the therapist meets with the family, she asks them about the problem that brings them to therapy. The family shares their story about the older daughter's ex-boyfriend, the leader of a local gang, who has harassed, threatened, and beaten the teen, her mother, their extended family, and their friends.

During the interview the therapist helps the family tell their story by asking questions that elicit greater detail about the clients' familiar story and to clarify the clients' understanding of a term or situational context. For example, when the oldest daughter fearfully talks about how she has dropped out of school because her ex-boyfriend's friends harassed her, the therapist asks questions that maintain consistency with the client's current story about the fear of being at school: "Can you tell me more about being 'harassed'?," "How did you feel when you knew his friends were watching you?," and "What did you fear would happen when they told him what you were doing?" The content of the therapist's questions is less vital to the process than ensuring that the questions respect and validate the client's reality. These questions, or any others that fit with the client's current story, allow the client and therapist to explore the story in greater depth and evolve new understandings.

The therapist avoids questions that try to force another story on the client, such as "How are you getting your required schooling now?," "Do you plan to graduate from high school?," or "Did you try talking with the principal?" These types of questions subtly suggest to the client that there is a better way that she should be handling the situation. These questions may be appropriate in a different conversation when the client is talking about how she wants to change her situation. Thus, starting with the familiar requires the therapist to keep pace with the client rather than trying to force the client to adopt the therapist's schedule for change.

CONTRAINDICATIONS

There are no contraindications for this intervention in the traditional sense because it is part of the therapist's philosophical stance. However, certain situations may require special attention. Therapists who work with clients required to attend counseling by an outside source, such as a court, federal agency, or school, may be given predetermined treatment goals and expectations. In such cases, the therapist may feel constrained by external demands. The therapist can make these expectations "public" (Anderson, 1995) and use them to begin a conversation about the client's view of the story. When the therapist allows the client's story to coexist with differing stories from outside sources, the client is free to nondefensively explore the situation and make meaningful changes from a familiar framework.

REFERENCES

Andersen, T. (1995). Reflecting processes: Acts of informing and forming. In S. Friedman (Ed.) *The reflecting team in action: Collaborative practice in family therapy* (pp. 11-37). New York: Guilford.

Anderson, H. (1995). Collaborative language systems: Toward a postmodern therapy. In R. Mucocele, D. D. Lusterman, and S. McDaniel (Eds.), *Family psychology and systems therapy* (pp. 27-44). Washington, DC: American Psychological Association Press.

Anderson, H. and Goolishian, H. (1992). The client is the expert: A not-knowing approach to therapy. In S. McNamee and K. J. Gergen (Eds.), *Therapy as social construction* (pp. 25-39). Newbury Park, CA: Sage.

Bateson, G. (1972). The logical categories of learning and communication. In *Steps to an Ecology of Mind* (pp. 279-308). New York: Ballantine.

White, M. and Epston, D. (1990). *Narrative means to therapeutic ends.* New York: W. W. Norton.

24

A Picture Is Worth a Thousand Words: Use of Family Photographs to Promote Parental Nurturance in Family Therapy with Adolescents

Susan K. Mackey

INTRODUCTION

Family therapy with adolescents most frequently focuses on issues of individuation, hierarchy, conflict, power, and control. The nurturance of adolescents by their parents has been relatively ignored in the literature (Mackey, 1996). This is despite considerable theoretical and research data supporting the importance of parental nurturance to adolescent identity formation and self-esteem (Mackey, in press). Parental nurturance is one avenue to address attachment/connection problems between parents and adolescents. Parental nurturance can be easily incorporated into most treatment approaches with adolescents and usually serves to enhance the therapist's effectiveness. This chapter will demonstrate how family photographs can be used to facilitate parental nurturance in the context of family therapy with adolescents.

Nurturance is defined as a subset of behavior within the more general classification of attachment behaviors. Attachment theory suggests that secure attachment is characterized not solely by the amount of contact between parent and child but by how well the behavior of the parent toward the child fits both the personal rhythms of the child and the child's developmental stage (Bowlby, 1982). This means that a nurturant act is successful only when the parent can discriminate between the parent's own needs and emotions and those of the adolescent. For example, a successful nurturant act might be a friendly jostle in the hall but not asking for the traditional good-bye kiss in front of an adolescent boy's peers.

ASSESSMENT OF ATTACHMENT

Five factors indicate that the attachment between parents and adolescent is in trouble and that parental nurturance might be an appropriate focus in treatment. The first factor is the chronicity of any power struggles ongoing between the adolescent and his/her parents. The longer the history of a power struggle, the more likely it is that the attachment is insecure or damaged. A related factor is the amount of anger or bitterness that has accumulated over the course of the ongoing struggle for power. The deeper the anger on both sides, the more difficult it will be to make progress on any other issues before shifting the quality of the relationship between the adolescent and his/her parents. A third factor is the degree to which the adolescent is connected to his/her peer group to the exclusion of the parents. The more the adolescent has become accustomed to having his/her needs met through peer as opposed to parental interactions, the less the motivation on the adolescent's part to cooperate with parental requests. This is especially true of those requests involving limit-setting, since they are likely to interfere with the typical ways the adolescent meets his/her needs. The fourth factor is a history of attempted solutions using limit-setting approaches that have failed. Even when it is clear to the therapist that the previous attempts were flawed in some important ways or not adequately carried out, the family will feel discouraged by these failures. Therefore, they will not be predisposed to revisit these approaches without some shift in focus. Finally, indications of abuse or neglect clearly indicate damage to the parent-child relationship, which will need to be addressed prior to any limit-setting approaches with the adolescent.

BUILDING THE FOUNDATION FOR INTERVENTION

The presence of any of the aforementioned factors indicates a damaged attachment. This means that the patterns of behavior are likely to be entrenched and strained. A new approach is called for that will break the typical patterns of mutual angry exchange and/or accusation and silent withdrawal that occur both in and out of the session. The therapist should first establish the ineffectiveness of the current behavior on the part of the parents as well as the previously attempted solutions. The next step is to invite them to consider a new approach. It should be stressed that while no guarantees of success can be offered, the cost of the new effort to the participants is minimal. Further, even if the adolescent's behavior does not improve, the family might benefit from a less hostile atmosphere. The therapist can further stress how exhausting the power struggle is and how the parents might enjoy some relief from it. Having established the rationale for a new treatment approach, the therapist can directly make reference to difficulties in the parent-child relationships. The therapist can follow up with the assertion that it is unlikely that the adolescent will change his/her behaviors without some improvement in these relationships.

USING PHOTOS TO PROMOTE NURTURANCE

Family photographs can be used initially as a means within the session to interrupt the current patterns of behavior and to elicit different kinds of interactions. Photographs frequently record family rituals and/or positive interactions and therefore may provide an opportunity to elicit memories of different, more connected behaviors between the parents and the child. The act of looking at them in session with the therapist in itself interrupts the usual sequence of behavior between parents and adolescent.

Subsequent to the discussion of the current difficulties in the relationship, the therapist can ask when is the last time when the family members remember that their relationships were good or better. Not infrequently, the family will report that the connection with the adolescent was good up until preadolescence. Once the "better" relationship point in time has been identified, then the family can be directed to talk in concrete detail about what was different at that time. Here family photographs can assist concretely in the discussion of daily activities and rituals in which the family participated. This discussion will hopefully elicit details that the family members have forgotten. The family members should be asked to bring in photographs from the period in which they last remember having good relationships as well as any favorites they wish to contribute to the session. The viewing and discussion of the photographs not infrequently provokes humor and fond reminiscences, which provide a welcome break from the typical interactions between adolescent and parents. Other important data about family relationships are often brought out in a nonthreatening atmosphere; for example, the centrality of grandparents or roles of siblings in the family.

The content of the photographs can then be used to help inform out-of-session tasks designed around parental nurturance. Specifically, old patterns or daily rituals can provide the basis or ideas for what might reconnect the parents and adolescent now. For example, a photo reminds the family how they used to give each other backrubs up until pubescence and that they could reinstate this practice.

CASE EXAMPLE

Joanne and Michael (both thirty-eight), brought their sixteen-year-old daughter, Leslie, to therapy because of difficulties at both home and school. Leslie had begun to have difficulties in the sixth grade. The parents and Leslie fight constantly about Leslie's homework and outside activities. Joanne reports that Leslie has become a chronic liar and is not to be trusted about schoolwork or to be where she says she is going to be.

Leslie reports that she hates her parents, and that all her friends agree that her parents are totally "lame." Any discussion about areas of conflict in the session quickly escalated to Leslie shouting profanities, Joanne looking helpless, and Michael becoming angry and threatening.

Previous attempts at therapy focused on a "tough love" approach that everyone reported as not having been successful. The parents agreed that they would like to improve their relationship with Leslie. Leslie remained skeptical about therapy but agreed to participate "for now." They agreed to bring photos from "better times."

At the next session, they reported a better week. Joanne said that Leslie had actually reminded her about the photos and had helped her pick some out. While cooperative, Michael was distant and seemed preoccupied in session until Joanne brought out a photo of him playing basketball with Leslie. At this point, father and daughter talked about how they used to "shoot hoops." When I inquired if they could reinstate this activity, Leslie and Michael simultaneously exclaimed that the other would not make time in their schedules. When mutually challenged, they agreed to play for fifteen minutes each weeknight and on Sunday.

It took several weeks for Michael to live up to his commitment, but it turned out to be the focal point for change, resulting in Michael's realization of how distant he had become from his family, which recapitulated his relationship with his own father.

SUMMARY

This case study illustrates how family photographs can be used in session to break negative behavioral sequences and promote more positive interaction between parents and their adolescent. The photos can then be used as the basis for the cocreation of an out-of-session task. In the case example, the task was small, concrete, and agreed upon by all family members—important elements of its success. With adolescents, dyadic interactions are advised; each parent can try a separate, small experiment that can be done several times during the week rather than one larger activity. The experiments should be separated from the adolescent's behavior during the week, whether positive or negative.

The success of shifting the focus in treatment of adolescents from power and control issues to improving the parent-child relationship through the promotion of parental nurturance serves both as a healing experience for the family and as the basis for further change for all family members.

REFERENCES

Bowlby, J. (1982). *Attachment and loss*. New York: Basic Books.
Mackey, S. (1996). Nurturance: A neglected dimension in famly therapy with adolescents. *Journal of Marital and Family Therapy, 22,* 489-508.

—25—

A Fairy-Tale Ending

Sharon A. Deacon

Terminating a case is often a very difficult task for both clients and therapists. It can be difficult to know when termination is appropriate. Is it appropriate only after clients have reached their goals? Or do you terminate when clients have the tools they need to reach their goals? Perhaps you terminate when clients say "enough." In any case, the actual act of terminating is tricky too. How does the therapist go about setting up some kind of closure for the therapeutic relationship that has developed? A fairy-tale ending would be just perfect, wouldn't it?

"A Fairy-Tale Ending" is an activity therapists can use as a method of closure at termination. The idea behind it is to help clients create a story of their therapeutic experience, write it down, and use it as a reminder of the changes they made in therapy, and as a souvenir of their therapeutic journey. For clients who have a difficult time seeing the positive, and who expect therapy to lead to a perfect life, this intervention helps them validate their progress and feel competent to go on without weekly therapy.

THEORETICAL BASIS

This intervention stems from ideas based in narrative therapy and experiential therapy. Clients end therapy when they feel they have been successful. Success requires the ascription of meaning to unique outcomes that can be plotted into an alternative story or narrative (White and Epston, 1990). In writing their own fairy tale about their therapy experience, clients are actually generating an alternative story, about their success, for themselves. Clients add new meaning to their progress, while externalizing their experience enough that they can see all the changes that were made and plan for the future.

Clients learn by doing. Actively creating a fairy tale of their own lives, clients are able to reexperience all the progress they have made. In doing so, clients often come to the realization that they worked hard, and termination seems like the natural next step. They utilize their creativity, and reaffirm their growth in a symbolic way—through a fairy tale (Connell and Russell, 1987; Piercy, Sprenkle, and Associates, 1986).

THE INTERVENTION

As the therapist and clients near termination (in whatever way you establish that termination is appropriate at that specific time), the therapist can begin to reflect on all the changes and growth the clients have achieved. The therapist may even begin to paint a picture, for the clients, of where they were and where they are now, including all the steps in between. As the clients start to realize all the progress that was made, the therapist can discuss the possibility of termination and introduce this intervention:

When I look back on the clients I have worked with, each case enters my head as if it were a story to tell. I think about how the clients were in the beginning, when they first entered therapy. Then I start to reflect on how the plot thickened, as I learned more and more details about the clients, and we started defining what the conflict was— because a good story always has some kind of crisis or conflict, you know. The case always seems to reach some high level of suspense, when the clients are anxious, and then a turning point usually occurs, when a change is made, and the story line shifts. Soon, the suspense or conflict is resolved somehow, and the plot begins to descend to a conclusion. That's where I feel we are right now, at the descent to a conclusion of your therapy story.

Clients are usually amused by this metaphor and tend to listen, like little children being told a story. I then continue by presenting the activity to the clients, as follows:

Something that I like to do with clients is to actively create a fairy tale of the time in therapy. We could start with a beginning, where we describe the setting and characters in the plot. Then we could move into building the suspense, defining the conflict that needed to be resolved. Finally, we could reach the turning point and resolution and then begin our progression to a conclusion. Do you think you could find that creative side of yourselves, to write this fairy tale with me?

After overcoming any objections, and making clients comfortable with being creative and imaginative, I send clients off with homework. I instruct them to start thinking of what type of fairy tale they would write about themselves and therapy. I allow them to use any type of symbolizations they want for the setting, characters, and conflict. I ask them to return to the next meeting with an outline and idea for the story. (Sometimes it is helpful to read to clients the fairy tale of another client, one that does not risk any type of confidentiality issues, as an idea of how to go about this activity.)

When the clients return, we sit down with art supplies and write and draw out the fairy tale they constructed. It is a joint experience shared by everyone involved in the therapy. While doing this, I am constantly reaffirming the progress they made, the resolution they have come to, and the need to conclude. I also like to ask them where they think the story may go from this conclusion ("sequels"), and how they can direct it in the way they want it to go.

I end the activity by making two copies of the story we created, one for the clients and one for myself. I discuss how the story can be used as a memento of their therapy and as a reminder to keep the changes going. The fairy tale is a trophy of their accomplishment. (This is also a good time to ask permission to use their story as an example for other clients.)

CLIENT RESPONSE

Most clients respond very favorably to this activity and manner of termination. It is a fun way to end therapy that allows for an appropriate closure to a temporary relationship. Some clients need assistance in accessing their right-brain and creative talents. This is when past fairy tales can come in handy. It is also okay for therapists to start the story and help the clients develop their ideas.

This activity is a great way to get a whole family involved in a collaborative project, and for children to take a lead role. It helps build cooperation, communication skills, and creativity in problem solving. The finished product is evidence that the family can work together and produce great outcomes.

CONTRAINDICATIONS

When clients have initiated termination themselves, and are in a hurry to end therapy, this intervention is perceived as too time consuming. Clients may drop out before finishing such a project, and therefore the intervention is not helpful in bringing some type of closure. Also, when clients are totally unwilling to accept that therapy was successful in any way, or if the therapeutic relationship is ending on poor terms, this activity is inappropriate and may only lead to more tension. Clients who do not feel comfortable being creative may become anxious when asked to complete such a project and may need a more concrete, simplified version of this activity, such as a verbal narrative.

REFERENCES

Connell, G. M. and Russell, L. A. (1987). Interventions for the trial of labor in symbolic-experiential family therapy. *Journal of Marital and Family Therapy,* *13*(1), 85-94.

Piercy, F. P., Sprenkle, D. H., and Associates. (1986). *Family therapy sourcebook.* New York: Guilford Press.

White, M. and Epston, D. (1990). *Narrative means to therapeutic ends.* New York: W. W. Norton.

26

The Wall of Defenses

Sharon A. Deacon

It is not uncommon for clients to enter therapy with a reservoir of defenses that they have used to protect themselves from being vulnerable to others. Many times, clients describe themselves as stuck behind a brick wall or having built a wall around themselves to keep intruders out. Therapists, too, often reframe their clients' behavior as an effort to protect themselves and hide behind a "wall." Therefore, therapy may focus on how to come out from behind the brick wall in order to build more satisfying, two-way relationships. This intervention serves to help clients identify their defenses, their reasons for needing protection, and how to become more open in relationships. Clients symbolically construct and destruct their wall of defenses.

The Wall of Defenses intervention can be used with any type of client, child or adult, who has difficulty expressing inner feelings and being open, honest, and somewhat vulnerable in relationships. For couples, this intervention can be extremely useful as a means for identifying underlying feelings and cognitions and the behaviors associated with each. This activity can serve as a guide for therapy, as well as an exploration of the client's past and how significant events have affected the client and his/her current behavior. It is a powerful tool for externalizing (White and Epston, 1990) the client's problems and helping clients to look at themselves honestly.

THEORETICAL FOUNDATION

The construction and deconstruction of the wall of defenses is an intervention that incorporates experiential therapy, art therapy, narrative therapy, and cognitive restructuring. Clients are given an opportunity to externalize their problems and trace the roots of the problem by drawing and labeling the wall they are stuck behind. Cognitively, clients gain a new understanding of the reasons behind their behavior as they examine the beliefs and attitudes that allow the wall to remain standing. Right-brain activities are used to produce spontaneity and creativity (Piercy, Sprenkle, and Associates, 1986). The primacy of the experience of drawing the wall and deconstructing it in the present is emphasized.

The basic focus of any experiential technique is to stimulate affective involvement through dramatization and symbolization, and encourage growth (Connell and Russell, 1987; Whitaker and Keith, 1981). The wall of defenses serves as a physical externalization and symbol of the foundation upon which clients' defensive behaviors are built. Seeing their defenses externally, by viewing the wall, provides clients with an alternate cognitive perspective of their problems. Just as in narrative therapy, the problem becomes a separate entity, outside the client (White and Epston, 1990). The client metaphorically works toward deconstructing the wall, rather than directly deconstructing themselves, their ideas, or their behaviors. Therapy becomes more of a task and less of a personal threat to one's esteem.

THE INTERVENTION

Before the actual activity can begin, the therapist must first reframe the clients' problem in terms of "being stuck behind a brick wall." The therapist and client can discuss what it feels like to be behind an obstacle (both the advantages of safety and invulnerability, and the disadvantages of not being close to anyone and unable to see or be seen by others should also be discussed). Once the client and therapist have established this reframe of a "brick wall of defenses," the actual drawing can begin.

Give the client a large sheet of paper and crayons. Ask the client to mentally picture the brick wall, and then draw it. As the client draws, ask the client to label all the bricks on the wall (the events in his/her life or reasons for which the wall was built and needed). Some examples of brick or event labels could be child abuse, divorce, being "dumped" by a girlfriend or boyfriend, losing a job, being criticized by parents, being overweight, fear of intimacy, and so forth. (I like to help the client construct the wall chronologically, such that the bottom, or foundation, of the wall serves as the basis for all the other bricks. Without this foundation of defenses, the other bricks would not have anything to build upon. If the foundation were removed, the wall would fall apart.) As the client draws each brick, discuss the associated event and what happened. Ask questions concerning what surrounded each brick as protection, how it is protecting the client now, what behaviors the client engages in that serve to keep the brick in place, and how the brick defense affects the client. Discuss which bricks build upon each other, and how the defensive behaviors are related. Be sure to include some bricks that represent simple, natural defenses that everyone has and that are normal. (I call these "N" bricks, for natural defenses.)

Allow clients to leave holes in the wall, where they have given themselves some room to be seen honestly by others and to be vulnerable with others. These spaces may also be past ways the client has tried to escape from the wall to be close to others. These spaces can be labeled too, such as drug use, running away, going to college, entering therapy, and so on. Every client will construct a different brick wall. Some may have many smaller bricks, while others may have a few enormous bricks making up their walls, depending on the size of the problem or defense. Let clients choose their own design and colors. You may even want to question them about their choices and what certain colors symbolize to them. This drawing may take several sessions.

Once the drawing is complete, ask the client how it feels to be behind the wall. (This may also be a good time to reiterate the advantages and disadvantages of having such a wall.) Then ask the client how he/she wants to begin deconstructing the wall. Discuss strategies that can be used to take the wall apart. For example, the client may choose to go brick by brick, from one side of the wall to the other, always leaving room to hide; top to bottom, shrinking the wall; randomly picking bricks all over the wall, by topic; or right at the bottom, forcing the whole wall to crumble (I do not suggest this, unless the client is prepared for the extreme consequences).

Each time the client picks a brick for discussion, the therapist can use various other interventions that apply to the defensive behavior labeled on the brick to create change. In some instances, it is helpful for the client simply to talk about how that brick got into the wall. Discuss the events that happened, how the client felt vulnerable, and why the client felt the need to protect him/herself. Some cognitive restructuring may be helpful, leading the client to realize that the brick may not be useful or needed anymore. It is also important to help clients think of other ways they can protect themselves besides hiding from a potential threat.

Utilizing the externalization aspect of this intervention, therapists can reframe clients' problems as something to "fight against," rather than placing the problem within the client. Clients are able to view the problem differently, seeing it outside themselves, and open up new possibilities for dealing with these "externalized problems." Once a problem is "dealt with," the client may feel confident in removing a now-useless brick from the wall.

Other experiential interventions are helpful when it comes to deconstructing the wall. Visualization, in which clients actually picture themselves beating on the wall with a hammer, may be helpful. In this manner, clients can release some of the aggression surrounding the circumstances of why the brick was placed on the wall to begin with. At the same time, clients are cognitively and symbolically destroying part of their walls.

Experiential sculptures may also be useful (see Simon, 1972 for further explanation of family sculptures). Have the client create a sculpture of the people listed on a particular brick, and include the brick wall in the sculpture. Ask clients to discuss how they feel in relation to others and the wall. Also, ask clients to surmise how the other people in the sculpture feel in relation to the wall. What would happen if the wall was removed from the sculpture? Discuss what the function of the wall is and possible alternatives that could be used, in place of the brick wall, for self-protection. Once some alternatives are explored, clients may feel more able to give up some bricks that relate to the sculpture.

Every time the client feels that the problem on the brick has been resolved or is no longer needed, the brick can come off the wall. Clients can symbolize the destruction of the brick however they wish (most choose to color it in). As a brick is removed, discuss how the other bricks are affected. Removing a brick that supports other bricks can cause those bricks to crumble too—as one change is made, others naturally follow. Always remind the client that although some bricks are falling, the "N" bricks will always be there, and the client will never be left completely vulnerable, without any protection. Constantly refer to the wall to see the progress the client is making, and to keep track of the goal for which the client is striving.

Throughout this whole process, clients may also wish to add to their pictures. Some clients add scenery ("it's always brighter on the other side") or a sun, as more light is let in on their side of the wall. A picture of an axe or hammer may used to symbolize the effort the client is putting forth. A ladder my be drawn as a symbol of escape from the wall, and the rungs may be labeled as steps necessary to see over the wall or destruct the wall.

The length of therapy using such an intervention depends on the severity of the client's problems and the client's motivation to work quickly. This intervention should not be rushed. The client should dictate the speed at which he/she is comfortable progressing.

CLIENT RESPONSE

Client response often depends on the way the therapist presents the intervention. With adults, it is important for the therapist to feel comfortable doing art therapy and engaging in experiential activities that can evoke strong emotional responses. Most clients who are open to experiential therapy enjoy the activity. They are able to see their problems, understand their behavior, and actively work to see the wall come down. It is a very gratifying experience that clients often choose to share with others.

CONTRAINDICATIONS

This intervention is not suggested for crisis situations that require more rapid intervention and/or resolution.

REFERENCES

Connell, G. M. and Russell, L. A. (1987). Interventions for the trial of labor in symbolic-experiential family therapy. *Journal of Marital and Family Therapy, 13*(1), 85-94.

Piercy, F. P., Sprenkle, D. H., and Associates. (1986). *Family therapy sourcebook.* New York: Guilford Press.

Simon, R. M. (1972). Sculpting the family. *Family Process, 11,* 49-57.

Whitaker, C. A. and Keith, D. V. (1981). Symbolic-experiential family therapy. In A. S. Gurman and D. P. Kniskern (Eds.), *Handbook of family therapy* (pp. 187-225). New York: Brunner/Mazel.

White, M. and Epston, D. (1990). *Narrative means to therapeutic ends.* New York: W. W. Norton.

27

Single Women and the Grief Circle

Karen G. Lewis

Single women may be the fastest-growing clinical population, yet only recently have they received much clinical attention. The intervention described here is for women who are depressed about being single, a depression that has not abated with grief work, therapeutic support, nor practical suggestions. But before considering this, it is important first to recognize that there is no consistency when talking about single women. There are more than twenty-eight different ways of being a single woman, depending (for example) on age, dating and/or prior marital status, religious or sexual preference, or parenting (Lewis, 1994). For simplicity's sake, single women can be divided into two categories: Always Single (AS) and Single Again (SA).

It is also important to recognize that being "single by choice" may only mean women don't like their choices (Lewis and Moon, 1997). Most would prefer to be in a committed relationship (with or without marriage) but *only if* the man were emotionally available and willing to take mutual responsibility for nurturing the relationship. Most women claim they do not "need" a man. He is the "icing on the cake," not the whole cake (Anderson and Stewart, 1994).

SINGLE WOMEN AND THERAPY

The image of the old maid has been replaced with the new image of the glamorized professional woman. Yet, many single women report they still hear messages, albeit subtle, reinforcing the old image and blaming them for their singleness (Lewis and Moon, 1997): "You're not trying hard enough," "You're too choosy," or "You don't give a man a chance." Many women, then, find a reason to explain their lack of a husband, and come to therapy to fix the "problem" they have self-identified, such as their weight, fear of intimacy, low self-esteem, or a difficult childhood. It is as if this is one way to take control of a situation that feels out of their control.

As therapists, we are not immune to societal ambivalence about singleness (Schwartzberg, Berliner, and Jacob, 1995). How does our bias about single women affect what we hear and how we intervene clinically? Do we help them see they can lead fulfilling lives without a man, or do we help them consider the personal problems that interfere with their finding a man? "Ah," you say, "we may need to do both." True, but which one gets attention first; which one gets more emphasis? Our clients are very attuned to the messages we are sending them about their singleness.

DEPRESSION AND SELF-DISTORTION

Women may come to therapy depressed about being single. Yet the depression may be a result of their failure to meet society's and their family's expectations that they would marry. The depression may be apparent or may underlie presenting symptoms. Even women who are content if they never marry may carry remnants of this depression.

Joyce, a thirty-eight-year-old AS, is a bright, highly successful stockbroker who has had relatively good relationships with men in the past. She sought therapy when her new lover complained she was frigid. After ascertaining that she has been orgasmic with former lovers, I said, "Tell me about the man with whom you are frigid," avoiding a discussion about her failure with this man. Her description depicted a man who was keeping her at an emotional distance. Within a few weeks, Joyce was clear that her lack of sexual response was a statement about the level of emotional closeness she felt with him. She hoped that by agreeing with his definition of her as frigid, he might be able to give more of himself to her. She was pushing to make the relationship work so she would have a relationship.

Knowing this made no sense, Joyce asked:

What's wrong with me? I must be doing something wrong since I'm still single. I've had a lot of therapy already. I'm probably healthier than most of my married friends. I think I have accepted the possibility I might never marry; yet I get myself in situations like this with Harold because—I don't want to be single!

Joyce started with the wrong question. Assuming her singleness is a result of something wrong with her does not give credit to her emotional growth. A better question might be "Why does fear of being single cause me to distort who I am, to define myself as frigid, or to accept someone else's description of me?"

Feminist literature (Jordan et al., 1991; Walters et al., 1988) suggests that women often carry the emotional feelings for others who are not dealing with their own feelings. This can be an important factor in single women's depression, for their lack of a husband may affect the lives of so many other people. For instance, Joyce's mother, father, and sister may have their own sadness related to Joyce's singleness. Her mother and father are being deprived of their next developmental life stage, grand-parenthood; her sister can't be an aunt. Joyce's depression may be more intense because she is carrying their sadness as well as her own.

THE GRIEF CIRCLE

In an effort to help women ascertain how much depression is theirs and how much belongs to others, I devised the Grief Circle. Almost invariably, women will claim the pain is all their own, but I gently push them to try the exercise, anyway.

Here is the way it worked with Joyce. I asked Joyce to take a large piece of paper and to draw a circle representing the size of her sadness or grief about being single.

> **TH:** Look at your circle and make sure it really does represent the full size of your pain. Now, think of all the people who also may be affected by your singleness, perhaps your mother, and your father. You may need space for siblings, grandparents, aunts, uncles, godparents, cousins, neighbors, teachers, or religious leaders. Your list is uniquely yours. Divide the circle, giving each of them the proportion of the pain that you imagine belongs to each of them.
>
> **J:** This doesn't make sense. Of course it's all my pain.
>
> **TH:** Perhaps, but perhaps not. I know this may seem silly, but would you be willing to draw the circle anyway? Then just look at it for a bit.

Joyce picked up the crayon and drew a large circle. After a few minutes of silence, she drew the circle shown in Figure 27.1. Joyce was stunned. She was surprised that she could divide her circle at all, and she was astounded that such a small portion of the circle actually belonged to her. She said, "I can't believe this. I never even thought about it. You mean, I may not be as sad as I think I am? That's odd!"

FIGURE 27.1. Joyce's Grief Circle

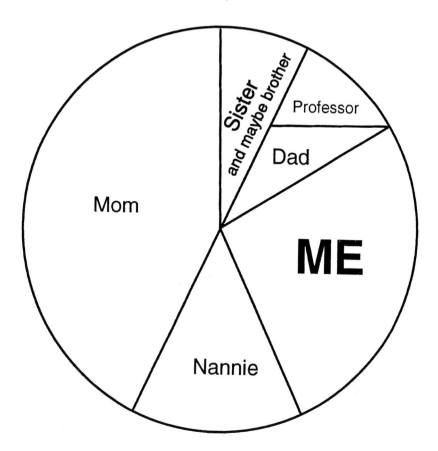

We then began talking about ways to let others take responsibility for their own feelings. She practiced conversations she would have with each person in the circle, how she would broach the subject and what she would say to each.

Less than two months later, she is amazed to say:

> You know, I am still sad, no, I'm angry that I'm single. I can't stand the thought I may never marry, but something feels different inside me now. I don't feel like I'm walking around with a ten-ton weight

inside me. I don't start weeping at the thought of not having children or when I see a happy couple holding hands on the street. I feel sad, almost wistful, but not that awful feeling I used to have. I also note that I'm not so defensive with my mother. When she makes a comment about me and men, I am able to hear it as her sadness without feeling responsible.

OTHER USES OF THE GRIEF CIRCLE

The Grief Circle is described here for single women who are depressed about not being married or partnered. However, it can be used when a client is carrying feelings for other people or is experiencing an intense feeling that has not abated with other interventions. Any strong emotional feeling, such as anxiety, anger, competitiveness, fear, may be visually clarified by using the circle concept.

Bob's financial irresponsibility was destroying his second marriage. In response to the question of whose irresponsibility he was carrying, slightly more than half of his circle was his father who died a pauper; the rest was his highly successful, "perfect" brother.

Ten-year-old Kathy worried incessantly. To everyone's surprise, the largest segment of her worry circle was her little brother. Only through this discussion did she speak of her fears that he was being sexually abused.

As a result of Mark's circle, he was able to give his "angst" back to his deceased, "long-suffering" grandparents who had raised him from birth. While he had been discussing his indebtedness to them, the circle helped him visually see how he continued to repay that debt—by being as deprived of pleasure as they had been.

As with any exercise, the way it is introduced and used is of utmost importance. Most clients hold firmly onto their view of their problem and resist another perspective. When that happens, talking about the problem is often less useful than finding an abstract or metaphoric representation of the problem. Helping them consider this new format takes skillful subtlety and persistence.

There are at least four useful components of the exercise. Picking the size of the circle to represent the size of the feeling (e.g., sadness, depression, anxiety, and fear) in itself can be useful. Second, clients may be relieved to see their feelings contained inside a circle, no matter how large. Clients may also be reassured by seeing how much their family members' feelings impact them. And, finally, clients may be relieved to visualize what percentage of the overwhelming feelings actually belongs to them.

Contraindications

I can think of no situations where such an intervention would be harmful; at worst, it might be meaningless and a waste of time.

REFERENCES

Anderson, C. and Stewart, S., with Dimidjian, S. (1994). *Flying solo: Single women in midlife.* New York: W. W. Norton.

Jordan, J., Kaplan, A., Miller, J. B., Stiver, I., and Surrey, J. (Eds.) (1991). *Women's growth in connection: Writings from the Stone Center.* New York: Guilford.

Lewis, K. G. (1994). Heterosexual women through the life cycle. In M. Mirkin (Ed.), *Women in context: Toward a feminist reconstruction of psychotherapy* (pp. 170-187). New York: Guilford.

Lewis, K. G. and Moon, S. (1997). Always-single and single-again women: A qualitative study. *Journal of Marital and Family Therapy, 23,* 115-134.

Schwartzberg, N., Berliner, K., and Jacob, D. (1995). *Single in a married world.* New York: W.W. Norton.

Walters, M., Carter, E., Papp, P., and Silverstein, O. (Eds.) (1988). *The invisible web: Gender patterns in family relationships.* New York: Guilford.

28

Slaying the Wild Things

Debra W. Smith

And when he came to the place where the wild things are
they roared their terrible roars and gnashed their terrible teeth
and rolled their terrible eyes and showed their terrible claws . . .

—Maurice Sendak, *Where the Wild Things Are*

INTRODUCTION

Helping clients create and execute a healing ritual has always been one of my favorite and most effective interventions, particularly when the presenting problem is grief or loss. I have found rituals particularly useful with children because the creation and staging of the ritual allows the child to take charge of his own healing and to experience a degree of control. Children generally find rituals comforting and healing. The breadth and scope of their rituals are limitless, since their imaginations seem to know no bounds.

Target Population

Although rituals are effective with individuals, couples, families, and groups, and with all ages throughout the life cycle, this particular ritual is targeted at children between ages four and seven. Children between these ages are in the middle of Piaget's preoperational stage of thinking and development, and as such are typically predisposed to rituals and to magical thinking more than other age groups (Stone and Church, 1984). They naturally create rituals in play, in games, and in their daily routines.

The ritual I will describe is helpful for children who are experiencing anxieties and fears related to normal developmental issues, or for children whose normal developmental fears are exacerbated by the stress of family changes, such as separation or divorce. The ritual is not intended to be used without concurrent treatment.

Theoretical Foundation

This intervention is based on the work of Evan Imber-Black, PhD and Janine Roberts, EdD, in their popular book *Rituals for Our Times* (1992). Additional information on the use of rituals can be found in *Rituals in Families and Family Therapy* by Evan Imber-Black, Janine Roberts, and Richard Whiting (1988).

THE PRESENTING PROBLEM: WILD THINGS IN THE NIGHT

Mr. and Mrs. S came to see me when they decided to end their marriage. They wanted me to help them prepare to tell their children, Lisa (age three) and Sean (age five), about the divorce, and also to help them create a stable joint custody situation. The children would be spending half the week with their dad, in their original home, and the other half of the week with their mom, in her new home, which would be in the same town.

Despite their inability to resolve their marital differences, Mr. and Mrs. S worked very carefully and cooperatively to iron out the details of the joint custody arrangements and to make the transition as smooth as possible for Lisa and Sean.

Shortly after the children began sharing the week with both their parents, Sean began to develop a variety of fears during the nights he spent with his dad. Although Sean kept his own bedroom, and most of his toys were at his dad's, and although his after-school and evening routines followed much the same schedule, Sean became fearful of many things including taking a bath alone, being alone upstairs or downstairs, and above all, he began to fear the "wild things" that came out when he tried to go to sleep each night.

The Intervention

The intervention was intended to help Sean destroy the wild things so that he would once again be able to go to sleep in his room without fear. As preliminary activities before creating and implementing the ritual, I had Sean draw pictures of his bedrooms at both his dad's and his mom's homes. He also drew pictures of the wild things that were scaring him and we talked about his fears and fantasies of what they would do to him.

Next, we talked about what it would be like to spend time at his home without the wild things. Sean admitted that it felt sad and strange to be in his home with his dad without having his mom present as well. He talked about his typical bedtime routine before the divorce and said that his mom was always the one to get him ready for bed and tuck him in at night. Now that his dad was doing this it felt "different and unsafe."

I involved Sean's dad in the ritual to foster and strengthen the connection between father and son and to show Sean that he could count on his dad to protect him and keep him safe. As Sean's dad sat with him in the sessions, I had Sean describe and draw pictures of the wild things. His dad was an active participant, asking questions and clarifying details about the wild things as Sean described and drew them. Because he did so, it became clear to Sean that his dad was totally familiar with the creatures that were scaring him and would not mistake them for something else. Initially, I had Sean draw the pictures on $8\frac{1}{2} \times 11''$ paper. As he drew each successive picture, I gave him incrementally larger sheets of paper, until the final picture was drawn on a sheet of paper that was large enough to make the wild thing seem quite realistic to a child Sean's age. When it was done, Sean cut it out.

We discussed what fate would have to befall this wild thing to make Sean feel safe once again. He felt that if it were slain with a sword and buried, he would once again feel secure enough to go to sleep in his bedroom.

Sean's dad assisted by "slaying" the wild thing with a paper sword that he created and decorated in the session according to his son's specifications. Once slain, Sean and his dad took the wild thing home, and as per our plan, put it in a shoe box and buried it out in a field.

Outcome

Sean and his dad returned to therapy for several additional sessions. They completed the work with the presenting problem by creating a new bedtime ritual for the nights Sean spent with his dad. It was quite different from the routine Sean had before his parents divorced and it was also different from the routine Sean had when he stayed at his mom's house. The therapy involved Sean and his dad writing and illustrating a short story called "When We Slayed the Wild Things," which they read before bedtime.

CONTRAINDICATIONS

This intervention may not be effective with children who have a poor imagination or who may be very depressed and therefore too constricted to use their imaginations freely. Children who are developmentally delayed or those who have an inability to separate reality from fantasy are also poor subjects for this intervention. This intervention is not suggested for children who have witnessed or experienced severe trauma, such as physical or sexual abuse or domestic violence. Such children may experience a reawakening of the original trauma through creating and acting out aggression toward the wild thing. Finally, if a child is very angry or is acting out aggressively toward a parent, it may not be wise to use this intervention as it may inadvertently encourage the aggressive behavior.

The therapist should have established a solid relationship and a safe environment for the child before attempting this intervention. Time should also be spent dealing with the child's feelings of anxiety, fear, anger, and loss surrounding the change that has occurred in the family before implementing the ritual.

REFERENCES

Imber-Black, E. and Roberts, J. (1992). *Rituals for our times.* New York: Harper-Collins.

Imber-Black, E., Roberts, J., and Whiting, R. (1988). *Rituals in families and in family therapy.* New York: W. W. Norton.

Stone, L. J. and Church, J. (1984). *Childhood and adolescence: A psychology of the growing person,* Fifth Edition. New York: Random House.

29

The Nightmare Question: Problem Talk in Solution-Focused Brief Therapy with Alcoholics and Their Families

Norman H. Reuss

"Men's courses will foreshadow certain ends, to which, if persevered in, they must lead," said Scrooge. "But if the courses be departed from, the ends will change. Say it is thus with what you show me!"

—Ebenezer Scrooge to the Ghost of Christmas Future,
A Christmas Carol by Charles Dickens

INTRODUCTION

The first time I asked the nightmare question was on November 22, 1994. I was working with a client and we were both completely stuck. She could make no movement toward her goal to stop drinking. I was using a solution-focused approach and she seemed to enjoy exploring those exceptions when she wanted to drink and was able to stop herself. We had, however, exhausted the use of exceptions without making a significant change in her drinking. She was frustrated by the lack of progress and was beginning to become disinterested in further therapy. I thought about a structured intervention, a technique used to get the alcoholic to stop drinking by submitting her to an increasingly painful series of confrontations about the negative consequences of continued drinking. The force and content of a structured intervention is so personally invasive and dogmatic, however, that many clients meet its force with resistance and may even deny the problem exists. We were stuck but I didn't want to make matters worse with a backslide.

Fortunately for both of us, it was the holiday season. Charles Dickens' *A Christmas Carol* was on television. In the story, Scrooge shudders in horror when he sees his own negative future in the message from the Ghost of Christmas Future. I knew what my client needed: a nightmare of her own making. It was with this idea in mind, a client-focused negative vision of the future, that the first nightmare question was constructed and asked in this manner:

> Suppose you go about the rest of today just doing what you usually do. You go home, go to bed, and fall asleep, and sometime in the middle of the night . . . some kind of a disaster happens . . . and all of the fears, all of the worries, all of the concerns, all of the problems that brought you here today . . . come true. This would be a nightmare I suppose. But because this nightmare happens in the middle of the night, you can't really know it has happened. What would you notice when you woke up tomorrow morning? What would be the first thing you would notice that would let you know your life had become unmanageable—that you were living a nightmare?

My client was intrigued by the question. She talked about drinking in the morning and a loss of interest in life. She talked about loss of hope and thoughts of suicide. Together we talked about ways her nightmare was already happening. We talked about the one sure way to prevent it. The nightmare worked; she stopped drinking.

PROTOCOL FOR ASKING THE NIGHTMARE QUESTION

At the Community Health Plan's Burlington (Vermont) Health Center where I first experimented with the nightmare question, we have learned that asking it has more impact when it follows several sessions exploring exceptions and the miracle day. We have also learned that it works best to ask the nightmare question early enough in the session to allow the therapist and client time to provoke and explore the powerful negative feelings a vision of the negative future may contain. Once these feelings have been appreciated it is the solution-focused therapist's job to help the client prevent the nightmare events by developing a homework assignment designed to promote movement in a positive direction.

The nightmare question is most appropriate and effective with clients who come to therapy with a problem and a goal they just can't reach on their own. The typical nightmare question candidate might present something like this; "You know, it's not that I don't want to stop drinking. I've tried. But every time I try, I just go back. Maybe it's my friends. They all drink. They don't make me drink. But when I stop it's just not the same. I want to stop drinking. I know I have to stop. My job depends on it. But I don't want to stop seeing my friends." By looking into the nightmare future this client can see that to keep the drinking means losing more than a job, it may mean losing everything.

We have also found that the nightmare question works well with families and couples. Families and couples can get just as stuck as individuals and for the same reasons. One course of change may require unattractive choices while staying the same is the reason they are seeking help. Like individuals, families and couples are often unable to see past the immediate difficult decisions and find it impossible to muster up the motivation to do the hard work making a change requires. When we use the nightmare question with a family or a couple we will entertain only one nightmare. We ask the question of all present. We use the nightmare of the first individual who speaks. We quickly involve everyone, however, by asking all individuals about how this nightmare will affect them, what they will notice about themselves and other family members, and how this nightmare will harm them as individuals and as members of the family or couple. If two or even three nightmares are discussed at the same time, each nightmare can lose its personal impact. In these situations the therapist must work very hard to connect the nightmares into one cohesive nightmare that everyone can own and examine.

We also use the nightmare question with mandated clients. In our work with mandated clients convicted of a first offense for driving while intoxicated, we insist they explore a nightmare day as part of group treatment. In one such group each client agreed their nightmare day would be to wake up to the realization that they had become hard-core alcoholics. One client added that he would have killed someone while driving in a blackout. When asked how they would feel on this nightmare morning, their list of feelings included anger, disappointment, confusion, despair, shame, and depression. Further discussion focused on their unanimous amazement that they would have let their drinking get so bad. One client summarized the group's feeling by saying, "I would feel ashamed to allow myself to get that way." We continued to explore the consequences of becoming hard-core alcoholics by asking, "Who else will notice you are living a nightmare day?" Responses ranged from everyone who read the newspaper headlines of a DWI fatality to friends, family, and co-workers. With the nightmare day developed in this manner we concluded by asking, "Are there warning signs that this nightmare is on the horizon?" One client conceded that the idea of a DWI conviction could be understood as a wake-up call. As he put it, "I don't see it happening ever but if I hadn't been stopped now my drinking could have gone on to get worse." With this admission the group joined in a discussion of how they were each responsible for their arrest, conviction, and changes they must make to lower their risk for future drinking problems. Seeing a negative picture of the future allows the mandated client to understand they will have a worse drinking problem *at some time* if they do not take the opportunity *at this time* to make some changes.

WHEN IT'S MIDNIGHT ALL DAY LONG

Jennifer is a working mother of two preteen boys. She is a heavy drinker in an unhappy marriage. During a recent binge of heavier-than-usual drinking she had an affair. Jennifer and her husband agreed she should be in therapy to talk about her problem drinking.

The initial interview began following the standard solution-focused format with agreement on a problem statement and goal, exploration of pre-session change, and a search for exceptions. Though Jennifer wanted to stop drinking she believed this was impossible because she used her nightly six-pack of beer to cope with a demanding, authoritarian, and judgmental husband.

With no viable exceptions, I asked the nightmare question. After a pause Jennifer said, "I would be drinking in front of my kids." We continued by exploring what she would notice about her feelings, her children, her children's feelings, their interactions, and how these things would harm her. As Jennifer experienced this nightmare day, without prompting she said, "They probably already know." Given this opportunity, we switched our focus to what was already happening. Jennifer confessed that even though she had tried to hide her drinking from her children, she believed she had failed. "They must know, because I'm just different every night. It's already happening in the nighttime. I don't want it in the daytime." Jennifer concluded by adding, "I think I can stop it, because for my kids I have to."

WORKING WITH THE FAMILY OF A TEENAGE MARIJUANA EXPERT

Jason and his parents were referred for family therapy. Jason's use of marijuana was the presenting problem. Jason would not budge from his position that marijuana was a harmless drug that should be legalized.

Jason's parents were just as convinced that marijuana was only a gateway drug that would lead their son to even more harmful substances. I opened the interview with the nightmare question. Jason's mom was immediately intrigued. Her quick answers indicated she had already entertained her own version of the nightmare many times. Jason simply said, "Oh my God, I'm a burnout." We spent the next twenty minutes exploring Jason's nightmare day, paying particular attention to his amazement that he would ever let marijuana get the upper hand in his life. Jason was willing to concede he had no rules to govern his use of marijuana and rules would be one way to prevent his version of the nightmare day. He accepted the challenge to come up with ten rules to govern his use before a scheduled follow-up interview.

During the follow-up interview, Jason not only presented his ten rules, but confessed to violating two of the rules (in the past) and admitted that perhaps he was closer to a nightmare day than he thought. Jason's parents were pleased by both his thoughtful attention to the task and his ability to critically evaluate his own use of marijuana. Though the conflict between Jason and his parents had not been resolved, the conflict had been altered enough that they thought they could handle it without further therapy.

CONTRAINDICATIONS

As helpful as I've found the nightmare question in focusing my clients' attention on the negative emotional consequences of problem drinking, there are situations in which I will think carefully before asking it. Perhaps it is obvious, yet it bears mentioning that when a client is already in an emotional crisis and is making the connection between drinking and the crisis, the nightmare question need not be asked. The crisis is the nightmare and can be successfully mined for motivation to change. I am also reluctant to ask the nightmare question with clients who are having difficulty coping with depression (the dually diagnosed client). Because the nightmare question encourages clients to experience painful feelings before it explores ways to prevent those feelings from occurring, I am concerned about increasing these patients' risk for self-harm. I will introduce the nightmare day in relationship to their drinking only after I am assured they can effectively cope with the imagined negative scenario.

MIRACLES AND NIGHTMARES

The more I work with the nightmare question and follow clients as they create their own alcoholic bottom the more I am convinced that this solution-focused problem talk is an effective spark that ignites change. While most of our clients are motivated by a positive picture of the future, a picture in which they see themselves acting effectively to meet their needs, some of them are at times motivated by negative pictures of their own futures. When they see themselves fumbling through their own lives, messing everything up, causing pain not only to themselves but to others, they don't like it. Our clients do not like living in a nightmare. They become highly motivated to get on with the business of doing something different to make their lives better. When clients are able to experience the logical conclusion of both miracles and nightmares I believe they are in a better position to make decisions and take that first small step that will make a big difference.

BIBLIOGRAPHY

Berg, I. K. and Miller, S. (1992). *Working with the problem drinker: A solution-focused approach*, New York: W.W. Norton, 75, 77.

30

I Rewrite with a Little Help
from My Friends

Frank N. Thomas

I have found through the years that my earliest attempts to alter my
approaches in therapy have often been the most informative and creative.
As my work evolves, I have found that clients are rich sources of wisdom,
providing opportunities for my own growth as we cooperatively seek to
reauthor their lives. The work of Michael White and David Epston has had
a terrific effect on my therapeutic stance and my interaction with clients.[1]
My movement toward a more narrative focus while remaining sensitive to
context opened up the following story.

An overview of this particular intervention is in order here. First, the
client is recruited to include friends and/or relatives in the helping process.
These people may be present in the therapy room or they may be others the
client identifies. Second, persons (preferably two or more) are selected by
the client as those who will be helpful. These "informants" should know
the client well and be known by the client as honest *and* kind. Next, the
client interviews informants with a simple question: "What do you *value*
about me?" and (if needed) the prompt, "Go on!," simply writing down
verbatim the terms used by the informants. (I would write down this
question on a blank sheet of paper and send it home with the client for use
in the interviews.) Next, the client brings the list of adjectives to the next
session, and the therapist and client sort out those that fit from those that
do not fit the client's experience of him/herself. The next step is to place
each adjective at the top of a piece of paper because the client is going to
collect experiences that illustrate each adjective in the coming week (the
"fact-finding mission"). Informants might be recruited to add to the evidence list as well. This "book of revealing evidence" can be utilized in
many ways, some of which will receive attention at the end of this chapter.

CASE EXAMPLE

Jill (all names are fictitious, of course) was referred by a local physician because of her chronic pain and depression.[2] Jill had suffered a severe injury in an accident and, while hospitalized, she was diagnosed with cancer. She had had surgery for the cancer and had completed her first round of radiation therapy as well. In Jill's first visit, she reported severe depression accompanying her chronic pain. In addition to her spinal injuries, which left her unmarred but had rendered her physically disabled, she reported isolation from family and difficulties in her marriage. She rarely moved in her chair due to pain, and her vacant stare and blank facial expression made connecting difficult. Jill insisted that her husband be excluded from our sessions at that time because she "didn't want him involved." I promised to support her wish but reserved the right to ask for reconsideration in the future—so much for the family therapist involving others!

Jill called her primary initial complaint "lack of self-worth." She related that she had no sense of who she was and felt she had nothing to contribute to the world. She felt as though she could "disappear, and no one would miss [her]." I felt that developing a significant therapeutic bond was essential at that point, and most of our time was spent reflecting on what had been useful in her past therapies, who she felt she could trust, and how we could work together toward success in her life.[3] I assessed for suicidality and received a firm (and believable) agreement that she would meet with me at the same time the next week. I began to think of ways for Jill to reconstruct a sense of self, utilizing her context and the relationships she already cherished in her life. The ideas of White and Epston were closely connected to my own struggle that week.

When Jill returned for our second session, she related that her depression had not improved but she felt hopeful that therapy would improve her lot. I related my desire to work with her to improve her sense of self-worth while being sensitive to the fact that we both needed ideas from others she valued to create a self-image that could "stand the test of time." I asked Jill to consider a task that would allow others to inform us about her strengths and worth without having them join us in the session. The dialogue went like this:

> **Frank:** Tell me who knows you well, a couple of people you could approach this week to help us out . . . people who will be honest with you, yet kind.
>
> **Jill:** Well . . . [long pause] . . . I think my husband . . . [another pause] and my physical therapist.

> **Frank:** OK. Do you think these two people would be willing to give you a few minutes of their time this week?
> **Jill:** Oh, yes. I'll see my physical therapist three times this week.
> **Frank:** OK. I'd like you to consider doing the following. Get a small notepad and pen to take along with you—something that will fit in your purse. Then I'd like to have you ask Peter [husband] and Ken [physical therapist] the following question: "What do you value about me?" Let them think, much like you and I do here! Then, simply write down everything they tell you without interrupting them. This might take two minutes, or it might take twenty. It's very important to me that you write down *everything* they say; so, if they speak too fast, ask them to slow down. Will you do that for me—for us—this week?
> **Jill:** [pause] Yeah—I think I'd enjoy that.

We then spoke about when she would interview Peter and Ken separately. She wrote down the question because I wanted to make sure she used the word *value* (not "like") in the interview. She agreed to return for our next session with their responses.

The next week, Jill had two pages of adjectives in a spiral notebook, one list from her husband and another from her physical therapist. She smiled as I read them aloud, and she revealed how pleasant it was to do such a task. Every adjective could be interpreted as positive. (*Note:* If there had been obvious or potentially negative descriptors, I probably would have avoided them in the following interventions.) Then, I read one adjective at a time to her, asking her if she agreed "51 percent or more" with the descriptor. Every adjective that fit 51 percent or more we left on the list, and any portrayal she did not "half agree" with I crossed out. In a few short minutes, we had a list of eight adjectives that (1) had been used to describe her by people who knew her well and (2) she agreed with. Continuing my "not-knowing" stance, I asked her to write each of the adjectives at the top of separate pages in her spiral notebook, skipping two pages between each adjective page.[4] The following dialogue took place as we formed this "rewrite" together:

> **Frank:** OK, this helps . . . but I feel like I'm still in the dark. I'd like to know more about how these words "fit" in your life. Would you be willing to help me out with that?
> **Jill:** Sure, no problem!
> **Frank:** What would really help me understand your "worth" is for you to write down examples of how you are "warm," "hon-

est," "humorous," and so on. I guess I assume that, if these are *you*, then you will have lots of examples even this week that you could write down for me. In fact, some things that you do will probably need to be written under two or more adjectives as examples, right?

Jill: Oh, I can think of one that happened today that needs to be written down in at least two places! [She related an event that she believed illustrated both humor and kindness.]

Frank: That's perfect! I can see you will have no problem supplying me with examples of how these words fit you. How long do you think you'll need to give me a pretty good list for all eight words?

Jill: Oh, not long. [She spoke about how some would be easier than others.]

Frank: Great! That'll be very helpful for me because I think I'll know a lot more about what gives you "worth" when I get that list. We'll have evidence of what you're made of!

Jill left enthused, remarking that her depression had "gone up" (improved) and remained tolerable all week in spite of her continued pain.

The following three sessions were spent reviewing incidents that illustrated her "honesty," "kindness," "loyalty," and other "parts of herself." Since the categories fit with both her own experience and the experience of those who knew her well, it was an effortless task to add example after example. The second week we added Peter and Ken to this "fact-finding mission." Jill asked them to give her examples whenever they observed her "revealing evidence" that supported the descriptors. In fact, at the end of three weeks, she had to start using additional pages in the back of the notebook to "record the evidence."

A few months later, as we were completing therapy, Jill asked me to write a summary letter to the physician who referred her. I wrote the following letter to her, giving her permission to forward it to her physician if she agreed with it. She sent it on without correction.

Dear Jill,

Just a note . . . I have been so gratified by the courage you have shown in the short time we have spent talking, and I want you to know how much change I have seen you make. Taking on your pain problem may be the most recent and most difficult, but I have seen many, many other significant changes during the past few months. Let me see if I can recount a few:

- Your self-worth has increased dramatically. I see this in my interactions with you, but I also see this in your ability to make new friends, talk openly with others, and forgive your shortcomings.
- You have continued to thrive despite your bout with cancer. It seems that you are living a day at a time and making the most of it! This was very clear in our last session, in which you talked about all the dreams you have for the next two years and how you are starting to make your dreams into reality with practical little steps.
- You found that people perceived you as honest, loving, loyal, competent, and valuable . . . all significant to the changes you have continued to make.
- You have taught yourself to be assertive when it was the right way to interact. Most people take years—you learned and experienced positive ways to assert yourself in a few short weeks. I remember [here I related events that support this].
- You display a level-headedness during a difficult time that most people have difficulty keeping up . . . and you should be commended for it.
- You have tackled your difficulty with _____ in a responsible and courageous way. Going to the support group, working with Dr. Zeus [the referring physician], and moving forward in spite of the recent hit-and-run you experienced shows great inner strength and resources that even I didn't know you had in you!
- Finally, you have beaten the depression that was running your life when I met you in February. Even though you have some down days, you are "severely positive" and hopeful, and I sense your joy each time we have a session. Bravo!

I believe you can continue to change in positive ways . . . and neither you nor Peter nor the medical professionals around you know the limits of your abilities! I look forward to hearing about your progress in the next few weeks . . . my hat's off to you!

Sincerely,

Frank Thomas

Jill reached her three-year milestone following aggressive cancer treatment. Her self-worth is still closely tied to the evidence we so thoroughly explored together. My hat is still off to her.

I have found this intervention to be a wonderful way to cooperate with clients. Families pick up on this quickly—they say that "catching" others performing evidence of their descriptors often resembles a detective movie in which everyone is writing (positive) notes on everyone else! The key ingredients seem to be: (1) an honest curiosity and position of not-knowing, (2) asking people who will be "honest, yet kind" to reflect on "what they value about" the client, (3) negotiating agreement on descriptor "fit" with the client, and (4) gathering behavioral and interactional examples as evidence that the person "really has" particular characteristics.

The only contraindication regarding the use of this intervention might be tied to the potential for negative descriptors to surface during interviews with informants. Although the client and her informant might find being "submissive to men" to be a valuable descriptor, you as the therapist have the option to focus on other, less subjugating or pejorative descriptors from the list. The risk is there, but the risk of having oppressive themes surface is found in any therapeutic dialogue and must be managed by the therapist.

This novel approach has also added to my supervision.[5] The supervisee/therapist can utilize friends, relatives, or even clients in the creation of a personal notebook of competency. Asking others what they "value" about you seems to bring out adjectives that can be utilized as both story and evidence. Be cautious—you may find this exercise so popular it takes on a change-producing life of its own!

Therapists and clients can cocreate meaningful narratives and involve significant others in the process through this intervention. I hope you will modify/revise/alter/adjust this to fit your unique style, remembering that each client's strengths and resources provide the details necessary to successful reauthoring of the self. It's possible, with a little help from your friends!

NOTES

1. White, M. and Epston, D. (1990). *Narrative means to therapeutic ends.* New York: W. W. Norton.

2. For an in-depth treatment of this case, see Thomas, F. N. (1994). The experience of solution-oriented therapy: Post therapy client interviewing. *Case Studies in Brief and Family Therapy, 8*(1), 47-58.

3. As in the solution-focused approach. See Walter, J. and Peller, J. (1992). *Becoming solution focused in brief therapy.* New York: Brunner/Mazel. Regarding ongoing evaluation, see Barnard, C. P. and Kuehl, B. P. (1995). Ongoing evaluation: In-session procedures for enhancing the working alliance and therapy effectiveness. *The American Journal of Family Therapy, 23,* 161-172.

4. See Anderson, H. and Goolishian, H. (1992). The client is the expert: A not-knowing approach to therapy. In S. McNamee and K. J. Gergen (Eds.), *Therapy as social construction* (pp. 25-39). Newbury Park, CA: Sage.

5. See Thomas, F. N. (1996). Solution-focused supervision: The coaxing of expertise in training. In S. D. Miller, M. A. Hubble, and B. Duncan (Eds.), *Handbook of solution-focused brief therapy: Foundations, applications, and research* (pp. 128-151). San Francisco: Jossey-Bass.

31

Time and Couples, Part I:
The Decompression Chamber

Peter Fraenkel

OVERVIEW: TIME AND RHYTHM AS AN IMPORTANT DIMENSION OF COUPLE FUNCTIONING

In this chapter and another appearing in this book (Time and Couples, Part II: The Sixty-Second Pleasure Point), I describe interventions that center on the relationship between couple satisfaction and distress, and the dimension of time. Elsewhere I have argued that the manner in which couples organize themselves in time often provides a ready "window" into issues of power and closeness between the partners (Fraenkel, 1994). Questions that assess how partners have decided to allocate time often reveal one or both partners' underlying concerns about the degree of connectedness between them, as well as feelings that the other is controlling him/her through time demands. These issues of power and closeness often underlie decisions about the amount of time partners are together versus apart from one another, how they balance and sequence leisure activities versus career and work (including household chores), and how partners perceive each other's punctuality and pace. For instance, one partner may feel distanced by the other's seemingly greater devotion to work than to being together as a couple; another may view the partner's consistent lateness to social engagements as a sign that the partner doesn't really want to participate in these activities; another partner may feel "pushed around" or controlled by the other's fast (or slow) pace of walking. Persistent differences between the partners in time allocation, pace, punctuality, and other temporal aspects of behavior may result in a sense of being "out of sync" with one another, which may represent a major source of a couple's distress.

That lack of temporal coordination or "rhythmicity" between partners might often result in distress is not surprising, if couple interaction is viewed from a broader, systemic perspective. Other types of relationships—for instance, those of musicians and dancers in performance (Scheflen, 1982), the biological systems that comprise the relationships among the organs and functions of the human body (Moore-Ede, Sulzman, and Fuller, 1982; Pittendrigh, 1972), and social and economic institutions in societies (Lomax, 1982)—all rely on regular, rhythmic coordination of each element with the others for the whole to function effectively. The temporal coordination of elements in a system is known as the process of *entrainment* (McGrath and Kelly, 1986; Pittendrigh, 1972). During times of stress, the rhythms of each element may fall out of entrainment, but eventually will "reentrain" with one another.

In the remainder of this chapter, I discuss one example of how lack of temporal coordination or entrainment between couple partners can be associated with distress, and I describe an intervention to assist couples to entrain with one another.

AIDING THE TRANSITION FROM APART TO TOGETHER TIME: THE "DECOMPRESSION CHAMBER"

With couples, one of the daily stress points that may lead to a lack of temporal coordination or entrainment is the transition from time apart to time together, typically at the end of the day as one or both partners return from work. Although some couples fall into a mutually satisfactory coordinated rhythm fairly easily, others may struggle with this period of reentrainment. Each partner may have expectations and preferences about how s/he will or should be greeted by the other, and about how time should be utilized once the partners come home. Differences in partners' expectations and preferences need to be discussed openly—otherwise a great deal of misinterpretation of each other's intentions can occur. For instance, hurt feelings may occur when Partner A hopes for a kiss and conversation when Partner B returns, while Partner B typically runs right for a shower, followed by a half hour of watching the news. Viewing this behavior, Partner A may believe Partner B is avoiding him/her. Partner B may actually want to kiss and talk, but only after a few minutes of private time, and feels Partner A is being controlling and won't give him/her a minute alone.

The first step in my intervention is to offer the metaphor of the Decompression Chamber (which I sometimes also call the Depressurizing Chamber), often accompanied by a drawing (see Figure 31.1), as a way of normalizing and demarcating this often challenging daily transition. I explain that many couples have difficulty smoothly reconnecting after a

FIGURE 31.1. The Decompression Chamber

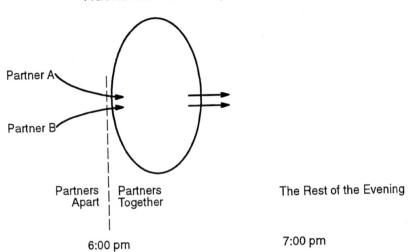

Partner A

Partner B

Partners Apart   Partners Together   The Rest of the Evening

6:00 pm   7:00 pm

day apart, and each may be feeling the pressures of the day and wish to release them prior to engaging in other activities for the rest of the evening. I compare this process to that of scuba divers, who need to emerge slowly from depths of higher water pressure to the surface, lest the change in pressure cause them physical harm.

I then encourage the partners to have an open discussion about their hopes and expectations for this transition period—what they would fill this depressurizing time with—and often have them write these ideas in the drawing. These ideas may include activities to do together—a discussion about the events of each partner's day, holding each other for a few minutes, sharing a snack or drink, or watching TV together—as well as activities each partner prefers to do alone. I usually find that partners are surprised to discover each is open to the other's preferred activities, but may disagree about the *sequence* and *duration* of these activities. I then encourage them to derive a sequence to try out during the next week—one that will incorporate most or all of each partner's preferences. In a sense, the intervention engages couples to develop a transition ritual (Imber-Black, Roberts, and Whiting, 1988).

For example, I worked with a couple in which the husband, Tim, commuted an hour and a half to and from work (three hours total), and when he returned, his wife Laura, who was at home with their two-year-old daughter, had wished he would immediately dive into the remaining housework. Although he believed it fair for him to do this housework, he had found it left him with no time for himself, and over time he had come to resent it. By the time he finally expressed his desire for some private time, he had become so frustrated that he could envision that only a full night away from the family (each night!) would satisfy him. His wife noted that she had no private time either, which led him to feel guilty and bury his resentment until this and other issues brought their conflict to a head and they sought therapy with me.

After an exploration of their expectations and frustrations, we engaged the idea of the Decompression Chamber, and came up with a plan in which Tim, upon arriving at home, would first affectionately greet Laura and their daughter, then immediately spend a half hour playing his guitar alone in the bedroom. Tim and Laura would then spend fifteen minutes discussing the day, and then Tim would do chores. The following week, the couple returned expressing true amazement at the effect that this seemingly minor intervention had on their quality of life. Tim reported feeling much better—"I feel like I have a life now!"—and that after one evening practicing his guitar alone, he spent the remaining evenings doing so in the living room, with their daughter climbing in and out of the guitar case. Laura was so inspired by the effect this had on Tim's mood and on decreasing their level of tension that they arranged to hire a baby-sitter two hours a day, so that Laura could pursue her interest in weaving.

CONCLUSION

I have found this intervention useful with a broad range of couples, at all levels of distress. Often, establishing a more mutually satisfying joint rhythm at the end of the day becomes a kind of action metaphor for other forms of joint effort, encouraging the partners to compromise on other problems to which they seek solutions. When one or both partners continue to struggle or refuse to compromise in developing a joint rhythm, this can usefully reveal more about the couple's issues around power and closeness.

REFERENCES

Fraenkel, P. (1994). Time and rhythm in couples. *Family Process, 33*, 37-51.
Imber-Black, E., Roberts, J., and Whiting, R. A. (Eds.) (1988). *Rituals in families and family therapy.* New York: W. W. Norton.
Lomax, A. (1982). In M. Davis (Ed.), *Interaction rhythms: Periodicity in communicative behavior* (pp. 146-174). New York: Human Sciences Press.

McGrath, J. E. and Kelly, J. R. (1986). *Time and human interaction.* New York: Guilford Press.

Moore-Ede, M. C., Sulzman, F. M., and Fuller, C. A. (1982). *The clocks that time us.* Cambridge, MA: Harvard University Press.

Pittendrigh, C. S. (1972). On temporal organization in living systems. In H. Yaker, H. Osmond, and F. Cheek (Eds.), *The future of time* (pp. 179-218). New York: Anchor Books.

Scheflen, A. E. (1982). Comments on the significance of interaction rhythms. In M. Davis (Ed.), *Interaction rhythms: Periodicity in communicative behavior* (pp. 13-22). New York: Human Sciences Press.

32

Time and Couples, Part II:
The Sixty-Second Pleasure Point

Peter Fraenkel

It has been said that for couples and families in the 1990s, the commodity most in demand is *time* (Ventura, 1995). Whatever other issues they may be struggling with—communication, in-laws, childrearing, sex life, money, household responsibilities, and the like—most of the couples I see privately and those whose therapy I supervise mention lack of time as a major issue and frustration. Couple partners complain about lack of time to fulfill work or household responsibilities, lack of time together, lack of time apart, lack of time with extended family or friends, lack of time with their children, lack of time for sex and intimacy, and lack of time just to do nothing. My informal research on couples that I, my colleagues, and my students have seen over the past few years suggests that this perceived lack of time cuts across socioeconomic, racial, ethnic, and sexual orientation lines, and is experienced at all stages of the couple life cycle.

Although in some cases, one or both partners may exaggerate or create extrarelationship time commitments as a means of distancing from each other, for most of the couples with whom I have worked in therapy, their time constraints—often centering around work, homemaking, and childrearing demands—are real. These time pressures often seem so overwhelming and unchangeable to the couple that they preclude more time for the relationship, particularly for the types of pleasurable activities that are believed to be central to maintaining commitment (Markman, Stanley, and Blumberg, 1994). Time constraints may directly affect therapy as well, in that, no matter how motivated they are, couples may experience such time pressures that they believe they have little or no time to try to institute any of the changes that emerge from the therapy.

They may fail to follow through with interventions in which the therapist suggests even what seems to be a minor addition of fun time—an evening off ("we can't get a baby-sitter"), a weekend away ("we don't have money for that"), or even dinner together ("our rhythms are off—she's home three hours before me, and can't wait to eat").

In an earlier chapter of this book (Time and Couples, Part I: The Decompression Chamber), I presented an outline of a theory on the relationship between couple distress and functioning, and the dimension of time (described in detail in Fraenkel, 1994). This theory forms the conceptual background of the work described in the present chapter as well. Here, I will describe an intervention I use with couples who genuinely want to increase their sense of closeness, but who have become immobilized by their seemingly immutable, unyielding time constraints. I will also discuss how, when it does not lead to increased closeness, this intervention can be useful to begin a dialogue about issues that may be blocking one or both partners' desire to spend more time together.

FINDING TIME FOR FUN AND CONNECTION: THE "SIXTY-SECOND PLEASURE POINT"

The Sixty-Second Pleasure Point challenges the notion, often held by busy couples who have all but given up trying to spend time together, that they need large amounts of time in order to restore, build, and sustain a sense of daily intimacy. The intervention is designed to create a sense of connectedness with a minimal investment of time. Although it is not a substitute for the benefits of larger amounts of time together, the Sixty-Second Pleasure Point can serve as a first step for couples who have found it difficult to locate any time for conjoint pleasurable activities. Doing the Pleasure Point exercise often generates a renewed sense of hopefulness about the relationship, and stimulates the partners to be more creative in how they find time for each other. Some couples may then build the exercise into their daily routines, whereas others may use it to provide a sense of connection during exceptionally busy periods.

To initiate the Sixty-Second Pleasure Point intervention, I first assess what the couple has tried already in terms of building in more fun time. When it seems it has been truly difficult for them to make time, I then ask them to do a free-flowing brainstorm in response to the following question: "Think of all the fun and pleasurable things you could do with one another *in sixty seconds or less*. Include in the list things you could do when together and those you could do with each other when physically apart (by using the phone, e-mail, fax)." Couples typically smile at this question, and then readily list ideas. Some examples I have heard in my practice and in couple workshops I run include:

Read a poem or something interesting from the newspaper, give a neck/back/foot/hand massage, kiss, hold each other, stroke one another with feathers, share an apple, tell (or send by fax or e-mail) a joke, brush each other's hair, listen to music, dance, have a glass of wine, feed each other something delicious, tell each other (in person or by the phone) "I love you and miss you," whisper something erotic in each other's ears, light a candle together, pray, smell some perfume or a flower, watch the end of a sunset, list all the things we would like to do if we had more time.

After the brainstorm, I then ask couples to imagine doing *ten* Sixty-Second Pleasure Points with each other across the day—a few if and when they see each other in the morning before one or both leave for work, a few during the day while apart, and a few more when they come back together at the end of the day. Using a pad of paper or chalkboard, I then write a flat line and mark it by the hours of the clock, beginning at 6 a.m., placing a line for each hour in sequence, and ending at 6 a.m. If working with a group of couples in a workshop, I then give an example of how a couple might distribute the ten Pleasure Points across the day; if working with a couple privately, I will ask them to place their planned Pleasure Points across the day.

Next, I ask the partners if they remember ever doing some kind of connect-the-dots activity as child, and ask them how it felt. Almost invariably, tapping this referent experience appears to bring to both partners a further sense of familiarity and comfort about trying this idea. I then suggest that human beings seem to have a cognitive need to connect dots, find contours, put things together. This assumption is based on a large body of thinking and research in perceptual and cognitive psychology, including the early contributions of the Gestalt psychologists (see Köhler, 1969, for review), as well as the theories of Gregory Bateson (1972). Next, I draw (or have the couple draw) a line connecting their Pleasure Points (see Figure 32.1), and I suggest that by doing these ten Sixty-Second Pleasure Points on a daily basis, they *may* find, although it is an imperfect solution to their time-pressured lives, that they will experience an "arc of pleasure and connection" across the day.

Couples generally will attempt to carry out this activity between sessions—after all, it requires them only to dedicate ten minutes of time per day, so it is hard for one or the other partner to say "we have no time"— and in most cases couples report that it greatly relieves each partner's concern that they could never find *any* time for each other. Often, it

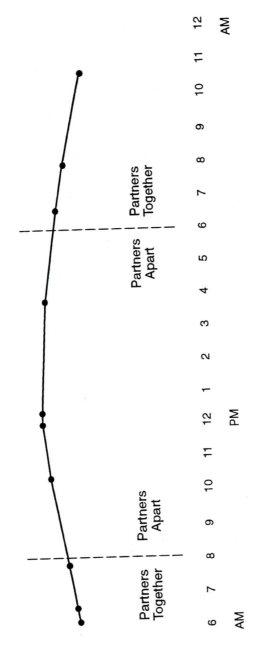

FIGURE 32.1. Sixty-Second Pleasure Points Across the Day Creating an "Arc of Connection"

● = Pleasure Point Activities

generates enough renewed hope and energy on the part of the partners that they spontaneously find or make even more time for each other.

CONTRAINDICATIONS

I have used the Sixty-Second Pleasure Point intervention with a wide range of couples and problems. In general, it has been quite successful in demonstrating to couples that small changes in how they use time can lead to surprisingly large outcomes of increased satisfaction, cohesion, and decreased conflict. I would not use it with couples whose level of conflict is extremely high, or whose level of commitment is extremely low. The intervention requires collaborative effort by both partners to approach the dimension of time more creatively, and assumes that both partners do want to spend more time together. Because the time required for the exercise is so minimal, failure to complete it almost always indicates an unwillingness on the part of one or both partners to carry it out, rather than an *inability* to do so because of external time demands. In such cases, exploration has generally revealed more pervasive issues for one or both partners about the degree of closeness they wish to share with each other. Thus, if carried out, the Sixty-Second Pleasure Point exercise usually increases the couple's sense of connectedness, and if not carried out, the exercise stimulates an important discussion about expectations and desires for closeness and intimacy.

REFERENCES

Bateson, G. (1972). *Steps to an ecology of mind.* New York: Ballantine Books.

Fraenkel, P. (1994). Time and rhythm in couples. *Family Process, 33,* 37-51.

Köhler, W. (1969). *The task of gestalt psychology.* Princeton, NJ: Princeton University Press.

Markman, H., Stanley, S., and Blumberg, S. L. (1994). *Fighting for your marriage.* San Francisco: Jossey-Bass.

Ventura, M. (1995). The age of interruption. *The Family Therapy Networker, 19,* 18-31.

33

Debunking Addictive Religious Belief Systems in Marital Therapy

Thomas W. Roberts

Although for most people religious faith is meaningful and rewarding, for some it may be an enslaving and guilt-producing experience. It may inhibit rather than enhance family relationships and create barriers that prevent intimacy. A religious experience that interferes with the development of healthy relationships and is characterized by compulsive rituals, avoidance of reality, dependency on supernatural powers, magical thinking, and rigid compliance to a set of principles can be described or labeled as addictive (Armor, Polich, and Stambul, 1978).

THEORETICAL BACKGROUND OF THE TECHNIQUE

One of the ways of understanding religious addiction is to apply concepts developed in understanding and treating physical addiction to drugs and alcohol. A number of points are important in applying the dynamics of substance addiction to religious addiction. First, both religious addicts and substance-abusing addicts attempt to escape a painful reality (Lenters, 1985; Simmonds, 1977). Religious addicts tend to be influenced by unexplained experience rather than critical exploration of experience. The conversion experience they so desperately desire fails to socialize them toward psychologically healthier behavior. Second, both substance and religious addiction are characterized by dependency on something external to oneself (Allport, 1970). Third, the religious addict fails to take responsibility for his/her own behavior, rarely taking credit for either functional or dysfunctional behavior (Denzin, 1987). Fourth, religious addicts are considered addictive personalities who are susceptible to other addictions. It is not uncommon for an alcoholic or drug addict to exchange substance dependence for a religious high. Fifth, religious addiction is characterized by denial. Most religious addicts deny their addiction to religion and, instead, condemn the behaviors of others in a self-righteous manner. As with substance addiction, denial is an issue that must be addressed in therapy. Sixth, religious addiction is related to a decline in intimate relationships because of rigid and dissatisfying communication patterns (Markowitz, 1983).

Murray Bowen's (1978) concepts about the dynamics of alcohol addiction and family functioning are also helpful. For Bowen, when two persons marry, there is a tendency for them to fuse together. This fusion comes from the lack of being "differentiated," which is the degree to which a person has solidly held principles by which he/she lives. Bowen believed that the most common way a couple handled emotional fusion was through one spouse becoming dominant and the other becoming adaptive. When this pattern continues over time, the adaptive spouse becomes a "no-self," who will develop symptoms. In the case of the religious addict, the symptoms are developing a belief system based on excessive religious principles.

SUITABILITY OF CLIENTS
FOR USE OF DEBUNKING TECHNIQUE

Clients suitable for the debunking technique are couples or families in which one member adheres to a rigid religious system that contributes to frequent arguments and misunderstandings. The relationship dynamics in a couple with a religious addiction problem may be organized in several ways (Roberts, 1992). First, a common pattern is that the religious addict maintains a one-up position because of the moral sense of self-righteousness. In this scenario, the nonreligious spouse is more apt to develop symptoms of depression, agitation, and anxiety. These symptoms may be viewed as co-dependent because they are linked with religious overinvolvement. A second dynamic is the spouse who must adapt or give in to the partner. As this spouse participates less and less in marital decisions, a more profound sense of being "de-selfed" develops. The spouse in the underfunctioning position may use religion as an attempt to maintain functioning. As this "borrowing" from religion continues, excessive and compulsive adherence to religious dogma and behaviors increases. Third, religious addiction might represent a strategy for responding to a traumatic life event.

DESCRIPTION OF THE INTERVENTION

The debunking technique includes six steps (Roberts, 1992). First, the couple must be guided in addressing the relationship dimensions of the symptomatic behavior. A spouse's response to the addicted spouse is as much a problem as the religious ideation. Second, each spouse is asked to take responsibility for his/her behavior that is contributing to the marital problem. Third, after the spouses have been able to initiate issues individually and religion has been raised as an issue, the therapist begins to challenge the religious belief system. Tying the religious ideation to the person's coping mechanism may be a significant step for that person in rethinking his/her relationship to God. Fourth, the relationship issues are addressed when the couple is asked to make agreements that can be executed as part of the homework assignments. Fifth, relating the religious preoccupation to particular situations or life-cycle events may help decrease the religious preoccupation. Sixth, establishing new nonreligious and religious rituals that enhance the relationship is necessary because the void created by challenging the religious system must be filled.

CASE EXAMPLE

Mary and Bob sought therapy because the spark had gone out of their relationship and they had little in common. They had been married for twenty-five years and had two grown children, the youngest of which had just gone away to college. About six months before seeking treatment, Mary had had surgery to remove a tumor in her abdomen. The tumor was benign, but Mary turned to religion to help her cope with this problem. Although healthy throughout most of her life, Mary had been addicted to prescription drugs during a period of heavy stress early in their marriage. Bob described the recent change in Mary by saying that she went away one weekend on a spiritual retreat and came home a religious fanatic. Mary simply stated that she "found the Lord" and prayed daily for Bob to do the same. She was concerned that Bob was not "saved" and believed that she might have to end the twenty-five-year marriage. Bob had taken over much of the household and joint social functions because Mary spent most of her time in religious activities.

The debunking technique involved the following steps with Mary and Bob. First, the therapist reframed the problem as relationship issues to undermine the blaming and recrimination of each other. Second, both Mary and Bob were guided in addressing their own individual issues that contributed to the marital discord. Third, the therapist tied the religious belief system to the problem by describing it as a coping mechanism for Mary and identified Bob's coping mechanism as overfunctioning. This allowed each to be less blaming of the other and to feel less blamed. Mary agreed to not pursue Bob about his "relationship with the Lord" and Bob agreed to not do Mary's work in the home. Fourth, the religious addiction was linked to normal life-cycle events of children leaving home and the extra stress of Mary's surgery. Mary began to understand how she had used prescription drugs to cope with stress early in the marriage. Finally, Mary and Bob began to establish new rituals such as going away to the mountains. Mary's religious addiction was not replaced, but no longer led to symptoms in the marriage.

CONTRAINDICATIONS

Debunking clients with religious addiction in marital couples is appropriate for couples in which one spouse is using excessive religious activities to help cope with life. Persons who develop religious addiction probably have others addictions as well. This technique would not be appropriate for individuals who are actively psychotic or persons with a basic paranoid-type personality disorder. Religious ideation in psychotic and paranoid persons is reduced through the use of psychotropic medication.

REFERENCES

Allport, G. W. (1970). *Individual and his religion.* New York: Macmillan.

Armor, D. J., Polich, J. M., and Stambul, H. B. (1978). *Alcoholism and treatment.* New York: John Wiley & Sons.

Bowen, M. (1978). *Family therapy in clinical practice.* New York: Jason Aronson.

Denzin, N. K. (1987). *The recovering alcoholic.* Newbury Park, CA: Sage.

Lenters, W. (1985). *The freedom we crave.* Grand Rapids, MI: William B. Eerdmans.

Markowitz, B. (1983). *Magic, science, and religion.* New York: Doubleday.

Roberts, T. W. (1992). Marital therapy and religious addiction. A presentation at the annual meeting of the National Council in Family Relations, November 7, Orlando, Florida.

Simmonds, R. B. (1977). Conversion or addiction: Consequences of a Jesus movement group. *American Behavioral Scientist, 20,* 909-924.

34

Ceremony to Memorialize Old Hurts

Stephanie Brooks

INTRODUCTION

Inhibited sexual desire (ISD) is a complex and common sexual problem couples present with in treatment (Kaplan, 1979; Weeks, 1987; Knopf and Seiler, 1990; Brooks, 1994). For many years we have known that only a few couples respond to behaviorally oriented sex therapy (Kaplan, 1979). The literature supports the use of a combination of intrapsychic, intergenerational, interpersonal, and cognitive-behavioral approaches to treatment (Knopf and Seiler, 1990; Leiblum and Rosen, 1988; Lazarus, 1988).

The Intersystem Model developed at Penn Council for Relationships (formerly known as the Marriage Council of Philadelphia) requires the clinician to assess and integrate these dimensions (Weeks, 1987, 1989, 1994). The Intersystem Model provides a comprehensive, integrative and multilevel framework that organizes treatment. The model emphasizes treatment of the client system from the individual, interactional, and intergenerational perspectives. Also, the therapist must consider larger system issues such as class, race, ethnicity, sexual orientation, and multiagency involvement when working within this model.

RATIONALE FOR INTERVENTION

This intervention can be used with recently committed and married upwardly mobile heterosexual couples. The couples have ranged from ages twenty-five to thirty-five, have diverse ethnic and racial backgrounds, and are highly successful in their respective careers. Some couples have young children, but most do not have children and they have little time for intimate activities and sex.

Besides their disinterest in sex, another common dynamic is chronic anger. This is a result of not having time to or feeling emotionally safe to resolve hurt feelings. Fatigue also plays a major role in sustaining the ISD as a symptom. These individuals are accustomed to being in control of their lives, which becomes a critical element in the treatment process. Some individuals in these couples could be said to have difficulty with cognitive flexibility and have become entrenched in old patterns and belief systems. Another important dynamic is that despite the educational achievement of these couples, they have archaic beliefs and myths about sexuality. It is not uncommon for individuals in these couples to hold beliefs that they do not need to talk about their sexuality. They sometimes hold romantic notions that their partners should know their needs and fulfill them in spite of the obvious demands on their time and energy.

INTERVENTION

The therapist must do a full evaluation using the Intersystem Model and have ruled out medical causality for the ISD. Sensate Focus and/or a series of touching exercises must be prescribed and deemed unsuccessful by the couple and therapist. The couple needs to attempt to comply with the prescribed exercises three to six times before the prescription of the ritual. During this time, the therapist needs to determine whether the couple is struggling with performance anxiety or resistance.

The therapist supports the couple's frustration about the lack of progress and offers no interpretation, but encourages the couple to discuss the state of their relationship. The therapist generally needs to take a one-down position, accepting blame from the couple regarding the choice of intervention. This is done in an attempt to support and strengthen the couple's relational commitment and function as a unit.

The therapist reframes the presenting problem (ISD) as a rite of passage that many couples undergo, which has the potential to strengthen their relationship. The therapist invites the couple to take advantage of and celebrate this opportunity to recommit to each other emotionally and sexually.

To participate in the celebration, the couple must be willing to create a ceremony in which they examine what they learn from their experience and how things are going to be different in their relationship, and discuss and create ways to resolve old hurts and recommit to a future together. The couple has total freedom to celebrate anyway they choose.

CASE EXAMPLE

Kathy (age twenty-seven) and Ronald (age thirty), a Caucasian couple of Jewish descent, dated for two years and were married for approximately one and a half years. They met when both were in law school at a competitive university. For approximately seven months, Kathy and Ronald reported an absence of consistent sexual intercourse. Over the months, Kathy lost interest in any sexual contact and subsequently this became the focus of many arguments.

The Intersystem Model was used to complete the multilevel assessment. Although it appeared that the ISD was situational, Kathy was asked to see her physician to have a complete physical evaluation to rule out medical disorders. The ISD was organized around relational/interactional, individual/intrapsychic, and intergenerational issues. This was presented to the couple, who were overly focused on their lack of sexual intimacy. They felt strongly about resuming their sexual relationship, hoping this would make them feel close again. The therapist outlined a treatment plan that recommended couples and sex therapy. The sexual relationship was the last issue to be addressed in the plan. However, despite the insight of this couple, they did not see the connection between the couple dynamics and their sexual relationship and were eager to solve the sexual problem.

The therapist prescribed sensate focus and a series of touching exercises as a way to gradually resume their sexual contact. It was recommended that they go slowly, as they had not had much intimacy in seven months. They were strongly advised against moving quickly at this stage of treatment. The therapist discussed with the couple the importance of feeling emotionally safe and comfortable within the relationship and the role it played in sexuality. The couple was invited to let the therapist know if they thought this approach did not work for them.

Kathy and Ronald tried the sensate focus exercise about six times over three weeks and failed. The therapist supported their frustration and agreed that perhaps this was not the best route to resolving their problems. The therapist also pointed out that although this approach had not worked to resolve their sexual relationship, she thought they had made some progress. During the three-week period they had spent a considerable amount of time alone discussing their relationship. They agreed on being less polarized and were getting along better than before treatment. The therapist then suggested that in cases such as theirs, it can sometimes be helpful to view the struggle as a rite of passage that many couples undergo, which had the potential to strengthen their relationship. The therapist invited the couple to take advantage and celebrate this opportunity to recommit to each other emotionally and sexually. Kathy and Ronald were amenable to this suggestion.

Upon returning to treatment the following week, the couple had completed their homework and were eager to share their progress with the therapist. The couple spent many hours discussing what had happened to their relationship over the past year and how that unresolved conflict created the ISD. They discussed the hurts created by their behavior, identified a way to acknowledge and bury old hurts, and memorialized the importance of their recommitment. The primary goal was for this experience to be meaningful to them. It was recommended they consider including a place, items, or an event that have special meaning to them. The couple enjoyed picnics and walking in the park. Since it was late spring they decided to have a picnic at a nearby park in a spot they enjoyed spending time with each while they were dating. They chose a day and planned the event to include a ceremony to memorialize the old hurts. Kathy and Ronald wrote their experience on paper. They listed their respective hurts and their recommitment to each other. Then the couple put their lists in a bottle and tossed the bottle in the lake at the park. This was a fun but emotionally charged way for them to dispose of the old hurts and rekindle intimacy and closeness in their relationship.

Over the next few sessions, therapy focused on how they could maintain these positive feelings. The couple learned how to anticipate and predict when each would begin to feel rejected and inadequate in the relationship. Within the next few weeks, the couple resumed sexual intercourse on their own. They continued to have intercourse as they discussed what they wanted from their intimate and sexual relationship.

CONTRAINDICATIONS

This intervention is best done with couples who carry the diagnosis of situational or secondary ISD. It is not recommended for individuals who suffer from psychiatric illness such as depression, post-traumatic stress disorder, or anxiety disorders. Individuals with unresolved or never-treated sexual traumas often require additional psychotherapy and supportive treatment before they are engaged in this type of intervention.

REFERENCES

Brooks, S. (1994). Treating inhibited sexual desire: The Intersystem Model. In G. Weeks and L. Hof (Eds.), *The marital-relationship therapy casebook: Theory and application of the intersystem model.* New York: Brunner/Mazel.

Kaplan, H. (1979). *Disorders of sexual desire.* New York: Brunner/Mazel.

Knopf, J. and Seiler, M. (1990). *Inhibited sexual desire.* New York: William Morrow.

Lazarus, R. R. (1988). A multimodel perspective on problems of sexual desire. In S. Leiblum and R. C. Rosen (Eds.), *Principles and practice of sex therapy.* New York: Guilford.

Leiblum, S. and Rosen, R. C. (1988). *Sexual desire disorders*. New York: Guilford.

Weeks, G. (1987). Systematic treatment of inhibited sexual desire. In G. Weeks and L. Hof (Eds.), *Integrating sex and marital therapy: A clinical guide*. New York: Brunner/Mazel.

Weeks, G. (1989). An intersystem approach to treatment. In G. Weeks (Ed.), *Treating couples: The Intersystem Model of the Marriage Council of Philadelphia*. New York: Brunner/Mazel.

Weeks, G. (1994). The Intersystem Model: An integrative approach to treatment. In G. Weeks and L. Hof (Eds.), *The marital-relationship therapy casebook: Theory and application of the Intersystem Model*. New York: Brunner/Mazel.

35

Strategic Journaling

Mary E. Dankoski

THEORETICAL BASE

Strategic journaling is based on the strategic therapy of the Mental Research Institute group (Watzlawick, Weakland, and Fisch, 1974). Often the way clients attempt to cope with problems becomes problematic itself. In effect, the attempted solution becomes the problem. Strategic journaling is designed for clients who find themselves ruminating about problems or bothered by repetitive, intrusive thoughts and images that seem to be out of control and unstoppable. Many clients attempt to solve this problem by cognitively telling themselves *not* to think about the problem, or to *stop* feeling or thinking a certain way. Unfortunately, what often happens is that the more clients tell themselves to ignore their thoughts, the more they find themselves thinking about their problem. They become stuck in a cycle in which their solution perpetuates the problem by increasing their thoughts about the issue.

Strategic journaling is designed to interrupt this patterned thought process by assigning the client to write about the issue in a journal or diary for a set period of time each day. By limiting him- or herself to a specific time period, the client begins to exercise control over thoughts and feelings when they previously believed they had none. Having a time set aside to think about the problem also helps cap the thoughts or feelings when they come up at other inopportune times of the day and interfere with daily tasks. The intervention communicates that the therapist believes the client can gain some control over these intrusive thoughts and images as well.

TYPES OF CASES IN WHICH STRATEGIC JOURNALING MAY BE HELPFUL

This intervention has been particularly successful with clients trying to stop their thoughts and feelings about incidents over which they had no control. Some examples are sexual assault, miscarriage, and the death of a family member. This intervention may also be helpful for those coping with natural disasters, accidents, and other traumas in which clients lack any real control of the situation.

THE INTERVENTION

Strategic journaling can be introduced as follows:

> You seem to be having a lot of thoughts and feelings about [client's problem] but you are fighting yourself about working through them. You need to let yourself process and work these feelings out. A good way to do this is to put them into words on paper by writing in a journal or diary. It's important that you don't overwhelm yourself, however. You have been stopping yourself from really thinking and working out your emotions about this for a while. Because of this, I think you should write about [client's problem] in your journal for only a short time each day, such as half an hour. Try to stick to this amount of time; with a shorter time you may not have enough time to really process the thoughts and a longer amount of time may overwhelm you. Try to make it the same time period every day; it should become your personal journal time. When you have thoughts or feelings about [client's problem] at other times of the day, try to tell yourself to wait until your journal time to work them out. Do you understand what I'm asking? Do you think you could try this for a week and see how it goes?

The same amount of time should be encouraged for many weeks to emphasize that the client has control over the issues. Once progress has been made, clients can stop journaling according to the recommendations, although they may choose to continue on their own.

Feedback from Clients

Clients have responded well to this intervention. The idea of "working through" emotions seems to fit with common expectations of the therapeutic process. The above instructions tap into this widespread expectation.

The ability to exercise control over emotions and thoughts is very powerful for clients trying to integrate experiences over which they had no control. By knowing that they have time set aside to write in a journal, clients have been able to effectively stop their thoughts when they creep up at inopportune times, such as at school or work.

Some clients have written letters to their loved ones or to the perpetrator of an assault, or have written poetry in their journals. One client wrote a poem and later shared it with her parents in a family session. Furthermore, clients who continue this process throughout treatment have a written chronicle of their therapeutic progress. One client who recently reviewed her journal marveled at the progress she had made since the start of therapy, stating that she sounds like a totally different person now. At termination, she had independently decided to continue journaling as a personal ritual.

CONTRAINDICATIONS

As with many strategic interventions, careful assessment must be conducted prior to implementing this intervention. Strategic journaling is not recommended for persons with suicidal ideation or with intent to harm others due to the possibility that journaling will increase the ruminations about inflicting harm on oneself or others.

This intervention has been helpful to adults but has been particularly successful with teenage clients, possibly due to the adolescent's developmental urge for self-expression. It is not recommended for the very young nor those who are not verbally inclined. The possibility of a pictorial journal could be pursued with those who are illiterate or prefer to express themselves through visual means.

REFERENCE

Watzlawick, P., Weakland, J. H., and Fisch, R. (1974). *Change: Principles of problem formation and problem resolution*. New York: W. W. Norton.

36

A Solution-Focused Guessing Game for Children

Mary E. Dankoski

THEORETICAL BASE

This intervention is an adaptation of the prediction interventions used in solution-focused therapy (de Shazer, 1988, 1991). An elemental process of the solution-focused model is to track solutions and exceptions to the presenting problem. Clients are often able to point out exceptions or "good days" when their problems are not present or are not as severe. Some clients are able to hypothesize about why these days are better than others, although many clients are not and maintain that their exceptions are random. A prediction intervention is designed to promote client awareness of their own agency in their exceptions. In these assignments, clients are asked to predict each day whether the following day will be a symptom-free or symptom-reduced day, or whether it will be a symptomatic day. Predicting an outcome tends to create a self-fulfilling prophecy because of the tendency for the client to behave in ways that increase the likelihood of the predicted outcome. Through an increase in symptom-free or symptom-reduced days, the client comes to understand that these exceptions are not random and that they have some control over their problems. This intervention also communicates the important message that the therapist believes the exception is predictable and thus controllable. This intervention can be framed as a guessing game for use with children.

TYPES OF CASES IN WHICH THE GUESSING GAME MAY BE HELPFUL

Children between the ages of approximately seven and twelve often respond positively to games. This has been a helpful intervention for children with anger management problems or temper outbursts in which they feel out of control. It is a versatile intervention, however, and could also be used effectively with families presenting children with various problems.

THE INTERVENTION

Prior to implementing this intervention, the problem and exceptions to the problem must be thoroughly assessed. If exceptions are noted yet are thought to be random, then the guessing game may be a helpful homework assignment. It can be introduced by asking the child if he or she likes or knows any guessing games and would like to play one during the coming week. The child is asked to guess whether he or she will have a good day (i.e., symptom-free or -reduced) or a bad day (i.e., symptomatic). The child is to monitor the guesses on a sheet of paper kept in a public place, such as the refrigerator. A calendar on which the child can record the predictions is also an effective way to document the intervention. The parents are to make their own predictions on a separate sheet of paper. For the child, the idea of guessing about his or her own behavior seems somewhat mysterious and silly. The child is often further excited about the possibility of proving his or her parents wrong by behaving differently than they would predict. The family is to bring the list or calendar to the next therapy session.

CASE EXAMPLE

The J family was an intact family that presented with their oldest son as the identified patient. He was a young-looking boy, ten years of age, named Billy. He had two younger sisters. They presented for therapy concerning Billy's "tempers," in which he broke things and hit his sisters, as well as his difficulty doing his homework independently and his tendency to manipulate his parents into doing it for him. The first part of therapy focused on the homework problems, and throughout their progress in this area, the parents' handling of Billy's "tempers" was also assessed. Because his "tempers" did not seem to be specifically related to problematic parenting, such as inconsistent discipline, the guessing game intervention was implemented.

The exceptions to Billy's temper outbursts were fairly consistent. He did not have many "tempers" at school nor at his baby-sitter's, yet neither Billy nor his parents could identify what made the difference between these situations and essentially thought of them as random. Billy noted that on his good days he "listened to his heart instead of to his anger." I asked Billy if he liked to play guessing games and began describing the intervention. He was to guess if the next day would be a day when he would listen to his heart or to his anger. At the end of the day he and his parents were to decide whether he guessed right based on his behavior that day.

While I was describing the game, Billy began to smile. He became involved in planning the details and offered to keep track on the calendar he kept in his room. He decided that he would write an "A" for the days he guessed that he would listen to his anger, and an "H" for the days that he guessed he would listen to his heart. He would then note whether he guessed correctly at the end of the day by writing another "A" or "H." He giggled at the thought of proving his parents wrong if they guessed an "A" day and he ended up having an "H" day.

Billy brought his calendar with him to the next session. He had consistently followed through with the assignment each day and was excited to discuss it. He had guessed an "H" correctly for the majority of days and his parents agreed that it was one of the most peaceful weeks they had experienced in a while. They had guessed many more "A" days but Billy proved them wrong. On the days when he had guessed an "A," he and his parents agreed that his "tempers" even seemed to be less intense than previously. On one day he had guessed an "A" but ended up with an "H," and I spent a lot of time asking him how he had turned this day around. Billy enthusiastically stated that he told his anger to "go away because I'm in charge and you can't tell me what to do!" We spent the rest of the session roleplaying what he could do and say to keep himself from listening to his anger. At the end of the session Billy and his parents were instructed to keep the calendar going until the next session.

When the family returned for the next session we looked at Billy's calendar and it again showed many more "H" days than "A" days. The "A" days also continued to be less severe and his parents indicated that his "tempers" were now less frequent and at a more tolerable level. Everyone agreed that Billy had made great changes. By the end of the session everyone agreed that Billy had learned how to listen to his heart and keep his anger from getting too loud. Therapy was terminated after one more session.

CONTRAINDICATIONS

As with other interventions aimed at children as identified patients, prior to implementing this intervention assessment should include parenting skills and other systemic issues in order to intervene at the appropriate level. This intervention could also be incorporated with other interventions throughout therapy that are directed at these other issues. For example, in the J case, interventions directed at the homework problems were implemented prior to the guessing game intervention.

Older children, such as teenagers, may think this intervention a hoax. Children who are too young may not understand the central idea of guessing about their own behavior or may be unable to track their own guesses and outcomes consistently. Moreover, not only must children be able to understand and agree to follow through with the intervention, parents must also be willing to follow through themselves in addition to encouraging their child. Parents may be more willing to do so if the therapist explains the thinking behind the intervention to them without the child present. Parents may be more willing to follow through when they understand that this communicates to the child that he or she can control his or her own behavior. They may feel more in-the-know, and thus less likely to question the intervention and more likely to follow through with the assignment.

REFERENCES

de Shazer, S. (1988). *Clues: Investigating solutions in brief therapy.* New York: W. W. Norton.

de Shazer, S. (1991). *Putting difference to work.* New York: W. W. Norton.

37

The Problem Box Ritual:
Helping Families Prepare for Remarriage

Israela Meyerstein

THE CHALLENGE OF REMARRIAGE
AND PRE-REMARITAL COUNSELING

The joining of families through remarriage is a complex process, particularly when children are involved. Remarriage is a significant developmental transition involving the entire family structure and organization. Family members are often ill prepared for the challenges of remarriage; witness the higher divorce rate (over 60 percent) in second marriages and the statistic that second marriages with children present are twice as likely to end in divorce as remarriages without children (McGoldrick and Carter, 1988). There are many changes for family members to accommodate to, such as different living arrangements, rules, and styles of communication. A host of ambivalent feelings, role changes, marital adjustments, and challenging new tasks must be faced (Einstein and Albert, 1986). Adjustment may be impeded by unrealistic expectations and myths about stepfamily life (Visher and Visher, 1982, 1987). The presence of children in and out of the household and complex relationships with ex-spouses, siblings, and grandparents create a far more dynamically changing environment.

For all these reasons, remarriage requires a creative preventive approach. Pre-remarital counseling that is brief, systemic, educational, and task focused can help to provide some essential preplanning, problem solving, and validation for families' struggles in the absence of societal support or a clear paradigm to follow. Pre-remarital counseling can provide normative education about realistic expectations, can improve family communication, anticipate stress, provide coaching in skills of negotiating, and create constructive tasks and rituals.

THERAPEUTIC RITUALS FOR TRANSITIONS

Since remarried families are the epitome of families in transition (Minuchin and Goldner, 1984) and rituals are useful tools in defining and easing transitional states (Imber-Black, Roberts, and Whiting, 1988), it seems only natural to look to rituals as a therapeutic resource. Rituals are viewed as "humankind's original form of therapy" because of their classic capacity to facilitate change and stability simultaneously (Davis, 1994). They can promote the task of providing family members with opportunities for balancing autonomy and connection. Rituals have also been used to symbolize losses and gains, help bond participants, and solidify identity. Because remarriage is full of anticipated changes and evokes ambivalent feelings of loss and gain, it is a particularly suitable arena for the use of rituals.

Application of the Problem Box Ritual

The use of a "problem box ritual" is most effective within the context of brief, systemic pre-remarital counseling. It is most suited for families whose primary issues are adjusting to the blending within the framework of a committed new couple relationship. The adults need to be clear on their commitment and on the plans to integrate families. Major conflicts between the adults and strong ambivalence about actually forming the new unit, combined with cross-generational coalitions, would compromise the ritual. The ritual is most helpful as a means of facilitating emotional adjustments before, during, and after the wedding ritual of remarriage. The ritual can be used for a variety of family situations, but is best suited for clients with the conceptual/developmental capacity for symbolization, the ability to follow tasks, and openness to creativity and play. The ritual is also more potent on the heels of a discussion about and legitimization of ambivalent feelings, fears, and worries about approaching remarriage. The ritual is best introduced with all family members present, including children whose active participation is most desired.

DESCRIPTION OF THE INTERVENTION

Following a discussion about remarriage as born of loss and the naturalness of ambivalent feelings arising in response to major life changes, family members are invited to describe feared losses and anticipated changes and are invited to participate in a prenuptial ritual (although it can occur after marriage as well). The ritual is framed as an additional way that may be helpful in preparing as a family for the anticipated changes.

Family members are asked to find a large cardboard box or container and to agree on a time to do the ritual. They are asked to prepare for it by gathering a variety of objects to put in the box. Each object represents something that each person felt he/she might have to give up, get, or change in the remarriage. The hope is that by giving space and voice to the negative and ambivalent feelings, family members will be better able to move forward. Ideally the ritual functions as a projective expression of individual and family themes and issues. Family members generally perform the ritual at home, but could also be asked to bring their objects into a therapy session and put them in the problem box there and describe them. After the ritual is performed, a discussion can ensue about some of the concerns raised and plans made to address these concerns.

CASE EXAMPLE

One such experience involved the L family, consisting of Cindy, the mother; her fiancé, Ken; teenage daughter, Anna; and son, Tony. The family had recently requested help because of an upsurge in fighting between Cindy and Anna over Anna's lack of cooperation and enthusiasm for the wedding. The family had previously been in treatment as a single-parent family, and adjustment to the divorce was stable. After a broadening of and a normalizing of the ambivalent feelings from only Anna to include all members, a discussion ensued about remarriage as born of loss. Family members were invited to describe what they each feared losing in anticipating changes brought about by remarriage. I suggested a prenuptial ritual to help further prepare them for the changes. I asked family members to find a large cardboard box or container, select a time, and prepare a variety of objects to put in the box that would represent what each felt he or she would have to change in the remarriage.

The family came to the next session several weeks later, pleased at the completion of the ritual and eager to tell what had transpired. Each family member listed what objects he or she had put in the box to symbolically represent their concerns. For example, Tony put in a stuffed cat (representing Ken's new pet who was joining the household), an old Walkman radio (representing having to share choice of stations more), and a lock (to indicate his growing need for privacy). Anna put in underwear (to represent her feared loss of privacy and the female-headed household), a favorite picture of herself and Cindy (to say, "we've changed, but will still be mother and daughter"), and her own initials (to signify keeping her own name). Ken, the new stepparent, put in his driver's license (to represent his own identity and feared loss of independence after a long bachelorhood). Cindy put in a picture of her and her new partner (to represent their new special bond). Each family member explained the symbolism of the objects he or she put in. After family members described their items representing anticipated loss or change, the therapist clarified that these were largely beliefs and fears of loss; they did not represent nonnegotiable situations. The therapist suggested that family members might want to discuss things they valued and wanted to hold onto. A discussion ensued over issues such as privacy arrangements in the new household, private versus public displays of sexuality, preserving important bonds between the mother and each child, and other issues that were highlighted by the ritual.

The ritual also facilitated the emergence of positivity, such as mother and daughter noticing recent constructive actions taken by the other. I asked how they could make the problem box useful in the future, so that family members could recognize problems earlier, or evaluate how they were doing on the adjustments described. The family decided to put the box in a visible location and to cover it with plastic wrap so that the symbols could be contained yet visible.

Subsequent sessions of pre-remarital counseling addressed some of the myths of stepfamily living (such as the myth of instant love). I shared some self-help tapes and readings. Follow-up sessions after the wedding were held to focus on the couple and coparenting issues.

USE AND CONTRAINDICATIONS

The problem box ritual has its greatest utility within a framework of brief preventive systemic pre-remarital counseling with families who are actively solidifying their remarital adjustment. It is most effective when combined with normative education, communication skills, and systemic family counseling. It is less suited, and may not be at all effective, if attempted while there are major conflicts between the adults regarding commitment to the new marital unit. For example, in one family the mother was gung ho about the blending but her fiancé had more than cold feet; he could not make a permanent commitment. Another contraindication for the use of the problem box ritual is the presence of strong cross-generational coalitions or areas of intense conflict impeding adjustment. In these situations family members are simply not yet ready or may not be able to utilize the ritual's potential. For example, there was a family in which the father promised his youngest son he would not remarry without the son's permission. The father then moved his future wife-to-be into the home, but could not understand why or believe that a campaign of guerilla warfare was being conducted by his son to scare away his future wife. Family therapy would be needed before such a ritual to address the conflicts. The problem box ritual helps family members seal the adjustment process by articulating fears, receiving validation, and understanding how remarriage requires a family-wide adjustment. Fostering collaboration and communication makes it easier for the family members to move forward in their lives.

REFERENCES

Davis, J. (1994). The Bar Mitzvah Balabusta: Mother's role in the family's rite of passage. In M. Sachs (Ed.), *Women in Jewish Culture*, University of Illinois Press.

Einstein, E. and Albert, L. (1986). *Strengthening your stepfamily*. Circle Pines, Minnesota: American Guidance Press.

Imber-Black, E., Roberts, J., and Whiting, R.A. (Eds.) (1988). *Rituals in families and family therapy*. New York: W.W. Norton.

McGoldrick, M. and Carter, B. (1988). Forming a remarried family. In B. Carter and M. McGoldrick (Eds.), *The changing family life cycle: A framework for family therapy* (pp. 402-432). Second Edition. New York: Gardner.

Minuchin, S. and Goldner, V. (1984). Quartet: Patterns of remarriage. In S. Minuchin (Ed.), *Family kaleidoscope: Images of violence and healing*. Cambridge, MA: Harvard University Press.

Visher, E. B. and Visher, J. S. (1982). *How to win as a stepfamily*. New York: Dembner.

Visher, E. B. and Visher, J. S. (1987). *Old loyalties, new ties: Therapeutic strategies with stepfamilies*. New York: Brunner/Mazel.

38

Using Batacca Sticks in Couples Therapy

Geoffrey L. Smith
Maureen Semans

Carl Whitaker will be remembered for his "crazy" antics in the therapy room. He encouraged his clients to learn about themselves and their family members through the symbolism inherent in interpersonal experience (Whitaker and Keith, 1981). Gary Connell (1996) related this experience with Carl Whitaker: "[Carl] once gave me a bumper sticker which read 'Anything worth knowing can't be taught,' to which he added, 'It must be experienced.'" Batacca sticks are one of the experiential tools that Whitaker found useful in his symbolic-experiential mode of therapy (Kaye, Dichter, and Keith, 1986; Whitaker and Garfield, 1987).

Our favorite time to use the batacca sticks is when we have clients in a couple who are particularly adept at blaming and/or who communicate with each other in a disrespectful, hurtful manner. Generally, we begin the intervention by asking the couple to talk to each other about their relationship or any other emotionally charged issue that is relevant for that particular couple. As cotherapists, we tell them that we will listen to them and act as their alter egos. We hold the batacca sticks and when the person for whom we are acting says something that is insulting or debasing we thump our cotherapist with the stick. We try to hit each other equal to the amount of hurt that one partner verbally inflicts upon the other; e.g., a small tap for a minor insult, and a stronger strike for an exceptionally rude comment.

We have found that this technique is particularly useful because the family can viscerally experience how they interact in a symbolic way rather than having us describe and explain their interactions to them. This provides the experiential component that the symbolic-experiential approach deems so important. We recently used the batacca sticks in this manner with Erick and Monica, a couple in their early thirties who had been married for six years. We chose to use this intervention with them because they were both rarely able to complete a sentence without being verbally abusive to each other. Many times we punctuated their hurtful communication pattern, but the cognitive explanations were inadequate in helping them comprehend to what extent they were mutually abusive.

When the technique was explained to them, they thought that it was a silly idea, but said that they would try anything if we thought it might help. It only took half of Monica's first sentence before one of us whacked the other with the batacca stick. The response was immediate; she rephrased her sentence. The new sentence was not much better than the previous, but it was a start. It took a few more whacks than we might have preferred, but they soon began communicating in a new way. The "I-messages" that we had been trying so long and hard to teach them were finally becoming a part of their interpersonal communication. It was not until the batacca stick intervention that they were able to symbolically see what they were doing to each other, and thus begin to use more positive communication patterns. Virginia Satir's comment that "[people] are often revolted by being asked to do openly what they secretly fear they have been doing all along" (Satir, 1988, p. 106) appears to apply in this case.

CONTRAINDICATIONS

Although we feel that this intervention can be used in a wide variety of situations with many couples or families, we do believe that there are at least three important contraindications to using this intervention. First, we prefer not to use this technique with any couple that has a history of interpersonal violence. Using the batacca sticks with such a couple could be construed as our symbolically approving of violent means of conflict resolution. We abhor violence and avoid giving them any excuse to be violent. Second, we do not use this intervention with new clients. We prefer to build a positive relationship with them so that there will be stronger transference when they see us modeling their verbal expressions by batting each other with the bataccas. Last, we do not use this approach when at least one of the clients appears to be a sadist. Although we do enjoy hitting each other with the sticks because it allows us to release some of the aggression that we feel toward each other regarding our disagreements about the course of therapy, we fear that a sadistic person would enjoy seeing us hit each other. The batacca stick intervention would lose much of its impact if one or both of the clients derived some pleasure from seeing us continually whack each other.

We have found this technique beneficial in assisting couples to understand how they are treating each other and useful in helping them develop new patterns of communication. Creative therapists will be able to think of many variations on our use of the batacca stick. Helping clients to think in new ways is an essential part of the therapeutic process and the symbolic experience provided by the use of batacca sticks can be an effective therapeutic tool.

REFERENCES

Connell, G. M. (1996). Carl Whitaker: In memoriam. *Journal of Marital and Family Therapy, 22,* 3-8.

Kaye, D., Dichter, H., and Keith, D. (1986). Symbolic-experiential family therapy. *Individual Psychology, 42,* 521-536.

Satir, V. (1988). *The new peoplemaking.* Mountain View, CA: Science and Behavior Books.

Whitaker, C. and Garfield, R. (1987). On teaching psychotherapy via consultation and cotherapy. *Contemporary Family Therapy, 9,* 106-115.

Whitaker, C. A. and Keith, D. V. (1981). Symbolic-experiential family therapy. In A. S. Gurman and D. P. Kniskern (Eds.), *Handbook of family therapy* (pp. 187-225). New York: Brunner/Mazel.

39

Necessity's Way

Celia B. Ferguson
Beverly McKee
S. Carolyn Patton

Necessity is the mother of *intervention*. Needed was a way to "treat" the client's stories with reverence and respect—but within a brief time period. And ways were needed, too, for the client to continue her/his own self-attending process for *when* the "brief time period" was to be over. Thus emerged Necessity's Way, grounded in Bowen's family systems theory (Bowen, 1978; Friedman, 1991; Kerr and Bowen, 1988) and revolving around the framework of the Internal Family Systems (IFS) model (Schwartz, 1995).

NECESSITY'S WAY

Necessity's Way is an eight-session intervention and is the brief portion (A) of a larger construction (A + B), the design of which deepens intra-psychically as A progresses through B. The clinician and client study the presenting problem and choose a focus for this brief therapy component, the primary goals of which are to: (1) establish safety for the client, (2) organize the influences/messages of the external system by using a genogram, (3) begin to deal with family-of-origin issues in nonreactive ways, (4) introduce the idea of multiplicity of parts, (5) identify and begin to study internal structures, systems, parts, etc., using the IFS model (see Glossary), (6) begin to release *managers* and *firefighters* from their extreme roles (Schwartz, 1995), (7) begin to increase self-leadership, and (8) name and establish a cognitive understanding of the *exiles*. Through Necessity's Way's eight goals, the immediate presenting problem will be addressed; also, the groundwork will be laid for another phase of therapy (if needed), encompassing deeper intrapsychic work.

The construction of the external family system genogram (McGoldrick and Gerson, 1985) is followed by the mapping of the client's internal family system (Schwartz, 1995). The genogram allows for assessment of the external environment and its influences, while the IFS map enables the client/therapist dyad to study how the client has reacted to and internally organized those external experiences.

Session 1

As the client begins to tell her/his story, the therapist uses "parts" language (Schwartz, 1995) in exploring the client's presenting problem and recording personal and familial history. A genogram is constructed as the client reports family events, births, deaths, cultural influences, world events, and so on. The therapist notes any current traumas or crises in the external system that might contraindicate brief therapy in general and Necessity's Way in particular.

Session 2

An emphasis on safety is continued, as is the intentional use of "parts" language and genogram construction. Influences of the family of origin (FOO) on the presenting problem are explored as further information is gathered regarding decisions for the treatment plan. A crucial, ongoing process is the recording of powerful messages the client heard from the patterns of the FOO, the culture, and world events.

Session 3

The IFS model is introduced as a way to look at the messages described above and as a way we all internally organize our reactions to life experiences (see Figure 39.1). The components of the IFS model are explained and the client's IFS map is begun. *Exile, manager,* and *firefighter* parts are delineated onto this IFS map, using the client's already identified messages. By the end of the third session, a decision needs to be made regarding the appropriateness of brief therapy. Also, the client and the therapist develop treatment goals specific to the genogram and IFS map information.

Sessions 4 Through 6

The next three sessions are spent guiding the client in becoming better acquainted with his/her managers and firefighters and their protective functions. Also, a link is made between the stressors in the external envi-

FIGURE 39.1. Internal Family Systems Map

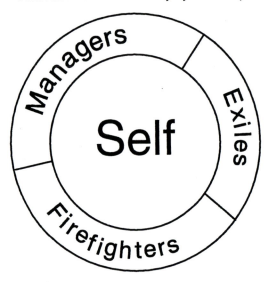

ronment and the client, the firefighters, and the managers. While the presence of firefighters and/or exiles may be acknowledged, Schwartz (1995) emphasizes stabilization of the external system and working with the protective managers to gain their cooperation before actively studying the rest of the system, that is, firefighters and exiles. In fact, prolonged contact with the exiles is a contraindication for the brief therapy intrinsic to Necessity's Way and should be reserved for later phases of therapy.

Sessions 7 and 8

Termination is the focus for these last two sessions. This includes a review of and plan for maintenance of progress, identification of troublesome areas indicating parts that may need additional attention, and giving permission to self-reliant parts to do the next piece of work in the future or to reengage in therapy if needed. Clients may benefit from having a copy of their IFS map to jog their memories when confusion again occurs; therefore, providing this tool is recommended.

CASE EXAMPLE

A forty-five-year-old male client presented with depression after making a job and community relocation. Although he was pleased with his chosen situation, he was concerned about a job performance evaluation regarding his poor communication with other members of his work group. He had been retired from the military for about five years. In his previous job he thought he had interacted adequately. He wanted to be successful in his present job and was puzzled about the problem.

During the construction of the genogram, much information was generated about his first family as well as about his marriage. He described his childhood in his parents' home as "typical," with his mother at home and his father away working most of the time. One of his few memories of childhood was that of being criticized by his father if he did something wrong. He also remembered that he enjoyed toys with which he could build objects. He remembered feeling pleased when he could successfully analyze the construction of an object and reproduce it. During the discussion of the genogram, words and phrases such as "likes to figure things out—positive" and "criticizes—negative," were noted. He reported no unusual childhood traumas, and he expressed regret that he had not been able to form a closer relationship with his stepson or feel closer to his wife.

When the IFS mapping began, he identified an *achieving, hard-working manager* who was always busy and focused on finishing some project. He also identified an *analyzer manager* who continued to enjoy "figuring things out." As the positive side of the *achieving* manager was explored, he identified liking his ability to do many things very well. His ability to learn new skills had been appreciated on work teams, plus he and his wife enjoyed renovating their house together. He recognized that he felt positive about himself when a project was in progress and particularly when it was finished to his satisfaction. The positive qualities of the *analyzer* manager were also explored. He enjoyed a career that made use of this quality, and he was known as a problem solver in work situations. This manager wanted to understand more about the depression the client was experiencing and gave permission to continue examining the internal system.

The negative sides of the managers were then investigated. The *achieving* manager sometimes kept him from his family, and he regretted that he had seldom taken time to stay in touch with friends. At times when things didn't go just right at work or on a home project, he became extremely irritable. Regarding his analyzer manager, his wife had told him on numerous occasions that she wanted him just to talk more and share his feelings with her rather than focus so intently on figuring out how they could fix situations and problems. She also saw him as insensitive to the feelings of others.

As the exploration of the positive and negative qualities of the two readily identified managers progressed, the client became able to differentiate from them and regard them from the *Self*. Although he had reservations about being too emotional, he was also uncomfortable with thinking he had become distant and critical like his father. Therefore, he was willing to continue and to begin to study the depression that had brought him into therapy in the first place.

His depression was tentatively mapped as a firefighter. Since the client was most familiar with the negative qualities of the *depression* firefighter, those aspects were explored first. He enumerated typical depression symptoms. Although he was willing to consider that there might be positive qualities to his depression, he was unable to identify those; therefore, that question went unanswered for the time being.

My client knew very little about parts of himself that had been exiled. He was able to see that a child who had been repeatedly criticized would feel hurt, so he was comfortable naming a *criticized* child "exile." He also identified keeping thoughts and opinions to himself and doing things well as ways to avoid criticism; therefore, he was able to conceptually understand how the analyzer and achieving managers had developed as attempts to protect the *Self* from the hurt of this criticized child exile.

Although a general treatment goal of reducing symptoms of depression had been agreed upon earlier, more specific objectives were now identified based on the regrets that he had expressed about lack of closeness with friends and family. Using his ideas for initiating contact, he implemented weekly homework assignments, noticed positive reactions from family and friends, and began to question his assumption that in the present he would be criticized as he had been in the past. Specifically, he worked toward the treatment goals of (1) releasing the analyzer and achieving managers from their extreme roles as he (2) increased Self-leadership and (3) increased appreciation for and cognitive understanding of his criticized child exile.

As therapy ended, the client had begun to feel closer to those he had contacted and had plans to continue to be more active in initiating socially. He identified overwork and analyzing versus contributing his own thoughts and feelings as problems that would probably arise again; however, he now recognized that they served the purpose of protecting him from a fear of being criticized. Since he could now examine whether the fear was in the present or past, he had more choices about being involved with others.

CONTRAINDICATIONS

Necessity's Way assumes many of the same ideas as other brief approaches. Intrinsic to most brief therapies is the notion that a focus on intrapsychic phenomena is not conducive to quick change (Segal, 1991; Watzlawick, Weakland, and Fisch, 1974). When using Necessity's Way, however, the clinician mindfully introduces the concepts of intrapsychic elements that most other brief therapy models tend to minimize. Thus, this psychoeducational component bridges the brief therapy with the longer-term intrapsychic therapy.

Clearly, Necessity's Way is one brief therapy approach for which there are some contraindications. Not unlike other intrapsychic models, if the client's external environment is volatile, then Necessity's Way is inappropriate. Specifically, if there are significant others in the client's external system who would likely escalate violence or abuse in reaction to any change in the client, then the goal of therapy needs to be stabilization of the external environment. Similarly, it would be unethical to try to work with those hurt, shamed, abused, or neglected exile parts in the client's internal system before stabilizing, calming, and gaining the cooperation of the internal managers and firefighters or without enough time to increase Self-leadership. Thus, shortage of time when working with certain diagnoses such as PTSD, MPD, major depressive disorders, or borderline personality disorder contraindicates the use of Necessity's Way.

The most important criterion for using Necessity's Way has to do with the therapist. It is imperative that the therapist have the capacity to lead primarily with her/his Self, that is, the differentiated leader aspect of the therapist's own internal family system (Schwartz, 1995, p. 22). Since it is inevitable that, at times, some internal part of the therapist will be activated within the client-therapist system, the therapist must be able to pay attention to her/his own internal system for treatment to be successful.

CONCLUSION

As an eight-session introduction to psychotherapy, Necessity's Way provides an immediately useful way for clients to view themselves and their problems. The therapist provides a cognitive structure for the internal world as the client collaborates in setting and meeting treatment goals, thereby increasing the likelihood of authentic and lasting change.

GLOSSARY

The **Self** is "the core of a person, which contains leadership qualities such as compassion, perspective, curiosity, and confidence. The Self is best equipped to lead the internal family" (Schwartz, 1995, p. 232).

Parts is "the term used in IFS for a person's subpersonalities. Parts are best considered internal people of different ages, talents, and temperaments" (Schwartz, 1995, p. 232), all of whom originate in attempts to protect the Self.

Exiles are "parts that are sequestered within a system, for their own protection or for the protection of the system from them" (Schwartz, 1995, p. 231).

Managers are "parts that try to run a system in ways that minimize the activation (upset) of the exiles" (Schwartz, 1995, p. 232).

Firefighters are "parts that go into action after the exiles have been activated, to calm the exiles or distract the system from them (dissociation)" (Schwartz, 1995, p. 231).

REFERENCES

Bowen, M. (1978). *Family therapy in clinical practice*. Northvale, NJ: Jason Aronson.

Friedman, E. H. (1991). Bowen theory and therapy. In A. S. Gurman and D. P. Kniskern (Eds.), *Handbook of family therapy*, Volume 2 (pp. 134-170). New York: Brunner/Mazel.

Kerr, M. E., and Bowen, M. (1988). *Family evaluation: An approach based on Bowen theory*. New York: W. W. Norton.

McGoldrick, M. and Gerson, R. (1985). *Genograms in family assessment*. New York: W. W. Norton.

Nichols, M. P. and Schwartz, R. C. (1995). *Family therapy: Concepts and methods* (third edition). Boston: Allyn and Bacon.

Schwartz, R. C. (1995). *Internal family systems therapy*. New York: W. W. Norton.

Segal, L. (1991). Brief therapy: The MRI approach. In A. S. Gurman and D. P. Kniskern (Eds.), *Handbook of family therapy*, Volume 2 (pp. 171-199). New York: Brunner/Mazel.

40

Couples Group Psychotherapy with HIV-Affected Gay Men

David W. Purcell
Nadine J. Kaslow

The problem addressed by this chapter is the psychological treatment of HIV-positive men and their partners in couples group psychotherapy. HIV and AIDS not only is devastating for the individual infected with the AIDS virus, but the disease also has a profound impact on one's family and friends. In the outpatient AIDS clinic of a large, inner-city hospital, a growing number of couples have presented for treatment, and we report on a short-term couples group formed to address this need.

THEORY

In developing a couples group for this population, we combined theories and techniques from family/marital therapy and group therapy, using systems theory as an overarching framework (e.g., Coché and Satterfield, 1993; Kaslow and Suarez, 1988). We also integrated the literatures on therapy with gay couples and group therapy with HIV-positive individuals (e.g., Carl, 1990; Friedman, 1991; Lego, 1993; Tunnell, 1994). Gay male couples have problems similar to and different from heterosexual couples. Any problems within a couple can be compounded by such serious medical complications as HIV infection (Friedman, 1991).

While couples group approaches are founded on the assumption that therapeutic change occurs in an interpersonal context, specific theoretical approaches and techniques may vary. Our group integrated interventions from object relations, structural, family of origin, and cognitive-behavioral approaches. The group was conceptualized as a "holding environment" that promotes behavioral change, normalizes relational problems, and offers alternative solutions to long-standing interactional difficulties through the

181

use of modeling, idea sharing, and feedback. Members learn about themselves through interactions with the leaders, their partners, and the other couples. In an AIDS clinic, group also provides support and encouragement and decreases loneliness and isolation by fostering attachments. Interventions address issues in the couples group at four levels: individual (intrapsychic and family-of-origin issues affecting the couple), couple (struggles within each couple), interpersonal (common conflicts for individuals and couples that highlight similarities and differences), and group ("group-as-a-whole" issues such as group norms, decisions, and conflict) (Coché and Coché, 1990).

THE GROUP SETTING

This group was conducted in the outpatient AIDS clinic of a large, university-affiliated, inner-city hospital. The clinic provides a wide range of services for patients including medical, psychological, social, and educational interventions. The initial reason for starting this group was the growing need in the clinic for another modality for couples that effectively utilized relatively scarce mental health resources. Another impetus for the group was the trainee therapists' desire to work together in a couples group (a psychology intern [DP] and a psychiatry resident) and the availability of an experienced couples group supervisor (NK).

GROUP STRUCTURE, SCREENING, AND RULES

Due to training schedules, time constraints, and the current health care climate, a short-term (twelve-week), closed group was formed. Our goal was to recruit three or four gay male couples currently in therapy. Three couples was a minimum for starting because fewer than three couples does not provide "the critical mass of dynamic material" that fosters group development and process (Kaslow and Suarez, 1988). Two gay male therapists led the group, thereby mirroring the model of a female and male suggested in couples groups for heterosexual couples (Coché and Satterfield, 1993). This allowed the therapists to model an egalitarian relationship with successful conflict resolution.

Regarding selection criteria, first we considered whether or not the usual selection criteria for couples groups applied in this low-income, medical setting. Common criteria for couples groups include: a committed relationship of some duration with sexual exclusivity, a presenting focus on couples issues, the absence of severe psychopathology and significant substance abuse, and a balance of homogeneity versus heterogeneity among the couples (Kaslow and Suarez, 1988). We chose to require a shorter duration of couplehood (six months) than traditionally is recommended, because AIDS patients often feel a strong press of time. We did require sexual exclusivity; although for long-term groups, this requirement is at odds with research that has found that sexual nonexclusivity is a distinctive feature of some gay relationships, although this may be less true today because of the AIDS epidemic (Kurdek, 1995).

Our two most difficult selection issues were the acceptable level of psychopathology and group heterogeneity. The majority of individuals seeking mental health treatment in the clinic manifested considerable psychopathology (particularly current and past substance abuse and Axis II pathology). Such individuals usually are excluded from groups either because of the possibility that they will upset a well-functioning group or that they will become more psychologically disturbed by their entry into the group (e.g., if a patient with Borderline Personality Disorder feels rejected by the group). Also, in a couples group specifically, if one member of a couple is particularly disturbed, focus on this person's individual psychopathology may divert from the couples focus of the group. However, in individual groups conducted at the same clinic, persons with more significant levels of psychopathology than is traditionally recommended have been managed successfully. Thus, in the couples group, we did not automatically exclude couples with substance abuse problems and significant character issues. Our standard was that couples in which one or both individuals reported current severe substance abuse or dependence or a history that predicted little ability to form successful relationships (e.g., a patient who had left three AIDS support groups due to interpersonal conflict) were not accepted into the group. Finally, we decided for homogeneity along some dimensions (e.g., gay male couples, HIV illness in at least one member) and heterogeneity along other dimensions (e.g., health status varied from serious opportunistic infections to asymptomatic, concordance of HIV status between partners varied).

Group structure and ground rules were similar to those in most groups, although a few important differences are notable. Members were asked to keep group information confidential, except with their partners. Both members of the couple were expected to attend sessions, although one partner could attend if the other was ill, a common scenario in HIV therapy groups. Long-term absences were not experienced by this group, although this issue could become complex in an ongoing group if one member of a couple was very ill for an extended period of time. If this issue had presented, we would have encouraged the healthier member to continue attending the couples group and to focus on couples issues at this final stage of the relationship, an experience that would be helpful for the other couples. Out-of-group contact was permitted in this group, a stance more consistent with the norm in HIV groups, where group members quickly come to rely on the group both inside and outside the session (Lego, 1993; Tunnell, 1994). This quick reliance on the group is facilitated by the fact that many patients have lost a significant portion of their support network to AIDS and they come to group specifically to form a new network to support them when they get ill.

THE WORKING GROUP

The group started with four cohabiting male couples who had been together for seven months to five years. All couples were in couples or individual therapy. Two couples were HIV concordant. The individuals in these two couples reported more significant substance abuse and exhibited more severe character pathology than in the two HIV-discordant couples. In fact, one concordant couple came to the first group high on marijuana and reported that it was part of their "healing regime." They did not use any other drugs and otherwise were committed to a health-focused life. They did not think that their marijuana use was a problem, but they did contract to not smoke in the four hours before group. The second concordant couple reported past use of many "designer" drugs, but currently they used infrequently due to physical illness.

As in all groups with persons with HIV disease and AIDS, each patient's HIV illness profoundly affected the group. The illness of one or more group members had an impact on the group process, content, and continuity in almost every session. While originally we attempted to solve the problem of absences, we came to view absences as an important metaphor for AIDS; it was always in the room in the guise of the empty chairs of absent members.

Over the course of the group, the couples shared many common issues and struggles such as: (1) acceptance of HIV status and its effects on jobs and relationships; (2) dealing with a wide range of emotions including rage, sadness, shame, guilt, jealousy, and helplessness in the face of personal health and the partner's health (whether worse off, better off, or HIV negative); (3) fear of both loss of a partner or abandonment if one's partner died first; and (4) differences within and between couples regarding openness about HIV status and sexual orientation. Because of the short-term nature of the group, the leaders were active in facilitating the group process and addressing issues on four levels: individual, couple, interpersonal, and group.

At the midway point of the group (which coincided with a Christmas break), the two HIV-concordant couples left with no warning. The group continued for the remainder of the twelve-session contract with the two couples who each had one HIV-positive member. Having to face the fact that they did not have a healthy member in their dyads may have threatened the two couples who dropped out, and hastened their departure. The two remaining couples were more psychologically stable, but one of these men was subsequently diagnosed with a very serious opportunistic infection. While two couples was not optimal, we did not have time to add couples before the end of the twelve weeks. Flexibility was the hallmark of the last few weeks of the group. During one group session, the ill member was in the clinic treatment room, an area of the clinic where the most medically ill patients are closely monitored. The other couple and the leaders spent part of the session with him and his partner in the treatment room (at his request).

INDICATIONS AND CONTRAINDICATIONS FOR PATIENTS AND THERAPISTS

Working with the HIV-affected population in a couples group format is potentially rewarding for both patients and therapists. Those couples who are committed to working on their relationship and do not exhibit severe character pathology or active substance use appear to benefit most from a couples group. In our experience, severe psychopathology appears to be more contraindicated in an HIV couples group than in groups for individuals from the same population, although further examination of this issue is warranted. Some difficulty for our group also may have been due to the differences in HIV status between some couples. It is likely that a combination of psychopathology and heterogeneity led to the two early departures in our group. Starting with couples who are all HIV positive or all discordant might help build cohesion and avoid sudden departures because of the very different types of issues faced by these two types of couples. However, in a group with less psychopathology, discordant and concordant couples might work well together and appreciate their many commonalities.

We would recommend the development of an ongoing group, rather than a short-term intervention, due to the unique issues dealt with in couples in which one or both members has a terminal illness. With issues of loss and death being very important in their lives, having to terminate the group after only twelve weeks was very difficult for group members. Also, from our experience in a long-term AIDS group for individuals, cohesion takes longer to develop in such groups because of the way that AIDS intrudes into the group process. It might be important to allow cohesion to develop over time and to allow group members to decide for themselves when to terminate from an ongoing group. Facilitating a healthy therapy termination while still alive could hold significant meaning for couples whose core issues ultimately center around terminations usually being due to death. While there are concerns about fostering unhealthy dependence in long-term groups (Kaslow and Suarez, 1988), in an HIV group encouraging appropriate dependence in the face of severe illness is one of the goals of the group.

Leading a couples group for men affected by HIV provides numerous opportunities for growth for mental health professionals including learning about therapeutic flexibility; facing existential issues such as death and life's meaning; and tolerating helplessness, ambivalence, illness, and loss. Therapists also can learn and benefit from exploring common cultural and countertransference issues. In a low-income setting such as our clinic, therapists become aware of their attitudes about different cultural backgrounds and illicit drug usage. Further, in a group with gay men, awareness of personal feelings about differences in sexual orientation, sexual attitudes, and sexual mores is fostered, even for gay male therapists.

Common countertransference issues that may arise in an HIV group include: (1) feelings of helplessness (due to the premature death of patients) that are defended against through either feelings of omnipotence and problem solving or depression and demoralization (Farber, 1994); (2) anxiety about death that leads to distancing from the group or denial around the topic of death; and (3) joining with the group members' strong feelings of anger or withdrawing when the members' intense anger is directed at the therapists (Bernstein and Klein, 1995). Addressing these issues in supervision or therapy is helpful. Finally, burnout is a distinct possibility when working in a clinic where many patients die. When working with an HIV group, mental health professionals should seek opportunities to nourish and nurture themselves while learning about their own limits to avoid burnout and enhance effectiveness during their work with clients.

REFERENCES

Bernstein, G. and Klein, R. (1995). Countertransference issues in group psychotherapy with HIV-positive and AIDS patients. *International Journal of Group Psychotherapy, 45,* 91-100.

Carl, D. (1990). *Counseling same-sex couples.* New York: W. W. Norton.

Coché, J. and Coché, E. (1990). *Couples group psychotherapy: A clinical practice model.* New York: Brunner/Mazel.

Coché, J. and Satterfield, J. M. (1993). Couples group psychotherapy. In H. I. Kaplan and B. J. Saddock (Eds.), *Comprehensive group psychotherapy* (Third Edition, pp. 283-292). Baltimore, MD: Williams and Wilkins.

Farber, E. W. (1994). Psychotherapy with HIV and AIDS patients: The phenomenon of helplessness in therapists. *Psychotherapy, 31,* 715-724.

Friedman, R. C. (1991). Couple therapy with gay couples. *Psychiatric Annals, 21,* 485-490.

Kaslow, N. J. and Suarez, A. F. (1988). Treating couples in group therapy. In J. C. Hansen (Series Ed.) and F. W. Kaslow (Vol. Ed.), *The family therapy collections: Volume 25. Couples therapy in a family context: Perspective and retrospective* (pp. 3-14). Rockville, MD: Aspen Publishers.

Kurdek, L. A. (1995). Lesbian and gay couples. In A. R. D'Augelli and C. J. Patterson (Eds.), *Lesbian, gay, and bisexual identities over the life span: Psychological perspective* (pp. 243-261). New York: Oxford University Press.

Lego, S. (1993). Group psychotherapy with HIV-infected persons and their caregivers. In H. I. Kaplan and B. J. Saddock (Eds.), *Comprehensive group psychotherapy* (Third Edition, pp. 470-477).

Tunnell, G. (1994). Special issues in group psychotherapy for gay men with HIV. In S. A. Cadwell, R. A. Burnham Jr., and M. Forstein (Eds.), *Therapists on the front line: Psychotherapy with gay men in the age of AIDS* (pp. 237-254). Washington, DC: American Psychiatric Press.

41

The Grid

Phoebe S. Prosky

This intervention is for use when a couple in therapy is teetering on the edge of separation. Frequently in such situations, indecision plagues the couple as well as the therapy, and many sessions may be spent in going back and forth between the two alternatives, the couple now moving toward each other, now apart.

The grid I bring to bear is a simple four-square and looks like this:

YY	NY
YN	NN

The first square represents the condition in which both members of the couple have some—even the smallest—wish to stay together. The squares below and to the right represent the condition in which one partner wishes to stay in the relationship but the other does not. The final square, diagonal to the first, represents the condition in which neither partner wishes to preserve the relationship.

I use the grid to determine a direction in the following way. If the couple falls into the first square, I propose that we bend our efforts to maintaining the couple. If the couple falls into any of the other three, I propose we begin to take the couple apart. At first blush it appears that therapy would be beginning mostly by dismantling couples. But in actual fact, most couples who come for therapy fall within the first square, and so it usually begins with an attempt at the restoration of the couple.

But why, in squares to the right and below, when only one of the couple wants to leave, does the therapy begin by dismantling? It does this on the principle that it takes two to make a couple. One just cannot do it alone.

The most dependable thing about working with this grid is that the starting direction of the work has no predictable bearing on the outcome.

Couples who begin dismantling will, as likely as not, discover an unappreciated strength in their structure and decide to stay together. Couples who begin restoring may well build their superstructure just high enough to make the discovery that there is no foundation to support it. You never know.

And that is the genie in the grid. It provides enough structure to move the couple and the work forward out of the frustration of indecision, but it does so in a transparent way that allows the couple's own process to prevail.

42

Revisiting the Subject of Emotional Highs and Lows: Two Interventions

Phoebe S. Prosky
Patricia M. Dyer

This chapter presents two interventions for people who experience life in extreme highs and lows and wish to develop a greater stability of emotion without turning to psychotropic medication. Commonly such people experience periods of time in which their thoughts are racing. This typically leads them to speak or act in an accelerated fashion, buying too much, calling too many people, cleaning too vigorously. They usually experience this phase as extremely uplifting and pleasurable. When this frenzy has exhausted itself, such people experience a descent into the depths of emotional experience, often becoming overwhelmed with feelings of hopelessness, or worthlessness, sometimes taking to their beds for days on end. The theoretical underpinning of the interventions presented here is the hypothesis that such cycles are addictive in nature: people become addicted to the highs or to the lows.

The prevailing view of this constellation in our culture is that swings in emotional states have a biochemical etiology. This view, however, is open to question: While it is true that body chemistry influences the emotions, it is equally true that the emotions affect body chemistry; these are covariables. It is as possible to address this problem by teaching people to influence their emotional states as through influencing the body chemistry with medication. One of the benefits of working from the emotional end is that it allows people to take charge of their own lives and relieves them of the notion that they have a chronic illness.

The symptom picture of emotional highs and lows is made up of two distinct groups of behavior: states in which the highs are the dominant mode and states in which the lows are dominant. The two must be approached differently. As is the case with all addictive behavior, the interventions that follow are not likely to be useful until the person in question has reached a point of despair with the behavior or "hit bottom."

We will begin by addressing those people whose predominant mode is high, and we will advance the hypothesis that they are addicted to the highs. They do everything in their power to generate and prolong them. The inevitable lows are simply the natural complement of the highs and reflect them in the opposite direction—they are a sort of vacuum created by the highs.

The relevant intervention looks like this:

It consists of asking people in this group to identify the behavior that ordinarily accompanies the *start* of an upward curve. When they have done this, they agree that when that behavior again occurs, they will interrupt it by doing *anything* else, or by doing something else specific. When they do this, their energy is diverted and the rise is capped. The accompanying low is only as low as the high was high. This gives an incentive to continue to interrupt the upward curve, and over time people are able to stabilize their emotional lives. They become aware of the start of the upswing earlier and earlier with each incipient rise, making it easier and easier to divert their energy.

This intervention does not work if tried at the start of the downward cycle. These clients want to stop the lows and keep the highs and would therefore prefer to practice on the down phase. However, the intervention is successful only when people are willing to give up the highs. It is contraindicated when this point has not been reached.

People who experience life in such cycles are often concerned that a more stable emotional life will be tepid and without excitement. This negative picture of emotional stability often acts as a powerful deterrent to these people's desire to take control of their lives. When this is an issue, the therapist may find it useful to use the following metaphor for the steady state. It is like a coaxial transatlantic cable, full of multicolored wires. It is not that all the color goes out of life in this steady state, but that all the color that this group currently experiences sequentially is brought together and experienced simultaneously. In that state it holds together as an integrated whole through its inherent balance. The experience is one of a stable self in technicolor.

Now we will turn to the people whose predominant mode of extreme emotional states is low, and here we advance the hypothesis that they are addicted to the lows. They do everything in their power to instate and perpetuate the lows. This group is afraid to feel happy and therefore they fixate on bad feelings—wrong things done to them in some way. To perpetuate the lows they push away any suggestion that could help them feel better. With them the highs are just the periodic breaking through of deferred good feelings. Paradoxically for this group, the highs bring about depression whereas the lows are the sought-after highs.

It is harder for this group to hit the bottom that they must before this intervention will be useful. People addicted to the highs are out getting themselves into trouble, and their motivation to change becomes increasingly strong with the accumulating consequences of their actions. People addicted to the lows, on the contrary, tend to isolate themselves from the public eye. They typically have a few people around them whose nature is to sympathize. These sympathizers help this group perpetuate the lows by confirming the wrongs done to them and feeling sorry for them.

This picture of the lack of motivation to change is compounded by the dynamics of any attempt they make to see a therapist. As the therapist moves to help them feel better, they drop out of therapy, because feeling better is not what they want. This group is less well understood by therapists than the first because they don't stay in therapy long enough for their patterns to be recognized. Part of their fear of feeling better is the specter of having no one to care for them. This group of people wears out most relatives and potential friends and is left with a few people whose need is to sympathize. They recognize that if they begin to feel better, these few remaining people will no longer be available to them; they do not believe that they could have real friends.

The relevant intervention for this group looks like this:

It requires intervention with the larger social group surrounding the person, bringing those related in various ways to the person into the intervention and educating them about the paradoxical effects of offering sympathy. The intervention involves asking them to stop offering further sympathy, and at the same time to enter into a contract reassuring the person in question that they will remain in contact, not because s/he is down and out but because of the person her/himself. Working in this way, this group begins to be willing to move upward emotionally into a more steady state.*

We can see that both groups—those addicted to the highs and those addicted to the lows—are acting to fracture their emotional experience, to experience it sequentially. All the feelings they express are in them all the time and are immanently available to a potentially more integrated emotionality. Ours is a culture that tends to think about emotions in just such a fractured way, assuming that a person who feels happy is not simultaneously feeling sad. These two interventions teach people to become more aware of the multitude of emotions at play within and to experience them in their natural simultaneity.

---

*This group of people can be distinguished from people experiencing straight depression by their craving for sad and tragic materials upon which to dwell.

43

Changing Hats
During Therapeutic Impasses

Judith Maria Bermúdez

INDICATIONS FOR USE OF THE INTERVENTION

It is common for therapists to experience impasses in therapy, especially for a beginning therapist. But what can you do when you run out of ideas, your client is still depressed, is making you crazy, and you want to see therapy progress before you get moved to a new practicum site? Could it be possible to have a little fun? This intervention was created with the hope of facilitating a playful atmosphere that could enable the therapist to amplify the client's "alternative and subjugated story."

THEORETICAL ORIENTATION

The primary theories that served as a base for this intervention were derived from Experiential Family Therapy, Narrative Therapy, and Solution-Focused Therapy. Based upon an interactive process of metaphorical language and personal interaction, Experiential Family Therapy enables personal integrity, such as congruence between inner experience and outer behavior, freedom of choice, independence, and an expanded experience (Malone et al., 1961). It is present-centered and its primary goal is growth (Niel and Kniskern, 1982; Kieth, 1987; Mitten and Piercy, 1993; Whitaker and Bumberry, 1988; Whitaker, 1992). In the spirit of Narrative Therapy, the style of this intervention also reflects the therapeutic form suggested by White and Epston (1990): (a) encourage a perception of a changing world through the plotting or linking of lived experience through time, (b) invoke a subjective mood in the triggering of presuppositions, establishing implicit meaning, and generating a multiple perspective, (c) invite a reflexive posture, and (d) encourage a sense of authorship and re-authorship of one's life and relationships in telling one's story. In addition, the therapist herself had to "do something different" (de Shazer, 1984), within a therapeutic impasse. The intervention was used in the following context.

INTERVENTION

Case History

An elderly woman sought therapy for support in dealing with painful issues in her life, primarily those pertaining to the death of her husband, who was a recovered alcoholic, her forced early retirement, her obese daughter, and her son's leaving for college and announcement that he was homosexual. She was overwhelmed with feelings of guilt, anger, confusion, fear and sadness; however, she could never directly deal with her feelings in therapy.

Wanting desperately to "facilitate change," my experience throughout the therapy process was one of exhaustion and I was losing the battle for structure. I could hardly get a word in edgewise as I sat and listened to her "dominant story." As much as I struggled to amplify her "subjugated story," she fought me all the way to convince me that she was a victim. Looking back now it seems as though she tried to stay focused on her children as a way to avoid facing her necessary and desired changes. After being unable to set goals for therapy and create a treatment plan for numerous sessions, I decided I had struggled for too long and was feeling frustrated over this laborious case. Unlike Whitaker, I wasn't having fun in therapy, and like de Shazer, I decided it was time to "do something different." What follows is my experience of changing my behavior in therapy, and resolving my therapeutic impasse.

Intervention

I decided that since my client seemed to be able to switch into therapy mode immediately by venting her unrelenting problems, she could also "switch hats" to talk about her subjugating story. Hats are always fun, and easy to change (unlike my client!), so I looked in my closet at home and took out all the ones I owned: a beach hat from the Virgin Islands, an olive-green hat with a feather, a baseball cap from the 1995 Chicago marathon, a small black hat with a net veil (similar to the ones used for funerals), a cowboy hat, and a wicker hat with a flower. I put them all in a bag and was on my way.

As the session began, I immediately told my client that I wanted us to do something different. I placed all the hats on a table and asked her to look at them carefully and think about which "type of person" would wear each hat. I gave her a few minutes to think about it and then asked her to describe the "type of people" to me. She did, and then I asked her to pick the hat that she wanted to wear. To my surprise she picked the baseball cap. When I asked her why she chose it she said, " because it was spunky and it could go with everything." So I asked her to put it on and asked how she felt wearing it. She said that she felt "young and ready to go."

I framed her choice of hat as a metaphor for the hats she wears in life. I told her how surprised I was that she didn't choose the black funeral hat since that was the "hat she wore in session." Then I chose a hat, the silliest one I could find (the green hat with the feather), and put it on. We both were amused by seeing the other in the hats and could not stop laughing as we sat and she seriously tried to continue "giving life to her dominant story." Of course it was difficult for her to do. I think it was the first time my client could feel free to let go of the image of the woman wearing the funeral hat and have the experience of being the "spunky lady in the baseball cap."

Discussion

Although this client was in enormous pain, I had established a great deal of trust and had joined with her. This intervention is contraindicated with someone who is not fully joined with you and does not trust your directives in session. This intervention would also not be appropriate for someone still needing to feel the pain of her losses and to process the meaning that they had in her life. It was clear this client was ready to move on and to explore and create a new way of being in her life. The combination of the Experiential, Narrative, and Solution-Focused components enabled the client to focus on her experiences so that they could be translated into symbols or internal representations, and to generate and re-author an alternative story that was more congruent with the way she wanted to be.

REFERENCES

de Shazer, S. and Molnar, A. (1984). Four useful interventions in brief family therapy. *Journal of Marital and Family Therapy, 10*, 297-304.

Keith, D. V. (1987). The self in family therapy: A field guide. *Journal of Psychotherapy and the Family, 3*(1), 61-70.

Malone, T. P., Whitaker, C. A., Warkentin, J., and Felder, R. E. (1961). Rational and nonrational psychotherapy. *American Journal of Psychotherapy, 15*, 212-220.

Mitten, T. and Piercy, F. P. (1993). Learning symbolic-experiential therapy: One approach. *Contemporary Family Therapy, 15*(2), 149-168.

Neil, J. R. and Kniskern, D. P. (Eds.). (1982). *From psyche to system: The evolving therapy of Carl Whitaker.* New York: Guilford Press.

Whitaker, C. A. (1992). Symbolic experiential family therapy: Model and methodology. In J. K. Zeig (Ed.), *The evolution of psychotherapy: The second conference* (pp. 13-20). New York: Brunner/Mazel.

Whitaker, C. A. and Bumberry, W. M. (1988). *Dancing with the family: A symbolic-experiential approach.* New York: Brunner/Mazel.

White, M. and Epston, D. (1990). *Narrative means to therapeutic ends.* New York: W. W. Norton.

44

Reciprocal Double Binds, Amplification of Constructions of Reality, and Change in a Training Context

Mony Elkaïm

The following pages describe an intervention that I make from time to time in training. This type of intervention, similar in some ways to Carl Whitaker's "psychotherapy of the absurd" (Whitaker, 1975), is based nonetheless on different premises. After outlining a model I developed to describe one type of couple interaction (Elkaïm, 1990) that may lead a couple to consult a therapist, I will show how the reciprocal double bind inherent in this model can be applied to the student-trainer couple. I will explain how this model could allow trainers to help students by amplifying their worldviews and by allowing them to reenact, in a new context, a scene that has been repeated too often in the past. After describing a specific intervention of this type and my student's reaction to it, I will go on to explain why I tend to restrict this type of intervention to training contexts rather than therapeutic ones.[1]

A MODEL OF COUPLE INTERACTION

The title of my book *If You Love Me, Don't Love Me* (Elkaïm, 1990) was inspired by those situations in which, for historical reasons, one person asks another for something he or she would like to have but, at the same time, doesn't really think is possible. When these cycles occur in a couple, a husband, for example, may say to his wife, "Love me." This explicit demand is what I call the person's "official program." At the same time, however, a fear of abandonment makes him afraid of being loved, so much so that he asks, on a nonverbal level, not to receive this love. This is the person's "worldview." In this model, when the official program contradicts the worldview, the partner is caught in a double bind. So, for example, if the wife responds to the request expressed on the official level, she goes against her husband's worldview. If she responds to his worldview, she ends up being criticized for not listening to the explicit request. In this perspective, a couple member manifests a particular behavior that has a function with respect to the worldview and the past of the other couple member.

For such a pattern to continue or get worse, it must have a function not only with regard to the past history of one of the protagonists, but also with respect to the couple system as a whole. Behavior will be repeated or amplified only if it plays a role in the wider systemic context, above and beyond the function it may have with regard to an individual's dynamics. In couples, this phenomenon occurs in both directions, given that the double binds are reciprocal. As a result, couple members frequently attempt to sculpt or model each other in order to reinforce their respective deep beliefs or worldviews. Each partner reinforces the other's worldview by taking the blame for something the other partner seems outwardly to want but doesn't really think is possible. In so doing, they protect their partners from having to face the consequences of the double bind in which they are caught; that is, they prevent them from discovering that they are imprisoned behind walls which they themselves helped build. The description of persons caught in a double bind and finding themselves acted upon by the system of which they are part could be equally valid in a training context.

A SUPERVISION SITUATION

The Intervention

Ten minutes before the end of a group supervision session, a student asked if she could speak about a problem that was worrying her. She wondered if she was capable of continuing her career as a social worker and psychotherapist. Her current phase of doubt wasn't unfamiliar. In her final year of high school, a teacher had warned the class that the year would not be an easy one, and that there was a chance that many of them would not succeed. Although she had never failed any courses in previous years, she felt that the teacher's warning was specifically directed at her. She therefore decided to give up the course of studies she was enrolled in for one that was less challenging.

As a trainer, I was faced with things that had been expressed by the student on two levels. One one hand, she said, "I don't believe I'm capable of succeeding," while on the other, "Help me to succeed." The hypothesis I can formulate is that the student is still caught in a preexisting double bind. The official program would be "I must succeed," while, for specific historical reasons, the worldview might be "Success isn't an option for me." If I respond to only one of the two levels, I will simply maintain the situation in its present state.

In accordance with my approach, I need first of all to verify my hypothesis about the student's worldview. Following this, I can investigate the context in which she became caught up in this double bind. It is not until I have done both of these steps that I can create a situation in training that responds to both levels at the same time to help her free herself from the double bind. In practice, my intervention was carried out in such a way that the two steps took place simultaneously.

I asked whether she had any children, which again was the case. I then asked her if she'd ever thought about making her husband and children her top priority, instead of having a career. She replied, "You sound just like my father. He never stopped telling me that I shouldn't have a career and that I should simply be a good wife and mother." I told her I did not see anything wrong with her protecting her father at a time when most people only think about themselves.

Throughout the exchange, the training group was astonished and perplexed by what was taking place. When one of the members remarked on the fact that she was accepting my provocation so easily, the student replied that what I had said to her was exactly what she told herself. During the first part of our exchange, the student helped me confirm my hypothesis about her worldview. By amplifying her fears to the extreme, I created an ambiguous situation. The exaggerated nature of my intervention was such that the student didn't quite know what to make of it.

On one hand, the training context implies by definition a contract of help and support. This, combined with the fact that my declarations were clearly designed to provoke her, made the student feel that I was trying to help her, so I was able to respond to her official program.

On the other hand, because the things I said to her were in keeping with her worldview, she couldn't completely dismiss them, and had some doubts about whether they were meant to be taken seriously. Thus, I responded at the same time to the second level.

This deadpan aspect of the intervention, when accompanied by warmth, is reminiscent of a technique described by Carl Whitaker (1975): he talks about continuing to build on the Tower of Pisa until it collapses under its own weight. I think nonetheless that the therapist who amplifies dysfunctional rules in a system or who exaggerates the deep-seated beliefs of a patient goes beyond the mere amplification of dysfunctional rules. There is an additional aspect, which is that of context: therapeutic contexts, which comprise an implicit contract of help, as well as training contexts, which imply both help and training, ally the therapist with the official program of the person with whom he or she is working. At the same time, the provocative aspect of the intervention allows the therapist to address the person's worldview, but in a novel way, one that does not contribute to maintaining this view. Thus, the therapist achieves the complex task of addressing both levels of the double bind concurrently.

Furthermore, in an almost psychodramatic way, the training system takes on aspects of the system in which the deep belief of the student originally arose. The ability of the trainer to accept the role that the student is trying to impose on him or her, while at the same time behaving differently from the person who filled that role in the past, combined with the emotional support of the group, creates a therapeutic system that allows whole realms of new possibilities to open up.

At one point during my exchange with the student, I made a slip of the tongue and said, "What's wrong with protecting your husband?" instead of saying, "What's wrong with protecting your father?" The student retorted vehemently, "My husband?! Never!" She then became thoughtful, and told us that when her husband's father was the same age as her husband, he became severely depressed, and his wife was forced to resume her career in order to support the family. Furthermore, it seemed that the student's husband was now showing signs that led her to fear that he might also have a breakdown.[2]

From this moment onward, the student stopped feeling that she was being torn apart by seemingly irreconcilable forces. She also started to see herself as someone whose symptom protected not only her husband, but also the rules of her own family.

The Student's Commentary

The student underwent a radical change after this session. She described her experience as follows:

> During the session, I remember that I felt sad, on the verge of tears, while expressing the doubts I had about myself. When Mony suggested I quit the training, I suddenly felt that I was both knowledgeable and capable.[3] I didn't reflect too much on what he was trying to get at. Very quickly, I found myself coming into contact with that

painful part of the family past I was always very afraid of confronting. I again felt the same old fear and sadness.

It was a very painful and unpleasant session for me. At the time, I thought I'd never get out of the difficulty I was in. But at the same time, in the back of my mind somehow, I had the impression that this difficulty, like others, would be overcome during my training with Mony Elkaïm.

A few weeks later, just after an unsatisfactory session with a family, I surprised myself by, for the first time, attempting to formulate hypotheses on what had happened during the session, and to envisage other approaches, rather than giving way to my familiar doubts.

From that moment onward, I never again experienced the "hesitation waltz," and although that phase of my life lasted for several years, today it seems very far away indeed.

What I Learned from the Student's Commentary

I had underestimated the specific role I played. Events that had occurred in the past during my student's training with me allowed her to believe that her current difficulties could be dealt with productively and overcome.

I thought that I had managed to respond simultaneously to the two levels of the double bind. My student's description of the situation taught me that, at various times, she felt that I was focusing primarily on one level rather than the other. So for example, the more I told her to give up her career, the stronger and more capable she felt.

There was not, strictly speaking, a sudden realization or change that occurred on the spot. Only afterward did the student become aware of the leap she had made and of her ability to react in a new way to situations that had in the past made her feel inadequate.

The student could hardly remember what happened during the training session, even though she was conscious of the results and pleased with them. I did not expect this "faraway" aspect and the partial amnesia that seems to have surrounded her remembrance of the session.

CONCLUSIONS

I have decided to restrict this type of intervention to supervisory situations. This is because I feel these interventions require the student to have the support of the group to be able to handle the trainer's provocation. In addition, the training situation allows one to engage in a detailed analysis of events, and to offer students tools that go beyond the mere intervention that allowed them to surmount a difficult moment in their history. There must be an alliance between the two parties involved in the intervention, and I think this is easier to achieve in a context where the group can both provide support to the student and constructively comment on what took place. In a therapeutic situation on the other hand, the patient may, for any number of reasons, take this provocative intervention literally, and experience an additional rejection as a result. Finally, even in a training situation, I think it is important that this intervention only be carried out with students who have an excellent alliance with the trainer and the rest of the group.

NOTES

1. A situation described and analyzed in a different manner in Elkaïm, 1985.

2. Particular attention should be given, I feel, to situations in which a slip of the tongue, traditionally assumed to be revealing only for the speaker, reveals an element that is also meaningful for the listener, even though he or she may not be not aware of it. A reflection on the function of a person's actions or utterances for the other members of the system of which he or she is part is central to my concept of "resonance" (Elkaïm, 1990).

3. At no time did I suggest that the student quit the training program, but it is interesting that she felt that it could have happened.

REFERENCES

Elkaïm, M. (1985). Double contrainte et singularites dans une situation de formation a la therapie familials. In M. Elaïm (Ed.), *Formations et pratiques en therapie familiale*. Paris: Editions ESF.

Elkaïm, M. (1990). *If you love me, don't love me*. New York: Basic Books.

Whitaker, C. A. (1975). Psychotherapy of the absurd: With a special emphasis on the psychotherapy of aggression. *Family Process, 14*, 1-16.

45

The Play Is the Thing: Using Self-Constructed Board Games in Family Therapy

Craig W. Smith
Sharon G. Renter

Interventions that involve children or the entire family can be particularly challenging, especially if the therapist relies on the expected modus operandi of therapy—talk. The following intervention provides a means by which talk is integrated into an activity that children and adults can easily relate to but in a way that is more directly relevant to their situation. Games have been used for many years in the area of play therapy and in working with children and adolescents (Ariel, 1986; Erickson, 1963; Moustakas, 1967; Singer and Singer, 1977). Yet, commercial games are, of necessity, limited in their content and application. The use of a self-constructed game is based on the use of metaphor (Roberts, 1987), whereby the game itself is isomorphic to the situation that the family or child is attempting to resolve.

This intervention is particularly suited to instances of conduct disorders, adjustment disorders, or parent-child problems in which there is a constellation of acting-out behaviors, difficulty with impulse control, a lack of appropriate social skills, or dysfunctional communication patterns in the family. It may be used with children alone or with the entire family. Although it might seem that there is a need for a high degree of creativity, this is not the case. Everyone has experience with games that they can rely on for their own special creation.

The goal in the construction and playing of board games is to assist the child or family to attain their identified goals for change. The therapist helps determine a theme for the game by helping identify the problems and goals of the client. The game construction should allow for as many choices as possible, utilizing the client's ideas, communication patterns, and artistic skills during the actual game design and creation.

CONSTRUCTING THE GAME

Materials Needed

Standard supplies for game construction should include:

- colored poster board, construction paper, old magazines, index cards
- pencils/pens, felt-tip markers, crayons
- scissors, ruler, glue, colorful stickers

Optional supplies may include:

- dice, game pieces, spinners
- art material (e.g., ribbon, lace, buttons, cloth, egg cartons, glitter, etc.)

Procedure

One or more sessions should have occurred before the game construction begins for purposes of establishing rapport and assessing the family. During the assessment process factors such as gross and fine motor skills, language development of the children, and the participants' perception of the problems should be determined, even if in a limited fashion. It is helpful to identify each of the family member's strengths in order for the process of game construction to be as successful as possible.

Ideally, there should be a table or large surface area on which to work during construction of the project; however, the floor works well and will probably be used anyway. All supplies should be out and ready to go prior to each session to maximize therapy time.

1. Gain a commitment for producing the game [the therapist might share with the child that he or she is working with another child with similar issues whose assistance with creating a therapy game would be helpful].
2. Establish a theme for the game. Children will usually find themes they enjoy: e.g., baseball, a trip to the ice cream parlor, a day at the fishing hole, etc. Specific problems may also be the focus, such as divorce, angry feelings, getting along with a new stepparent, or moving to a new home. The parents and children should jointly agree on a format for the game, with the children taking the lead.
3. Establish the intent or goal of the game. Some of the questions to be asked include:

- Will there be a winner of the game? How will winning the game be determined?
- How will the game be played? Will you use dice, draw a card, spin, etc.?
- What will the rules of the game be? How many players, who begins first, what kind of rewards or consequences/lessons will be learned?
- What ages are appropriate for this game? The game should be tailored for the youngest member who will participate but include aspects of interest to older children. The therapist should always help each child feel successful and take ownership for whatever parts they are able to accomplish with the project. This also serves as a model for the parents in their interaction with the children during the game construction and play.

4. Begin the game construction. The family [with the lead of the child] may choose a playing board that is circular or has connected boxes, a winding path, or doors that open and close. Remember to allow as much freedom as possible for the child to make the choices and the parents to support and contribute. This is an important part of the therapeutic process in which the family engages in problem solving, cooperation, modeling, and other behaviors that can be observed and modified.

5. The family or therapist and child [when the game is used in individual child therapy] can draw the format of the game on the poster board with as much skill as appropriate. Some children are determined that the squares all be exactly the same size and use great skill in producing the "perfect" board; others use a freehand approach, making mistakes or changing their minds partway through the process.

6. Use the theme chosen to decorate the board, make playing pieces, etc. If an approach using a "draw a card" is chosen, use therapy time for discussing positive and negative cards, activities, feelings, etc. This activity is especially helpful in linking therapy sessions together because working on the cards can be a homework activity. The creation of the game can take three to four sessions to complete and could easily take additional sessions if the child is slow with tasks or should situations arise that require different forms of intervention during the process.

7. The therapist should use the family's [particularly the child's] perception of the rules and the creative process as part of the therapy. By joining in with the family with coloring, cutting, and creating, the therapist allows the exchange of ideas and models appropriate behavior.

8. Upon completion of the game, it should be put aside until the next session before trying it out. This gives the family a fresh perspective on their work and lets them anticipate the culmination of their efforts. The game should be played for the first time in session in order to assist the family in the process. However, afterward the game is an excellent way for them to work on the issues at home, and they can even modify the game as new situations or issues arise.

When using this intervention with children alone or with families **remember the basics:**

- Allow the child(ren) as much opportunity for input and decision making as possible.
- Help the child(ren) feel successful about the process and take ownership of their finished product.
- Use all stages of the project to work toward the therapeutic goals.
- Games, especially for children, do not have to fit into the adult view of what is right or wrong.
- Most important, HAVE FUN!

CONTRAINDICATIONS

A study in which the use of self-constructed board games was the sole intervention strategy demonstrated significant changes in acting-out behavior in school-age girls (Renter, 1995). However, the use of the intervention alone is not advised. Rather, it should be part of a clearly devised treatment plan. While this type of intervention is particularly suited to facilitating the acquisition of effective communication and problem-solving skills, it is not advisable to use it in the early stages of therapy with violent or abusive families. Finally, while no studies have explored this area, it is likely that the use of this intervention with families with preschool children may be less effective due to the child's developmental level.

CASE STUDY: ANNA

Anna was not happy. She was eight years old and identified as "the problem" by both her mother and her teacher. Mom would not participate in therapy and expected the therapist to "fix" Anna. The target behaviors included temper tantrums, physical aggression, "being sad," and arguing and talking too loud and too much. The therapist was unable to dissuade the mother and teacher from including "being sad" as a target for intervention; so, it was included as a manifestation of the child's self-esteem.

The therapist worked with Anna to create a board game. The game she created was a "follow the path" design. The cards used during the game proved to be very useful in assisting Anna in identifying positive and negative behaviors and offered the opportunity for problem-solving skills to be used to address them. Over the course of the seven-week treatment period the targeted behaviors all declined in frequency. The intervention provided an environment for negative attitudes, feelings, or perceptions to be addressed in an indirect manner, allowing the reality of these feelings to be less intense. Anna used examples from real life as part of the game. For example, the use of the situational cards, which reflected positive and negative issues, allowed for the identification and discussion of problems without taking total responsibility for them.

By focusing on the game, Anna's mother and teacher were able to distance themselves from problematic issues while they were being dealt with through the game. Although initially reluctant to engage in family therapy, Anna's mother did enter treatment with her daughter after she had spent a session playing Anna's game with her. This indirect approach with Mom also provided a means of dealing with the problems differently. The metaphor of the game allowed Anna and her mother to put things in perspective and to diffuse anger. During the process Anna's mother was able to separate her own issues with Anna's teacher and other significant individuals in her life from Anna and her behavior. The acting-out behaviors continued to decline until termination occurred.

In summary, the use of self-constructed games can afford the child in everyone a means of dealing with issues directly relevant to his/her situation in a nonthreatening and constructive manner. The use of games is most successful in cases where social skills and interactional behaviors are the target of intervention.

REFERENCES

Ariel, S. (1986). Family play therapy. In R. van der Kooij and J. Hellendoorn (Eds.), *Play, play therapy, play research* (pp. 153-160). Netherlands: Swets and Zeitlinger.

Erickson, E. H. (1963). *Childhood and society.* New York: W. W. Norton.

Moustakas, C. E. (1967). *Creativity and conformity.* Princeton, NJ: Van Nostrand.

Renter, S. G. (1995). *Therapeutic use of self-constructed board games in work with children.* Unpublished master's thesis, University of Nebraska-Lincoln, Lincoln, NB.

Roberts, S. D. (1987). Therapeutic metaphors: a counseling technique. *Journal of the Academy of Rehabilitative Audiology, 20,* 61-72.

Singer, D. and Singer, J. (1977). *Partners in play: A step-by-step guide to imaginative play in children.* New York: Harper & Row.

46

Therapists Must Be EXPLISSIT

Robert F. Stahmann

A number of years ago, I became aware of a model for conceptualizing the different levels of intervention that are required in helping couples with sexual dissatisfactions or dysfunctions. This so-called PLISSIT model identified four different levels of expertise and intervention (Annon, 1976). The model was very useful in its intended field of sex therapy, and I have found that the model works well in generalizing beyond the practice of sex therapy to include much of what we do, or attempt to do, in marital and family therapy. The model also works well as a framework for providing feedback in clinical consultation and supervision.

As applied to sex therapy, the four different levels of expertise and intervention conceptualized by Annon's model are represented in the word PLISSIT or p-li-ss-it. "P" represents the "permission" level and consists of the therapist simply feeling comfortable enough to convey a sense of permission to clients so that they feel free to bring up sexual matters. The next level, which often blends with permission, is providing "LI" or "limited information." Many couples and individuals can be helped through merely providing some basic information such as an overview of the sexual response cycle. The third level of intervention is giving of "SS," "specific suggestions," which can be viewed as the sex counseling level. Here suggestions to deal with specific sexual problems may be offered or exercises such as sensate focus are introduced. The fourth and most complex level of intervention is "IT" or "intensive therapy." This is the level of sex therapy.

While I have found that the PLISSIT framework does guide the levels of intervention, for me there was an important missing ingredient. That is, simply put, the expectations about therapy that therapists and clients may have. All clients have some sort of preconceived expectation or idea about therapy as a process, or some expectation about the family therapist as a person. Family therapists have expectations that guide and direct their delivery of family therapy interventions. Thus, with the addition of "expectations," the model has become EXPLISSIT or EX-P-LI-SS-IT.

Consequently, in looking at the EXPLISSIT model for conceptualizing, designing, and delivering marital and family therapy interventions I first look at the (possible) expectations of both the client and the therapist. What does the client expect about the therapy process? Why are the clients here? What might indicate to the client(s) that therapy is (and has been) successful? What does the therapist expect? What does the therapist expect about the therapy process with this client? What does the therapist expect about outcome? In supervision and case consultation, what does the supervisor expect about the process and outcome? What about the trainee/ supervisee and his/her expectations about the supervision process and outcome? What are the expectations about the transfer of supervision or consultation to the therapy process with the client(s)?

AN EXAMPLE: THE AB FAMILY

Mrs. AB phoned the clinic seeking an appointment for herself and her son Mike, age nine. The family physician had recently diagnosed Mike with attention deficit/hyperactivity disorder (AD/HD). It had been suggested that they might find it helpful to meet with a family therapist, a professional who could help them understand and deal with Mike and this family phenomenon. Thus, client Expectations initially might have been that the family therapist would help Mike and the parents understand the AD/HD diagnosis and work with Mike to change his behavior at school that led to the visit to the family physician and the referral. Perhaps the parents were surprised and their expectations modified when the therapist asked them both to come along with Mike for the first visit.

Therapist Expectations may have been always to see the whole family for the initial assessment interview. The therapist may also have expectations that AD/HD is a system problem rather than an individual (medical) problem/disorder.

At the Permission level, the therapist may at times need to reassure the AB family that the "disorder" of AD/HD is something that they can discuss and deal with openly. The therapist can also help them accept that such a label or diagnosis is often upsetting until it is understood, and that their individual or collective anxiety is a normal reaction. Here the Permission and Limited Information levels often blend as the therapist imparts basic knowledge about typical patterns of child development and family interaction. Information about AD/HD as a variation of typical development and the usual outcome of AD/HD can be reassuring to the family.

Limited information provided by the therapist about the criteria for AD/HD diagnosis might assist the parents to understand that Mike's behavior is the basis for the diagnosis, and that behavior can be changed. Here, the idea of family systems and family interaction can be introduced as the basis for understanding and change.

The third level, Specific Suggestions, might be termed the family counseling level. Mr. and Mrs. AB might benefit from specific suggestions for responding to Mike's behaviors. The therapist might suggest books or other written materials about AD/HD that can be guides and references for them. Specific suggestions that help the parents see family system interaction and relationships as the "patient" or problem, rather than seeing Mike as the "identified patient," would likely facilitate movement of the family therapy process. Here, family counseling includes the ongoing providing of Specific Suggestions with application of them between sessions by the clients and follow-up and refining during later sessions.

The fourth and most complex level, Intensive Therapy, may be indicated if the presenting problem of Mike's AD/HD is found to be the symptom of underlying marital or family dysfunction or difficulties, or other problems that may not have initially been identified. In such cases the treatment plan would be modified to deal appropriately with the updated therapy plan. The IT, Intensive Therapy, may be done with Mike individually, his parents as a couple, the whole family, or some combinations of these. Thus, the EXPLISSIT model can help the therapist identify levels of intervention and the delivery of interventions.

SUPERVISION AND CONSULTATION

The EXPLISSIT model can be useful for the supervisor and supervisee (trainee). Of course, a major variable would be the setting in which the supervision would occur, but some example of how the EXPLISSIT model may apply follow.

Both supervisor and supervisee have Expectations about what may occur in supervision (or consultation) and how it may occur. Apart from their own expectations about the format, process, and content of supervision, supervisors typically have external expectations from an agency or a credentialing body such as a state licensing board or AAMFT that may direct the process. Supervisees will have many varied expectations about supervision, also influenced by the context of supervision and experience level of the trainee. The important point is that both are sensitive to expectations and both feel free to articulate, clarify, and modify them throughout the supervision process.

At the Permission level, the supervisor will often need to work hard to establish a safe relationship with the supervisee so that appropriate disclosure and openness about the supervisee's therapy can become the norm. Much of supervision, especially for beginning therapists, consists of the supervisor giving Limited Information. Information about the intake and screening process, office or agency procedure, treatment planning, and case notes, in addition to that dealing with the therapy process, are some examples. Usually when both supervisors and supervisees think of supervision, the idea of Specific Suggestions comes to mind. We look to supervisors for specific suggestions. Consultation, a process similar to supervision, also usually assumes Specific Suggestions. It is probably accurate to say that a major expectation of supervision is that specific suggestions will be provided. The fourth level of the model, Intensive Therapy, is what is being supervised. In the supervision process there is a learning and unfolding of what Intensive Therapy is and how it is done.

CONTRAINDICATION

I have attempted to show glimpses of how the EXPLISSIT model has been useful to me. It may be useful to sensitize students, therapists, and/or supervisors to potential levels of intervention. Hopefully such awareness would lead to better process and outcome. The model would be contraindicated if you, the student, therapist, or supervisor did not find it useful. If it has some validity and appeal to you, I am sure that you will amplify it beyond the examples here.

REFERENCE

Annon, J. S. (1976). *Behavioral treatment of sexual problems.* New York: Harper & Row.

47

The Relapse Is Your Friend

Joseph L. Wetchler
Debra L. Del Vecchio

The following intervention is part of a treatment model, Systemic Couples Therapy for Substance-Abusing Women (SCT) (McCollum et al., 1993; Nelson et al., 1996; Wetchler et al., 1994; Wetchler et al., 1993) that provides a relational treatment focus for substance abusers. The model integrates aspects of strategic (Haley, 1987; Watzlawick, Weakland, and Fisch, 1974), structural (Minuchin, 1974), and transgenerational (Bowen, 1978; Kerr and Bowen, 1988) family therapies. It has been tested over a five-year period as an addition to traditional drug treatment for substance-abusing women. While the approach has been tested on women, it is believed also to be helpful with men.

IDENTIFYING PATTERNS

A major component of the model is the idea that substance abuse is maintained by ongoing present-centered and transgenerational patterns. Therapists and clients assess the ongoing interactional sequences that maintain the substance abuse and then alter them. To assess a problem-maintaining sequence, therapists need to discover the pattern of events that surrounds those times when an individual abuses a substance.

Traditional drug treatment often views the relapse as a major problem that needs to be avoided. While SCT also is abstinence-based, it views the relapse as important information for successful treatment rather than as an "enemy" to be avoided at all costs. Many substance abuse clients are initially unaware of the relationship patterns that maintain their problem. During the early phases of treatment they may be unable to identify relational sequences that lead to drug use or provide a sketchy scenario at best. Many of them will relapse until these patterns can be identified and altered.

Minuchin (1974) states that families are most open to change during times of crisis. It is during a relapse that substance abuse clients are most upset about their problem and most open to evaluating it and working on it. Many clients who were initially unwilling to look at relationship patterns are more open to this assessment during this difficult time. Clearer problem-maintaining patterns can be more easily identified immediately after a relapse than in the initial phases of methadone treatment or while an individual is away from the family in an inpatient detoxification program. In effect, the relapse becomes the therapist's "friend" in resolving the problem. Therapists need to be aware that multiple relapses may be necessary before clients are sufficiently motivated to identify and alter their relationship patterns.

Identifying drug-maintaining patterns integrates aspects of Bowen systems and strategic therapies. Similar to Bowen's (1978) beliefs, clients can identify their role in problem-maintaining sequences and plot strategies to alter their behavior in a cycle. This then leads partners to alter their behavior.

CONTRAINDICATIONS

Therapists who take this stance need to be aware of when clients relapse during a legitimate attempt for sobriety and when clients are being manipulative. Many substance abusers enter treatment without making a legitimate commitment for change. Attempting to embrace a client's relapse as a friend will fail if that client is continuing to get high on a regular basis with no desire to improve. Substance abusers are notorious for triangling helping professionals against each other (Stanton and Todd, 1982). Therapists new to substance work can be easy targets for manipulative clients looking to get someone to back their strategies to maintain the status quo.

CASE EXAMPLE

Maria was a thirty-five-year-old IV heroin addict in a methadone-maintenance treatment program who entered the SCT project with her thirty-seven-year-old live-in partner, Fred. She was involved in weekly individual therapy with her drug counselor, weekly couples therapy with her SCT therapist, and daily methadone maintenance. She immediately stopped using heroin; however, at four weeks of treatment she began using cocaine two to three times per week. This continued for several weeks until she was in jeopardy of being kicked out of the treatment center for repeated relapses.

Her SCT therapist chose to deal with these relapses as a chance for getting information about her couple relationship and her drug use rather than confronting her about noncompliance with treatment. Discussions revealed that she got in a fight with her partner every time prior to using cocaine. She would stifle her anger and leave the situation. While alone, or with a friend, she would get high. Bepko (1989) believes that women use substances to block unwanted feelings of power, such as anger or demanding their needs. It appeared to fit for Maria because she would back off from Fred in the middle of a fight and anesthetize her feelings of need and anger with cocaine. After the pattern became clear to Maria, she was assigned to choose times in advance and talk to Fred about what she needed from him and how she wanted him to be responsive to her. Planning these talks in advance was a way of blocking their fights before they got started.

These talks went amazingly well. Both Maria and Fred reported that they felt understood and supported. They were able to resolve several problems and Maria realized that she could assert herself in a relationship. Further, she stopped relapsing on cocaine immediately following the start of the discussions. Maria remained drug free through the end of therapy and at a one-year follow up. She and Fred married and had a baby. She requested that her SCT therapist be the baby's godparent, but the therapist kindly refused.

DISCUSSION

Identifying the pattern around the relapse was the pivotal event in this therapy. Had the therapist focused on confronting the noncompliant behavior, much of this important information could have been missed. It took several relapses and several discussions before the pattern became clear to Maria, and it was at this time that she could finally begin to alter her role in the sequence.

REFERENCES

Bepko, C. (1989). Disorders of power: Women and addiction in the family. In M. McGoldrick, C. M. Anderson, and F. Walsh (Eds.), *Women in families: A framework for family therapy.* New York: W. W. Norton.

Bowen, M. (1978). *Family therapy in clinical practice.* New York: Jason Aronson.

Haley, J. (1987). *Problem-solving therapy* (Second Edition). San Francisco: Jossey-Bass.

Kerr, M. and Bowen, M. (1988). *Family evaluation.* New York: W. W. Norton.

McCollum, E. E., Trepper, T. S., Nelson, T. S., Wetchler, J. L., and Lewis, R. A. (1993). *Systemic couples therapy for substance-abusing women*. West Lafayette, IN: Purdue Research Foundation.

Minuchin, S. (1974). *Families and family therapy*. Cambridge, MA: Harvard University Press.

Nelson, T. S., McCollum, E. E., Wetchler, J. L., Trepper, T. S., and Lewis, R. A. (1996). Therapy with women substance abusers. *Journal of Feminist Family Therapy, 8,* 5-27.

Stanton, M. D. and Todd, T. C. (1982). *The family therapy of drug abuse and addiction*. New York: Guilford.

Watzlawick, P., Weakland, J. H., and Fisch, R. (1974). *Change: Principles of problem formation and problem resolution*. New York: W. W. Norton.

Wetchler, J. L., McCollum, E. E., Nelson, T. S., Trepper, T. S., and Lewis, R. A. (1993). Systemic couples therapy for alcohol-abusing women. In T. J. O'Farrell (Ed.), *Treating alcohol problems: Marital and family interventions*. New York: Guilford.

Wetchler, J. L., Nelson, T. S., McCollum, E. E., Trepper, T. S., and Lewis, R. A. (1994). Couple-focused therapy for substance-abusing women. In J. A. Lewis (Ed.), *Addictions: Concepts and strategies for treatment*. Gaithersburg, MD: Aspen.

48

Sculptural Metaphors
to Create Discontinuity and Novelty
in Family Therapy

Israela Meyerstein

"Sculptural metaphors" refer to the physicalizing of idioms of speech by using concrete objects to dramatize interaction. Expressing and externalizing a metaphorical description of a relationship in concrete sculptural form has the potential to create discontinuity (interrupt process), introduce novelty, and tap into deeper emotional experience.

METAPHORS AND FAMILY PROCESS

Family members interact with one another in repetitive, observable patterns that are often outside their own awareness, in which they mutually stimulate, constrain, and construct one another (Minuchin, Lee, and Simon, 1996). Since family members often perceive their own actions merely as responses to others' provocations, helping them to experience their mutual influence on one another is often a challenge, which can be facilitated when the therapist finds ways to step outside the verbal framework of therapy conversation.

Family sculpting, as developed by Virginia Satir (1972; Satir and Baldwin, 1983) and Peggy Papp (1976) and colleagues (Papp, Silverstein, and Carter, 1973), is one method of dramatizing, concretizing, and making overt and palpable interactional patterns. By involving family members in an experiential self-description, sculpting brings forth perceptions of the relationship as is and recasts it in a more desirable direction. The method can be used to bypass intellectualization or to involve less articulate family members. It can be used both diagnostically and as a therapeutic restructuring intervention.

Metaphor, with its multiplicity of dimensions (Combs and Freedman, 1990), has the capacity to tap into the uniquely personal, to operate indirectly, and to stimulate the random and creative. In particular, symbols, the smallest units of metaphor, such as words, objects, or mental images, work on the analogic level to set off powerful limbic associations and broader relationship meanings.

The introduction of sculptural metaphors in a session can create discontinuity. That is, they interrupt verbal process in therapy, changing channels to nonverbal, nonlogical dimensions. Carl Whitaker (1981) could perhaps be called the "father of discontinuity" because of his non sequiturs, crazy thoughts, primary process fantasies, and his use of the nonlogical and the absurd. His interventions emerged from deep within the self to interrupt process and introduce surprise and novelty.

APPLICATION OF SCULPTURAL METAPHORS

Sculptural metaphors have their best use as a tool in interrupting stuck communication and interaction patterns between family members that operate rigidly and without awareness. They can be used to highlight complementary and/or symmetrical patterns in couple relationships or parent-child issues. They can create a reflection process—similar to looking in a mirror—and make the covert overt. Changing channels to a concrete action metaphor may have its greatest impact on a predominantly verbal or intellectualizing family in helping them experience something directly. Sculptural metaphors may be well received by people who naturally gravitate to kinesthetic channels. In whatever situation used, sculptural metaphors require the therapist to have established a trusting relationship with individual family members first so they can more readily tolerate the more dramatic portrayal of family patterns.

DESCRIPTION OF INTERVENTION

A sculptural metaphor translates an expression into concrete, visible, palpable form. It can also summarize an ongoing relationship or capture a momentary interaction. The therapist observing family interaction can introduce sculptural metaphors to interrupt redundancy in several ways. The therapist can offer a reflection "in the mirror" of a couple's pattern for them to see and then set up a minisculpture, or pose. The therapist places family members in positions relative to each other that reflect, dramatize, or amplify the family's dynamics.

Alternatively, the therapist can use a sculptural metaphor to interrupt escalating process by taking an object and placing it in an expressive position for all to view. The object or prop is used to graphically illustrate an aspect of the relationship pattern, such as distance, hostility, dominance, submissiveness, or entanglement. Family members generally pause due to the surprising distraction. The therapist may then use positive connotation and reframing in describing the sculptural metaphor, or may simply label what it is and let family members react to it and to each other. The power of the metaphor is in the novelty and in the direct experiencing of it. Sometimes discussion may intensify its effect or dilute its impact. The sculptural metaphor may apply to relationships between family members or to therapist-family interaction.

CASE EXAMPLES

The following are several different examples of sculptural metaphors used to create discontinuity and novelty in couples/family therapy.

Ed and Kate had a rather traditional complementary relationship, in which Ed would criticize Kate's spending and Kate would sheepishly admit her error and then repeat her behavior when angry at Ed. Ed continued to lecture Kate as it if were a matter of her understanding better, and Kate did not connect her spending to a rebellion at Ed's overcontrol. I felt that creating a sculptural metaphor that reflected their complementary pattern might help because clearly they were unaware of how they triggered each other. I had Ed stand on the sofa, pointing a blaming finger at Kate, who was crouched down half-penitent, half-rebellious, holding her wallet. I asked them to act out their sculpture in motion. The sculptural metaphor had the effect of creating an internal recoil as each experienced visible discomfort at the extreme of his/her position and the stuckness of their roles with each other.

In another couple, Stacy verbally attacked John's lack of helping efforts and John defended himself, withdrew, and judged Stacy as unreasonable. Their angry bitterness seemed to escalate and cycle without end. To interrupt the pattern, the therapist suddenly took a large pillow and placed it between them to dramatize and label "warring trenches." The couple looked puzzled and perplexed as they stopped their verbal battling. The therapist offered John protection in the "trench," which he declined. The therapist defined Stacy as trying to "send missiles to grab John's attention" and John as running for cover from Stacy's demands. With this couple, the sculptural metaphor offered respite from the repetitive pattern of verbal battling.

Another family session involved a devoted, appeasing single-parent mother and her entitled oppositional teenage son who debated her attempts and challenged her right to set rules, while the mother continued to patiently explain, discuss, and try to convince him. The main intervention of the session was a sculptural metaphor repeated twice: each time the mother was about to waver in her resolve, the therapist stood up and got a tie to bind her hands, telling her, "Your son is trying to 'tie your hands' from setting rules as a parent." The experience of the tied hands prompted her to strengthen her resolve and not let her son have it his way. The mother was clearly affected by this metaphor, and was able to tell her son the discussion was ending with her decision in place. The son was annoyed but at least stopped the debating. After the session the mother revealed the deeper power of the metaphor: it reminded her of her childhood, when she often felt her "hands were tied," when she was a "hostage" in her parents' battles and unable to extract herself. She then connected that her son reminded her of her mother in the way he persisted in keeping her tied to him. This metaphor was a turning point in the mother's empowerment in relation to her son.

A final example involves Robert, who suffered for years from panic disorder, anxiety, and depression, resulting in work inhibition. His devoted wife, Rachel, would sit with him and mother him through these difficult situations. Tired and frustrated, Rachel resented his demands, but nevertheless obliged and tried to coach him. In a previous session, the therapist had evoked a fantasy of Robert sitting on Rachel's large lap for many years. After that session, Robert made some attempts to assert himself and participate more actively as a father in the family. However, Rachel began to disagree with Robert's perceptions, instead suggesting her way of dealing with the situation and giving him instructions. The therapist introduced a sculptural metaphor: she handed a baby teething spoon to Rachel, suggesting perhaps she needed to continue to spoon-feed Robert suggestions and correction. For the first time Robert insisted on his right to make his own judgment, including mistakes, without Rachel's help. The drama of the spoon-feeding scenario made both partners recoil from their overly dependent complementary relationship and Robert began to assert himself more constructively at home and at work. Rachel, able to see the futility and counterproductiveness of her helping, was able to back off and respect Robert's efforts and stumbling to learn on his own. The metaphor was used after much verbal discussion had produced no effect in the therapy.

USE AND CONTRAINDICATIONS

These exmaples illustrate some different uses of sculptural metaphors for couples and family sessions. The variety is endless, up to the imagination and playfulness of the therapist. Essential preconditions for use of sculptural metaphors are the therapist's prior effective joining with each member and the development of a basic trusting and respectful relationship. It is important that the sculptural metaphor challenge the role functioning, and not the person, who the therapist continues to support. To construct sculptural metaphors the therapist must be able to identify patterns of interaction, and to capture them metaphorically or through idioms of speech. Accompanying or following the action-oriented sculptural metaphor, the therapist may elect to use a reframing technique or create the possibility for family members to process the experience as well as discuss related issues with the therapist. Finally, I would advise caution when working with patients who might be threatened by action-oriented physical interventions, or have sensitivities due to prior abuse. In these situations, the therapist must use greater thoughtfulness about consequences and timing in employing sculptural metaphors.

REFERENCES

Combs, G. and Freedman, J. (1990). *Symbol, story, and ceremony: Using metaphor in individual and family therapy.* New York: W. W. Norton.

Minuchin, S., Lee, W. Y., and Simon, G. (1996). *Mastering family therapy: Journeys of growth and transformation.* New York: Wiley.

Papp, P. (1976). Family choreography. In P. J. Guerin (Ed.), *Family therapy: Theory and practice.* New York: Gardner Press.

Papp, P., Silverstein, O., and Carter, E. (1973). Family sculpting in preventive work with well families. *Family Process, 12,* 197-212.

Satir, V. (1972). *Peoplemaking.* Palo Alto, CA: Science and Behavior Books.

Satir, V. and Baldwin, M. (1983). *Satir: Step by step: A guide to creating change in families.* Palo Alto, CA: Science and Behavior Books.

Whitaker, C. A. and Keith, D. V. (1981). Symbolic and experiential family therapy. In A. S. Gurman and D. P. Kniskern (Eds.), *Handbook of family therapy* (pp. 187-225). New York: Brunner/Mazel.

49

A Therapeutic Remarriage Ritual

Florence W. Kaslow

In this chapter, some major problems that remarriage families face and that propel them to seek therapy will be summarized. Then a ritual developed to help such families resolve the dilemmas left over from their prior marriages, which impinge upon their new family's ability to become a cohesive, caring unit, will be discussed. It is hoped readers will find this a valuable additional intervention approach and will adapt it to suit their patient populations and personal styles.

PROBLEMS IN REMARRIAGE FAMILIES

Every year, millions of divorced individuals enter into remarriages. They commence these unions cautiously, hoping this one will be reasonably happy "'til death do us part." However, they bring with them unfinished issues from childhood and adolescence, such as incomplete individuation and/or cut-offs from their families of origin (Bowen, 1978). They are likely, also, to bring unresolved feelings and dilemmas from their prior marriages if they did not achieve the psychic closure (Kaslow, 1995) that comes from letting go of the former relationship.

They may still have various entanglements with members of their prior in-law families. For example, if someone has been and still is in business with members of his/her ex-spouse's family, the relationship is ongoing and his/her financial well-being may be contingent upon it remaining harmonious. This can make the former spouse and the new partner very uncomfortable; each may question where he/she fits and whether the work involvement perpetuates elements of the previous union (Kaslow and Kaslow, 1992). Conversely, if the party felt forced out of a position in an in-law's business because of the divorce, and resented this additional upheaval, the ensuing bitterness and downward economic spiral can spill over into the way the person and the new spouse interact with the former in-laws as the children's grandparents, and complicate special occasions such as children's weddings. Sometimes fear of hostilities erupting stymies a family's ability to celebrate important life events; therefore, these animosities need to be resolved so they can derive pleasure from these occasions instead.

Following their parents' divorce, many children have two residences: Mom's house and Dad's house (Ricci, 1980). If both parents remain single and uninvolved for a period of time, the children have a fine opportunity to bond with each parent separately. This can lead to deeper relationships and forge a closeness that exceeds what they formerly had. Children can adapt to two different sets of expectations and rules, especially when these are clear and consistent, and they feel loved in each home (Kaslow, 1988a).

However, in the next postdivorce phase, when either or both parents become involved with new partners, the children's relationship to that parent usually undergoes another shift. The children may again feel abandoned and hurt by the parent who originally moved out if the new love relationship overshadows the parent-child attachment. The new partner may resent the children's claim on the parent's time and affection, and become competitive. The seeds of dissension may be sown early and continue to plague the relationship long into the future. If the primary residential parent falls in love and the new beloved becomes an important part of his/her life, the children may feel rejected and unwanted by the very person who has been their main source of affection and stability. They may resent the intruder and even try to sabotage the relationship. Either scenario does not bode well for the prospects of a happy, blended family constellation (Sager et al., 1983).

If either parent has tried to alienate the children from the other parent (Palmer, 1988), the children are apt to get caught in a loyalty struggle (Boszormenyi-Nagy and Spark, 1973/1984). They realize if they love their Dad and express a desire to be with him, Mom will be hurt. Yet they do not want to lose contact with him or have to feel guilty when they have a good time with him. If Dad remarries and the children like his new wife, Mom may feel betrayed. This reaction may be exacerbated if Dad's relationship to his new spouse began before the divorce (Kaslow, 1988a). The ex-wife may believe such a person is morally unfit to be her children's stepmother, and may want to forbid visitation or ensure the children will not be taken in by her "devious wiles." The same dynamics are apt to prevail if the wife had the extramarital liaison and pushed for divorce. Her ex-husband may feel so humiliated and resentful that he does not want the children to love and respect their mother, or to have a positive attachment to their new stepfather. Jealousy, possessiveness, and moral judgments regarding fitness to be a proper parent are all factors that may make coparenting and holiday contact schedules complex, volatile issues.

In addition, one may bring into remarriage residual feelings of hurt, loss, anger, and resentment. Partners may be unwilling to risk being vulnerable again, and so may be guarded about becoming too close. If they have been cuckolded by their former partners, they may be unwilling to trust again; this cautiousness poses a barrier to achieving intimacy (Schnarch, 1993) and can prove frustrating to a spouse who is able to make a deep emotional investment. This problem is intensified if either feels guilty about their new union having begun in a predivorce affair.

Another factor is that the economic divorce, which entails the transfer of money for child support and alimony, is not coterminous with the legal divorce but continues for years after the decree is final, until the last mandated payment is made (Kaslow and Schwartz, 1987). Continuing financial obligations to the prior family, which are ethically and existentially valid, may still interfere with the new family's sense of unity and their ability to manage well financially.

In light of the foregoing, and the myriad other problems that characterize many stepfamilies (Visher and Visher, 1979, 1991; Kaslow, 1993), interventions that make a profound impact are often required. Previously, I described the divorce ceremony that I use (Kaslow, 1993a) any time two years or more beyond divorce to help couples integrate what was good in their marriage with what led to its demise, and to thank each other for what was meaningful. It can only be effective if both are willing participants and they are ready to move beyond anger to a more harmonious postdivorce relationship.

Yet even if they have undergone a divorce ceremony or have resolved their despair and rancor through another medium such as therapy, a different set of issues is likely to crop up when remarriage occurs. It is these issues that the remarriage ritual attempts to untangle and smooth out.

THE REMARRIAGE RITUAL

When the clients are a remarried couple/family and they seem unable to make progress with the utilization of various verbal psychotherapy strategies (Sager et al., 1983; Visher and Visher, 1991), I introduce the idea of doing a remarriage ritual. I explain that it entails having the former spouse and the new partner, if he/she has one, and children living in both households present. Often this suggestion meets with a response of "no way" or other forms of resistance. We explore their fear about what will happen if everyone is in the same room together, and also what the other options may be to get them unstuck. During the next few sessions I may try projective genograms (Kaslow, 1995) and/or sculpting, reframing, and other systemic or strategic interventions. If they continue to find that the children are frequently upset, withdrawn, and/or obstreperous before and after transitioning between houses, or that they seem unable to accept and relate to the stepparent after a normal time period for adjusting to the new family constellation, and given a stepparent who has been warm, patient, and nonintrusive or not harsh, then I am likely to again explore the possibility of creating a remarriage ritual session. Generally they agree the second time it is suggested.

The couple are then instructed about how to approach the other parent(s). This entails inviting them to attend a joint session that has as its purpose healing rifts and facilitating an improved coparenting arrangement—with all of its emotional, financial, and physical ramifications. They are encouraged to relate the reasons for the session in a nonhostile manner, and indicate that the tone will not be one of attack or criticism. If they have a great deal of trepidation about whether their invitation will be accepted, they may add that the therapist is experienced in doing these types of sessions and has had good success with them.

The couple/family in treatment is told that I will be adding a male cotherapist for the session, given the large number of people who will be attending. Fee amount and who is to pay are also discussed at this time.

The Day of the Session

Usually everyone arrives exhibiting some signs of apprehension and curiosity. They meet each other in the waiting room, and when everyone is assembled they come into the treatment room. The therapists introduce themselves and everyone selects a seat in a circle of chairs. The cotherapists sit across from each other to be able to maintain eye contact. We thank them for coming and may ask if everyone is clear on the reason for the session. An alternative way I sometimes proceed is to go around the circle and ask each person to tell what he or she would like to see happen in and from the session, that is, the outcome they desire. The strategy chosen depends on the dynamics of the particular extended family constellation. Whichever opening intervention is used tends to draw out the most pressing concerns immediately.

Depending on the amount of contention and strife expressed, and the ages of the children present, we decide whether to have the children remain in the session throughout, or to ask them to wait in the waiting room so that we can meet with the adults alone for a short period of time. Since we anticipate this might happen, if there are children under eight years of age and no responsible adolescent in the family, we will ask them to bring along a baby-sitter, "just in case."

This interval with the adults is used to help them understand why it is essential for the well-being of the children all purport to love, to handle the intrafamilial relationships in a more compassionate and constructive way. The fact that all have expressed, in response to our queries, their commitment to doing what is in the best interest of the children, is utilized as the core leverage for facilitating progress toward more harmonious sharing and interactions.

Later each biological parent is asked to reassure the children, if there seems to be any question about it, of their continuing caring for them and desire to remain involved in their lives in a variety of ways, including being available by phone to chat or talk about problems when the child is in residence with the other parent. Both parents are asked to affirm that the child is free to love the other parent without interference in the form of sarcastic or disparaging remarks about them, barriers set up to visitation and attendance at special events, or scenes made at activities like Little League games or school functions. When this is given, children visibly relax and perk up. Some are inclined to ask, "Do you really mean it?" An adolescent might blurt out, "It's about time! I don't ever want to hear another nasty remark about Mom/Dad. This war should have been over a long time ago." Next they are asked to give permission to the children to accept, like, even love the new stepparent (or live-in partner) without fear of interrogation, jealousy, or rejection. Frequently this request evokes strong emotions, as heretofore a parent may have been unable to relinquish the child from a bond that meant forming an attachment to the new stepparent would be perceived as a betrayal. When children hear this and believe the permission is given genuinely, they sometimes cry, run and hug the parent, go to the stepparent and take his or her hand, or behave in some way to solidify the possibilities that have been opened up. For many families this is a profoundly moving and healing aspect of the ritual session.

If the other parent has engaged in similar prejudicial behavior about the ex-spouse's new partner, the process is repeated. The adults are told that if they disagree regarding parenting styles and rules, and expectations for the children, we can have another session to try to make these more congruent, or at least compatible, but this is not the objective for this session. They tend to easily grasp why. Conversely, specific revisions on time in each household and for vacations may be done, with all expressing their needs and preferences, and doing this in a nonlegalistic fashion that takes into account the children's current developmental levels. When necessary, it may be suggested that modifications to a child custody agreement be filed in a nonadversarial way with the court.

If the children seem uncertain about a stepparent's interest in and affection for them, that individual is asked to convey his or her feelings to the child in this forum, and also when they are together at home. Sometimes this is the first opportunity they have had to express positive emotions openly, and this can help overcome seeming indifference or defensiveness.

These emotional sessions are drawn to a close by asking the participants to again go around the circle in the order in which they are sitting, and sum up for themselves what they derived from the session that was most significant for them. It is crucial that each person's voice be heard and their thoughts honored without rebuttal. Usually each person comments on something different that was meaningful, and these commentaries coalesce into a wonderful composite of what they gained from the time and energy each expended. As they listen attentively to one another, each is validated and better understood.

CONTRAINDICATIONS

This approach is not recommended for remarried families in which there is a psychotic member or someone with a severe personality disorder, particularly of the anti social, borderline, or narcissistic types (American Psychiatric Association, 1994; Kernberg, 1975; Solomon, 1996). Anyone with such personal pathology is likely to impede the collaborative process essential for the remarriage ritual to evolve efficaciously.

POSTSCRIPT

I have been using variations of this approach for the last dozen years. If the families are well screened, these less than two-hour sessions tend to be quite beneficial for all. In some ways, I'm still amazed at how much of depth and significance can be accomplished when such sessions are properly structured, planned, and implemented. The data on effectiveness are purely clinical and come from follow-up reports from families who have participated.

REFERENCES

American Psychiatric Association (1994). *Diagnostic and statistical manual of mental disorders* (Fourth edition). Washington, DC: Author.

Boszormenyi-Nagy, I. and Spark, G. (1973). *Invisible loyalties*. New York: Harper & Row. (Reprinted 1984, New York: Brunner/Mazel.)

Bowen, M. (1978). *Family therapy in clinical practice.* New York: Jason Aronson.

Kaslow, F. W. (1988a). Remarried couples: The architects of stepfamilies. In F. W. Kaslow (Ed.), *Couples therapy in a family context: Perspective and retrospective* (pp. 33-48). Special issue of Family Therapy Collections. Rockville, MD: Aspen Publishers.

Kaslow, F. W. (1988b). The psychological dimension of divorce mediation. In J. Folberg and A. Milne (Eds.), *Divorce mediation: Theory and practice* (pp. 83-108). New York: Guilford.

Kaslow, F. W. (1993a). The divorce ceremony: A healing strategy. In T. Nelson and T. Trepper (Eds.), *101 family therapy interventions* (pp. 341-345). Binghamton, NY: The Haworth Press.

Kaslow, F. W. (1993b). *Understanding and treating the remarriage family.* Volume 1 in *Directions in Marriage and Family Therapy.* New York: Hatherleigh Co., Ltd.

Kaslow, F. W. (1995). The dynamics of divorce therapy. In R. H. Mikesell, D. D. Lusterman and S. H. McDaniel (Eds.), *Integrating family therapy: Handbook of family psychology and systems theory* (pp. 271-283). Washington, DC: American Psychological Association.

Kaslow, F. W. and Kaslow, S. (1992). The family that works together: Special problems of family businesses. In S. Zedeck (Ed.), *Work, families and organizations* (pp. 312-351). San Francisco: Jossey-Bass.

Kaslow, F. W. and Schwarz, L. L. (1987). *Dynamics of divorce: A life cycle perspective.* New York: Brunner/Mazel.

Kernberg, O. (1975). *Borderline conditions and pathological narcissism.* New York: Jason Aronson.

Palmer, N. S. (1988). Legal recognition of the parental alienation syndrome. *American Journal of Family Therapy, 16*(4), 361-363.

Ricci, I. (1980). *Mom's house, Dad's house: Making shared custody work.* New York: Macmillan.

Sager, C. J., Brown, H. S., Crohn, H., Engel, T., Rodstein, E., and Walker, L. (1983). *Treating the remarried family.* New York: Brunner/Mazel.

Schnarch, D. M. (1993). Inside the sexual crucible. *Family Therapy Networker,* March/April, 40-48.

Solomon, M. (1996). Understanding and treating couples with borderline disorders. In F. W. Kaslow (Ed.), *Handbook of relational diagnosis and dysfunctional family patterns* (pp. 51-269). New York: Wiley.

Visher, E. B. and Visher, J. S. (1979). *Stepfamilies: A guide to working with stepparents and stepchildren.* New York: Brunner/Mazel.

Visher, E. B. and Visher, J. S. (1991). *How to win as a stepfamily,* Second edition. New York: Brunner/Mazel.

50

The Complaint Technique

Brenda Carroll

In the child and family services division of a large community mental health center, treatment is often brief and the treatment goals well focused. This kind of environment lends itself well to Solution-Focused Therapy techniques that, "Focus on people's competence rather than their deficits, their strengths rather than their weaknesses, their possibilities rather than their limitations" (O'Hanlon and Davis, 1989, p. 1). However, a common complaint of clients treated using this model is that they don't feel heard by the therapist. O'Hanlon and Davis clearly point out that becoming set in your own agenda (of being solution focused) to the point of failure to recognize client responses is a recipe for a therapeutic sticking point. To sidestep the impression that the therapist has suddenly mutated into Polly-anna, grafting the strategic intervention of the paradoxical prescription of complaining becomes an important intervention. The complaint technique allows the client to feel heard while allowing the therapist to continue focused, goal-directed brief therapy.

The complaint technique is well suited for both family and individual work but may be most helpful with those clients each therapist inevitably has who say, "I want to change, but don't make me change anything." Often this client wants to share his or her story and is unable to continue until all of their frustrations and irritations related to the identified problem or person have been hashed and rehashed.

However, more appropriate than defining the type of client for whom this intervention is most suited is defining the type of therapist. This intervention may be particularly helpful for the novice therapist who is intent on staying strictly solution focused to become unstuck without feeling the model has been compromised. The therapist motivated to follow the wide, straight path of treatment goals without meandering down alternative routes will feel a greater sense of control over the direction of the therapeutic process. Those side roads have still been followed but have been reframed to fit the therapist's epistemological bent.

Using the complaint technique, the therapist begins by setting aside the entire first session for the client to tell the story of the concerns, frustrations, and problems that brought them to therapy. This first step alone is a departure from the solution-focused premise that a complete understanding of the problem is not imperative for positive outcomes. In this session, the therapist refrains from looking for exceptions, normalizing, asking presuppositional questions, or other techniques typical in Solution-Focused Therapy, instead simply listening to the family or individual describe the problems. At the completion of the initial session, the therapist thanks the client for being thorough and then sets the stage for subsequent meetings. The therapist may explain:

> I know that you came here because you want things to be different in your [family, relationship, life, etc.], and so that will be our focus. But I also know it's really important for you to have time to share your concerns with me; so from here on out let's plan to reserve a portion of each session for that purpose.

With this introduction, the therapist explains the basis of the complaint technique. In each session, beginning with the second, time is set aside for complaining. The second session begins with thirty minutes of an hour meeting reserved for that purpose. At every session after, the time for complaining is reduced by five minutes and the time for focusing on solution patterns and positive changes increases. There is a clear demarcation between the two time periods. If the client begins to talk about positive changes or other noncomplaint-based topics, the therapist must respectfully say to the family, "I'm sorry but this is the time for you to share your frustrations and complaints with me. You have _____ minutes before your complaint time is up," emphasizing the therapist's desire for the family to feel heard. If necessary, the therapist must encourage the family to complain, make suggestions about possible topics, and generally prevent the family from sharing their successes. Often, having each family member come up with a complaint about every other member of the family, no matter how trivial, fills this time well. After the complaint time is over, the focus of the session shifts clearly to solution-focused questions and interventions. If any additional complaints occur during the second half, the therapist should respectfully remind the client to save that thought for complaint time the next meeting. By the seventh session, the client is down to five minutes of complaint time verses fifty-five minutes of solution-focused work in an hour session.

By this time in treatment, often the only thing left the clients want to complain about is having to fill complaint time. Typically, clients begin by relishing the time to have your undivided attention focused on their complaints but as early as the third or fourth session are sick and tired of hearing themselves talking about being sick and tired. When the therapist is faithful in pursing the complaint technique, often complaint time becomes filled with chuckling, eye rolling, and the fabrication of obviously ridiculous complaints. The family joins together around having to "get through" this time in the meeting and, in playful families, may egg one another on to see if they can slip a positive comment in without the therapist noticing.

The children in the first family with which this intervention was utilized (ages thirteen, nine, and six) could be counted upon to say, "Do we *have* to?!?" when asked to start complaining and began requesting very frequent updates on the amount of time left to complain. It felt much like having a child in the car who is anxious to reach a destination saying, "Are we there yet?" In essence, the complaint technique is just that: directing the client to anticipate and long for the experience of positive change. The focus on solution patterns becomes something the client requests rather something foisted on them by the therapist.

At first glance, it seems the complaint technique is appropriate any time the therapist determines solution-focused therapy is a suitable treatment modality. However, after receiving feedback from others in my workplace, there are some cautions to be noted. When a client presents in therapy, even with the most pure solution model the therapist will receive his or her story as part of the response to solution-focused questions. Discernment by the therapist between the desire to complain and the necessity of storytelling will be important. In some families, sorting the chaff of complaints from the grain that is their story will take several sessions and the complaint technique will have to wait. Finally, an insightful supervisor pointed out when complaining is an affliction of one family member rather than the entire system being treated, "In some instances this technique may further identify this individual as the problem versus the system encountering itself" (Gahm, 1996). As the complaint technique is designed to bring all members of the client system to a joint focus on solutions with the therapist, singling out any one family member and further identifying that person as the problem would be counterproductive.

REFERENCES

Gahm, T. (1996). Personal communication.
O'Hanlon, W. H. and Davis, M. W. (1989). *In search of solutions: A new direction in psychotherapy.* New York: W. W. Norton.

51

"Time Out"—Calming the Chaos

James Verser

Parents are often concerned about *what to do* when it comes to disciplining their children. Effective discipline results not only in improved behavior by the children, but also the creation of a warm and stable atmosphere within which children can grow. Effective parenting techniques are, therefore, essential to the creation of a stable family. Currently, "time out" is one of the most frequently used, but not fully understood, parenting techniques. There are many versions of it, many of which are quite effective. I have taught this version to many parents, and it is almost always effective in reducing the frequency and intensity of the targeted behaviors.

The ideas for this intervention have been drawn from two main sources. The first is systemic family therapy, especially strategic family therapy with its emphasis on an appropriate generational hierarchy; the parents need to be in charge of the family (Haley, 1976; Minuchin, 1974; Minuchin, Rosman, and Baker, 1978). The second is the social learning approach of Gerald Patterson (1975, 1976) and Logan Wright (1978); each of them provided initial descriptions of time out.

Time out is an appropriate technique for most families. It is not as effective with teenagers and severely disorganized families. Children with special needs (e.g., attention deficit disorder) will have more difficulty adapting to it. Parents who are unable to increase their level of consistency will be unable to make time out effective.

PURPOSE

The purpose of any technique of discipline is to teach children responsibility, self-discipline, and appropriate behavior. It also helps parents to demonstrate that they are clearly and firmly in charge of themselves and of the family. The specific purpose of time out is to give the parent an alternative to yelling, lecturing, screaming, scolding, and otherwise adding to the tension and chaos that is caused by certain misbehaviors. Each parenting technique needs to focus on certain specific behaviors, and time out is effective with the following behaviors:

- mouth offenses: yelling, screaming, talking back, twenty questions, bad language, name calling, hurtful comments
- inappropriate physical contact: hitting, punching, touching while walking by, stepping on feet, gouging, pinching, biting
- temper tantrums
- sibling rivalry
- open defiance

Parents must determine what is acceptable or unacceptable behavior in each of these areas. Once the standard is set, the parent is ready to use time out.

Time out is a specific period of time, based on the child's age, spent in the bathroom with the door closed. With children six years and younger, the time is three minutes; with children six years (or first grade) and older, the time is five minutes. Time out begins to be effective with children at approximately two and a half years of age and ceases its effectiveness at approximately fourteen years of age or upon entering high school. These small amounts of time are quite effective. In fact, research (Patterson, 1976) has demonstrated that lengthening time out for longer than ten minutes does not appreciably increase the effectiveness of the procedure.

WHAT TO DO

Time out should be explained to the children, and then the parent makes a clear response to misbehavior. When the child's behavior is considered appropriate, the proper response is either to ignore it, to praise it, or to be productively involved in it. When the behavior is inappropriate, the parent's response is to say to the child, "Go to time out." At that point, the parent begins to look at his/her watch, as the child has thirty seconds to go into the bathroom and close the door. If the child does not enter the bathroom within thirty seconds, then the parent adds one minute to the time out period. For every minute the child takes to get into time out with the door closed, the parent will add an extra minute. This means that if the child refuses for ten minutes, the parent will add ten minutes to the time out, and the child will serve fifteen minutes: five minutes for the time out, plus ten minutes for being ten minutes late. As indicated above, this additional time does not make time out more effective. The additional time is a separate consequence for not going to time out immediately.

Younger children may need to be assisted into time out. But certainly by the time the child is four years old, he or she can comprehend the rule well enough to earn extra time for being late. In my experience with hundreds of families, I have had only a handful of children who have resisted for longer than fifteen or twenty minutes. Most children do not resist at all. They may earn one or two minutes from time to time, but essentially when the parent truly enforces time out, the children go.

From the time the parent tells the child to go to time out until it is completed, the parent should discuss nothing with the child except how much time they have to spend in time out. This is not the time to talk about why the child has to go to time out or whether it is "fair." This is an attempt by the child to regain control of the situation, and the parent must maintain control. This is effectively done by refusing to have any discussion and simply insisting on compliance with time out. This technique also removes the need for physical intervention by the parent.

Once the child is in time out and the door is closed, there should be no communication through the door. What this really means is that the parent will not answer the child, who is likely to say many things while in time out. The child may yell, cry, call names, or talk about how unfair this is, but the parent is not to respond. Questions about how much time is left in time out are also ignored.

The most effective way to measure time out is to use a portable kitchen timer with a bell on it. Set it for the appropriate number of minutes and place it near the bathroom door. Then, when the timer rings, the child may come out. If the child does not hear the ring, the parent can inform the child that time out is completed.

When the child leaves time out and is not in control of his behavior, or immediately engages in other inappropriate behavior that merits time out, the parent should immediately place the child back in time out for another five-minute period. This means that if the child spends fifty out of the next sixty minutes in time out, it is not because he was put in for fifty minutes, but because he earned it ten times (a small consequence used frequently is much more effective than larger consequences used occasionally). This is one of the advantages of time out. It gives the parent frequent opportunity to use it, thereby demonstrating that the parent is in charge.

When the child's behavior becomes inappropriate, the proper response is to say "Time out." Give no warnings. A warning really is "permission to do it again." If the parent says to the child, "If you do that again, you are going to have to go to time out," the child is being given the go-ahead to continue misbehaving. The parent has said, "I am not yet ready to put you in time out."

While the child is in the bathroom, the parent should not try to control his or her behavior. It is okay if he or she plays, sings, cries, yells, or "uses the bathroom." Truly destructive behavior needs attention, but this is very rare. When time out is over, if the child has messed up the bathroom, then the door may be left open, but the child must remain in the bathroom until he or she has cleaned up the mess. Otherwise, the child is free to come out when his or her behavior is appropriate.

When the child comes out, he or she may be upset and may want further time alone. This is perfectly acceptable and often is desired. As long as the child is not continuing to be inappropriately mouthy, throwing a tantrum, or violating one of the other behavioral norms for which time out is appropriate, the child should be allowed to have the feelings and to go off alone to nurse those feelings. Typically, what will happen is that after a short period of time, which could extend to half an hour or more, the child will return to family interactions in a much more pleasant mood. It is not uncommon for a young child to wind up singing before time out is completed. When the child comes out of time out, he or she is often already in a good mood.

Parents usually have a strong need to talk to their children about why they have disciplined them. I have found over the years that it is not very productive to initiate conversations about why a child is being disciplined at the time that discipline is necessary or as soon as the consequence is completed. Instead, use the "thirty-minute rule." Simply stated, a discussion with the child about why the behavior was inappropriate should be delayed for at least thirty minutes after the consequence is completed. At the time of the misbehavior, and quite often at the time the consequence is completed, most family members are still upset. When people are emotionally upset, they usually cannot have a calm or reasonable discussion. Therefore, the discussion about the inappropriate behavior usually results in an argument rather than a discussion. The long-term result is that the child begins to experience discussion and conversation as "a consequence" and becomes less and less eager to have a conversation on any subjects with the parents. It can be determined that this has occurred when the child responds with "What did I do?" when the parent requests a talk. The child has already learned that conversation is a consequence, and any conversation means that he or she has done something wrong and now is going to be punished. This is mitigated greatly by the "thirty-minute rule."

Sibling Rivalry

Sibling rivalry is defined as any behavior between siblings that the parent determines to be inappropriate. When two or more siblings are behaving inappropriately, the appropriate response is to send all the children involved in the interaction to time out. The parents should not attempt to determine who started it or who was responsible. This only leads to more wrangling, arguing, and debating without calming the situation down or gaining control. If the parent directly observes the interaction and determines that one child has initiated it, then it is appropriate to send that child to time out. But most of the time, the parent is looking the other way, or in another room, or one child comes to tattle, or the parent overhears the inappropriate interaction. In these cases, it is much better to send both or all of the children to time out, each to a different location. Ultimately, this will help them to learn how to control their relationships more effectively than trying to play Solomon and figure out who started it. It greatly reduces the escalating interactions.

Alternative Time Outs

The basic idea of time out is that when the child has misbehaved in one or more of the areas for which time out is effective, then he or she should be isolated for a short period of time. This should occur immediately without yelling, nagging, screaming, and so on. This basic idea needs to guide the use of time out in whatever setting the family happens to be. Following are a few examples of how time out can be adapted to other situations.

Automotive Time Out

After the amount of time a family spends in the home, families tend to spend most of their time in the car. Misbehavior in the car is not only frustrating to the parent, it may produce a dangerous situation as the parent's attention is distracted from the complex task of driving the car. In setting up automotive time out, the parent must first decide what kind of behavior is acceptable in the car. Once this has been determined, when the child misbehaves, the parent should stop the car and pull off to the side of the road at the first safe place. Pull the car as far off the road as is practical or pull into a parking lot where it would be safe. Then put the misbehaving child out of the car. Have the child sit or stand by the side of the car away from the road by the front or back wheel. If placing two children outside the car, place one by the front wheel and one by the back wheel. Shorten the amount of time from five minutes to three minutes. At the end of time out, the children get back in the car, and the parent proceeds down the road. If the misbehavior continues, then the parent should stop the car again and perform another time out.

The story that describes how I invented automotive time out is both instructive and heartwarming. A number of years ago, the Blue family was struggling to establish more appropriate discipline within the home. After about three visits, they came in quite perturbed. While time out had been working effectively at home and the boys' behavior was improving, the parents were anticipating their vacation. The plan was that they would drive from New Jersey to visit their family in Michigan. They had three boys: Chad (thirteen), Sean (eleven), and Kevin (nine). Every time they got into the car, the boys would act out incredibly, and every driving experience became an ordeal for the parents. There was much yelling and screaming as the parents tried to get the boys to be more in control of themselves. Therefore, this trip to Michigan was being viewed with a great deal of trepidation. As we discussed what should be done, I came up with the idea of time out as described in the previous paragraph. The parents seemed mildly relieved since time out had been working at home.

Once they returned from their vacation about two weeks later, I received a marvelous report. The family left home on a Saturday morning and proceeded north to Michigan. It took them about two and a half hours to travel the first forty miles. It took them that long because the parents decided they were going to make automotive time out work, and they stopped the car quite frequently. They began to despair that they would ever get to Michigan, but they were also determined to demonstrate to their sons that their behavior in the car was not acceptable. By the time they traveled forty miles, the boys seemed to have gotten the message. Time out was not needed for the rest of the trip. They were in Michigan for ten days, and time out was needed only twice. On their return trip, which was longer than the trip going out, they only had to use time out once. All five of them reported that this was the most enjoyable vacation they had ever had. At that time, I knew that automotive time out worked.

Family and Friend Time Out

Often, traveling in the car leads to a friend's or relative's home. The parent can simply say, "Remember, Aunt Bertha has a bathroom." The basic rule here is that every home has a bathroom, and time out should be used just as it is at home.

Shopping Time Out

Another situation in which parents are often frustrated by their child's misbehavior is when the family goes shopping in public areas. Again, appropriate behavior needs to be determined, and violations need to be met with a time out. In a store or mall, the parent must choose a place where the child can be told to sit or stand alone. The parent must then walk away from the child a minimum of fifteen to twenty-five feet, depending upon the age of the child and the particular situation. The issue of safety must be kept in mind. In a public place, the child cannot actually be isolated as in the home. However, as the parent walks away from the child, the parent needs to *not* look directly at the child. The child must be watched, but with peripheral vision. The child needs to be placed in a location where the parent can observe who is approaching the child without having to look directly at the child. Again, the amount of time is reduced to about three minutes. When time out is over, the shopping expedition continues without further discussion of the problem. Time out is repeated as often as necessary.

Picnic Time Out

Picnic time out is used whenever a family is enjoying a leisure activity, such as a picnic. Essentially, a parent must locate a place, for example, a certain tree, and indicate to the children that that is the "time out tree." Then, whenever the child's behavior becomes inappropriate, he or she is sent to that place for the time out period. Again, when the time out is over, the leisure activities are resumed with no discussion of why the child was placed in time out. Time out is repeated as often as is necessary.

Discipline in a Public Place

A significant problem that parents experience with their children in public is shame. When a child misbehaves in public, parents tend to feel ashamed and believe that other people will be judging them negatively as parents. The result quite often is an ineffective attempt at hushing up the child or scolding him or her without any significant improvement in behavior. The parent continues to feel ashamed and a failure.

Parents need to develop a new attitude about discipline. A part of this is accepting the reality that a child will always test parents in any new situation to see whether the parent is going to continue to be loving enough to be in charge. If the child has seen that the parent is confused or afraid to use assertive discipline in public, then that child is going to act out even more. Parents must understand that this is normal behavior in children and must believe in themselves so they can use effective discipline in public. Parents must pretend that they have badges on their shoulders that say, "I am proud to be an effective parent." With that attitude, they can also say to their children, "I am proud to be able to effectively discipline you. I am proud to demonstrate it to anyone who is around. Therefore, when you misbehave in public, I welcome the opportunity to demonstrate for other parents how to effectively discipline their children." With this attitude, it becomes much easier to discipline the child in public without simply becoming angry at him or her.

As this attitude and new behavior take hold, the child begins to understand and realize that the parent truly is in charge no matter where the family is. As a result, with time the child's public behavior will begin to improve. It is also important to note, however, that from the ages of three to eight, children do not know how to behave in public and must be taught. The two ways of teaching are (1) to directly instruct the child in the desired behavior and offer rewards for that positive behavior; and (2) to consistently use time out when behavior is unacceptable. Because learning is a slow process, and because there are many, many different public situations, it does take a number of years of using these two methods before a child begins to fully understand how to behave in public. However, with consistent guidance about appropriate behavior, and consistent response to inappropriate behavior, the child will learn. As this learning takes place, it becomes more and more of a joy to take the child anywhere.

TIME OUT IN THERAPY

While many families can benefit from the mere instruction of how to perform time out, many families appear in therapy seemingly unable to make the needed changes. In the therapeutic setting, an additional component intended to get the child to monitor the parents' behavior greatly increases the effectiveness.

Once time out has been explained to the family, I turn to the children and say, "Would you like to help Mom and Dad learn not to yell, lecture, and nag?" Usually, they brighten up and say, "Yeah!" Then I say, "You can even make some money doing this." Now I have their full attention. I explain that for the inappropriate behaviors, the parents are to use time out, and they are not to yell, scream, nag, lecture, give warnings, spank, or use other consequences. If the parents do any of these things, the children are to write down the date and a description of the parent's "misbehavior." They are to bring the list to the next therapy session. I promise that we will go over it, and for each legitimate offense, I will fine the parent $1.00. I will collect the money and hold it until the end of therapy (or other appropriate time), when I will divide it among the children, keeping a little for myself as banker. This invariably increases the children's investment in time out. Occasionally, I encourage the children to act up as a way to give them more opportunities to catch their parents yelling and possibly making more money.

CONCLUSION

If time out is used consistently, then the negative interactions for which it is appropriate will be greatly reduced in frequency and intensity. Time out will never *completely* eradicate these behaviors because they are essentially normal. However, it will help to quiet the family environment, and it will contribute to a greater degree of peace and harmony, calming the chaos.

REFERENCES

Haley, Jay. (1976). *Problem-solving therapy.* New York: McGraw-Hill.

Minuchin, Salvador. (1974). *Families and family therapy.* Cambridge, MA: Harvard University Press.

Minuchin, Salvador, Rosman, Bernice, and Baker, Lester. (1978). *Psychosomatic families: Anorexia nervosa in context.* Cambridge, MA: Harvard University Press.

Patterson, Gerald R. (1975). *Families: Application of social learning to family life.* Champaign, IL: Research Press Company.

Patterson, Gerald R. (1976). *Living with children: New methods for parents and teachers,* revised. Champaign, IL: Research Press Company.

Wright, Logan. (1978). *Parent power: A guide to responsible childrearing.* New York: Bantam Books.

52

An Empirically Driven Marital Therapy Intervention

Stephanie A. Ross
Ana Ulloa Estrada

CONCEPTUAL OVERVIEW

In the United States, one-half to two-thirds of all first marriages are expected to end in separation or divorce (Castro-Martin and Bumpass, 1989), and subsequent marriages are even more likely to fail (Brody, Neubaum, and Forehand, 1988). Marital distress and dissolution have been shown to compromise the emotional and physical well-being of all family members. Marital and family therapists have firmly believed in the efficacy of marital therapy to address some of the problems that have been found to contribute to marital distress and divorce. Although marital therapy cannot help all couples to repair their marriages, and may actually help couples to separate, overall it has been proven to be helpful (Jacobson and Addis, 1993). Guided by social exchange theory (Thiabaut and Kelley, 1959), empirical research on marital interactions has identified behaviors that actually lead to a deterioration in communication and eventual divorce among couples. The following intervention draws on these research findings and attempts to utilize what we have learned about the predictors of marital distress and divorce to enhance the practice of marital therapy.

The intervention involves the use of a brief videotaped interaction task, which is completed by the couple at the outset and can be repeated periodically through the course of marital therapy. The goals of the proposed intervention are threefold: it provides (1) a useful therapy assessment device; (2) a tool for the therapist to use in treatment with the couple; and (3) a measure of therapy outcome. The ultimate goal of the intervention is to maximize therapeutic effectiveness. The intervention could be used with almost all couples who present for marital therapy. Couples who present as highly distressed, that is, couples who indicate divorce as a possibility, would be especially good candidates for this intervention. Similarly, couples who might benefit from a structured therapy format may also respond well to this intervention.

The intervention identifies and directly addresses the husband's and wife's interaction patterns that have been shown to predict short- and long-term harm to a marriage (Gottman and Krokoff, 1989). Gottman (1993a) found that a husband's defensiveness, contempt, and stonewalling (defined as the husband's withdrawal from the interaction) predicted divorce, while a wife's criticism was related to separation, and her criticism, defensiveness, and contempt actually predicted divorce.

Gottman (1993b) proposes that stable and happy marriages rely on a behavioral ratio of roughly five to one, with the couple engaging in approximately five positive behaviors or exchanges for every negative exchange. Furthermore, he suggests that negativity appears especially dysfunctional when it is coupled with high levels of complaining, criticizing, defensiveness, contempt, and disgust.

MARITAL INTERVENTION

The proposed intervention is as follows: in the first session, after the logistics of treatment have been worked out and before formal therapy actually begins, each spouse separately completes the Dyadic Adjustment Scale (DAS) (Spanier, 1976), a brief, self-report measure of marital adjustment and satisfaction. From the couple's responses on this measure, the therapist locates an area of continuing disagreement for this couple (e.g., family finances, children, sex) and then asks the couple to engage in a fifteen-minute conversation with the goal of resolving this area of disagreement. The therapist leaves the room and the conversation between the couple is videotaped.

The therapist utilizes this "sample" of the couple's behavior in a number of ways. First, the therapist can view the videotaped interaction to identify specific destructive behavioral patterns (e.g., complaining/criticizing, defensiveness, contempt, stonewalling) as well as positive sequences (e.g., positive presentation of issues, engagement, assent, agreements, humor, and positive listening behaviors) as defined by the Rapid Couples Interaction Scoring System (RCISS) (Krokoff, Gottman, and Hass, 1989). Second, the therapist can also scan the videotape specifically searching for the ratio of positive to negative behaviors and exchanges between the couple.

CASE APPLICATION

A brief case example* illustrates the potential utility of this intervention. In this case, the therapist initially viewed the videotaped interaction privately, to gain a better understanding of the couple's interactional patterns. Then, the videotape was used as a psychoeducational tool during sessions. In conjunction with the couple, the therapist specifically identified and addressed the relative strengths and liabilities associated with their exchanges. Therapy homework assignments provided rich opportunities for the couple to practice recognizing and subsequently modifying their problematic behavior. The therapist had the couple repeat the interaction after about eight therapy sessions, and again at termination. In this way, the intervention served as a measure of both therapeutic progress and outcome.

In the following figures, we have plotted the positive minus the negative RCISS behaviors (identified earlier) across fifty conversational turns between a wife and a husband prior to entering marital therapy (see Figure 51.1) and after eight therapy sessions (see Figure 51.2). Both of these conversations focused largely on the couple's communication problems. The pretreatment graph depicts the negativity of the wife's statements while the husband remains relatively positive throughout the problem-solving conversation. Specifically, note the seemingly synchronous and positive flow of the beginning of the conversation. At about the fifteenth turn, the conversation becomes unregulated, with the wife becoming increasingly negative and the husband remaining relatively positive.

In Figure 51.2, after eight sessions of marital therapy, both wife and husband are consistently positive, reflecting a regulated interaction. Consistent with other observational and self-report treatment indices (e.g., DAS, observer ratings of therapy) we have collected, this couple is observed to be more happy and stable in their marriage across time in therapy.

LIMITATIONS OF INTERVENTION

We realize that videotaping the couple's interaction and coding the interaction in its entirety is not feasible in all clinical settings. We have found that audiotaped interactions can be useful as well. Although the use of audiotaped recordings eliminates some valuable information gleaned from observing nonverbal cues (e.g., stonewalling, facial expressions), ver-

---

*The clinical data in this case have been somewhat altered to preserve the anonymity of the couple.

FIGURE 52.1. Case example of RCISS speaker point graph for couple at pre-treatment. (Positive-Negative = ratio of positive to negative behaviors.)

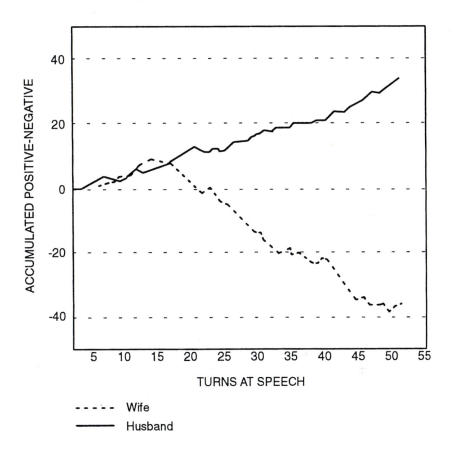

bal interactions effectively expose corrosive patterns of interaction and the positive to negative ratio of behaviors. This interaction can be easily incorporated in training settings where audio recording of sessions is a common method of clinical supervision. While behavioral coding is typically not feasible in clinical settings, specifically identifying and tracking these identified behaviors over the course of treatment is quite possible. Similar to the use of videotaped interactions, we recommend that therapists integrate these audiotaped interactions into their overall assessment and treatment plan, specifically as a measure of the couple's therapeutic progress and outcome.

FIGURE 52.2. Case example of RCISS speaker point graph for couple after eight sessions of treatment. (Positive-Negative = ratio of positive to negative behaviors.)

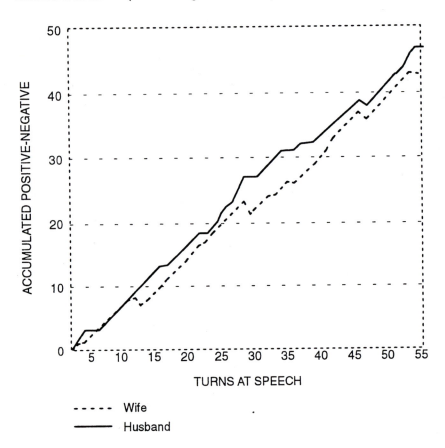

Although videotaped and audiotaped interactions are useful in the assessment and treatment of most couples, there are situations in which this intervention may have limited success. Given that some of the behaviors that have been empirically demonstrated to predict marital dissatisfaction and divorce are gender specific, this intervention may have limited usefulness or relevance for gay and lesbian couples. One must also consider the unique structure and dynamics of gay and lesbian relationships. While presently there are no data to support this recommendation, we suggest that the task may be useful in capturing the ratio of positive to negative behaviors and exchanges between gay and lesbian partners, which are likely to be related to the success of any relationship.

Also, this task may not be suitable for couples whose native languages are not English. If the task is completed in a language other than English, the therapist must be aware of the nuances of the particular language such as varied tones and inflections. Furthermore, the therapist should consider the racial, cultural, and ethnic background of each couple, as these factors likely have profound influence on communication patterns and their interpretation by spouses. Although the intervention is intended for use with diverse populations, the therapist should always be aware of cultural variations, and should even feel free to inquire about the influence of culture when viewing the tape with the couple. Socioeconomic status and the economic power that each spouse maintains in the relationship may also affect their communication patterns.

Also, the therapist may have a difficult time with some camera-shy couples who strongly oppose being videotaped. Although some couples may absolutely refuse to complete the videotaped task, many can be reassured by the therapist's explanation of the usefulness of this task in assessing treatment progress or effectiveness. It has been our experience that once the couple is engaged in the problem-solving discussion, they quickly forget about the videotape equipment. Indeed, one or both spouses' refusal to participate may be diagnostic in and of itself.

The videotaped interaction for assessment and treatment purposes should not be used in isolation. Clearly its effectiveness is maximized when used in conjunction with standardized questionnaires and traditional information gathering techniques and treatment strategies. Although it may take a bit of extra time and effort on the part of the therapist and the couple, this intervention is a rich and valuable assessment method and psychoeducational tool. With the changes that managed care has thrust upon the practice of marital therapy, therapists need to develop creative interventions that not only are derived empirically, but that can be implemented swiftly and effectively. Given the negative consequences of divorce and the potential utility of this intervention, the extra energy required to apply this intervention seems worthwhile.

REFERENCES

Brody, G. H., Newbaum, E., and Forehand, R. (1988). Serial marriage: A heuristic analysis of an emerging family form. *Psychological Bulletin, 103*, 211-222.

Castro-Martin, T. and Bumpass, L. (1989). Recent trends and differentials in marital disruption. *Demography, 26*, 37-51.

Gottman, J. M. (1993a). A theory of marital dissolution and stability. *Journal of Family Psychology 7*, 57-75.

Gottman, J. M. (1993b). The roles of conflict engagement, escalation, and avoidance in marital interaction: A longitudinal view of five types of couples. *Journal of Consulting and Clinical Psychology, 61*, 6-15.

Gottman, J. M. and Krokoff, L. J. (1989). The relationship between marital interaction and marital satisfaction: A longitudinal view. *Journal of Consulting and Clinical Psychology, 57*, 47-52.

Jacobson, N. S. and Addis, M. E. (1993). Research on couples and couple therapy: What do we know? Where are we going? *Journal of Consulting and Clinical Psychology, 61*, 85-93.

Krokoff, L. J., Gottman, J. M., and Hass, S. D. (1989). Validation of a global rapid couples interaction scoring system. *Behavioral Assessment, 11*, 65-79.

Spanier, G. (1976). Measuring dyadic adjustment. *Journal of Marriage and the Family, 38*, 15-28.

Thiabaut, J. W. and Kelley, H. H. (1959). *The social psychology of groups.* New York: Wiley.

53

Symbols in Relationships

Don G. Brown

OVERVIEW

In a long-term relationship some behaviors get elevated to symbolic status; that is, they stand for something far more important to the relationship than they appear to an outsider. The power of the symbolic behavior can bring forth a strong positive or negative emotional response and the outside observer might be amazed that a simple statement or action could cause a reaction of such magnitude. The marriage and family therapist often encounters these symbolic behaviors that produce negative consequences and continue to persist in spite of therapeutic interventions, even though both partners sincerely want to change the emotional fallout of these interactions. If a divorce occurs, then the symbolic meaning of the interaction may be lost and not necessarily transferred to a new partner.

An analogy from baseball is appropriate. A very good player may fall into a slump—not performing up to standards for an extended period of time. The press has reported friction on the team, between player and manager. The team wants the player to get out of the slump, the ballplayer wants to get back to the old form, the manager tries everything in his bag of tricks, but all efforts fail. Finally a "trade" takes place—a new team, new management, new fans, new teammates. The slump ends and everyone is happy.

A marriage is not like a team sport where we can or should easily change/trade partners in order to end a set of interactions that lead to a slump. Family therapists look for other ways to change these interactions that produce marital discord and strategic family therapy has developed innovative approaches to this problem.

CASE ILLUSTRATION

The following case illustrates how a behavior becomes laden with symbolism and maintains it in spite of efforts to change. The intervention comes out of strategic therapy, but the course of therapy following the intervention is psychodynamic.

Betty and John have been married for thirty-five years and have three grown children. For the past fifteen years the marriage has been in a slump. Betty sought counseling first. John's episodic drinking created major problems for her. In therapy she revealed, for the first time, that her alcoholic father had sexually abused her as a small child. She felt angry and helpless in dealing with John's drinking, and often reverted to childlike behaviors. She had tried several things. They were now sleeping in different rooms and had developed parallel lives. When he was not drinking they would resume some normal interaction, but when he drank she would stop fixing meals, refuse to go anywhere with him, and even sing or hum when he would try to talk to her. The drinking seemed to appear when things were beginning to get better in the relationship—often it followed a good weekend. John would usually attribute it to some minor general stress.

John expressed a desire to have a better marriage and he also began therapy with me. They were seen separately and concurrently for a brief period. He, too, said that the drinking was a problem. It had affected his job in the past and he knew it could affect his future plans. He said he wanted to stop. Therapy started with a straightforward and conventional approach to staying sober. He would give up alcohol for brief periods, the relationship would improve, and a bout of drinking would send them back to their former slump. This pattern continued for several sessions. It became evident that the drinking had some symbolic meaning in the relationship. John was not unable to give it up, since he did so often. Rather he appeared unwilling to give it up.

During one session, John recounted a story about a late-night conversation with Betty. It was about a christening dress for a new grandchild. The son had refused his mother's offer of the dress (in which he had been christened) and her push to have the religious ceremony performed. The mother kept up the subtle pressure. Finally one night the son called and relented. As Betty was telling John this, for her, good news, John replied, "Well, you won—now are you happy?"

I filed this vignette away and in a later session, as John and I were discussing his drinking, I said, "You really aren't ready to give this up. If you do then Betty will win. And you feel that your drinking is the one place where she does not control your life." His smile was sudden and large—like a little boy who had been caught in a prank.

This strategic intervention would have been an appropriate one even if insight had not followed, since it would take some of the power out of the symbolism of his drinking. But in this case it was the opening of a door.

Drinking was recognized as a defensive weapon. Therapy continued, leading soon to couple work. Through Al-Anon the wife had already been learning different ways of responding to her husband.

Similar interventions reflect elements of strategic family therapy. In this case I had started with a traditional approach to outpatient substance abuse treatment—education, mild confrontation, and an encouragement to attend a twelve-step program. After a few sessions it became obvious that the episodic drinking played a major role in the marital interaction. The strategic approach opened the way to personal and relational growth.

What are the signs that a behavior pattern may have reached symbolic status? If both parties in a long-term relationship agree that they want to change the interaction, yet it persists intermittently even though therapy continues, then the family therapist might look to see if that pattern is symbolic of a deeper and more important issue in the relationship.

CONTRAINDICATIONS

This approach is not recommended in a case of chronic addiction. The long-term effects of regular substance abuse must be treated first before the marital interaction can be properly evaluated.

BIBLIOGRAPHY

Gurman, A. S. (1981). Integrative marital therapy: Toward the development of an interpersonal approach. In S. H. Budman (Ed.), *Forms of brief therapy* (pp. 427-430). New York: Guilford Press.

Madanes, C. (1981). *Strategic family therapy.* San Francisco: Jossey-Bass.

Nichols, W. C., and Everett, C. A. (1986). *Systemic family therapy—An integrative approach.* New York: Guilford Press.

Stanton, D., Todd, M., and Associates. (1982). *The family therapy of drug abuse and addiction.* New York: Guilford Press.

54

Use of Structural Family Therapy to Facilitate Adjustment Among Adolescent Leukemia Patients

Sharon Z. Johnson
Ana Ulloa Estrada

THEORETICAL RATIONALE

Recent advances in medical technology have increased the survival rates for children diagnosed with acute lymphocytic leukemia. For those who successfully complete maintenance therapy without relapse, the prognosis is good, with approximately 80 percent of patients remaining free of the disease. This has led to increased efforts aimed at understanding individual adjustment to this disease, as well as discovering interventions that facilitate adjustment in families with a member who has been diagnosed with acute lymphocytic leukemia.

An illness such as leukemia requires intensive medical management and places considerable physical, psychological, and social demands not only on the identified child patient but also on the family system. It is clear that parents of chronically ill or handicapped children experience more stress than parents of typically developing children (e.g., Wallander, Pitt, and Mellins, 1990), and that successful adjustment depends on the degree to which the family as a unit can accommodate to the major changes and demands brought about by the illness.

It is important to intervene with families with adolescent leukemia patients. Given the dramatic biological, psychological, and social changes that characterize adolescence (Feldman and Elliott, 1990), these patients are especially vulnerable (Holmbeck, Paikoff, and Brooks-Gunn, 1995). Further, despite the increased importance of peers during adolescence, the family is still considered to be the primary source of socialization and support throughout the second decade of life (e.g., Furstenberg, 1990). Adaptive family relationships may *enhance* the psychosocial well-being of a well-adjusted child (Lamborn et al., 1991) or *protect* children at risk from further difficulties (e.g., Masten, Best, and Garmezy, 1990). In contrast, less adaptive family relations may increase the vulnerability of a well-adjusted child to psychosocial dysfunction or *exacerbate* the level of psychopathology already present in an at-risk child (Cohen and Brook, 1987; Rutter, 1990).

Rolland (1994) argues that families who adjust most successfully to a child's illness are those that maintain family stability and provide a sense of continuity, while remaining flexible and adaptable to changing circumstances. Families that function in a chaotic manner or who rigidly strive to maintain their pre-illness roles within the family often have difficulties. Likewise, families who are enmeshed, allowing the illness to become the central focus of the family, or families who function in a distant manner by ignoring the demands of the illness and the need to provide individual support, compromise their adjustment.

Developmental periods such as adolescence have unique psychosocial developmental tasks that require different and sometimes conflicting changes from family members, particularly when faced with a chronic illness. For example, parents' increased attempts to physically care for their child in hopes of maintaining remission may conflict with the adolescent's developmental need to individuate and achieve an autonomous relationship with their parents. This creates something of a paradox for the family; families must strive to support the emerging autonomy of family members in the face of a pull toward mutual dependency and caretaking (Rolland, 1994).

In our experience, the structural approach to family therapy has been successful in treating families who are faced with adjustment issues brought about by the diagnosis of adolescent leukemia. Developed by Salvador Minuchin in the 1970s, this method of treatment has been used most often in treating structural malalignments in low socioeconomic families, in families of divorce, and in the treatment of families with a member diagnosed with anorexia nervosa or drug addiction (Nichols and Schwartz, 1995).

THE INTERVENTION

The goal of treatment is to predict and ameliorate rigid adjustment patterns in families with an adolescent leukemia patient toward creating more adaptive ways of family functioning and interacting. The therapist begins working with families by joining with them, in an effort to convey acceptance and an understanding of the way they function. Families with an adolescent diagnosed with leukemia are often overwhelmed and worried, and report a sense of hopelessness about the future of their child. In addition, some families may feel shame about having to obtain professional psychosocial advice. Successful joining occurs when family members are first reassured that seeking professional advice is a common occurrence. In addition, the strengths of the family for their efforts in coping with the illness should be highlighted. It is also important that the therapist be viewed by the family as a positive resource rather than an adversary, and the therapist must take care not to reinforce the family's feelings of shame and guilt (Rolland, 1994).

The therapist assesses the family structure by including all family members in the evaluation. The therapist attempts to interact with family members in a relational and nonblaming manner with the intent of identifying problematic relationships and desired changes. Rolland (1994) has identified a number of relevant assessment questions: How has the family needed to reorganize itself with the onset of the illness? How have each family member's roles changed? How much responsibility does the affected member have in terms of his/her illness? How does the family feel about this amount of responsibility, and are there other family members who share in the responsibilities? What are the expectations of each family member, and do these fit with what has been recommended by health professionals?

Once the desired changes have been identified, the therapist works to restructure family relationships by encouraging members to bring difficult or problematic issues into therapy. Through the use of enactments, family members are instructed to discuss a difficult issue while the therapist observes the family process. The therapist intervenes to modify maladaptive structures by establishing hierarchies, defining boundaries, and realigning family members to promote growth and flexibility.

For example, a common problem faced by families with an adolescent with leukemia is establishing reasonable developmental goals and expectations. Parents are particularly fearful of the future and are often resistant to the adolescent's emerging independence, frequently creating an overly protective, if not smothering, parent-child relationship. Often the adolescent feels invincible, and rebels by failing to comply with his/her medical routine (e.g., refusing to attend treatment sessions, or refusing medications). In response, parents often become even more intrusive and protective of the adolescent. In this situation, the therapist would underscore these conflicting patterns, and challenge the adolescent's and family members' expectations (invincibility and mortality, respectively) and behaviors (medical noncompliance and infantilization, respectively) in order to foster awareness and encourage new ways of relating to each other.

The Family's Response to Treatment

In our experience, families respond quite favorably to such structural interventions. Often an illness such as leukemia is associated with a stigma that prevents family members from communicating effectively. As a result, families often strive to maintain pre-illness roles rather than accommodating to the new demands created by the illness. Families are often relieved to discuss issues that are often feared, and welcome the opportunity to learn more effective ways of interacting with each other.

Contraindications

Although Minuchin was dedicated to treating ethnic minority families (Nichols and Schwartz, 1995), the described structural family therapy interventions may not be easily applied to certain ethnic minority families in which a member has been diagnosed with leukemia or another chronic illness. For example, it is not considered pathological for Italian families, or families of many other ethnic groups, to gather around the ill person in what may appear to be an overly involved or enmeshed manner. Family expectations related to medical illnesses in children and adolescents are culturally derived and can result in a range of behaviors and expressions that may be considered both appropriate and highly supportive. Thus, it is critical that the therapist is aware of cultural differences and variations in a family's response to illness, and be able to make informed distinctions along the continuum of normal and maladaptive family patterns and ways of relating.

REFERENCES

Cohen, P. and Brook, J. (1987). Family factors related to the persistence of psychopathology in childhood and adolescence. *Psychiatry, 50,* 332-345.

Feldman, S. S. and Elliott, G. R. (Eds.) (1990). *At the threshold: The developing adolescent.* Cambridge, MA: Harvard University Press.

Furstenberg, F. F. (1990). Coming of age in a changing family system. In S. S. Feldman and G. L. Elliott (Eds.), *At the threshold: The developing adolescent* (pp. 147-170). Cambridge, MA: Harvard University Press.

Holmbeck, G. N., Paikoff, R., and Brooks-Gunn, J. (1995). Parenting adolescents. In M. Bornstein (Ed.), *Handbook of parenting.* Hillsdale, NJ: Erlbaum.

Lamborn, S. D., Mounts, N. S., Steinberg, L., and Dornbusch, S. M. (1991). Patterns of competence and adjustment among adolescents from authoritative, authoritarian, indulgent, and neglectful families. *Child Development, 62,* 1049-1065.

Masten, A. S., Best, K. M., and Garmezy, N. (1990). Resilience and development: Contributions from the study of children who overcome adversity. *Development and Psychopathology, 2,* 425-444.

Nichols, M. P. and Schwartz, R. C. (1995). *Family therapy: Concepts and methods.* New York: Allyn and Bacon.

Rolland, J. S. (1994). *Families, illness, and disability.* New York: Basic Books.

Rutter, M. (1990). Psychosocial resilience and protective mechanisms. In J. Rolf, A. S. Masten, D. Cicchetti, K. H. Nuechterlein, and S. Weintraub (Eds.), *Risk and protective factors in the development of psychopathology* (pp. 181-214). New York: Cambridge University Press.

Wallander, J. L., Pitt, L. C., and Mellins, C. A. (1990). Child functional independence and maternal psychosocial stress as risk factors threatening adaptation in mothers of physically or sensorially handicapped children. *Journal of Consulting and Clinical Psychology, 58,* 818-824.

55

"We versus It"

Jan Osborn

INTRODUCTION

Individual issues and external events have the potential to become wedges in the couple relationship. Once a place of solace and comfort, the relationship can become a source of tension and thus something to be avoided. While the couple may have a sense of togetherness in some areas of their lives, they become polarized around these issues or events and adopt a toxic "me versus you" stance.

Through the use of experiential techniques, the meaning of the issue or event can be shifted for both members of the couple, while increasing the understanding of one's own and each other's position, thus decreasing reactivity and polarization. A together stance of "we versus it" (or ideally "we dealing with it") is thus established. This allows the couple to talk about once highly toxic issues without attacking one another. Rather, feeling supported, they can work collaboratively against the issue instead of against each other.

While experiential techniques can be easy to use and are often helpful in accessing emotion, they have a much more powerful impact if the therapist has a clear theoretical understanding of what she is attempting to accomplish. Therefore, this article will first outline the tenets of experiential theory that were instrumental in developing the use of this intervention. This will be followed by an explanation of the intervention and a case example.

EXPERIENTIAL THEORY

The focus of experiential therapy is on emotional experience rather than insight or cognitive knowledge as a source of change (Whitaker and Bumberry, 1988), although insight is often a result of change. Believing that most communication occurs on an affective level that is often unconscious and nonverbal, experiential therapy deals with the representational system beneath verbal communication, and thus takes place at the level of living, not thinking, talking, or reasoning. Emotions play an important part in family functioning and are honored and encouraged in the therapeutic process. Struggle and passion are important components of growth and the experiential therapist works to foster an atmosphere in which struggle and passion are heightened so that growth can occur (Whitaker and Bumberry, 1988).

Experiences occur on two levels, the individual or internal level and the external or relational level. The internal process of the individual determines how an event will be experienced. This internal process, however, is affected by external processes such as witnessing how others experience the event. Thus, experiences are created through relationships with other people. The family system is the main external context for experiences that develop the individual's internal thoughts, feelings, and behaviors. Children learn to define themselves in relation to others based on the experiences they have in their families. These experiential learnings are passed from generation to generation and enhanced by an individual's tendency to look for characteristics in a mate that are either familiar or diametrically opposed to those of the family of origin (Satir, 1983).

Families of procreation become subcultures of each mate's family of origin, and are in a constant state of struggle and negotiation. This struggle occurs through symbolic experience. Dysfunction occurs when the struggle over whose family of origin the new family will use as a model is not successfully negotiated. Families are unsuccessful, according to experiential therapists, when their views are oversimplified and they are locked into a rigid view of reality. This limits all the other varied and wonderful possibilities, and emotional energy is blocked. Thus, the central issue in therapy is expanding the significance of experience and broadening perspectives. The therapist works at complicating the family members' oversimplification and expanding alternative ways to think about the family and be in the world (Whitaker and Bumberry, 1988).

Bringing family experiences alive in therapy exposes the representational system underneath cognition as these experiences are an external expression of family members' internal lives. By bringing the symbolism alive in the therapy room, blockages to the free flow of emotions can be removed and perspectives can be expanded. Because dysfunction occurs when the expression of emotional intensity is blocked, for family members to experience health, they must have open access to feelings.

As Satir (1983) suggests, individuals often defend against the emotions elicited by shifts in meaning. Through recognition of one's own meaning-making process and defenses each is better able to understand self and other and move from the pain of blaming each other to the pain of recognition of one's own internal process (Satir, 1983). Each member of the couple can then attend to her/his own pain, while not interpreting the other's expression of pain as an attack. They can soothe themselves and each other and work collaboratively.

THE INTERVENTION

The power of experiential techniques comes not from the intervention itself but from the process. Thus, the intervention itself is simple. The difficulty comes in assisting the clients to push through their defensiveness and tendency to blame and hang in with the process. This is less difficult if the client has hope that the process will lead to less pain. The therapist may need to hold that hope for the clients until they have the faith themselves.

In this particular intervention the couple sit next to each other facing an empty chair, symbolically representing the "we versus it" stance. They are asked to place the toxic issue in the chair. One at a time each describes the attributes of the issue as it takes on life (color, size, etc.) and then tells the thing how s/he feels about it. After they have done this each is assisted to talk about how the exercise was and how it was to watch the partner. Time and time again I have watched couples be amazed at their own and each other's responses to the thing in the chair. Almost always a common ground is found, creating the foundation of "we-ness." The couple is then invited to talk together about how they can face the thing together, as opposed to having the thing between them. This process can be much more clearly experienced through a case example.

CASE EXAMPLE

Sarah and Marie came in for couples treatment, troubled that though they loved each other very much they had vicious fights. Each was in individual therapy working to resolve traumatic past histories, and each was very reactive to the other. Marie was having great difficulty with the way Sarah was treating her, which she attributed to Sarah's abusive past. Sarah agreed that some of her behavior was related to her history, and would also get defensive when it was brought up because she felt that Marie was being critical of her and how quickly she was moving in her individual therapy. They each saw the behavior of the other through their own lenses of hurt and inadequacy, thus seeing the behavior as proof that they were not worthy of love, and could never be good enough to receive love. Cognitive understanding that the other was acting out of her hurt place and protecting herself was not enough to shift the meaning of the behavior. Though both were suffering and wanted desperately to be helped by the other and to help the other, they were not able to do so.

In an attempt to establish a "we against it" stance, Sarah's sexual abuse was placed in the chair. Sarah went first and described the abuse and rage associated with it as blackness and evil. She yelled at the abuse and told it that she hated it, she did not want it to be part of her, and that it was destroying her relationship with Marie by causing her to act badly and avoid closeness out of the fear that it had instilled in her. She yelled through sobs and listed for the abuse all the ways it had robbed her of things (spontaneity with sex for example), thus robbing her relationship with Marie. Later, when discussing the experience, she cried and said that she was so angry that she was left with the impacts of her abuse and she had to clean up the mess in her life that her perpetrator created.

Marie stated that she felt much freer to scream at the abuse because she had watched Sarah do so. Her focus was much more on how angry she was at the abuse for causing the woman she loved such pain. She, too, placed the blame with the perpetrator for interfering with their lovemaking and told him that she wanted him out of their bed. Marie stated that it was a great relief to yell at the abuse. Before the exercise she had said that she felt that discussing the impact of the abuse was taken as criticism of Sarah for having been affected. She also stated that she was very moved to hear Sarah talk because she had no idea that Sarah was so pained by her own behavior or its impact on the relationship. Sarah struggled to accept Marie's compassion for her because of her shame that the abuse was a part of her. The two then "ganged up on the abuse" and together yelled at it and told it how wrong and bad *it* was. They then, for the first time, were able to grieve together the impact the abuse had had on Sarah and the relationship. They were eventually able to discuss their sadness at impacts that were previously toxic to talk about, such as their sex life, without Sarah feeling attacked. They developed a "we against it" stance. The homework was then to remember the "we" when "it" appeared to be getting in the way.

Through the exercise Sarah also became clear that as much as she did not want the abuse to be a part of her, it was. Thus, she would now have to take responsibility for her behavior. The "we versus it" stance became a valuable resource to her. She was able to stop her old ways of coping (which included shutting Marie out) and ask for help. Rather than picking a fight with Marie, she was able to put the abuse in the chair (actually it was usually the tissue box), and fight with it instead, sometimes inviting Marie to help her.

This couple found this experience so helpful that many other issues were placed in the chair and similarly addressed, including Marie's past abuse issues. They have been able to adopt a "we versus it" stance on many issues and when they find themselves blaming each other, one or the other will say, "We have to be together on this, put it in the chair," and they take themselves through the exercise at home. Each is still struggling through resolving family-of-origin issues, but they have become allies in the healing process. They are significantly less reactive to each other; thus the frequency, intensity, and duration of their fights are greatly reduced, while compassion and understanding are greatly increased.

CONTRAINDICATIONS

Both members of the couple must be able to think abstractly and work safely in metaphor. Thus, if either of the clients is thought disordered or intellectually challenged, the therapists would need to assess the clients' individual capabilities to both tolerate and understand the intervention. Systemically, this intervention is designed to bring couples together as "we." Thus, if the couple is in the process of deciding whether to separate, this intervention is not recommended. Also, if the couple has a history of violence, this intervention should be used with caution.

CONCLUSION

Both individual and systemic change come out of a shift in meaning, belief, or attitude and this can both result from and lead to a different emotional experience of an event. A cognitive shift in meaning may lead to a different experience, or a different experience may lead to a shift in meaning. Because we take in information according to our belief system, if our beliefs change we can see things differently. If we see things differently, we will experience them differently. Similarly, a change in experience may bring about a change in meaning or belief. Once the event is experienced differently, it can never be experienced in quite the same way again.

The safety of the therapeutic relationship can provide an environment in which people can risk being honest with themselves about their unacknowledged beliefs and can have a different experience. If this can happen within the couple relationship, and each is able to be open and honest about his/her own beliefs and meanings and understand those of the other, then systemic change can occur within the relationship.

REFERENCES

Satir, V. (1983). *Conjoint family therapy.* Palo Alto, CA: Science and Behavior Books.
Whitaker, C. A. and Bumberry, W. M. (1988). *Dancing with the family: A symbolic-experiential approach.* New York: Brunner/Mazel.

56

The Many Colors of Divorce

Pasha D. Blundo

Structural family therapy addresses the necessity of focusing on the reorganization of adult relationships after a divorce (Minuchin and Fishman, 1981). Rather than relating to each other as ex-spouses, adults should begin to formulate their relationship as coparents. If therapists think of the parents (residential and nonresidential) as a team working in the best interests of the child, it should follow that both adults should be included in the therapy process. Often, the idea of these sessions is met with hesitancy. Encouraging the residential parent to invite the ex-spouse requires creative interventions. The following intervention is one I have used to communicate to parents the complexities of life after divorce from their child's point of view.

Rather than creating a genogram to map the structure of the family, I prefer three-dimensional techniques. Based on an image of what is going on in the family, a sculpture of relationships can be created (Satir and Baldwin, 1983). Combining the sculpture with play therapy has proven useful for me, especially when working with young children. Rather than sculpt using the people in the therapy room (which may exclude the nonresidential parent), I ask the children to use Play-Doh to represent people. During this intervention, the adults in the room are to watch and not give suggestions or comments to the child. First, I ask the child to pick a color to represent Father (including him first immediately gives the relationship priority). The Play-Doh is shaped into a ball and is placed on the floor. Next, I ask the child to pick a different color for Mother. Another ball is formed and placed on the floor. The child is then asked to form a ball combining the two colors used for Mother and Father. I explain to the child that this represents him/her, as he/she is one half of each parent. The child places his/her own ball on the floor next to those for the parents. I note the amount of distance or closeness between balls to assess relationship patterns. If either parent has remarried, I will ask the child to form more balls representing stepparents, using colors different from ones already chosen. Once again, I notice the boundaries that may be apparent between members. Finally, I will ask the child to make balls for other members of the family, using the colors to represent relationships. For example, a half-sister would be the color of the child's stepparent and biological parent, stepsiblings take on the colors of their biological parents, and so on. If the child is very attached to the stepparent, he/she may want to have three or four colors in the ball. I encourage this combination, but continue to stress the primary formation of the ball—the colors of the biological mother and father.

After the balls have been formed, we talk about placing the balls in their respective homes. It is crucial to watch the process of the nonresidential parent being taken outside of the home where the majority of members live. Visitation schedules and holiday rituals can also be played out by having the child move his/her ball chaotically around the room according to the situation described. At this point in the intervention, the child is asked to place the balls according to how they see the family. I explain that balls placed close together can mean that the members should spend more time together, while balls far apart mean that those members do not get along well at all. More often than not, the child places him/herself in the middle of the mother and the nonresidential father. Typically, there is a moment when the child sits confused, wondering whether to place hostile parents farther apart because they always fight, or closer together so that the child can see both more often. The child can describe through the sculpture the feeling of being torn between parents and caught in the middle without expressing this directly to the adults present in the room.

Continuing to use the Play-Doh, the adults are then asked to determine options for change by moving the balls around the floor. In one incident, a mother who refused to allow the nonresidential father in the therapy room placed her and her ex-husband far apart on the floor. Her child, a nine-year-old boy, screamed, "Hey! That's not fair to put my dad way over there!" He ripped his Play-Doh ball in half and placed one side with Mom and one with Dad. Interestingly enough, the broken Play-Doh ball next to Mom had some of the Dad color in it. I used the opportunity to explain to Mom that no matter how much she did not want to cooperate with the father, his inclusion in the boy's life was inevitable. Cooperation between the parents was the only way to keep from tearing the boy in half. Mom later agreed to a session with the nonresidential father and their son.

In their book *The Difficult Divorce*, Issacs, Montalvo, and Abelsohn (1986) describe their structural approach to the divorcing family. One main principle of their theory is that therapy must be conducted with all subsystems in the family. It is suggested that therapists complete individual, parent-child, and parent-parent sessions before attempting a family session. Likewise, assessment of family subsystems is crucial to the timing of this intervention. A potentially hostile session can be planned and controlled and should not be rushed. Therapists may find it useful to repeat the intervention in separate parent-child sessions in order to communicate the importance of coparenting to both parties.

REFERENCES

Issacs, M., Montalvo, B., and Abelsohn, D. (1986). *The difficult divorce*. New York: Basic Books.

Minuchin, S. and Fishman, H. (1981). *Family therapy techniques*. Cambridge, MA: Harvard University Press.

Satir, V. and Baldwin, M. (1983). *Satir step by step*. Palo Alto, CA: Science and Behavior Books.

57

On a Scale from One to Ten . . .

Shannon B. Dermer

Solution-focused therapists utilize scaling questions to draw upon client perceptions of the intensity of situations or behaviors, provide a means for tracking progress, create expectations for change, clarify goals, and introduce circular thinking. However, at first glance scaling questions such as, "On a scale from one to ten, with one being problems at their worst and ten being no problems at all, where would your put your problems?" may appear to be dull, static questions that are too behavioral for many family therapists. Fortunately, with a little tinkering these questions can become an integral part of any imaginative therapy.

Modified scaling questions establish a source for meaningful metaphors and externalizing discussions (via narrative approaches). Because this process symbolizes powerful themes across a continuum of meaning, I refer to it as *allegorical scaling*. It establishes, at once, a tangible representation of client beliefs and a springboard for abstract thinking. Allegorical scaling is a creative process that emphasizes joining and therefore is enjoyable for both clients and therapists. The approach works with a wide range of people because it integrates the respectful manner narrative therapists employ in externalizing conversations. It draws upon meaningful concepts for the client, uses his or her language, and is aware of observer bias in deciding what works or does not work for families. In other words, the recipe for successful use of allegorical scaling includes a dash of creativity, a pinch of client language, and a cup full of assessment, all mixed with a good dose of careful conceptualization.

CASE EXAMPLE

Teri, age thirty-five, contacted the Family Center because she stated that she was "in love with an asshole." During sessions we discussed what she considered her strengths as well as her problematic areas. She identified her sense of humor, intelligence, and caring as sources of strength and her "codependent" behavior with men as her biggest problem. Teri described herself as feeling like a puppy dog who waits around to lick her boyfriend's face and fetch his slippers for him. When asked to, she named these feelings and behaviors "Lassie" because she felt like she was always waiting for Timmy to fall in the well so she could be useful and save him in order to get a pat on the head. We spent some time describing the associated feelings and behaviors that go along with being Lassie. In addition, we explored this theme along a continuum, designating anchor points along the way. (For purposes of writing, I will call these anchor points *concept assemblies* because they are interlocking ideas, beliefs, and actions grouped together for reference points). I asked her to give names to the concept assemblies (again I do not use this term in therapy), which she labeled Lolly and Cujo respectively.

APPLICATION

Each concept assembly is placed equidistant on a nine-point scale. Lolly is placed in the middle because it represents a balance between the more dissimilar concept assemblies of Lassie and Cujo. Conversations revolve around the continuum using each concept assembly as a point of reference. The client is then asked to mark where she would put herself on the scale overall, where she would like to be, and where she is today. Teri decided that she is usually closer to Lassie, but she has a tendency to vacillate between the two outer points. However, when I asked her where she would put herself on this day, she laughed, "Well, I've been good today. I've pretty much been *Lolly*gagging around!"

CONCLUSION

Allegorical scaling encompasses all the client-friendly assumptions of solution-focused therapy while highlighting affect and integrating aspects of cognitive and narrative therapy. This process tracks problems and alternatives, and connects past, present, and future behaviors. In addition, it can be used to emphasize the connectedness of life by having an individual or family think about where other people would place them on the scale or how they may move closer or farther from concept assemblies in certain situations. Basically, allegorical scaling establishes an arena to talk about difficult things in a meaningful, nonthreatening manner, but does not bypass personal responsibility. Not only can the scale be a source for externalizing discussions, but it also enhances joining by providing a common allegorical language for therapist and clients. It provides a basis for serious conversations as well as playful ones, as when Teri joked that she was lollygagging around.

There are no contraindications to using this approach; however, there are potential pitfalls. Therapists must be cognizant of using language in externalizing that promotes personal responsibility and choices. For example, this approach is appropriate for use with violence, but therapists should be alert to clients who try to use allegorical scaling as a means to bypass responsibility. In addition, when constructing the scale, make sure families externalize patterns and not specific people (i.e., do not let them name a concept assembly after someone participating in therapy). Names given to concept assemblies should be chosen based on their meaning, descriptive attributes, and affective components, not as an insult to someone participating in therapy. Finally, allegorical scaling can be utilized during stabilized time periods with clients who experience psychotic episodes; however, patterns within the clients' lives, not the actual voices or images, should be externalized. Because of the collaborative style of this approach I have not come across any contraindications, but red flags certainly appear that caution therapists to proceed with care.

In summary, allegorical scaling encompasses strongly held themes and places them within a context that fosters nonthreatening conversations around a continuum of central themes. Although I jokingly referred to the recipe for successful use of allegorical scaling, it is not be used in a cookbook manner. If employed merely as a technique, it diminishes many of the aspects that make it a respectful, useful process. Allegorical scaling must be accompanied by a genuine sense of curiosity and esteem for families.

58

Genograms in a Multicultural Perspective

Ana Ulloa Estrada
Penny Haney

Genograms are family-tree diagrams that record information about family members and their relationships over at least three generations. They provide a quick gestalt of complex family patterns, stimulate clinical hypotheses linking the clinical problem to the family context, and track the evolution of the presenting problem and family relationships over time. Because a comprehensive discussion of the origins, principles, and clinical applications of genograms is well beyond the scope of this chapter, the reader is referred to McGoldrick and Gerson (1985) for more on genograms. The purpose of the present article is to outline and demonstrate with brief case examples how genograms can be used in a multicultural (MC) context.

THEORETICAL UNDERPINNING OF GENOGRAMS AND THE MULTICULTURAL METAFRAMEWORK

Murray Bowen (1976) is consistently credited with the conceptual development of genograms. Bowen hypothesized that family patterns of functioning, relationships, and structure continue or alternate from one generation to the next, a pattern he called multigenerational transmission. In this theory, problems and symptoms reflect a system's adaptation to its total context at a given moment in time. The adaptive efforts of members in the system reverberate throughout many levels of the system—from the biological to the intrapsychic, interpersonal, nuclear and extended family, community, culture, and beyond (e.g., Bowen, 1976).

Bowen's (1976) development of the genograms reflects his fundamental belief that family problems derive normative and emotional meaning in relation to their *historical* context. Analogously, the Multicultural (MC) Metaframework presupposes that families are understood in relation to

269

their *sociocultural* context (Breunlin, Schwartz, and MacKune-Karrer, 1992). The MC Metaframework incorporates the sociocultural context of both unique (culture-specific) and similar (intercultural and universal) meanings that define the family and contribute to the rules, roles, and expectations for family members by framing sociocultural context into two levels. The first level, cultural transition, includes historical/generational sequences (cultural evolution), and immigration/acculturation processes. Historical/generational sequences and immigration/acculturation evolve over time, and influence the second level of sociocultural context: economics, education, ethnicity, religion, gender, age, race, minority/majority status, and regional background. We add three other important sociocultural contexts: spirituality, sexual preference, and physical challenges.

Because these sociocultural contexts define the family, they can guide systemic interventions. We propose that incorporating genograms into this multicultural perspective (i.e., recording sociocultural information into a genogram, a multicultural genogram) can result in a more meaningful understanding of the family, and, subsequently, more effective intervention.

SPECIFIC USES OF MC GENOGRAMS

In their text on genograms, McGoldrick and Gerson (1985) outline the clinical uses of the genogram. We expand their discussion by outlining four areas in which MC genograms can be particularly useful: (1) engaging the family, (2) assessing the family in a multicultural context, (3) reframing and detoxifying family issues, and (4) assessing the cultural fit between the therapist and the family.

Engaging the Family

The MC genogram interview can be used to demonstrate an interest in the family system, to engage the family in treatment, and to begin to build a therapeutic relationship with the family. It can provide a less threatening and more structured atmosphere during the first sessions of family therapy, facilitating an alliance between the family and therapist around a meaningful, familial, sociocultural sharing of information. Yet, it still allows the therapist to obtain access to complex emotional information and experiences associated with the presenting problem, and often in a more effective manner. The graphic representation efficiently captures meaningful, sociocultural information in a visual, concrete way that can be expanded and updated as the family reveals or becomes aware of more information.

Take, for example, a Hispanic, single-parent family who presents for therapy because of concern over the eldest daughter, age fourteen, who is five months pregnant. The use of a genogram can engage the entire family in a discussion of the present and past family structure and context. All members, even the youngest children, can contribute to the discussion, providing their own perspectives of their family's sociocultural context. The pregnancy is addressed in some detail, but is embedded within the entire task. The opportunity to share meaningful information that captures their entire (i.e., within a sociocultural context) sense of self and family leaves the family feeling understood, connected to each other and the therapist, and hopeful about the process of therapy.

Assessing the Family in an MC Context

The MC genogram assesses a range of critical family issues within the larger sociocultural context of the family. The therapist can begin to think multiculturally in assessing strengths and conflicts, hypothesizing about the presenting problems, and planning interventions with the family that consider its complex and evolving circumstances. Simple questions can lead to important family issues. For example, when the question, "How did you two meet?" leads to embarrassment or concealment for a first-generation Hindu couple who were reluctantly married by an arrangement between their parents, or the question, "Where does your son live?" opens up a dialogue with a lesbian parent who is cut off from her children, important information is conceptualized in light of the presenting problem.

The MC genogram task can also help shed light on more subtle or complex sociocultural aspects of the family that may be contributing to the problem or constraining a solution to the problem. For example, a question about differing levels of acculturation posed to a highly distressed American-Mexican couple who were seeking marital therapy revealed a tension surrounding the generational status and acculturation levels of the partners. When the therapist asked the wife about her ethnic background and identity, the husband replied, "She thinks she's white." The tension in this couple, related to her higher level of acculturation, increased independence, and desire for a more egalitarian relationship, was subsequently revealed as a threat to the couple's cultural identity and stability.

Therapists collecting MC genograms, then, use the information to continually develop, test, and revise clinical hypotheses based upon an emerging understanding of the family. The MC genogram can also help the therapist understand the family's conceptualization of the problem and provide a forum in which to listen to, address, and validate their conceptualizations. Families frequently come into treatment with a clear and, at times, rigid sense of the problem and about who (e.g., identified patient) or what (e.g., family pattern) needs to be changed. Understanding the family's conceptualization of the problem has important implications for working with the family and/or their potential resistance, as the next section demonstrates.

Reframing and Detoxifying Family Issues

When the family's perspective becomes resistant to change or to other ways of perceiving the behavior or situation, MC genograms can offer the family a fresh perspective, either spontaneously during the genogram task or through the therapist's questioning and input. In these ways, the MC genograms can be an effective tool for reframing family behavior and relationships across time and for normalizing or detoxifying the family's perception of itself.

The genogram provides many opportunities to do so. For example, in many non-English speaking, newly immigrated families, the eldest child, particularly the eldest male, is frequently responsible for the translation of English for the parents and grandparents. Plotting out the family genogram can highlight the importance and influence of the acculturation process on this behavior. This can normalize the experience for the child, who may be feeling burdened by the responsibility and feeling different from his/her peers. Likewise, it could normalize the behavior for the parents, who may have difficulty with the child being in a more adult/parental role. In the example of the Hispanic family described previously, discussing the pregnancy within the larger task of the MC genogram allows the family an opportunity to step back from the tension and intensity of the situation. While the issue of the pregnancy is no less important an issue, the atmosphere is detoxified, creating a context more conducive to intervention.

Reframing can occur when new information discovered during the MC genogram task provides both therapist and family with increased knowledge. This knowledge allows the therapist to interpret for the family a different meaning of the behavior within the sociocultural contexts of the system and enables family members to view themselves in a more positive light. Discussing, and often cocreating, alternative conceptions of the family's experience opens up new possibilities for change in the future.

Cultural Fit Between Therapist and Family

A common misconception is that only ethnic and racial minority therapists have cultural backgrounds. *All* therapists have a rich cultural heritage and background that can inform and guide their work. Furthermore, many of the therapist's sociocultural contexts can overlap with those of the family, even if therapist and family have different cultural backgrounds. At the same time, given advanced levels of training and education, most therapists belong to the majority or privileged society, rendering them more likely to be vulnerable to potential blind spots in understanding other cultural and ethnic groups.

MC genograms offer a means for therapists to come to understand the similarities and differences between their own and the family's cultural backgrounds. Similarities or matching between the sociocultural contexts of the family and the therapist can provide a strong beginning toward building a therapeutic relationship. Differences in sociocultural backgrounds and experiences of the therapist and family can expand and enrich respective views. Both similarities and differences can offer new hypotheses about the constraints maintaining the presenting problem. Furthermore, the increased knowledge gained about the family's sociocultural context can also reduce the likelihood of therapist blind spots.

For example, a Mormon couple seeking therapy for their marital problems and a Catholic therapist may share some similarities because both parties have a religious background. Doing an MC genogram may highlight the similarities in that the therapist may be more able to understand and align with the couple around the importance of a religious connection as a fundamental foundation of their marriage. The MC genogram task, however, would also provide an avenue for the therapist to obtain more information and clarity about the couple's particular alignment with the Mormon church, the history of that alignment, and the manifestation of the alignment in their marital interactions. The increased knowledge of both the similarities and differences can help the therapist avoid assuming that he or she understands the complexities of the couple's religious connection because of the shared importance in both the therapist and couple's lives or assuming that the differences between the Mormon and Catholic faiths preclude any similarities.

CONTRAINDICATIONS

While the MC genogram offers an effective and meaningful way to understand, assess, intervene, and align with a family, there are situations in which postponing or refraining from using this task is appropriate. Some families may have difficulty with this task if discussing family history and/or secrets is countercultural. For these families, the information typically discussed during an MC genogram task may include family history never before discussed with the children or information about a spouse's family of origin that may not have been shared with the other spouse. Therapists should describe the MC genogram task to the client and indicate their belief in its value, yet provide the family with an opportunity to postpone or refrain from the task if they feel extremely uncomfortable with it. The family's reaction to the task alone may provide valuable clinical information.

The MC genogram task should be also postponed or eliminated if it seems to make little sense to the family and/or to the therapist. In some cases, families may be unable or unwilling to see their presenting problem as part of a larger sociocultural context. Or, families may be particularly sensitive to questions regarding ethnic and cultural background, particularly if the therapist is of another culture. These families may need additional time in therapy to begin to do so.

In other instances, the family's presenting problems may render the task inappropriate, or at least better off postponed. For example, a family seeking treatment for their son's increasingly aggressive, violent, and dangerous behavior may need some immediate intervention to reduce the crisis situation. The MC genogram task may be inappropriate as it would interfere with implementing an immediate plan for reducing the behavior. Other problems may not be as critically urgent, but may be so emotionally laden for the family that they are unable to meaningfully engage in the task. They may perceive the task as unrelated to their immediate concerns and as hindering intervention for their presenting problems.

The essential aspect of these contraindications is that the therapist should be sensitive to the family's presenting problems and potential response to the MC genogram task. While the MC genogram is an efficient, meaningful, and productive task, its benefits are limited if the task is overwhelming or meaningless to the family, or if the clinical context renders it inappropriate. In these instances, the MC genogram can be postponed to a more appropriate time, or alternative ways of engaging, assessing, or intervening with the family around their sociocultural context can be used.

Therapy presents a rich opportunity to expand the family's and therapist's views and life situation, and it is important to enter the therapeutic domain with an open yet informed view of all sociocultural contexts. Curiosity and respect concerning the family's sociocultural experiences, their descriptors (including the language they use), and their family theories or explanations are the best tools therapists have for working with families from various sociocultural backgrounds. For the reasons elaborated in this paper, we offer the MC genogram as an effective, meaningful, and productive manner in which to gather this information. Furthermore, consistent with Hardy and Laszloffy (1995), we encourage therapists to examine their own sociocultural background and to seek out training opportunities to obtain the requisite MC knowledge and skills to effectively address the therapeutic needs of an ever-increasing number of culturally diverse families. Therapists may want to make their own MC genograms prior to using this task in therapy in order to understand the context of the task for their clients and to increase their awareness of their own sociocultural context.

REFERENCES

Breunlin, D. C., Schwartz, R. C., and MacKune-Karrer, B. M. (1992). *Metaframeworks: Transcending the models of family therapy*. San Francisco: Jossey-Bass.

Bowen, M. (1976). Theory in the practice of psychotherapy. In P. J. Guerin (Ed.), *Family therapy: Theory and practice*. New York: Gardner Press.

Hardy, K. V. and Laszloffy, T. A. (1995). The cultural genogram: Key to training culturally competent family therapists. *Journal of Marriage and Family Therapy, 21*(3), 227-237.

McGoldrick, M. and Gerson, R. (1985). *Genograms in family assessment*. New York: W. W. Norton.

59

Using Art to Aid the Process of Externalization

Thomas D. Carlson

TARGETED POPULATION

This intervention is designed to help both clients and therapists involved in the process of Narrative therapy (White and Epston, 1990). Narrative therapy places an enormous emphasis on both clients' and therapists' abilities to express themselves verbally. This may make the process difficult for many clients. Therefore, this intervention is targeted for those clients who have difficulty expressing themselves in therapy and is especially useful with adolescents.

THEORETICAL FOUNDATION

Narrative therapy assumes that as people go through their lives they form dominant stories about themselves and their lives. These stories become the basis of their identities. Problems develop as people adopt stories that are impoverishing (White and Epston, 1990). The driving force behind Narrative therapy is the principle of externalization (White, 1995). Externalization is the process of enabling people to rewrite the dominant stories in their lives. Three stages are involved: (1) determine the client's dominant story, including the perceived problem; (2) externalize the problem; (3) help the client find alternate stories that may be more empowering; and (4) help the client present this new story to an audience.

INTERVENTION

Since the interventions within this model are language-based, some clients may have difficulty engaging in externalizing conversations. To enhance the opportunities for externalizing conversations with these clients, I have found art therapy techniques extremely helpful.

When clients are having difficulty expressing their stories, I have found it helpful to have them draw a self-portrait, a view of themselves. This visual picture gives the therapist and client a very powerful tool in assessing the dominant story of the client's identity; a drawing may reveal certain aspects of self that the client is unable to describe in words.

The process of coming up with the appropriate externalization can be difficult when relying solely on language. Typically, to help clients externalize problems, the therapist constantly engages in "externalizing conversation" (White, 1995, p. 41). Using externalizing conversation means that the therapist refers to the problem as "it" rather than as residing in the client. Once the client and therapist have come to some agreement about what the problem is, the therapist can then refer to it with a label such as "anger." To externalize the problem, the therapist asks questions such as, "How is it that anger tempts you to follow its lead?" This type of questioning allows the client the opportunity to remove the problem from his or her own identity and in so doing puts them in a new position to fight against the problem.

Since people have a tendency to view themselves as the problem, a self-portrait is helpful in revealing to the therapist the extent to which less verbal clients have internalized the problem. The self-portrait may also help the therapist and client define the problem that is externalized.

As therapy progresses and clients begin to change their relationship to the problem, clients can be asked to redraw their self-portrait. This is an effective tool for the client in redefining their relationship to the problem and for the therapist to use in assessing the externalizing process. As the client begins using externalizing language, these new drawings should reflect this change.

Example of Client Response

Karen was having difficulty expressing her story. I asked her to draw a self-portrait of who she felt she was. The drawing revealed a person who was half angry and half happy. Karen expressed herself as a person who tries to be happy but who is often overtaken by anger. This was a turning point in the case. The drawing revealed a dominant story that anger had taken over her life and provided an opening for a possible externalization and alternate story.

Karen's drawing demonstrated that she had internalized anger and it then became a problem that could be externalized. To find out if "anger" would be a helpful problem to externalize, the therapist suggested, "So, most of the time you try to be happy but 'anger' comes in and takes over." Karen immediately responded, "Yes, that's it!" At this point, the therapist began using externalizing questions such as, "So, when you are feeling happy, how does 'anger' get you to go along with him?" The client was then able to discover how "anger" had recruited her into a lifestyle that she did not want for herself. Throughout the process of therapy, as change occurred, Karen was asked to redraw herself in relation to the problem. With each new drawing, "anger" became less and less a part of her identity. Eventually, she redrew herself standing above "anger" with her foot holding it down.

PREFERRED STORIES

As clients redefine their relationship to the problem, the changing self-portraits can be used to help define alternate stories that are preferred. If, for example, a client's drawing reveals that the problem is moving outside of his/her identity, the therapist can ask the client to discuss how it is that he/she has been able to take this important step in his/her life. With each new self-portrait, the therapist and client review ways that the client is taking back his/her life from the problem. Capturing these new self-portraits on paper is a very effective tool for helping clients actually see their new, preferred stories.

Client Response

Sean drew himself as partly "depression." As he described times when he had been able to overcome "depression," he was asked to redraw himself. As a new person began to emerge in the drawings, Sean was asked to give a name to this new lifestyle that he was living. He called this new lifestyle "the new me." "The new me" was a person who was in control of his life and choosing to live happily. Sean's drawings were highlighted by asking him how he accomplished these changes. Asking clients how they were able to change and what their accomplishments mean about them as persons is a vital part of Narrative therapy. It serves as a way for them to see their agency over their own lives.

PERFORMING BEFORE AN AUDIENCE

As clients create new identities for themselves, it is important for them to present this new identity to others. At the end of therapy, I like to have clients review all of their self-portraits to the audiences they have selected. Beginning from the first drawing, the clients are asked to describe how their relationship with the problem has changed and what they have done to take back their lives from the problem. Presenting these drawings to an audience not only presents a verbal account of the new identity, it also presents a powerful visual picture to the family.

Client Response

At the end of therapy, Karen was asked to review all of her drawings with her family. By reviewing her progress "over anger," she was able to take part in performing her new identity for the family. Presenting her new story to her family in drawing and in language served as a way to reify this new identity. Reviewing her progress also served as a way for the family to see her in a new light. If her new identity was going to take hold, her family needed to see and believe the changes she had made.

CONTRAINDICATIONS

It is important to consider the fit between any intervention and the client. The use of a self-portrait appears to be best suited for those clients who have difficulty expressing their stories in words and are somewhat talented in drawing. This intervention fits particularly well with adolescents due to their creative abilities and the difficulty they have expressing themselves verbally. This intervention may be contraindicated for those clients for whom talking seems to work. Although art is a helpful tool to open up conversation, it should not be used to replace it.

CONCLUSION

The use of the self-portrait can enhance the process of Narrative therapy by (1) helping the client and therapist better understand the client's dominant story; (2) aiding the process of externalizing the problem; (3) giving the client and therapist a tool for exploring alternate or preferred stories in the client's life; and (4) helping the client present a clear picture of her/his new identity to others.

REFERENCES

White, M. (1995). *Re-authoring lives.* Adelaide, Australia: Dulwich Centre.
White, M. and Epston, D. (1990). *Narrative means to therapeutic ends.* New York: W. W. Norton.

60

The "What Are You Prepared to Do?" Question

David Pearson

It has been noted that couples who bog down or become stuck in therapy are often involved in what has been called repetitive symmetrical exchanges (Jackson, 1973) or frozen, noncooperative positions (Fineberg and Walter, 1989). Such couples continue in such interactions because each blames the partner for their problems and/or each is waiting for the partner to make the first move toward change.

Systems-based couples therapists have been criticized for not demanding a focus on personal responsibility (Bograd, 1984, 1986). There has been increasing emphasis by some on developing theoretical frameworks that more explicitly integrate the concept of personal responsibility with systemic ideas (Cottone and Greenwell, 1992). In the meantime, some therapists have begun focusing more on personal responsibility in their therapy. Bowen (1978), has long promoted the idea that each person in a system can achieve a more differentiated sense of self by accurately observing his/her personal responsibility for the continuance of a problem. In the last decade, other therapists (Jenkins, 1990; White and Epston, 1990; O'Hanlon, 1987) have developed a variety of interventions and approaches to enhance the personal responsibility of clients in relationships. Weeks and Treat (1992) have noted that the development of a sense of personal power, which is crucial to the change process, is closely connected to an attitude of personal responsibility in clients:

> Systems change most often when an individual understands his or her contribution to the relationship dynamics *and works to alter his or her own behavior.* (p. 94; emphasis added)

Some couple interventions intended to increase the personal responsibility of each partner for change seem to focus on increasing couple awareness of their problem interactions (Weeks and Treat, 1992; Rae, 1993). Other interventions emphasize psychoeducational and communication techniques

(L'Abate and McHenry, 1983; Bernal and Barker, 1979; Walton, 1993). I have used a different question as an intervention with stuck couples with good success. I call it the "What are you prepared to do?" question. It is an intervention that not only focuses on encouraging work from the couple, but also emphasizes present and future possibilities, in contrast to present and past problems.

INTERVENTION

Although the "What are you prepared to do?" question may be worded with some slight variation, the typical way I ask it is as follows (numbers in parentheses correspond to numbers in the list following):

> [name] I'd like you to tell [partner's name] and me (1), based on what we've discussed (2), one (3) specific thing (4) you are prepared (5) to take personal responsibility (6) to do (7) on a daily basis (8), over the next two weeks (9), with the intention (10) of increasing the happiness of your partner (11), regardless of what your partner does (12).

1. Note that the question involves each partner committing to the other and the therapist, in words, what solution each is prepared to do. Making such a commitment in front of witnesses creates an expectation that the solution will be implemented. Rarely do clients wish to make a commitment that would later embarrass them if they should not follow through on it.
2. The question *must* be preceded by some discussion of attempted/ possible solutions for the couple's problems. All stuck couples are "experts" in identifying what each partner should change to make things better, but mere "novices" at identifying what they, personally, could change to make things better. I focus on what they are novices at.
3. Most couples can identify at least one thing they, personally, could do to help their partners feel happy. Clients often respond to this request by coming to the next session having implemented a variety of happiness-inducing behaviors daily.
4. It is important that the "thing" chosen be specific. Stuck couples often think in large, global terms about solutions. Requesting specificity and perhaps discussing some examples of specific behaviors they have previously mentioned may be helpful.
5. The term "prepared" is an important word to use; it suggests and reinforces for the clients that they have thought out and voluntarily decided to implement a self-change.

6. The term "personal responsibility" is at the core of this intervention. It has significance in Western cultures. Most clients understand they are entering into a contract for change when this term is used.
7. The use of "do" cements for the couple that the "thing" they are committing to needs to be a behavior. Stuck couples often are more comfortable discussing or arguing over thoughts, feelings, or ideas.
8. The responsibility of each partner to do a selected self-change behavior daily is intended to further the idea that self-change must be pursued regardless of one's emotional state, life stressors, or even the responses of one's partner. Daily implementation also improves trust and/or limits feelings of betrayal that are so common with stuck couples.
9. I usually suggest a two-week period between the intervention and the next session. This allows the couple and me to see the motivation and commitment of each partner to do the "hard work" of change. It also provides time for the relationship system to respond to the self-changes.
10. I have found the word "intention" to be important to use in this intervention. Couples tend to allow each other more latitude in their self-change efforts if they perceive the partner's heart to be in the right place. "Intention" can be used to reframe any behaviors that did not facilitate the receiving partner's happiness between sessions.
11. Although couples begin therapy with many possible presenting problems, my experience is that all such problems have brought unhappiness into the life of one or both individuals. It is universally appealing for each partner to accept the challenge of doing something to increase the partner's happiness. Appealing to the existing desires for love and happiness in a couple is a crucial motivation for self-change.
12. Disconnecting one partner's responsibility for change from the attitudes, actions, and comments of his/her partner is overtly stated in order to preempt the most common complaint in couples therapy (i.e., "My partner didn't change as much as I."). As the therapist questions quid pro quo as a necessary condition for change in a relationship, more options are opened for the couple.

CASE EXAMPLE

John (age thirty-three) and Susan (age thirty-seven) presented for therapy with the complaints that Susan was unhappy, was experiencing depressive symptoms, and felt there was a lack of communication and affection from

John. During the first two conjoint sessions, the couple agreed that a goal for therapy was for them to do more couple communication and activities. However, they never actually carried through on solutions they generated to achieve this goal. Rather, both at home and in the sessions they usually got stuck in discussions of who was most at fault, who needed to change the most, and how John was discouraged about ever being able to please Susan. Each felt the other needed to change in a variety of ways for the relationship to improve.

The "What are you prepared to do?" question was asked toward the end of the third session. I repeated the question slowly several times, emphasizing the key words and terms. Both accepted the challenge of this intervention and each identified one behavior they would implement according to the format.

By the next session, both John and Susan reported having done the "hard work" of the intervention on ten of the fourteen days. Significantly, each had actually done more than the one thing they committed to. Each reported feeling personally empowered as well as feeling more hope and optimism about their relationship. John concluded, "Perhaps we can work as a team if I keep this up."

CONCLUSION

I have noted that the "What are you prepared to do?" question works best with stuck couples who are in the middle phase of treatment, when the couple and therapist have a lot of possible solutions that simply do not seem to get implemented. The intervention can be a welcome difference for a couple and therapist who are involved in historical discussions, discussions that (despite the therapist's best efforts) do not promote the therapy goal, and discussions that center around mutual blaming. The question also seems to be more helpful with motivated couples who are both willing to be "customers" in the change process.

This intervention may not fit for therapists who do not feel comfortable taking a "demanding" position with a couple or for therapists who prefer to prescribe tasks, rituals, and so on for their clients.

REFERENCES

Bernal, G. and Barker, J. (1979). Toward a metacommunication framework of couples intervention. *Family Process, 18,* 293-302.

Bograd, M. (1984). Family systems approaches to wife battering: A feminist critique. *American Journal of Orthopsychiatry, 54,* 558-568.

Bograd, M. (1986). A feminist examination of family systems models of violence against women in the family. In J. C. Hansen and M. Ault-Riché (Eds.), *The family therapy collections: Women and family therapy* (pp. 34-50). Rockville, MD: Aspen.

Bowen, M. (1978). *Family theory in clinical practice.* New York: Jason Aronson.

Cottone, R. and Greenwell, R. (1992). Beyond linearity and circularity: Deconstructing social systems theory. *Journal of Marital and Family Therapy, 18,* 167-177.

Fineberg, D. and Walter, S. (1989). Transforming helplessness: An approach to the therapy of "stuck" couples. *Family Process, 28,* 291-299.

Jackson, D. (1973). Family interaction, family homeostasis, and some implications for conjoint family psychotherapy. In D. Jackson (Ed.), *Therapy, communication and change* (Fourth Edition, pp. 185-203). Palo Alto, CA: Science and Behavior.

Jenkins, A. (1990). *Invitations to responsibility: The therapeutic engagement of men who are violent and abusive.* Adelaide, Australia: Dulwich Centre Publications.

L'Abate, L. and McHenry, S. (1983). *Handbook of marital interventions.* New York: Grune and Stratton.

O'Hanlon, W. H. (1987). *Taproots: Underlying principles of Milton H. Erickson's therapy and hypnosis.* New York: W.W. Norton.

Rae, J. (1993). What is my part? In T. S. Nelson and T. S. Trepper (Eds.), *101 interventions in family therapy* (pp. 113-116). Binghamton, NY: The Haworth Press.

Walton, M. (1993). What, where, when, and how. In T. S. Nelson and T. S. Trepper (Eds.), *101 interventions in family therapy* (pp. 113-116). Binghamton, NY: The Haworth Press.

Weeks, G. and Treat, S. (1992). *Couples in treatment.* New York: Brunner/Mazel.

White, M. and Epston, D. (1990). *Narrative means to therapeutic ends.* New York: W.W. Norton.

61

Race in Family Therapy: Unnoticeable or Relevant?

Denise D. Daniels

Therapist: So how does it feel to be seeing an African-American female family therapist?

Husband: It's O.K.

Wife: Oh, I didn't even notice it until you said something.

Cross-cultural issues in mental health are an emerging field. Presently, theorists and therapists are investigating the influences of culture on human behavior, the family life cycle, and in the therapeutic process. Specifically, the importance of racial matching for clients and therapists in the therapeutic process has been a continually debated issue in clinical and counseling psychology literature (Helms and Carter, 1991). To further understand cultural issues in therapy, this chapter draws upon clinical and counseling psychology and family therapy theories in an attempt to more fully describe and develop a more comprehensive understanding of cross-cultural and intracultural (i.e., differences among people in similar cultural groups) therapeutic relationships with minority therapists.

Breunlin, Schwartz, and MacKune-Karrer's (1992) Metaframeworks model provides a foundation for understanding the fundamental concepts that underlie all family therapy approaches. In addition, Metaframeworks is used as a strategic system to determine the most effective treatment strategy. Six elements make up the Metaframeworks perspective: internal process, sequences, organization, development, culture, and gender (Breunlin, Schwartz, and MacKune-Karrer, 1992). I will focus on the Multicultural Metaframework as it relates to the beliefs that clients may present with when seeing a therapist of color, particularly an African American, and how their beliefs may influence the therapeutic process. This chapter will introduce the Multicultural Metaframework Model and define Cross's Racial Identity Development Model using personal clinical experiences to illustrate how intracultural differences can affect the therapeutic relationship. Finally, I will present an intervention supported by these models.

MULTICULTURAL METAFRAMEWORK

When examining the Multicultural Metaframework, Breunlin, Schwartz, and MacKune-Karrer (1992) point out many levels that define culture, including economics, education, religion, gender, race, age, regional background, and minority/majority status. In addition to the ever-present levels listed, there are cultural transitions that evolve over time as a result of historical events and changes in ideology and circumstance. Historical/generational sequences examine present and past cultural themes that contribute to the meaning and interpretation of societal and family events. Similarly, immigration/acculturation sequences deal with ethnic minorities adjusting to American mainstream culture and are frequently expressed through racial identity development. These sequences are important cultural transitions that are a significant part of understanding the effects and influences of culture on the everyday life of minority and majority people.

From the very beginning of therapy when I am attempting to develop rapport, the foundation for a therapeutic relationship, cultural elements are notable. As an African-American female therapist, I meet clients who come into the office with many beliefs and assumptions about African Americans. When some clients initially meet me, they see an African-American female and all of the stereotypes that are associated with African-American females. Frequently, I receive questions that either indirectly or directly address my competence and my educational training. Although this may be common when people are entering therapy, at times, people have asked me questions about how I *financed my education.* A Caucasian male client offered, "It must be expensive to go to graduate school. How do you afford it?" He commented on how much he was struggling to finance his dental school education and wanted to know how much I was paying. I believe he was indirectly asking if I was the recipient of an affirmative action quota or funding program. He obviously had some presumptions about African Americans in higher education and probably some negative feelings about affirmative action. Even though I have the same academic credentials as my colleagues or more, my competence is questioned because African Americans typically "are not respected by the dominant groups" (Breunlin, Schwartz, and MacKune-Karrer, 1992). Therefore, regardless of the accomplishments and credentials that many ethnic minority professionals achieve, our competence is questioned because of our ethnic minority status, which for many people is synonymous with inferior ability.

The Multicultural Metaframework also enters into the therapeutic process throughout the course of therapy. For example, a Jewish female client came to her second session talking about her brother's girlfriend, who was African American. Her basic concern was accepting this woman and working on her views about and her family's response to her brother dating outside of their race and religious affiliation. It quickly became apparent to me that she was actually talking about *our* relationship. When I asked her, "What is it like for you to see an African-American therapist?," we began to develop two of the most important elements in a therapeutic relationship—honesty and openness. We discussed what it meant for her to see an African-American therapist and if she felt that she could work with me. The client felt that she could work out her struggles about her brother's girlfriend as well as her personal issues by seeing me. She disclosed that she knew that I was African American when she spoke to me on the phone and decided to attend our first meeting. Her goals in therapy were now twofold: to work out her discomfort and negative feelings about African Americans and to work on her personal problems. Once we directly addressed our cultural differences, race rarely emerged as an issue during our next year together in therapy. This example demonstrates how cultural issues may be addressed openly and dealt with in the context of the client's presenting problems. This client was both aware of her issues and had the courage to bring up the issue of race early in the therapeutic process. Many people are intimidated or lack insight and may take longer to talk about racial issues. Others may never have the courage to address it. Therefore, racial beliefs and stereotypes will always be a constraint to developing a truly open and safe therapeutic environment.

Spurlock (1985) suggests that ethnic minority therapists introduce the subject of racial identity to clients at the initial appointment. She believes that therapists should ask their clients, "How do you feel about seeing me, a black woman?" (Spurlock, 1985). She suggests that addressing race puts both African Americans and Caucasians at ease and lets them know that the issue is open for discussion. In my own practice, this discussion has opened up communication with my clients from a range of cultural backgrounds (e.g., African Americans, Irish Americans, and others). It gives them an invitation to discuss their stereotypes, concerns, and expectations. Addressing race is very important for all clients because there are intercultural and intracultural differences and similarities in American society.

IMMIGRATION/ACCULTURATION SEQUENCES AND RACIAL IDENTITY DEVELOPMENT

Intracultural differences can be explained by variations in the immigration/acculturation sequence described by the Multicultural Metaframework. W. E. B. Dubois (1903) suggested that African Americans experience a duality of identity or a "double consciousness," illuminating the reality that African Americans incorporate both African and American culture, values, and beliefs (Cross, 1981). The acculturation process for African Americans can be understood using the theory of racial identity formation and development originally proposed by William Cross (1971) and recently applied by other theorists to capture the experiences of other ethnic minority groups. Briefly, the first stage of Cross's Racial Identity Development Model is the Preencounter stage, which is characterized by adopting the dominant European-American culture's negative view of African Americans. The second stage is termed the Encounter stage and reflects an increased awareness of one's African-American identity and validation of oneself as an African American. This is followed by the Immersion stage, in which an African American becomes immersed in his/her culture to the exclusion of the dominant European-American culture. Finally, in the Internalization stage, the person gains a sense of inner security, realizes the relevance of all cultures and begins to focus on other issues. The reader is referred to Cross's (1981) article for a more in-depth review of this model.

Racial Identity Development theory allows therapists to hypothesize and predict African American clients' range of views and reactions to African-American family therapists. For example, I recently posed the question, "How do you feel about seeing an African-American female therapist?" to an African-American woman who came in with concerns about her son's behavioral problems in school. She sighed with relief and discussed her nervousness about seeing a therapist who would understand her needs, perspectives, and issues as an African-American woman. However, all African Americans may not share her enthusiasm and level of comfort. Intracultural differences may lead some African Americans, particularly in the Preencounter stage, to reject an African-American therapist because of their negative feelings about their racial identity. However, there are a variety of reasons why people react to racial identification and the best way to find out what clients are thinking and feeling is to ask them how they feel about seeing an ethnic minority therapist.

HISTORICAL/GENERATIONAL SEQUENCES

In addition to intercultural and intracultural issues, there are salient historical and present events that may affect the therapeutic relationship.

With the use of the Multicultural Metaframework, one can define these events as historical/generational sequences. An example of how historical/ generational sequences may affect the therapeutic process is the recent uproar about the O. J. Simpson murder case, which was extremely publicized and in which racial differences were magnified. As an African-American female family therapist, many clients assumed that I had certain opinions or even asked me about them during the therapy sessions. My opinions about the Simpson case are interesting but of little therapeutic value. However, racially dividing issues may bring tension into the therapy room when clients have particularly strong feelings about the event. I found that briefly acknowledging the racial divisions surrounding the case, rather than completely ignoring these issues, seemed to reduce the tension in therapy, particularly with clients who had strong feelings about the court proceedings. Therefore, major societal events that are salient for ethnic minority and majority communities and have racial implications may enter into therapy sessions and cause racial issues to be brought to the forefront in therapy.

MULTICULTURAL INTERVENTION

An intervention to address racial differences and similarities is to ask clients within the last fifteen minutes of the first session, "How does it feel to be seeing an African-American female family therapist?" The family therapist can then explore the beliefs and values associated with the therapist's and/or clients' racial group membership. Finally, the family therapist and clients can process the way cultural similarities and differences may affect their therapeutic relationship.

CONCLUSION

In the previous case examples, historical events, societal issues, personal racial identity development issues, stereotypes, beliefs, and presumptions can all influence our clinical experiences. It is my belief that ethnic minority family therapists should directly address the obvious issue of race in the first session in order to give the client permission to discuss a sometimes difficult subject with the goal of providing a safe and healthy therapeutic environment. Therapists of color need to be aware of and equipped to address their racial identity even with clients of the same race because people may be at difference stages of minority identity development. Furthermore, because family therapists deal with families and couples, we cannot assume that family members' intercultural or intracultural beliefs are similar and must take individual variation into account. In conclusion, cultural and racial issues are prominent in America in the past and present and enter into therapeutic relationships, particularly with therapists of color.

REFERENCES

Breunlin, D. C., Schwartz, R. C., and MacKune-Karrer, B. (1992). *Metaframeworks: Transcending the models of family therapy.* San Francisco: Jossey-Bass.

Cross, W. (1971). The Negro to black conversion experience. *Black World, 20,* 13-27.

Cross, W. E. (1981). Black families and black identity development: rediscovering the distinction between self-esteem and reference group orientation. *Journal of Comparative Family Studies, 12,* 19-49.

DuBois, W. E. B. (1903). *Souls of black folk.* Chicago: A.C. McClurg.

Helms, J. E. and Carter, R. T. (1991). Relationships of White and Black racial identity attitudes and demographic similarity to counselor preferences. *Journal of Counseling Psychology, 38*(4), 446-457.

Spurlock, J. (1985). Assessment and therapeutic intervention of black children. *Journal of the American Academy of Children Psychiatry, 24,* 168-174.

62

The Extramarital Affair:
Honesty and Deconstructive Questioning

Peter Lehmann
Donald K. Granvold

Michael White (1991) has suggested that the stories we have about our lives extend across time. For example, stories provide a map of the world that shapes beliefs about gender and culture; values about family, marriage, and work; and views of self. People make meaning out of life by organizing significant life experiences into stories which are then incorporated into a larger life narrative (E. Bruner, 1986; J. Bruner, 1986; Combs and Freedman, 1994; Hoyt, 1994; White and Epston, 1990). The dominant stories in which one is living may be restrictive, painful, shortsighted, negatively biased, debilitating, and the like. Other stories remain unexpressed or tacitly held (Guidano, 1988); stories that reveal strengths, resources, and competencies. The goal in constructive therapy is to guide the client's generation of new stories in which current dominant themes are abandoned for those that are more empowering, sensitive to, and consistent with desirable life goals, and more aligned with one's "preferred self."

This chapter presents a method of deconstructive questioning (Freedman and Combs, 1996) in which a male client is invited to attend to an alternative story of himself. Deconstructive questioning is akin to a Socratic dialogue whereby the client is asked about the meaning and effect of certain events with the hope of arriving at a different perspective of self. In this case, questions probed views of self based on guilt, truth, and self-responsibility.

CASE EXAMPLE

Bonnie was in the midst of an amiable three-year separation from David when she referred herself for individual counseling. She felt stressed as a single mother and anxious about her feelings toward David. Bonnie loved her husband very much and had many hopeful fantasies about a reconciliation. Yet, she also believed that she was likely "holding on to David" for security despite her growing appreciation for life independent of him. In particular, Bonnie was confused about David's eight-month ongoing extramarital relationship with Clare, a woman he had met through work. Bonnie said that, according to David, his affair with Clare was over and that he loved his wife. She found it curious and of great concern that David was unwilling to return home. Further, David was unable to explain his reluctance, except to say that he needed more time.

After three months of weekly individual sessions with Bonnie, David asked for marital treatment sessions with the goal of reconciliation. Bonnie responded positively, although with hesitation. Again, she stated some ambivalence about the likelihood of a successful reconciliation because David had made a number of overtures in the past and had failed to follow through. Bonnie expressed further reluctance based on her view that each of David's reconciliation overtures corresponded with messages from her that she was becoming increasingly independent from him and moving more comfortably toward a new single life.

When marital treatment was initiated, David was seen individually for several sessions prior to conjoint treatment. In an early session with David, it was clear that the intimate relationship with Clare was not over. He professed that the relationship was platonic, while admitting a deep love for her. At the same time David agonized over his love for Bonnie. He was in love with two women and felt guilty about it. David loved Bonnie for her nurturing and caretaking, along with her willingness to give him time to "work through his indecision regarding the marriage." Furthermore, he considered sex with Bonnie to be superior to any encounter he had ever experienced including his contact with Clare. Clare's intelligence, easy communication style, and carefree lifestyle formed the basis of his love for her.

In a number of sessions, David wept openly, professing his confusion about what to do. Attempting to sort out these feelings, David provided a story of a man frozen, incapable of making a decision. He felt guilty about his inability to be truthful and weak in failing to responsibly disclose his true feelings about Clare to Bonnie. In effect, David's dominant story of himself was of a man, husband, and father who was guilt-ridden and indecisive and therefore weak and dishonest.

THE INTERVENTION

Over a number of sessions, David was asked a series of deconstructive questions with the objective of rewriting his stories in ways reflecting a more honest, responsible, and strong person. These questions also attempted to provide a window of opportunity for considering some actual stories of his life representative of preferred values and behaviors. On the basis of these narratives, it was anticipated that David would experience empowerment, clarity of direction in life, and a renewed sense of integrity.

Guilt

- What effect might truth and honesty have on limiting feelings of guilt?
- Would you see yourself differently as a father figure or as a partner if you were more guilt-free?
- What qualities do you have that you know could counter some of the effects of guilt?
- You have shared that your father knowingly promoted guilty feelings in you and that you have greatly overcome the effects of these efforts. What did you learn in this process that you could use in dealing with your current guilt over loving two women?
- In what ways is guilt valuable or alternatively hurtful to you?
- What consequences have you experienced as a result of your feelings of guilt these past months?

Truth

- Were you to talk openly and truthfully with Bonnie about your feelings toward Clare, what bearing do you think this would have on your views of yourself . . . about your predicament . . . your emotional responses to your current dishonesty?
- What do you think being truthful with Bonnie might tell her about you as a person?
- What legacy of yourself would your children learn if they knew you were truthful with Bonnie?
- If there was to be a future for you and Clare, do you think it would make a difference in her feelings for you knowing that you had been open and honest with Bonnie?
- What is your history of being a truthful person?
- How does being deceptive "fit" with your views of yourself?

Responsibility

- Do you find yourself intrigued with responsibly telling Bonnie the truth about your honest feelings for Clare? If so, describe your thoughts.

- What and how have you tried to teach your kids about self-responsibility that they may be likely to carry with them into adulthood?
- What do you think taking responsibility for yourself would say to Bonnie about you that she already knows?
- If your tears had a voice, what might they be saying to you about the choices you have made?
- What other life experiences illustrate your accepting responsibility despite the outcome?

OUTCOME

Deconstructive questions can be very powerful and revealing in stimulating the shaping and development of new meanings (Freedman and Combs, 1996). Through the deconstructive questioning process, David began to connect his current experience with a number of past events in which he behaved in ways that reflected the self he preferred to be. For example, he reconnected with the business/personal side of himself that was fair and ethical. Also, through reconsidering some of the conclusions he had reached about himself as not such an honest or responsible person, he realized a connection with family-of-origin rules of dishonesty and deceit. He traced the history of these stories to a father who himself had been involved with other women while maintaining a religious lifestyle and professing wholesome values. He began to reconcile his own duplicity as he rediscovered his strong disdain for his father's hypocritical ways.

Through the process of reconstruction, David began both to alter his views of himself and to behave in ways more consistent with his new narrative. Specifically, he decided to take greater responsibility for his behavior and to be truthful with Bonnie about his feelings for her and for Clare. In a number of highly emotional joint sessions, David told Bonnie that he continued to love both her and Clare, and that the relationship with Clare had indeed been physical. He decided not to return home for the foreseeable future. David was relieved by his disclosure and felt particularly grateful that Bonnie did not hate him. Shortly thereafter, David agreed with Bonnie's request that contact between them be less frequent and more structured. Specifically, Bonnie expected drop-in visits and spontaneous encounters to cease. Conjoint marital treatment sessions were terminated at that time. David ended treatment with the therapist while Bonnie continued individually for four sessions. During the last sessions with Bonnie, her story slowly changed from holding on to "letting go." David's truthfulness allowed Bonnie to more accurately see and appraise his relationship with both Clare and herself. While she professed that she really had known that David was highly intimately involved with Clare, hearing it allowed her to dispel the illusions under which she was living—that David was truly committed to her and not to Clare; and that exclusive marital recommitment was forthcoming. In place of these illusions, Bonnie relatively comfortably concluded that she could love David for being a father to their children but not as a partner.

REMARKS

The method presented in this chapter represents a constructionist view of psychological distress that asserts that people are active participants in the creation and construal of their personal and social realities (Mahoney, 1988). Rather than viewing the presenting problem as the target of intervention, it is considered to represent a perturbation to the individual as a social system. As such, the problem is an opportunity to explore new meanings of self, the world, and the relationship between the two (Granvold, 1996). Deconstructive questioning is a means of rewriting the individual's story and producing change in his/her life narrative.

There are problems that contraindicate the use of the method described above. Problems of an acute nature in which assessment reveals risks such as self-injury, suicide, or aggression toward others obligate the therapist to use interventions that are more direct, including crisis intervention procedures as indicated (Dattilio and Freeman, 1994; Granvold, 1997). Furthermore, the issues and associated contextual factors a client presents may call on the therapist to take a more proactive stance in confronting, challenging, informing, or posing specific options to the client. In these circumstances deconstructive questioning, if used at all, would necessarily be incorporated with other more directive, therapist-centered procedures.

The process of deconstructive questioning may be contraindicated should the therapist see his/her role as hierarchical in nature to that of the client; in this case the therapist takes a moral stand against infidelity, claiming the behavior is wrong. Questions would less likely reflect a curious and inquiring position interested in the details of the client's story. Instead, exploration would reflect the values and beliefs of the therapist's narrative, thereby taking the solution out of the client's hands.

REFERENCES

Bruner, E. (1986). Ethnography as narrative. In V. Turner and E. Bruner (Eds.), *The anthropology of experience.* Chicago: University of Illinois Press.

Bruner, J. (1986). *Actual minds, possible worlds.* Cambridge, MA: Harvard University Press.

Combs, G. and Freedman, J. (1994). *Symbol, story, and ceremony: Using meta-phor in individual and family therapy.* New York: W. W. Norton.

Dattilio, F. M. and Freeman, A. (Eds.). (1994). *Cognitive-behavioral strategies in crisis intervention.* New York: Guilford.

Freedman, J. and Combs, G. (1996). *Narrative therapy: The social construction of preferred realities.* New York: W. W. Norton.

Granvold, D. K. (1996). Constructivist psychotherapy. *Families in Society, 77*(6), 345-357.

Granvold, D. K. (1997). Individual cognitive-behavioral therapy with adults. In J. R. Brandell (Ed.), *Theory and practice in clinical social work: A handbook for the 1990s and beyond* (pp. 164-201). New York: The Free Press.

Guidano, V. F. (1988). A systems, process-oriented approach to cognitive therapy. In K. S. Dobson (Ed.), *Handbook of cognitive-behavioral therapies* (pp. 307-354). New York: Guilford.

Hoyt, M. F. (1994). *Constructive therapies.* New York: Guilford.

Mahoney, M. J. (1988). The cognitive sciences and psychotherapy: Patterns in a developing relationship. In K. S. Dobson (Ed.), *Handbook of cognitive thera-pies* (pp. 357-386). New York: Guilford.

White, M. (1991). Deconstruction and therapy. *Dulwich Centre Newsletter, 3,* 21-40.

White, M. and Epston, D. (1990). *Narrative means to therapeutic ends.* New York: W. W. Norton.

63

Three Excellent Agreements:
Wynona and the Eighteen-Wheeler

Maria T. Flores

The presenting diagnosis was post-traumatic stress disorder (PTSD) with agoraphobia. Wynona, a ten-year-old girl, was constantly having nightmares. She would wake up crying, then would awaken her mother and stepfather. She would crawl into bed with them and seemed fine for the rest of the night. Her parents thought these episodes would gradually decrease. After three months without change, they tried medication. After three more months, Wynona's parents' worry reached a peak and they came in for therapy on the advice of their family doctor.

Wynona's mother explained that Wynona had been a good student and very outgoing. She stated, "Now Wynona is afraid to get in a car and does not want to leave the house for school, which is extremely unusual for her."

It all happened so fast. How the eighteen-wheeler caught the top back of the car is not explainable. Wynona was sitting in the back of the car on the left side. She saw the "big black wheels" coming down to crush her head. The roof of the car cracked as it bent toward her. She ducked to avoid the danger. She heard a horrible sound of metal on metal and the sounds of screaming people and honking horns. The smell of burning tires lingered. This was her nightmare: the black wheels coming to crush her head, the terrible screaming sound from which she awoke in a state of panic. Nothing soothed her until she saw her mother.

When I work with PTSD or panic attack patients, I rely on M. Erickson's ideas of three "excellent agreements." These agreements dispose clients to move steadily in the direction of health (Erickson and Rossi, 1981). These consecutive agreements tap into the symbolic meaning (Bertalanffy, 1968) and the induction process of the clients. I extrapolated the intervention for Wynona, creating three distinct "soothing" situations on which she could agree for her own health. My hypothesis was simple. Wynona did not know how to soothe herself internally to get over her traumatic fear. It seemed to be my job to create this possibility for her. If she could soothe herself, the problem would eventually decrease and with time, disappear.

I learned that after the accident Wynona continued with her plans and went to work with her uncle and cousin. She did not see her mother until later that night, around 9:00 p.m. By that time, Wynona's mother had already heard the details of the accident as seen by the uncle. Mom hugged her daughter in relief and, since it was late, began to put the kids to bed. I theorized that too much time had elapsed between the accident and the comfort from her mother. Also, the comfort and soothing from the mother was short-lived because it was late and the mother had made her own adjustment before seeing her daughter. Mom did not take the time to soothe her daughter and hear about the accident from her perspective, as she normally would have.

The first excellent agreement and the third session was with the entire family. How to get over the nightmares was the topic. Each member had a specific approach. Dad suggested thinking different thoughts or positive thoughts when Wynona got scared at night. Her older brother thought when she awoke startled she might want to simply look around the house to see that she was safe. Her "twin" brother (same-age stepbrother) suggested telling herself she was safe and singing a song to go back to sleep. Mom suggested calling on God to comfort her, and then thanking God for saving her and her uncle and cousin. I added some basic behavioral techniques of breathing and counting to settle and calm herself.

Wynona began a process of soothing herself. She agreed to try her family's suggestions when she awoke. Wynona tried these approaches as her first excellent agreement successfully for about two and a half weeks. Then suddenly the nightmares returned, but not every night. She said singing, doing her breathing exercise, and telling herself things worked, but only sometimes.

Wynona described how she awoke staring at the "big black tires" over her head to the left of the car. She could smell the burning tires. At this point she felt paralyzed and could not get the picture of the tires out of her mind. She also admitted that when this happened in school, she would stop doing her work.

In the next few sessions, I began to introduce the second excellent agreement, a soothing technique for the purpose of getting Wynona to claim some personal power. I worked with her on how to take some power in a powerless situation so I could symbolically help her move the tires. I asked her to describe in detail the actions she took to get out of this dangerous situation. At first, she could not remember, but slowly she pieced together the details. She remembered bending her head down to keep the car's roof from hurting her. She had to unbuckle her seat belt and crawl over the seat into the front and out the passenger side. Then she waited two or three hours in the parking lot and practiced her cheerleading exercises until they went with her uncle and cousin to work. She talked about how she wanted more than anything to talk to her mother. She explained how a "trembling fear" stayed with her all day until she saw her mother that night.

With her mother present, I underlined how quick and smart Wynona was in bending down when the tires crushed the car's roof. I asked her how she thought to do this. She explained her automatic process. Wynona's mother listened with interest, which Wynona visibly appreciated. I asked her how she managed to unbuckle her seat belt. Did she have help or did she do this herself? She explained no one could crawl to the backseat so she did this herself. I praised her and encouraged praise between mother and daughter. Her mother also applauded her actions. Mom and I listened to all the details and soothed her every step of the way.

I ended the detail sessions by asking her how the story ended (Parry and Doan, 1994). Wynona hesitated and then said, "I don't know." "Well," I asked, "was it a good or bad ending?" She responded, "Good." Her mother added, "Yes, good you were not hurt. You were safe." I then asked, "When did the story end for you? Was it getting out of the car, playing in the parking lot, working with your cousin or seeing your mother?" She responded, "It was seeing . . . no . . . it was hugging my mother."

I pulled out my old (Minuchin, 1981) enactment intervention and asked Wynona to show me how she hugged her mother. We then practiced in her mind seeing the tires, unbuckling the seat belt, crawling out of the car, playing in the parking lot, working, and finally hugging her mother. This hug was real. We did this several times. The first few times it was difficult for Wynona to move past the image of the tires, but she eventually did. At first she said, "I can't," but then she did. Refocusing her mind on the story form, with one thing following another, made it easier, especially since she had a hug at the end.

Thus Wynona soothed herself in different ways. She claimed her power of escaping from death or injury. It was Wynona who ducked to avoid a collapsed roof. It was Wynona who unbuckled her seat belt and crawled out over the seat. This gave her a sense of doing something, which was a definite affirming process for her. Her second excellent agreement was claiming her own power in what she did to escape injury.

Then she soothed herself by hugging her mother. This process helped collapse the time lapse between the time of the accident and the time of the complete relief of hugging her mother. Wynona could then internalize this action as a personal process of soothing herself. Basic family systems work makes getting over trauma easier.

I left Wynona and her mother with instructions that they could practice this process during the day when Wynona became frightened or did not want to leave the house. I also explained to Wynona that at night she had to add this process to the other things that worked to get her over the nightmares. I told her if this did not work we would stop this during the day and try something else. Both mother and daughter agreed to try this process: a third and final excellent agreement, a hug.

And basically that was it. Mom called and cancelled her next appointment because Wynona was no longer having nightmares and was going to school without hesitation. Wynona still did not want to spend the night away from home but that was the only residual left from the accident.

The only negative effects with Wynona occurred about six months later. While on the expressway one afternoon, Wynona grabbed the wheel of the car as her mother was passing an eighteen-wheeler, almost causing an accident. Wynona had taken too much power. Mom scolded Wynona, and her daughter promised not to do this again. Wynona explained she had become frightened of the eighteen-wheeler. Mom understood Wynona's fear and proposed to keep her distance from large trucks but admitted this could not always be avoidable. Other than this incident, Wynona was doing fine. She was no longer having nightmares and her grades were back to normal. This case was closed but I must admit, after these sessions, I also keep my distance from eighteen-wheelers while on the road.

Using three excellent agreements is a process of collaboration with clients that solidifies change, especially with clients suffering from post-traumatic stress syndrome or panic attacks. Three excellent agreements are like pathways that help clients move from a traumatized state of being, locked in the past, to living in the present. Clients find in their own stories things that they can agree lead to brighter futures. I have successfully used this approach with Vietnam veterans and rape victims. Wynona's case was easier than most because it was one event and because of the quick response by her parents to get her therapy.

REFERENCES

Bertalanffy, L. Von (1968). *General systems therapy*. New York: George Braziller.
Erickson, M. S. and Rossi, E. L. (1981). *Experiencing hypnosis: Therapeutic approaches to altered states*. New York: Irvington Publishers.
Minuchin, S. (1981). *Family therapy techniques*. Cambridge, MA: Harvard University Press.
Parry, A. and Doan, R. E. (1994). *Story re-visions: Narrative therapy in the post-modern world*. New York: The Guilford Press.

64

Functions of Behavior in the Adolescent Family

Scot M. Allgood

One of the more interesting types of clients to work with are adolescents and their parents. By the time most families reach my office the battle lines are well drawn. The parents often have well-developed cases of righteous indignation and the adolescent is convinced that the parents will never understand him/her. These cases can be among the most enjoyable or dreaded of the week.

By combining some basic ideas from the established family therapy models, a framework for mutual understanding between family members can be developed. This intervention assumes that the initial joining has been successful to some extent with all family members. A second assumption is that the therapist is comfortable and skilled in dealing with both overt and covert hostility. The last assumption is that the therapist is an expert on family functions and may be able to identify problems or potential problems that the family could not see themselves.

The basic framework for this intervention is drawn from functional family therapy (Alexander and Parsons, 1982). In this model the behavior of family members is conceptualized as meeting one of three functions: merging (attempts to get closer), separating (attempts to distance oneself), or midpointing (maintaining the status quo). To identify these functions, the therapist makes a map of them between the initial and second session. Each family member and the relationship function with other members is identified. This map is based on the observed and reported family interactions, and sequences are discussed. In large families, older and younger siblings who will not be participating in therapy would not be put on the map.

INTERVENTION

Conceptually, examining functions of behavior can be very useful. Instead of the therapist alone creating the map, however, in this case the entire family helps in clarifying the relationship functions. With the simple map, it becomes useful to draw upon the Milan model for circular questioning (Boscolo et al., 1987). Each member can hypothesize about the functions of the behavior between other members.

Open discussions on the types, frequency, or outcomes of the mismatched functions of behavior help clarify the problematic sequences. It is not unusual to have overt or covert hostility as the family discusses these functions. If the therapist is aware of the interactions and manages the session, the hostility adds another point in the assessment. Likewise, open discussion on the matched functions helps identify familial strengths and resources.

There are several advantages to using this intervention. The first is that it involves the entire family. Second, the views of each family member are considered, which aids in the process of joining and assessment. Third, each person has the opportunity to express his or her views of the familial relationships in the roles of both observer and participant. Last, the discussion on the differences in how individuals see the same relationships gives the therapist an idea of how family members respect each other, compromise, and recognize differences in perceptions.

The second part of the intervention, which usually works best as a homework assignment, involves sending the map home with the assignment to write in two areas. Areas of agreement (two members midpointing, merging, or separating) are noted and the skills, beliefs, or behaviors needed to maintain the agreement are noted. Secondly, differences between members in the functions of behavior are noted. Each family member is requested to identify ways in which potential compromise may be reached in resolving those disagreements.

The main purpose for this part of the intervention is to give family members a chance to begin seeing the problem in a systemic way. As the various relationships are examined, influences on other relationships are noted. At this point it is important to ensure that individuals or subgroups are not blamed. Focusing on the relationships throughout the initial meeting sets the stage for future sessions, underlining that it is counterproductive to identify scapegoats or identified patients.

Families typically respond favorably to the therapist when strengths of each person and his or her relationships are noted. A balance in the number or type of compliments helps solidify the therapeutic relationship and subtly reframes the "problem adolescent" into a family concern.

In the case of two parents and one adolescent, the map would be very simple. Each person would be identified by some mark on the paper (I typically use circles with initials). Arrows with the points meeting halfway between the circles are then added. The functions are defined and then an open discussion is initiated to try to build a consensus on which one is being used. Thus the functions from the adolescent to each parent would be identified, and then from each parent to the spouse and the adolescent. The consistencies and differences would be discussed homework prescribed as noted above.

An example of how this intervention was successfully used occurred when a couple presented with a sixteen-year-old son who kept running away. There were other children in the family, but they did not have "severe" problems, so the parents did not want them involved. The son had been adopted at birth and the parents were "almost convinced" that was the underlying problem for his behavior. After the initial joining was done this intervention was used. The three family members each had a chance to express opinions about the functions of behavior both involving themselves and between the other dyad. The functions between each parent and the son were consistent (mother was merging with the son, father was midpointing with the son, son was midpointing with the mother and separating from the father). There was, however, an inconsistency in how the marital relationship was conceptualized. The husband reported he and his wife were both merging. The wife and son, however, both reported the mother was separating and the husband was midpointing. Discussion on the differences in perception highlighted an earlier observation of good communication skills and that the family was respectful of each other. The end result was a discussion of how the family business was affecting the entire family, with the largest consequences being evident in the marital relationship. At the conclusion of the discussion, the couple wanted a few days to talk and consider if and/or how they wanted to address the marital concerns.

The homework for the family was then focused on areas of agreement and disagreement in the differing functions between each parent and the son. Each was to come up with strengths and potential areas of compromise relative to the differing functions of behavior. At the beginning of the next session the family reported that they had "jumped the gun" and tried to resolve the differences. In the discussion, the conclusion was drawn that the differences were more related to perception than problematic behavior and that they could manage the desired changes by themselves.

While I clearly recognize the above example is not the norm, the principle of having the family be their own expert is very consistent with many models of family therapy. The idea of identifying strengths and systemic relationships with the underlying premise of compromise can bring about desired changes very quickly.

The contraindications relate to therapist skill and type of presenting problem. If the therapist is uncomfortable in dealing with adolescents and/or conflict, this intervention may result in a loss of control in the session. As noted previously, discussion of the mismatched functions is likely to bring out some level of hostility, which the therapist needs to manage. Other contraindications relate to the type of presenting problems. Those problems related to potential harm to self or other family members need to be addressed before this intervention is used.

REFERENCES

Alexander, J. and Parsons, B. V. (1982). *Functional family therapy*. Pacific Grove, CA: Brooks/Cole.

Boscolo, L., Cecchin, G., Hoffman, L. and Penn, P. (1987). *Milan systemic therapy*. New York: Basic Books.

65

Together and Apart: Daily Rituals in Divorced and Remarried Families

Janine Roberts

Scraps of folded paper were being tossed by Teresa (fifteen), Ramon (thirteen), and Sally (six) into a lovely off-white ceramic bowl decorated with small enamel hearts in intense colors. It graced the middle of the table where the three children were eating dinner with their parents. Teresa Cabezas and her brother Ramon had just come back to their dad and stepmother's house for one of the five-day spans of time that they lived there each month. Sally, the offspring of Ramon and Teresa's father's second marriage with Ellen (forty-one), lived in the home all the time.

Above each person's place setting were colored markers and paper. Periodically the parents or children would write something down and flip the paper into the bowl. Over dessert, the bowl was passed around and each person read out loud what others had written:

- One thing I am looking forward to this weekend is having Sally read to me and seeing what new words she has learned (Teresa).
- I'm going to miss having our own TV room like we have at Mom's. It means having to share TV time here. That's the pits (Ramon).
- Something we kud all do is go on the padle boats in the park (Sally).
- Last time all five of us were together I appreciated how we worked out the hassle about whether when kids did the dishes it meant doing the pots and pans too. Everyone hung in with the discussion even though it was hard (Ellen).

The Cabezas-Austin family used to find the transition time when the two teenagers came back into the household chaotic and fraught with the potential for misunderstandings and hurt feelings. It goes more smoothly now—not perfectly, but with a better sense that they can manage all that the shift entails.

As Juan Cabezas, the father, said:

> Since we started this ritual at the first meal that we all have together
> when the two older kids come back into the house, we've reset our
> focus. It helps us to anticipate changes that people have to adjust to,
> think about and plan one or two things to do together that are fun, as
> well as give ourselves credit for things we have already managed
> well. The tone is established that we are working on this together.
> Along with the adjustments we get some goodies too.

Simple therapeutic rituals such as this can be easily inserted into the
ongoing ritual life that all families have. They are a powerful resource for
divorced and remarried families to help them manage the unique tasks and
transitions that occur when individuals move in and out of different kinds
of family situations. Familial roles and rules, household rhythms, presumptions, shifts from one part of the day to the next, might be quite
different in one living arrangement than another. For instance, Annaliese,
who shares custody of her three children with her husband, Ben, has two
weekends a month when she is alone with no responsibilities for her
children. When she has the kids, her days feel packed with many demands,
but also happy, busy activities that keep her connected to others in the
community where she lives. When the children are not present, there is a
dramatic shift to the quiet that she cherishes, but there is an element of
loneliness in it as well and she finds she needs to reach out and structure
her time much more intentionally.

Because our daily rituals, such as mealtimes, bedtimes, and how we say
hello and goodbye so centrally mark movement through the day, and highlight the values, beliefs, and membership of each family, they are a rich tool
for therapists and family members.[1] Furthermore, rituals offer easy access
to complex dynamics with a resource focus, and can be used with any
model of treatment. Working with rituals is also a frame that is very sensitive to different cultural nuances and ethnic patterns because it is built upon
the family's own day-to-day experiences. The symbols and symbolic
actions of rituals, such as throwing comments into the off-white bowl in the
opening example, also contribute possibilities of accessing meaning that are
not always verbalized but are potent and important to families. The bowl
was given to the Cabezas-Austin family when Juan and Ellen married and
so had particular meaning about the five of them coming together.

MORE THAN HELLO AND GOODBYE

Daily rituals are a good place to start with divorced and remarried
families because they can quickly address developmental tasks common to

people in these situations. Entrances and exits in these families offer special concerns because children often are moving in and out of two or more households (not just leaving and reentering one house).[2] Movement from one living arrangement to another frequently has embedded in it concrete reminders of the losses family members have experienced. When I separated from my daughter's father when she was six, my old study with its distinctive purple rug and violet walls was a constant reminder to her that I was not there. Parents can remake life in one place, whereas children many times have to remake it in several places.

The transition from one space to another is also a physical marker that children and adults are going to have to adapt to different sets of rules and expectations. Dynamics for parents may also get set off as they see or talk to ex-spouses and/or their new partners. Children may feel particularly caught in loyalty binds during this time as well.

As stepfamilies and divorced families see that movement between houses is much more than just the physical change, they understand better the intensity of emotions and reactions that can accompany these times. Small changes in the rituals that surround these kinds of transitions can give people access to these feelings and ways to work with them. Five-year-old Danny was very agitated whenever he needed to make the weekly transition into his mother's and maternal grandmother's house from his father's. His mother and grandmother found that it was not until he sat down and made something for his father (a drawing, painting, or Play-Doh figure) that he was able to settle into routines with them. He would carefully explain to them what he had made for his daddy, put it on the window shelf near the front door, and when he returned to his father's he would carry what he had made. This seemed to help him hold a sense of connection to his father, even while in his other home, as well as aid him in making the transitions.

BEDTIMES: NIGHT LIGHTS, STORIES, AND A GLASS OF WATER

Bedtime rituals help us to slow down from the active pace of our waking hours and make the transition to sleep. They are often a time for cuddling and closeness between adults and children—to reflect upon the day and to offer a sense of safety and reassurance as children go into their nighttime world.

With families that have experienced a separation and/or divorce, children may be reminded at bedtime that the parent they were living with before is not there, especially if there was an ongoing ritual of getting them a glass of water, tucking them in, and/or saying goodnight to them. It may be important to acknowledge this openly to help children name the feelings they may be having, as well as make any changes in the ritual to mark the new circumstances. Sarah Wu's nine-year-old twins, whose father lived two towns away, had a phone call to their father each night before they started getting ready for bed. Chris Mehta, a single-parent father, found that for six-year-old Ben, making contact with his mother before bed was too disruptive and unsettling. Instead he started sleeping with a bright-eyed tiger that his mother had given him, as she called Ben her "bright-eyed boy." This was a concrete reminder that she cared about him.

Remarried families have to find a way to incorporate and honor each other's styles and ways of saying goodnight. Members who have been living together previously may have unique and intimate ways of expressing their connection to each other at bedtime. These often involve some kind of communication just between two people as well as physical contact that may or may not be comfortable yet for stepparents and stepchildren to do with each other. For Matisse and her daughter, it was a long hug on the right side and then one on the left side. They had lived in Spain and learned there to greet each other with a kiss on each cheek, which had grown into this double hug for their goodnights.

As Visher and Visher (1993) have highlighted, building strong dyads across previous familial boundaries can be central in making new links in stepfamilies. Bedtimes can be one small way to start to build some of these connections. Christina brought two daughters, four and eight, to her second marriage with Samuel. They had lived together as a single-parent family for almost four years and Samuel was finding it hard to have a relationship with the girls. The therapist began asking him questions about times during the day that he might do one or two small things differently to feel more involved. Samuel described himself as saying "goodnight" from outside the open bedroom door to the two girls' room while Christina was in there tucking them in. The therapist asked the couple to discuss ways they might bring Samuel into that time and they came up with the idea that after Christina had read the girls their story, and as she was putting them in each of their beds, Samuel would come in to say goodnight with a simple phrase or two about what he appreciated about each of them that day. Over time, as this became more comfortable, Samuel moved to giving them goodnight hugs, a kiss, and finally to reading stories to them as well.

MEALTIMES: WHAT'S ON THE TABLE?

When people gather to eat together it is a visible marker of membership—of who is in the family. It is also a key time when many of the convictions and customs of the family are enacted, such as what topics can be talked about, allowable affect, and gender roles about giving and receiving care. When there are major changes in families, mealtimes sometimes fall by the wayside. Sitting down with some previous members absent or with new people can be too painful. Stress and chaos levels may be high enough that there is not energy or focus to get people together for meals. People in new configurations may not have renegotiated the rules about who needs to do what to get meals on the table.

Yet, if people are able to continue to gather for meals, even one day a week (for example, at a Sunday brunch), it provides a place for the family to acknowledge their changes as well as mark and affirm who they are currently. Remarried families may have the coming together at mealtimes of two households with quite different expressions of what is important to them as family members. John did not expect his sixteen-year-old son Zachary to help with meals, but he did expect him to stay at the table until all were done eating. John also liked to start meals with a grace said by him or his son. In contrast, his new partner, Patrice, expected both of her teenagers to help with the meals and had a rotating chore chart which they followed carefully. When they sat to eat, people simply dished up their food and began eating it as soon as it was on the plate. "So that it doesn't get cold!" said Patrice. People could also get up and leave the table when they were finished eating, even if others were not done. As these different ideas about families collided, dinner times were not pleasant for any of them.

The therapist first inquired about how often they ate together and found out it was usually four nights a week. She asked if they would be willing to do an experiment. The teenagers were intrigued and the parents were willing to go along, so the therapist suggested an odd days/even days ritual (Palazzolli et al., 1978) She invited them on two of those nights to do it as Jake and Zachary had been for the last five years, and for Patrice and her two children to be like anthropologists studying what the rules and regulations were for Jake and Zach. On the other two nights, they were to reverse roles and learn about what was important to Patrice and her family. After they began to understand what their differences and similarities were, the therapist worked with them to choose what they wanted to keep from each of their previous mealtime rituals, and to create their own family dinners.

TAPPING INTO RITUALS

There are several simple but important ways that therapists can help divorced and remarried families tap into rituals as a resource. One is to ask them questions that help to highlight aspects of ritual life that are working well and to see the ways in which they can contribute positively to familial connections. Families do not always recognize daily rituals for what they are, nor their power to affect and inform their relationships. As twelve-year-old Martin said, "I never thought about it before that I always sit on the same side of the table with my mom and never with my stepdad and stepbrother. It was like us looking at them."

Questions can also be asked of children who live in two or more places, to elucidate what the key changes are between household expectations, roles, and rules. This can help the adults to understand that their children often have quite different day-to-day experiences because they need to go back and forth between different living arrangements.

Rituals that are already in place in some way can be an anchor point from which to make modifications (as in the opening vignette). Rituals that are working well in one area, say bedtime, can be a model for thinking about how to get rituals going in another part of the family's life (such as meal-times). The role of the therapist is not to prescribe set interventions, but to help people experiment and explore to uncover new possibilities. Ways to help them draw on their inventive capacities include encouraging people to think of small, easy changes. Humor and playfulness can be key ingredients. The use of symbols and symbolic actions can be concrete ways to access intricate levels of meaning. Asking people to bring in found objects from their apartment or house, neighborhood, work, or school that represent a hope or wish they have for their family life can be a simple way to introduce symbols. Some of these objects might then be incorporated into one of their daily rituals as a way to highlight the significance of particular ideas.

When daily rituals are not working well, people can get a little distance from them by studying what about them is uncomfortable. Encouraging people to be in-house anthropologists, as in the last example in the section about meals, can help them to be curious about family dynamics. This kind of observing often helps people to be less emotionally drawn in and gives them a well-situated place to start from in thinking about ways to modify and change their rituals.

While there are no particular contraindications to working with these types of interventions, there will be situations in which it is harder to institute them. For instance, if two households of separated or divorced parents are not talking with each other, are fighting over visiting arrangements, and/or their children are brought into ongoing disagreements between them, a therapist will need to be attentive to how these dynamics affect ritual possibilities. Intervention may first need to be at the level of helping people talk directly to each other, reducing conflict, and getting children out of the middle. Likewise, when people in remarried families find themselves in dilemmas including intense conflict and/or questioning whether to stay together as a family, it may be difficult to plan and carry out daily rituals. At the same time, making space for them can provide a different arena for people to interact, one in which they can remember the hopes and dreams that brought them together.

Working with daily rituals centers divorced and remarried families inside their ordinary experiences but at the same time takes them outside. It locates them in the landscape of their lives, and gives them many ways to see, hear, feel, and express who they are as unique people creating family.

NOTES

1. It is beyond the scope of this short chapter to talk about other rituals in divorced and remarried families such as family traditions (birthdays, anniversaries, vacations, reunions), holiday celebrations, and life-cycle rituals. See *Rituals for Our Times: Celebrating, Changing, and Healing Our Lives and Our Relationships*, by Evan Imber-Black and Janine Roberts, New York: Harper Collins, 1992.

2. In presentations that I have done on rituals and divorced and remarried families (such as at the Family Therapy Networker Conference in March of 1995 in Washington DC with Elana Katz), I have focused on three different kinds of living and visiting arrangements: (1) a lot of ongoing contact between households; (2) long time spans between any visiting and contact; and (3) little or no regular contact with children or others from household to household. Each of these situations has very different implications for daily rituals. In this brief chapter, I have chosen to focus on the first set of conditions. I am currently working on a longer article that addresses working with rituals in the second and third kinds of living arrangements.

REFERENCES

Imber-Black, E. and Roberts, J. (1992). *Rituals for our times: Celebrating, healing, and changing our lives and our relationships*. New York: Harper Collins.

Selvini Palazzolli, M., Boscolo, L., Cecchin, G., and Prata, G. (1978). A ritualized prescription in family therapy: Odd days and even days. *Journal of Family Counseling, 4*(3), 3-9.

Visher, E. and Visher, J. (November, 1993). Keynote address on remarried families at AAMFT National Conference in Los Angeles.

66

Trance and Transformation: Intervention with Verbally Combative Couples

D. Kim Openshaw

Couples often carry out combative behavior, common to their daily interaction, within the therapy setting. It is as if they are saying, "You are the expert, listen to us persuade you who is right, then you can pass judgment." While a variety of techniques may be appropriate in altering a combative dynamic, it is logical to assume that couples will only be able to manage conflictual issues when the emotional climate has been neutralized and the interactional dialogue has been altered. Trance and transformation is an intervention strategy designed for verbally combative couples and involves two intervention strategies, Take Five and Empathy Training. Although these intervention strategies may be carried out together or separately, this chapter suggests that the most effective and efficient method to move couples towards practical conflict management strategy involves their combined use.

TRANCE

Take Five

Take Five (Alman and Lambrow, 1992), a common metaphor for "kicking back" and relaxing, is a quick method of trance induction, which leaves the client in a calm mild-to-moderate trance state without interrupting her/his ability to carry out an interactive process. Several hallmarks of the verbally combative couple, prime candidates for this intervention strategy, include: argumentativeness, hostile verbal and nonverbal behavior, increased tonality, and blaming sequences. Moreover, this interactive style can usually be assessed within ten to fifteen minutes of the first session.

While the content brought by combative couples to therapy is affectively laden, the interactional process suggests a self-reinforcing cycle of accelerated hostility. Avoiding an acceleration of the abusive behavior requires implementation of a therapeutic strategy that inhibits a "more of the same" phenomenon. Take Five is an effective and efficient method to neutralize the atmosphere in preparation for communication and conflict management. Six steps comprise Take Five:

- **Step One:** Couples identify, then write out a description of a "serenity place"—a mental "holding environment" that permits them to escape the immediate stressor and to image a calm, safe, and secure environment in which they can contemplate, meditate, and/or just reenergize.
- **Step Two:** The couple is instructed in how to take five deep breaths, breathing in through the nose, filling the lungs completely, and holding the breath for a count of three. Next, they exhale out the mouth until the lungs are emptied, again holding for a count of three.[1] This process is continued until they have completed five deep breaths, at which point they begin normal breathing.[2] To facilitate the deepening process, which encourages an increase in the relaxed state, the couple is instructed in formulating a "mantra" or chant, which they use as they exhale. This chant, which is mentally repeated, is of their own choosing (e.g., "How relaxed can I become?").
- **Step Three:** At the conclusion of the fifth deep breath, the couple is trained to create a mental image of their serenity place as they resume normal breathing. Imagery of their serenity place can be enhanced by encouraging them to engage one or more of their sensory modalities (i.e., sight—"What do you see around you?"; auditory—"What sounds do you find comforting?"; olfactory—"What aromas are particularly pleasant and represent your serenity place?"; kinesthetic—"What can you touch or feel that reminds you of this calm and peaceful place?"; and gustatory—"Are there particular flavors that might enhance your knowledge of where you are?").

It is not uncommon to create a Take Five tape for the couple to use at home to increase their expertise in the use of this technique. This may practiced individually or as a couple.

- **Step Four:** A cue (e.g., red handkerchief, time-out sign, etc.) is agreed upon and is initiated at any time either person is feeling an increase in negative emotion. It is further agreed that no matter who initiates the cue, both parties will engage in the Take Five process.

- **Step Five:** A written contract regarding the use of Take Five in session is formalized. This contract may be expanded to include use of the Take Five technique outside of therapy, especially after the couple has successfully applied the technique.
- **Step Six:** While in session, the couple is instructed in the use of the Take Five technique at least twice under the direction of the therapist. Initial implementation of Take Five is enhanced when lights are dimmed and soft music is played. Once the couple has practiced Take Five, they are encouraged to implement it on their own while in session.

TRANSFORMATION

Transformation entails the implementation of two intervention strategies designed to alter the interactional process by increasing understanding and empathy during a period of decreased emotional involvement.

Enhancing Understanding: The Written Diaglogue

Understanding precedes empathy and as such, becomes the initial focus of the transformation process. The written dialogue sustains the neutralized emotional environment, acquired through the implementation of Take Five, in that it literally slows dialogue down.

Writing out a dialogue inhibits, then alters the current spontaneous interactional process. A topic[3] is selected by the couple that involves low to medium emotional intensity, yet is relevant to the couple. The individual with the greatest interest in the topic is instructed to write out, in a specific and positive manner, what it is he or she would like the partner to understand concerning the issue.

Once the initial dialogue has been written, the couple reinitiates interaction in the following manner: first, the sender of the message is encouraged to read the message carefully and determine if what he or she will be saying is what he or she wants the receiver to hear. The written dialogue is read to the receiver. Next, the receiver is instructed in writing out what was heard so that it can be accurately reflected. The responsibility of the receiver is to parrot or paraphrase back to the partner what he or she heard with 100 percent accuracy. Should there be misunderstanding, the sender repeats the message until it is accurately understood. The receiver then reflects the message until a "shared understanding" is achieved (Miller et al., 1988). Finally, having achieved a shared understanding, roles are reversed and the receiver becomes the sender. The aim is for the new sender to write out a response regarding the topic that reflects his or her opinion and position on the topic. The written dialogue continues, with the goal being to create a process in which understanding, not agreement, is accomplished.

Empathy: The Final Frontier

The understanding process continues, and is guided by the clinician, until the couple has focused the specific issue into a systemic perspective. While understanding is a necessary component of conflict management, it is not sufficient. Empathy, it is suggested, is the critical condition for effective and efficient implementation of conflict management skills. Thus, the final step in the transformation process is to foster empathy so that the issue under consideration can be synergistically resolved, and a true win/win solution achieved (Covey, 1989).

Accuracy of Verbal and Nonverbal Expression

Although nonverbal expression tends to be under subconscious control, couples can learn to accurately coordinate verbal and nonverbal statements (Stuart, 1981). In fact, it has been demonstrated that verbal and nonverbal synchrony increases the likelihood that messages will be accurately understood (e.g., Miller et al., 1988; Stuart, 1981). At this point, the couple is taught how to share their written messages with one another while incorporating nonverbal cues consistent with the spoken message.

Facilitating Empathy: Implementing Role Reversals

Four basic steps are involved in fostering empathy. First, the concept of role reversal is introduced, with a discussion of how being in the other person's place could facilitate both logical and emotional understanding of the concern they are examining. Role reversal can be introduced through a simple method such as having them read the story *I'm My Mommy. I'm My Daddy* (Wilcox, 1975). Second, both parties write out a scenario that accurately incorporates their perspectives (i.e., beliefs, how it affects them, etc.) on the issue. Next, scenarios, following the format of the written dialogue, are shared with one another. The goal is an accurate understanding of what it would be like to live out the scenario from the perspective of the partner.

Finally, the scenario is rehearsed in session with the clinician commenting on the process, emphasizing the importance of integrating the "acting as if" role.

These intervention strategies, composed of many metalevel interventions, set the foundation for altering the emotional context frequently encountered when combative couples engage in therapy, while at the same time providing them with a method of slowing down their present communication process. Successful implementation of these interventions provides a foundation upon which the therapist can teach conflict management skills. It is recommended that couples continue to use Take Five, while utilization of the written dialogue may be more dependent on the degree of emotional sensitivity the issue may evoke. Regardless, the couple now has a set of skills which, if implemented, will provide a means for problem resolution with minimal hostility.

CONTRAINDICATIONS

Although no contraindications have been specifically identified with this technique, resistance to the trance portion of the intervention may be experienced. Antagonism to trance is significantly reduced when four factors are considered. First, the amount of training the clinician has in the use of guided imagery and/or hypnosis is important. Knowing that the clinician is skilled in the technique is not only a comfort to the client, but allows the clinician to implement the intervention with confidence. Education and preparation of the client is the second critical factor. Providing the client with a clear understanding of what they are about to experience, the rationale for the intervention, and demythologizing the technique decreases misconceptions and normalizes fears. Next, the therapeutic alliance needs to be sufficiently developed so that empathy and trust form the foundation of the intervention. Finally, the timing of the intervention, with the desired outcome in mind, must be considered.

NOTES

1. Holding the breath for a count of three, and then holding at the end of the exhale for a count of three, reduces the likelihood of hyperventilation.
2. "Normal" implies a return to a less-agitated state where it is noticeable that the client's breathing is smooth and even, there is a recognizable decrease of muscular tension, pulse rate tends to slow, etc.
3. The concern is not content, but alteration of the interactional process.

REFERENCES

Alman, B. D. and Lambrow, P. (1992). *Self-hypnosis: The complete manual for health and self-change.* New York: Brunner/Mazel.

Covey, S. R. (1989). *The 7 habits of highly effective people.* New York: Simon and Schuster.

Miller, S., Wackman, D., Nunnally, E., and Miller, P. (1988). *Connecting with self and others.* Littleton, CO: Interpersonal Communication Programs, Inc.

Stuart, R. B. (1981). *Helping couples change: A social learning approach to marital therapy.* New York: Guilford Press.

Wilcox, D. (1975). *I'm my mommy. I'm my daddy.* New York: Western Publishing.

67

Many Small Steps Instead of One Intervention

Tom Andersen

. . . observations which no one has doubted, but which have escaped remark only because they are always before our eyes.

—Wittgenstein, 1953, p. 125e

NOISY ENTRANCE

The room had six empty chairs, and we could hear some people coming in. They were talking and laughing and giggling—intensively.

One said: "Have an open mind, be open."

All found chairs.

The six persons that gathered in the room were four from a family and two professionals—one local therapist and one consultant. I was the consultant. The first was an old woman; a grandmother to one of the others and mother to two of them. The second was a thirteen-year-old granddaughter, and daughter to one of the two others. The third was a daughter of the first one and a younger sister to the mother of the thirteen-year-old. The fourth was the mother of the thirteen-year-old girl and the oldest daughter of the first one.

The noise was so intense that I thought we would never be able to have a talk. "Be prepared to give up the session!" was what I told myself in my inner talk. I have some overruling ideas. One is: "Don't try to do what is impossible!" And sometimes talking is impossible.

The oldest daughter wanted her mother to be there. "She would not come. But I thought it was important. I feel it is important that we all are together." Her mother, the grandmother of the thirteen-year-old, gave many signs that she did not like to be there.

I have only a few guidelines in my way of working, and one is: Those who want to talk should have a chance, but more important is that those who do not want to talk should have a chance not to talk (Andersen, 1995).

I therefore asked the grandmother, "Do you think they will accept if you sit and listen for a while?" The grandmother said, "I am all right." I said, "Maybe you will listen quietly for a while?" She said, "I will listen to them without saying anything." I asked the others, "Would that be OK with the rest of you?" They accepted. And I was very relieved.

I thought at first that a meaningful talk would be impossible. However, I thought I could try to talk with the local therapist first, with the others listening to that talk. Maybe that would give some kind of ease in the room. By that I felt I was strategic. Actually. Even though I don't like to be strategic and take the lead.

I determined to talk with the local therapist with the other four women listening to that talk. Listening to others talking will sometimes give ease and even useful ideas for one's own inner talk.

"How would you like to use this session?" was my question to the local therapist. "I, and we, don't know how to proceed," she said.

My job, I thought, was to talk with everybody present in such a way that the local therapist could find an answer to her question: "How can we proceed?"

The local therapist told that she had mostly met with the thirteen-year-old girl and her mother, or the thirteen-year-old alone, during the last year and a half. The therapist had tried to meet all the four (present today) twice, but those talks had been abandoned both times.

The granddaughter had been out of balance, mostly sad, and had difficulties in concentrating her mind over the last year and a half. The local therapist, looking at the granddaughter, said, "At one point you said things were like a black cloud . . . it seemed to be a strong statement about how you feel sometimes."

I never take it for granted that a person can speak with whomever about whatever at any point in time. Human beings are very often strongly selective when finding one or more others to talk with, particularly when a sensitive issue is raised. "Black cloud" was a strong statement, and should therefore be treated with care.

> I: Did the conversations you had say what was in that black cloud or . . .
> **Local therapist:** Well . . . it came in a session when we had been talking . . . I am feeling protective of her [the granddaughter] . . .

I: Is that black cloud something everybody here can easily speak about
... or would it be the first time to speak about it here . . . or . . . would
there be anyone who would feel uncomfortable speaking about that
black cloud . . .

After we discussed it a while, the local therapist thought all were ready
to talk about what was in that black cloud. And that was much anger
toward the thirteen-year-old's father. She and her mother were angry, but
for different reasons. Talking about the anger toward the father turned into
talk about the anger between the grandmother and her oldest daughter and
the granddaughter. During this the grandmother could not resist talking
anymore and said in a strong voice to her granddaughter, "We are two cats
on the roof fighting for the balance and a piece of the roof, and I am just
about to have had it. You got to stop that because I have gotten very very
put out about it. One thing I tell you right now, I was not in Dublin. I don't
feel responsible for what happened to you in Dublin." The granddaughter
said, "I never said you were." The grandmother said, "I love you a great
deal but I don't like you. You understand what I am trying to tell you?"
The granddaughter said, "I noticed that." The grandmother said, "And I
get so mad at you sometimes and you were such a nice kid before this stuff
happened."
What happened in Dublin was that the oldest daughter, who divorced
from the thirteen-year-old's father, found a new man, and he battered her
and her daughter as the first man had done. Every time the grandmother
spoke the other three of them laughed intensely, so much that it was hard
for me to hear the words they were speaking. They laughed particularly
when she spoke in anger, as she did here.
About the same time these things happened in Dublin, Frank, the grandmother's second husband, died. They all still missed him very much
because he was such a special and central person to all of them. The
granddaughter said on behalf of them all, "When we say his name we have
to cry."
My thinking is that laughing is not a result of something, but a way of
being-in-the-world. Life consists of small steps from one moment to the
next moment. And in every moment we are being-in-the-world (Heidegger, 1962; Bakhtin, 1993). I told myself that maybe laughing is the only
way they could be here now. If so, then I could not possibly take the
laughter away from them. But, on the other hand, the laughter was so
strong that I could not hear what they said. I thought that maybe the local
therapist and I could talk about the laughter, with the four women listening

to that talk. By listening they could have their own inner talks about what they heard us talk about.

> **I:** There is one thing I have been noticing when we have been speaking. There has been some laughter in the room, even when these seem to be very very serious issues . . . and I have been wondering all the time . . . if laughter could speak what would the words be? Do you have any ideas what those words would be?
>
> **Local therapist:** I have been very aware of that laughter . . .
>
> **I:** Are they happy words or sad words?
>
> **Local therapist:** No . . . they are sad . . . I think they are really discomfort . . . so uncomfortable talking about this kind of . . . very sad.
>
> **I:** Is it so uncomfortable that we should avoid talking about that?
>
> **Local therapist:** I don't know . . . I think different people in this room have different feelings about that . . . and again I am being protective of the thirteen-year-old.
>
> **I:** I feel very uncertain . . . if laughter had words and the words were sad words . . . how could we proceed?
>
> **Local therapist:** I don't know . . . that may be the impasse . . . that may be it . . . that may be what I am asking.

The grandmother moved on the chair and we understood she was ready to talk once more. "We are here to talk about it. If we cannot talk about it . . . how we can get it out and sort it all out and try to deal with it? We got to talk about it. Some are uncomfortable . . . so am I. I haven't been through this . . . it is not exactly easy to me to talk . . . we cannot keep it under cover to protect my granddaughter. We will not get it sorted out unless we get it in the open. She is only thirteen . . . I had a lot to deal with when I was at your age [to the granddaughter]. I had none to go to either . . . if you don't get it out in the open how can you deal with it?"

Then the grandmother talked about having cancer. The prognosis was poor. And it was particularly hard for her to think of not being able to take care of herself. She had been on her own since she was thirteen, the same as her mother had been.

All four most probably knew about the cancer, but nobody could speak of it for different reasons. The person who was closest to being able was the grandmother's oldest daughter, the person who so strongly wanted this meeting. And the grandmother said, "My oldest daughter and I have never been fighting so much any time as we have done lately . . . I am scared like everybody else."

It is often hard to bring the inner voices to the open. Sometimes very painful. The words being spoken to one's own outer ear in an open talk have a stronger emotional impact than when the same words are spoken to the inner ear in an inner talk (Penn and Frankfurt, 1994).

I therefore asked them if this might be enough, and we might stop here, or if they would be interested in listening to what the team had been thinking when they heard our talk. They were interested, and here are some of what the team members said: (1) "Finally at the end of her speech the grandmother said . . . I have finally said it . . . maybe it was easier for her to come here to a group to talk about her fears of cancer than without the support of the group." (2) "I wonder how the thirteen-year-old is feeling about her grandmother having cancer . . . how that must be for her . . . and I wonder if she is angry . . . and coming out toward her grandmother . . . is that she doesn't want to lose her." (3) "How can the thirteen-year-old find a way to deal with her own sadness when her mother is dealing with sadness and her grandmother is dealing with sadness? Who can help her? They all need help . . . she is a very young person to find a way to deal with that." (4) "I found myself initially in the thought of courage and determination that the grandmother was showing." (5) "I was experiencing in many ways they were enwrapping each other and embracing . . . with laughter or in anger or in speaking or in the ways they tilted their heads or were silent. I felt very much in the presence of a family of four women who were with each other." (6) "I was thinking when the thirteen-year-old said that we are thinking of my grandfather every day . . . and the grandmother said he went too early . . . he went too early . . . he said he should be here all her life . . . so I wondered would it be somehow possible to include him and hear his voice in the conversations in the family somehow?" (7) "In proceeding I thought it is important that these mothers and daughters keep coming together."

Listening to such a second talk about one's own first talk might be very moving, so I cannot take it for granted that they want or are able to speak. The local therapist and I therefore asked what would be the best, either to keep their thoughts for themselves or to talk about them.

The grandmother: I was kind of embarrassed actually. I don't know which it was . . . the woman said something about courage . . . I . . . I couldn't understand how she got that out of . . . how I . . . how we all . . . how I was talking . . . because I don't think I have been taking it so well. I don't give myself any credit. I mean, I . . . I feel you got to do what you got to do. So I do it, you know, the hit or miss . . . it gets done. I kind of get embarrassed when someone says . . . takes courage or where did she get the courage from.

The oldest daughter: I was . . . I was very . . .

The teenager: . . . touched . . .

Her mother [the oldest daughter]: That is a good word . . . someone said. Frank is still here . . . that relationship . . . the loss of Frank for my mother and my daughter might be a concern for my daughter losing my mother as for myself . . . and I never really . . . it never crossed my mind . . . I never thought about it . . . but that might be a concern.

The teenager: I have lost one grandparent and I don't want to lose another. I have two more left . . . my grandmother [pointing to her] has been there for me thirteen years . . . I can count on her but I can't count on my grandfather who lives so far away . . . God I can't believe it, I said that.

Her mother [when all laugh]: They would probably not believe you said that even if they heard you say that.

The local therapist: I always felt very moved and there is a privilege to be with the four of you . . . and . . . I wonder if that would be something that you consider doing again. I know we tried it . . . somehow it stopped.

The grandmother: I got very aggressive. I got an attitude . . . but now . . . because I understand . . . I realize I need help.

The teenager: We all do.

The grandmother: Yes . . . but ot for the same reason. I just didn't want to admit it . . . and no tnat I have admitted it I can get involved.

The youngest daughter of the grandmother: What I heard today helps me understand the situation better . . . now I understand what she [the thirteen-year-old] went through . . . because she used to hide a lot . . . you know she talked to me on the phone . . . no, no, nothing wrong . . . and she always laughed and smiled and I did not know.

The grandmother: And I did not understand it.

The teenager [pointing to her mother]: She didn't even know . . . I mean . . .

The grandmother: Usually a mother is the last to know.

CLOSING WORDS

It is most significant to work in many small steps and to be sure that, from moment to moment, those who want to talk can have a chance to talk. But it is even more important that those who do not want to talk should have a chance not to talk. And that those who want to talk, can talk about what they would like to talk about. But it is even more important that they shall not talk about what they would not like to talk about. This is so obvious, but it has escaped our attention, because it is all the time there, right in front of our eyes (Wittgenstein, 1953).

REFERENCES

Andersen, T. (1995). *Reflecting processes, acts of informing and forming: You can borrow my eyes, but you must not take them away from me!* In Friedman, S. (Ed.), *The reflecting team in action.* New York, London: Guilford Press.

Bakhtin, M. (1993). *Toward a philosophy of the act.* Austin, TX: University of Texas Press.

Heidegger, M. (1962). *Being and time.* New York: Harper & Row.

Penn, P. and Frankfurt, M. (1994). Creating a participant text: Writing, multiple voices, narrative multiplicity. *Family Process 33*(3), 217-233.

Wittgenstein, L. (1953). *Philosophical investigations.* Oxford, UK: Blackwell.

68

Metacommunication and Role Reversal as an Intervention

Lee N. Johnson
Kim Hander

Premarital counseling has long been difficult for marriage and family therapists. The exploration of patterns and issues that is common in many cases becomes difficult due to the clients being in "love" or the perpetual myth that all married people live "happily ever after." This chapter will talk about an intervention that was used by a cotherapy team in working with a premarital case. However, the concepts may be useful to a couple who have become stuck in therapy, parent-child dyads, and parent-adolescent dyads. Concepts from behavioral sex therapy (sensate focus; Masters and Johnson, 1970), intergenerational therapy (Friedman, 1991), and functional family therapy (Alexander and Parsons, 1982) were employed in forming the hypothesis and designing an intervention.

This intervention may be useful in situations in which the couple seems to care about each other but does not communicate. For example, when communication styles are different, feelings of stress and frustration often arise. One person may open a flood gate of information and ramble on and on, while the other person may prefer a style of communication that controls the information (i.e., if I don't ask about it, I don't want to know unless it is very important). It is also helpful to understand the emotions the current pattern evokes. Feelings of frustration, insecurity, and neglect may be an indication of such a pattern. Clients learn a style of communication in their families of origin and expect that style to continue in their significant relationships. Furthermore, the communication style they use serves as a model for their partner. Finally, similar to clients' discovery during sensate focus that they touch their partners as they would like to be touched, this intervention was employed to help couples communicate as they would like to be communicated with.

THE INTERVENTION

The intervention involves a two-step reversal of communication styles. The first step is to have the couple completely reverse roles. She is to play him and he is to play her. The next step is to have them converse about a very common topic, such as what they did that day. Remember they are not to talk about what they did that day but about what the partner did that day (i.e., in every way they are to play the partner). This step comes first because they have already thought about what the partner does, and it is easy to mimic. It can also be more fun if they exaggerate the behavior. The second step is to have them remain in the role of the partner but to use information about themselves (i.e., they are using their own information but communicating with the partner's style). The second step is practiced during the session and then assigned as homework once a day. Finally, the couple is asked to come up with their own code word or sign to indicate that they need to switch roles. The code word allows the couple to communicate in their usual roles but to be able to switch communication styles when either of the spouses needs it. As stated earlier, the communication pattern can evoke emotions of frustration, insecurity, and neglect. When either spouse has these feelings, a reversal of communication roles can be helpful. Additional times to use a reversal may include when either spouse wants to share some important news or has something important to discuss. These additional times may also be helpful in preventing negative feelings associated with the presenting communication pattern.

CASE EXAMPLE

John and Mary, a self-referred couple who had been dating for about two years, were planning to get married in approximately six months. They both were very busy and had little time together. When they finally had time, it started with arguing. For example, Mary would try to find out what happened in John's day by asking numerous questions, and then ramble on about what she had done during her day. Any information about John's day was given by him selectively answering a chosen few of the numerous prying questions asked by Mary. They both described this interaction as something "to get out of the way" so they could spend time together. Neither found the interaction enjoyable and described the feelings associated with it as discouraging, confusing, and unimportant. Both agreed that it did not bring them closer together. On the surface it might appear that they were avoiding or afraid of intimacy.

The cotherapy team used many interventions to try to facilitate changes in the interaction. The teaching of "I messages" and "reflective listening" slowed down the interaction but did not change it. Next, a paradoxical intervention was used, prescribing the interaction for a specific amount of time per day as homework. As they completed the homework they realized that the interaction was "stupid." However, even though they chose to not participate in the previous pattern, the relationship remained distant, the communication was no better, and the negative feelings remained.

It was hypothesized that this couple had learned their patterns of communication from their families of origin (Mary's family talks a lot while John's family asks questions). These communication patterns were familiar to each partner and they most likely expected them to continue in their present relationship. Therefore, we hypothesized that their behavior (the communication pattern) was to model or show the partner the style of communication each thought should be employed in the relationship. Like clients who participate in sex therapy and learn that they touch their partners in ways they would like to be touched, they were communicating in ways they wanted to be communicated to (i.e., Mary wants John to just tell her everything about his day and John wants to ask questions and not hear everything all at once).

The intervention described previously was employed. First, John was asked to be Mary, and describe how Mary's day had been just as Mary would do it. While John was doing this Mary was to act as John did when Mary described her day to him. They were also instructed to exaggerate the behavior to allow the other person to experience it. John began to ramble like Mary, and Mary began to stare at the ceiling like John. While they each experienced what it was like to be the partner, it was still not enough to facilitate the hypothesized change. In the next step, John was instructed to act like Mary but to tell her about his day, not hers, while Mary was to play John again. He began rambling about his day while both were exaggerating the behavior as before. About halfway through the scenario John slowed down his speech so that he was no longer rambling and Mary began to ask follow-up questions in a manner that did not seem prying. Without prompting, John began to ask questions about Mary's day. Both described this new pattern as something that they could do, and found it much more enjoyable and equal. As a homework assignment they were asked to tell each other about their day using the other person's communication style. In the next session they devised a code word that they could use at any time that would tell the partner they needed to switch communication styles.

In this case the hypothesis was confirmed; the couple was trying to communicate about their preferred communication style through their participation in the pattern. The intervention was successful in teaching them what each was trying to teach the other and giving them a way to communicate when this needed to happen.

The fact that this was a self-referred premarital case may have made a difference in the couple's willingness to explore other alternatives to their communication style. This type of intervention may also be used in marital and other relational (e.g., parent-child/adolescent) difficulties as well. A contraindication for the employment of this intervention would be extreme feelings of animosity toward one's partner. As with many interventions, this technique would not be useful in domestic violence cases because the potential to cause an escalation in violence is too great. Also, a high level of conflict may also contraindicate this intervention. Finally, an additional contraindication would be a great imbalance of power in the dyad. With the case described above the couple was not caught in power struggles but simple misunderstandings.

REFERENCES

Alexander, J. and Parsons, B. V. (1982). *Functional family therapy.* Monterey, CA: Brooks/Cole Publishing.

Friedman, E. H. (1991). Bowen theory and therapy. In A. S. Gurman and D. P. Kniskern (Eds.), *Handbook of family therapy,* Volume II (pp. 134-170). New York: Brunner/Mazel.

Masters, W. H. and Johnson, V. E. (1970). *Human sexual inadequacy.* Boston: Little, Brown.

69

Sticks and Stones Can Break My Bones: The Verbally Abusive Child

Allison Waterworth
Maureen L. Minarik
Carol L. Philpot

INTRODUCTION

The past decade has witnessed an increase in the incidence of verbal and physical abuse enacted by children against their parents. Once relatively rare, cases of child aggression against parents have appeared with alarming frequency in both the media and in clinicians' offices. This emerging trend likely reflects a structural breakdown of the family, in which parents no longer maintain a position of authority over their children. Thus, when such families seek professional assistance, restoration of parental authority and utilization of healthy disciplinary principles should be primary therapeutic goals. The following is a family therapy technique used to support parents in dealing with verbal abuse, particularly insults, from their children. The technique itself will be presented first, followed by a theoretical explanation of its origin and utility.

DESCRIPTION OF TECHNIQUE

Across relationships, verbal insults are most effective when the recipient perceives the insults as containing a grain of truth. In parent-child relationships, insults directed by children at their parents may be particularly damaging, for such insults may prey upon a parent's insecurities in the role of parent and as a person in general. Further, single parents may find such insults especially challenging, in light of the absence of adult support when presented with a child's verbal onslaught. However, single or married, parents who are vulnerable to the insults directed at them by their children are less likely to respond appropriately when a conflict arises. The purpose of our technique is to teach vulnerable parents to emotionally disengage when their children begin to hurl insults.

Implementation of the technique requires at least three individual therapy sessions with the parent. First, the therapist asks the parent to mentally review several episodes that involved verbal insults from the child, and then asks the parent to write down the insults frequently employed by the child/adolescent. The therapist and parent review episodes in which the insults were used, exploring the sequence of parent and child behaviors. Such examination will likely reveal common underlying patterns across the different instances and will permit the therapist and parent to identify the antecedents that precipitate a verbal barrage from the child.

For example, a parent may discover that when s/he sets a limit and blocks the child from obtaining a desired goal, the child responds with verbal abuse and insults. These insults may be quite painful to the parent, and after prolonged exposure to hurtful barbs, the parent may recant and give in to the child's initial demand. In doing so, the parent is rewarded, via negative reinforcement, with a cessation of insults. The child is rewarded as well, because the child gets his/her original goal. The parent thus learns to give in when presented with insults, and the child learns to use insults as a tool for gaining desired outcomes.

Once such a pattern is identified, antecedents and consequences should each be included on the list of typical insults. The parent should then be instructed to review the list each time the child begins to use verbal insults. During a verbal assault, the parent should record the number of times that the child makes each insult and add any new insults the child makes. The parent should also review the identified pattern in order to remind her/himself of the child's goal, as well as her/his own behavior that has typically maintained the abuse.

In the second therapy session, two new columns are added to the client's list: "My Beliefs" and "Painfulness of Insult." For the first column, the therapist asks the parent to reflect on each abusive statement listed and to indicate to what extent s/he believes that statement to be true, on a scale from 1 to 10 (1 = completely untrue, 10 = absolutely true). For the second column, the therapist asks the parent to rate the perceived painfulness of each of the insults on a scale from 1 to 10 (1 = not at all painful, 10 = extremely painful). The correspondence or discrepancy of the ratings in these two columns can be a valuable point of discussion for the therapist and client. Insults with high ratings on both dimensions are likely to be most effective in producing the child's goal (parental capitulation) and thus should be targeted first in the following session. After this session, the therapist instructs the parent to continue recording the child's insults as they occur.

When the parent returns for the third session, the therapist asks her or him to make a fourth column titled "Seeing It Differently." The therapist works with the parent to evaluate each insult, particularly those rated to be most true or most painful. Insults are examined by parent and therapist to establish potential credibility. A child, for example, who says to her or his parent, "You are weak!" may in fact be correct in the assumption that the parent disciplines ineffectively. In this instance, the parent and therapist identify alternatives to the parent's behavior to remediate the behavior and thereby reduce the truthfulness of the child's insults. However, if parent and therapist determine that the child's insults are incorrect and unwarranted, they generate alternative ways of thinking about each insult and/or create arguments about why the statements are not necessarily true.

THEORETICAL UNDERPINNINGS

Our technique draws largely from two theories in family therapy: two subtypes of cognitive-behavioral therapy, behavioral parent-skills training (Patterson et al., 1975) and functional family therapy (Alexander and Parsons, 1982); and strategic family therapy (Haley, 1963). The overarching notion that the family with an abusive child is hierarchically out of balance reflects the structural theory of Salvador Minuchin (1981). Although we borrow concepts from Minuchin to understand families with verbally abusive children, we do not utilize specific interventions in the technique presented here.

Behavioral parent-skills training (Patterson et al., 1975) posits that cognitive, behavioral, and environmental determinants are in constant reciprocal interaction, and that the child behaves defiantly in response to the parent's behavior (Patterson et al., 1975). The child's abusive behavior then reinforces the parent's maladaptive actions. The therapist's primary task in this model is the identification of antecedents and consequences of the problematic behavior, and the subsequent development of new contingencies for the parent and child. The therapist then teaches the parent about behavioral principles, based on the assumption that the parent is the most effective change agent due to her/his contact with the child. Further, placing primary responsibility for changing the child's behavior on the parent, rather than the therapist, builds a sense of competence in the parent.

The functional family therapy model (Alexander and Parsons, 1982) is a second type of behavioral family therapy that contributes to the theoretical basis of our technique. This model assumes a greater cognitive component than BPT and helps the parent grasp an increased awareness of the motives for the child's deviant behavior. Within this paradigm clients learn to understand the function of the abusive behavior and the role it plays in regulating relationships.

Although our technique draws largely from the cognitive-behavioral models of family therapy, it also reflects some of the basic tenets of strategic therapy (Haley, 1963). According to this model, a symptom (verbal abuse) is believed to be a strategy for controlling a relationship, but the symptomatic person denies that s/he is attempting to control the other's behavior via the symptom (Haley, 1963). The therapist's goal is to direct each family member toward healthier methods of negotiating control such that the symptomatic behavior can be relinquished. As with our technique, the strategic model uses directives and prescriptions to elicit change based on the assumption that insight is not a sufficient ingredient for change. The goal of the therapist is to understand the power behaviors occurring in the relationship and to make a prescription that realigns these behaviors in a more adaptive fashion for the clients.

APPLICATION OF THEORY TO TECHNIQUE

When both the child's motives and the parent's dysfunctional responses are identified, they are written on the piece of paper containing the list of typical verbal insults. In an actual argument the parent is instructed to return to the list in order to provide an alternative behavior to the parent's typical response (yelling, crying, threatening). This allows the parent to remain affectively detached from the insults, focusing more on cognitions and behaviors. Also, the parent is reminded to review the columns titled "My Beliefs" and "Seeing It Differently" to reinforce her or his ability to respond appropriately to the child. The parent is asked to use the insult list for one week to continue recording various insults, and to simultaneously be aware of her/his own beliefs regarding these statements. Optimally, the parent will realize that the statements perceived to be the most true and painful are the ones that result in negative responses to the child. These are the insults that degrade the parent's ability and resolve to respond effectively with the child.

During session three of this technique the parent either gains greater insight about these beliefs, or generates alternative beliefs to each insult. At this level the therapist can use her/his judgment to determine whether insight or cognitive shifting will be the most effective intervention with the parent. The "Seeing It Differently" column will support the parent in using positive self-statements when the child uses verbal insults. With self-esteem intact, the parent will be more likely to use adaptive and appropriate responses toward the child.

CASE EXAMPLE

Jessica is a fourteen-year-old female who has been viciously swearing at her mother for two years. Because she was sexually abused, she frequently uses statements such as, "It's your fault I was abused," and "It never would have happened if you would have protected me." Jessica's mother Sara responds by crying, yelling, and threatening to send her away. Sara also attempts to defend her previous actions and refute blame for her daughter's abuse.

After an intake and two conjoint sessions to assess family dynamics, the therapist requests to work with Sara alone for the next three sessions. In the first individual session Sara is asked to recount a typical scenario and is then asked what happened right before the verbal outburst and how she responded to this. Sara states that she eventually becomes so exhausted from fighting with her daughter that she just gives in to whatever her daughter wants for the rest of the day. A recent trip to Kmart provides a typical example. While waiting in the checkout line Jessica asks if she can have a candy bar, and Sara replies that she may not since they will be eating dinner soon. This initiates a cycle of increasing insults and threats by Jessica. First she states that her mother "never lets her have anything." As her mother continues to hold the limit, Jessica searches for increasingly hurtful and effective insults. She screams that her mother is a "fucking bitch" and that she never would have been "beat up by her father" if her mother had protected her. Sara becomes increasingly embarrassed and in an effort to stop the attention being drawn to them in the checkout line agrees to buy Jessica the candy bar.

In week two, Sara returns with her paper and reports that Jessica's insults actually increased when Sara ignored her and attended to her paper. The therapist responds that this is to be expected because negative behavior actually increases before it is extinguished. The therapist reinforces Sara for persevering and asks her to make the columns "My Beliefs" and "Painfulness of Insult."

In this session Sara is asked to reflect on how much she believes each of the insults to be true as well as the painfulness of each insult. This increases Sara's awareness that she is often her own worst enemy and that she secretly holds many negative beliefs about herself. Sara is asked to take the paper home and continue recording the number of insults for the week. She is reminded to think about Jessica's motive, her typically negative responses, and the degree to which she believes the insults.

She returns in session three and reports that Jessica's verbal insults have still not ceased. At this juncture the therapist educates her further regarding behavioral principles including extinction. She is told that extinction may take several weeks or months, and that it will not occur continuously or indefinitely. However, Sara is asked to reflect on what she is learning about herself and her own sense of power. Sara replies that she is feeling more in control of herself and likes the fact that she has not behaved as negatively with Jessica. She is glad that the therapist has given her permission to not respond to Jessica at all, and that she does not have to defend herself to Jessica, only to herself. Using the "Seeing It Differently" column, Sara begins the process of creating new and different beliefs that are incongruent with the insults. The therapist helps Sara be objective and take responsibility only where appropriate. Because Sara's sense of power has moderately increased, she is able to acknowledge that she is "weak" at times by giving in to Jessica when she should not. The therapist applauds her insight and reinforces her to stand firm when she knows she has made a good choice for herself and Jessica.

Once she is educated about reinforcement contingencies and begins to feel more confident and powerful, Sara is able to establish limits with Jessica and not be manipulated to change them. As Jessica comes to finally believe that her mother is not going to be swayed or manipulated, she learns that her verbal insults no longer are effective. Jessica's verbal insults decrease markedly and, secretly, she feels relieved that her mother has finally begun to set limits.

CONTRAINDICATIONS

In the example presented here, the parent responded to her child's verbal abuse with grief and barbs of her own. Yet, in many families, parents use physical rather than verbal means to respond to vocal provocation. Obviously, in such instances, it is imperative that the therapist perform an extensive assessment of the abuse and/or violence and intervene appropriately. It must also be noted that some children proceed beyond verbal abuse to physical aggression against their parents. The technique we present here would not be an adequate method for realigning the family boundaries; indeed, this technique may unfortunately serve as provocation for physical aggression in such families.

It is also essential that the therapist evaluate a parent's capacity for implementing this technique in a suitable manner. Some parents have unfortunately passed the threshold where they are unable to forfeit their own need to "win" in order to benefit the child and the family as a whole. Such parents are likely to use this technique as a vindictive weapon rather than a constructive tool.

Finally, this method is not appropriate for children to implement, particularly those who are being verbally abused by their parents. Not only would this promote the deterioration of the family structure, but children who attempt to gain control over their parents by using this technique may meet with a violent reaction, particularly if the parents are already engaged in verbally destructive behavior.

REFERENCES

Alexander, J. and Parsons, B.V. (1982). *Functional family therapy.* Monterey, CA: Brooks/Cole Publishing.

Haley, J. (1963). *Strategies of psychotherapy.* New York: Grune and Stratton.

Minuchin, S. (1981). Structural family therapy. In R. J. Green and J. L. Framo (Eds.), *Family therapy: Major contributions* (pp. 445-476). Madison, WI: International Universities Press.

Patterson, G. R., Reid, J. B., Jones, R. R., and Conger, R. E. (1975). *A social learning approach to family intervention: Families with aggressive children.* Eugene, OR: Castalia Publishing.

70

Binuclear Family Therapy: Conflict Reduction Through Agreeing to Disagree

Donald K. Granvold

The relatively high rate of divorce has produced families posing unique challenges to both children and parents. From a child's perspective there is the requirement to accommodate living in two separate family systems, each with its defining characteristics. The divorced parent is thrust into a parallel parenting role with the ex-spouse, a condition which for most makes parenting even more difficult. When remarriage takes place, new family members are added to this constellation, multiplying the requirements for change and adaptation in the newly constituted binuclear family system. When a divorced family presents for treatment, the therapist is confronted with remarkably different and, I believe, greater challenges than those presented by intact families. As noted, there are more familial relationships to be considered in divorced families and family system components are less well defined (e.g., rules, roles, boundaries, relationships, resources, environment, etc.).

The goal in treating the divorced family is the functional reconstitution of the family in its binuclear form. In seeking this goal the family therapist promotes interpersonal relationships among family members in which negative outcomes are most limited and the positive potentials are most realized. The tendency in postdivorce treatment has been to focus on the child(ren) or on single parent/child relationships to accomplish the reconstituted family (Atwood, 1992; Granvold, 1994; Johnston and Campbell, 1988; Rice and Rice, 1986; Textor, 1989). The treatment format, accordingly, has excluded members of the binuclear family constellation. For some families there are valid reasons to include in treatment only part of the binuclear family. Geographical constraints, high levels of conflict between ex-spouses or between ex-spouse and current mate, intractable unwillingness of one parent to participate, and curtailment of parental involvement resulting from physical or sexual abuse represent reasons to exclude family members. Furthermore, the treatment objectives may more narrowly focus on one subsystem—on parent/child relationship or stepfamily relationship within one remarried (REM) nucleus. There are some families, however, where the treatment of choice is to include *both* parents and possibly to include members of remarried family units—stepparent and stepsibling.

A myriad of reasons exists to support the advisability of including both biological parents in family therapy, including such issues as dispelling the child's illusion of parental reconciliation; helping parents separate their previous marital conflicts from their ongoing parental responses; promoting effective lines of communication and appropriate content for children to transmit between parents (avoid use of child as a pawn between conflicted ex-spouses); limiting interference and undermining of the childrearing practices of one biological parent by the other (confusing, emotionally unsettling, and fosters manipulative behavior in the child); addressing the child's concern that a positive relationship with a step-parent is not an act of disloyalty to the biological parent; and effecting collaborative problem solving and greater coordination of efforts between biological parents in relation to child problem behaviors, disabilities, and maladaptive emotional responses. In short, there are many problems, issues, and concerns in divorced families that can be far more effectively addressed with both biological parents present in treatment with their child(ren) than if a biological parent is absent.

CHILDREARING DIFFERENCES

One of the more common issues in binuclear family functioning is childrearing differences. The likelihood is fairly great that rules, boundaries, roles, and the like will be markedly different in the two households that constitute the binuclear family. It is quite common for a parent to identify in therapy his/her upset feelings with the ex-spouse over differences in such areas as bedtime, curfew time, chores, and homework. Oftentimes the couple did not agree in these areas *before* the divorce! This is a great opportunity to restructure expectations. In essence, if the couple tended to disagree before the divorce they are at *least* as likely to disagree after divorce.

In the scenario that follows, Jim and Susan (ex-spouses) have been having conflict over an appropriate bedtime for their eleven-year-old son,

Jerry. Jim, Susan, and Jerry have been discussing these conflicts in family therapy to attempt to reduce the dissension among them and thereby promote a more adaptive environment for all family members. It has been determined that Jerry functions adequately whether he goes to bed at an earlier or later time. Jim and Susan have reached an impasse on the issue and each has expressed emotional distress over the ex-mate's stance.

CASE ILLUSTRATION

Therapist: Jim and Susan, did you agree on bedtime for Jerry when you were married to each other?

Jim: No, not really. I always thought that Susan was too liberal with Jerry, and, of course, I still do.

Susan: And I think you have always been too restrictive. We'll never agree.

Therapist: [to Jim and Susan] What do you think the likelihood is that you two will agree *more* on bedtime and other such issues after the divorce than you did before you divorced?

Susan: Probably very little.

Jim: Slim and none.

Therapist: I agree. Furthermore, there is actually some evidence that children can adapt well to differing sets of rules in the two households as long as the rules are consistently applied. Given this information and the great likelihood that the two of you will continue to disagree, how could you revise the expectation that you *should* agree on bedtime and the like?

Susan: I suppose that we could agree to disagree.

Therapist: I think that that's an excellent idea. Is it possible that you accept one another *with* your differences?

Jim: Yes, I suppose so.

Susan: I'll try as well, as long as you [Jim] don't become too restrictive of Jerry.

This brief cognitive restructuring interchange requires repetition and additional discussion of differences in childrearing and other areas to effectively promote the acceptance of differences between ex-spouses. The reduction of conflict between ex-spouses, reduction of independent criticism of one another by ex-spouses to the child or in the child's presence, and the development of greater supportiveness of one another by ex-spouses are viable means to effect greater positive potential in the binuclear family. Cognitive restructuring of expectations and informative discussions guided by the therapist are ways to accomplish these outcomes.

There is a body of literature including findings from many studies that can be drawn upon to more effectively inform members of divorced families of preferable ways to function postdivorce. The following is a brief sample of helpful findings that Jim and Susan found meaningful in revising their expectations and, ultimately, in changing their interpersonal behavior related to parenting Jerry.

It is helpful for divorced parents to know that children have the capacity to display adaptability and differential responses in two households where markedly different rules and roles exist. For example, in one household children may be encouraged to be highly expressive and direct with the parent and in the other household be expected to be polite, respectful, and deferential (Goldsmith, 1982). On the surface, this appears to be problematical. There is evidence, however, that children learn to switch from one set of expectancies, rules, and roles operative in one household to highly dissimilar characteristics in a second household without major psychological disruption if the two households maintain *clear* and *consistent* characteristics (Galper, 1978). Minuchin (1974) notes that it is clarity rather than symmetry of parental expectations that is the more important ingredient in the child's adjustment. Furthermore, children display better postdivorce adjustment when parents are mutually supportive and cooperative even though they may differ in parenting styles and expectations of the child.

In conducting binuclear family therapy, or other forms of divorce therapy focused on parenting issues and children's adjustment for that matter, the therapist is advised to inform parents of the findings on postdivorce parenting. While the inclination of divorced biological parents may be to attempt to force agreement on parenting issues and to gain behavioral compliance from one another in the enforcement of unilaterally-based expectations, rules, and the like, the merits of this practice are questionable. Divorced parents should be encouraged to:

1. weigh more heavily the significance of consistency of parenting *within* each household than commonality *between* households;
2. explicate parental expectations, rules, and roles in their respective households;
3. tolerate parenting style differences;
4. refrain from criticizing the ex-mate in front of the children; and
5. support the ex-mate despite their differences in parenting.

These modifications can be expected to enhance the adjustment of children who are attempting to adapt in two households.

CONCLUSION AND CONTRAINDICATIONS

When working with families entering the separation and transition phases of divorce and on into postdivorce recovery and beyond, therapists are encouraged to include both biological parents with their child(ren) in treatment. While there may be a reluctance to orchestrate opportunities for biological parents and children to experience further conflict or to endure repeated expressions of hurt, anger, sorrow, and the like through involving them conjointly in treatment, the benefits may be remarkable. There are, however, many divorced and divorcing couples whose level of acrimony is so great, whose conflict management and impulse control skills are so deficient, or the level of psychological disturbance of family members is so high that it would be strongly ill-advised to attempt to treat them collectively. In the latter circumstance alternative treatment formats may more effectively serve family members.

REFERENCES

Atwood, J. D. (1992). A systemic-behavioral approach to counseling the single-parent family. In J. D. Atwood (Ed.), *Family therapy: A systemic behavioral approach* (pp. 191-205). Chicago, IL: Nelson-Hall.

Galper, M. (1978). *Co-parenting: Sharing your child equally.* Philadelphia: Running Press.

Goldsmith, J. (1982). The post-divorce family system. In F. Walsh (Ed.), *Normal family process* (pp. 297-330). New York: Guilford.

Granvold, D. K. (1994). Cognitive-behavioral divorce therapy. In D. K. Granvold (Ed.), *Cognitive and behavioral treatment: Methods and applications* (pp. 222-246). Pacific Grove, CA: Brooks/Cole.

Johnston, J. R., and Campbell, L. E. (1988). *Impasses of divorce: The dynamics and resolution of family conflict.* New York: The Free Press.

Minuchin, S. (1974). *Families and family therapy.* Cambridge, MA: Harvard University Press.

Rice, J. R., and Rice, D. G. (1986). *Living through divorce: A developmental approach to divorce therapy.* New York: Guilford.

Textor, M. R. (Ed.). (1989). *The divorce and divorce therapy handbook.* Northvale, NJ: Jason Aronson.

71

The Use of Rogerian Techniques in Marital Therapy

David L. Fenell

Many readers of this book on family therapy techniques will have limited experience in working conjointly with couples. Yet individually oriented as well as novice therapists are frequently presented with opportunities to work with couples in therapy. Often the therapists would like to work with the whole system but elect to work with only one member of the system because they have not been trained in systems theory and are uncertain about their ability to help the family change through systems work (Fenell and Weinhold, 1997). The intervention described here provides one solution to help therapists begin working conjointly with couples.

CARL ROGERS' PERSON-CENTERED THERAPY

Most therapists have studied Carl Rogers and the person-centered theory of counseling. Moreover, most have been trained in employing the critical relationship skills that are essential to this theory in their work with clients. These critical relationship skills discovered by Rogers in his work in individual therapy are: (a) the therapist's ability to be genuine in the relationship with the client; (b) the therapist's ability to be caring, non-judgmental and fully accepting of the client; and (c) the therapist's ability to demonstrate accurate empathic understanding of the client's thoughts and feelings (Rogers, 1961).

When the therapist is able to consistently demonstrate these three characteristics in the counseling relationship with the client, therapeutic change occurs. Thus, Rogers' theory postulated that the therapeutic relationship is both necessary and sufficient to bring about therapeutic change

(Rogers 1951, 1961). The intervention described here is based on the notion that marriage partners may provide these facilitative conditions to each other in the marital relationship.

Because basic Rogerian skills are taught and practiced in the early stages of many therapist training programs, the assumption is made that the approach described here can be implemented in the treatment of couples by most therapists.

USING ROGERIAN THEORY IN COUPLES THERAPY

When a therapist is contacted by a client presenting marital problems a decision about the unit of treatment is made. Often the decision is made to treat the couple concurrently in individual sessions because the therapist has not been trained to work in any other way. Some therapists would like to use conjoint marital therapy but do not feel confident in their ability to do so.

The use of Rogers' person-centered therapy offers a relatively simple and often effective way for therapists to begin working conjointly. When the decision is made to treat the couple conjointly as a system, the therapist must decide how to best intervene. Person-centered therapy offers a simple and effective way to proceed. The four steps used in this approach to therapy are described below.

Establish Genuine Relationships with Each Partner

The first step in the therapy process is critical. The therapist must establish a genuine, trusting relationship with *each* partner. During this stage of therapy, the therapist speaks to each partner using Rogerian techniques while discouraging the partners from talking to each other about their problems. Such discussions between the partners may escalate into arguments and hard feelings that will undermine this plan of treatment. In the process of establishing the relationships with each partner the therapist will demonstrate Rogers' facilitative conditions and is genuine with each partner; shows positive regard and caring for each partner; and ensures that an accurate empathic understanding exists concerning the position of each partner. To demonstrate empathy, the therapist accurately reflects the content of the client's communication and understands and reflects the spoken and unspoken feelings associated with the content being revealed. The therapist must accept the information nonjudgmentally and with positive regard for the partner disclosing the information. The therapist establishes an effective relationship while modeling the key Rogerian skills that the couple will eventually practice. Again, it is important that the therapist respectfully block the attempts of the other partner to intrude into this conversation.

In summary, the therapist is real in the relationship, truly cares about and demonstrates caring for each partner, listens to each partner nonjudgmentally with respect, understands each partner, and helps each partner identify thoughts and feelings associated with the presenting problems. A significant result of these therapist-client conversations is that the nonparticipating partner is often able to hear and understand the spouse with more accuracy and empathy from the observer position.

Obtain Feedback on the Client-Therapist Relationships

Rogers believed that when a person feels safe in a relationship, trust and positive regard emerge. After the therapist has established trusting relationships with each individual client, the second step in the treatment occurs. This step requires the therapist to obtain feedback from each partner on their perceptions of the therapist's communication style and resulting relationship with the *other partner*. For example, the therapist might ask the husband, "Bob, what is your assessment of my conversation with Sara? How am I doing?" Almost invariably the client will say something like, "You are really able to talk to her. She seems to open up when you talk to her. I learned some things about her just listening to you two talk."

Questions to Obtain Commitment to the Therapy

When one partner has described the therapist's conversation with the spouse in positive terms, it is time to seek a commitment to therapy. The therapist asks, "Bob, you say I was very effective in talking with Sara. Would you like to be able to talk to her in a similar way?" Again, the response from the client is invariably in the affirmative. Then a key question is asked to gain commitment. "Bob, would you like to spend a few weeks in therapy working with Sara (this treatment is brief, usually three to six weekly sessions) and learning how to talk to Sara as I have today?" Once again, the response is almost always in the affirmative.

In this example I began the intervention with the husband and later would use the same procedure with the wife. The goal is to obtain commitment from both partners to work toward learning to improve relationship and communication skills as modeled and taught by the therapist using Rogerian techniques.

Teaching and Practicing the Skills

During this stage the therapist teaches the three major Rogerian techniques described above and helps the partners practice the skills in therapy dealing with their current relationship issues. The therapist should be prepared to model and coach genuineness, nonjudgmental caring, and accurate empathy during this stage of treatment as initially the couple may be operating on preconceived notions about their partner rather than understanding what the spouse is actually saying, thinking, and feeling. It is important for the therapist to coach the partners in accurately understanding each other when these preconceived notions are in operation. For example, the therapist might intervene in this way: "I'm not sure I heard Bob exactly the same way you did, Sara. I thought Bob said he was worried about you when you work long hours, not that he was opposed to you working. Why don't we check this out with Bob and see what he hoped you would hear?" A few such interventions will usually help the clients move to a place in their relationship where they are better able to hear, understand, and accept their partner's intended messages.

When the therapist observes one of the partners accurately hearing the other, it is important to ask the speaker how it felt to be heard. The response will typically be something like, "He really heard me and it feels great to be understood and accepted by him." Through in-session practice with actual couple issues the therapist will have many opportunities to reinforce the couple for demonstrating Rogerian skills learned in therapy and to ask each to report to the other what it was like when the partner used these skills.

As the couple learns to become more genuine and trusting with each other, they are able to hear and understand each other in caring and nonjudgmental ways. As the partners' thoughts and feelings are heard and accepted, each becomes more willing to risk increased intimacy in the relationship. The increased intimacy then leads to increased commitment and marital satisfaction.

This couples therapy technique is rather simple and is easy for most counselors to employ whether they have been trained in systems work or not. It is very useful in many relationship counseling situations. However, like other interventions, it is not a panacea and may be contraindicated. This approach to couples therapy may be ineffective in situations where one or both of the partners are experiencing highly charged emotions or severe psychiatric symptoms that preclude their ability to understand and practice the concepts of genuineness in relationship, nonjudgmental caring, and accurate empathy. Likewise, it is ineffective without client commitment to change. In such situations more active and directive interventions could be more effective. Yet in many marital counseling situations where the couple desires a happier and more intimate relationship, this technique can be quite useful.

REFERENCES

Fenell, D. L. and Weinhold, B. K. (1997). *Counseling families: An introduction to marriage and family therapy* (Second edition) Denver: Love Publishing.

Rogers, C. R. (1951). *Client-centered therapy.* Boston: Houghton Mifflin.

Rogers, C. R. (1961). *On becoming a person.* Boston: Houghton Mifflin.

72

If You Can't Say Something Nice . . .

David L. Kearns

. . . then don't say anything at all. Many readers could quickly complete the phrase that serves as the title of this chapter without assistance. This expression is a fundamental notion that parents frequently impart to their children, used to encode at least the possibility that children will be kind and respectful in their dealings with others. And although this phrase calls for a standard of behavior that may be difficult to maintain consistently, its underlying theme is one that most people continue to support, to one degree or another, throughout their lives.

Despite what their parents may have told them, one situation in which this otherwise good advice seems to go unheeded is when spouses are experiencing chronic marital discord. Marital therapists routinely see couples who, with alarming regularity, say disrespectful, sometimes downright vicious things to one another, both inside and outside the therapy room. In their most problematic and destructive form, once these interactions have begun, they can quickly escalate to a point where each partner is saying things that often seem designed simply to wound the other as much as possible.

It is not the intensity of these interchanges that intrigues me, nor the speed with which attempted conversations can sometimes reach a point of utter futility. What I find intriguing is that by the time many couples enter therapy, they are saying things to one another—and saying them in ways—that they would rarely consider duplicating when interacting with others.

But, of course, not all verbal conflict is bad. One component of the family conflict literature addresses the adaptive functions that occasional conflict can serve (e.g., the clarification of rights and obligations, promotion of open communication, streamlined decision making, etc. [see Vuchinich, 1987]). The comparative frequencies of conflictual versus nonconflictual interchanges are critical, however. Conflicts that are too fre-

346

quent or too intense may of course negate the benefits that otherwise might result, to the point of eroding the overall quality of the marital relationship (Deutsch, 1973; Vuchinich, 1987). Therapists who work with couples who have already experienced considerable erosion know that the task is rarely as simple as getting people to say nice things to one another. If the therapist is to assist the couple in identifying and addressing the core issues that anchor their discontent, the verbal abuse in which they are engaged will need to be contained and ultimately minimized in some way.

THE INTERVENTION

In the sections that follow, I will present a defiance-based intervention (Papp, 1980) that I have used on occasion as an initial component of therapy with verbally abusive couples. Most clearly informed by the strategic and paradoxical schools of psychotherapy (Haley, 1988; Weeks and L'Abate, 1982), the intervention is primarily symptom prescriptive, although with evidence of fewer abusive interchanges, a restraint from additional change is also commonly employed. The steps of the intervention are outlined below. Comments about various steps are contained in parentheses.

Step 1: Justifying the Intervention

The intervention is used only after more compliance-based techniques have proved ineffective in containing and reducing the verbal abuse of the couple. I commonly suggest that the virtual absence of progress in therapy up to this point may be the result of inadequate information about the problem. It is proposed that their continued difficulty in gaining control over their fighting suggests that a crucial element of the problem has probably gone unrecognized, and that a concerted effort must be made to learn from the difficulty they are trying to escape (Weeks and L'Abate, 1982). I propose, however, that because they have fought with one another with such obvious regularity and intensity, they may have habituated to the battle to such an extent that even with careful observation of the fights they have with one another, they may be incapable of learning new and critical information that may be of use in solving the problem. I stress the importance of doing something different, and with their agreement, proceed with the following steps.

Step 2: Identifying Others

In this step I ask each marital partner to identify someone they see regularly, whom they like and respect. I ask them to identify someone other than the spouse. (Couples sometimes identify a number of people. When this occurs I have each of them narrow their choice to the person they like and respect the most.)

Step 3: The Task Prescription

Once each spouse has identified one person, they are asked to arrange face-to-face meetings with these people. During their respective meetings, they are directed to insert into the ensuing conversation words and phrases that they sometimes exchange in their verbal confrontations with one another. Whenever the opportunity arises, they are asked to use a tone of voice that is common during arguments with their spouse. If interruptions are common in their arguments, each partner is asked to interrupt as often as possible the comments of the person with whom they are conversing. If the verbal interchanges of the couple typically involve unhelpful references to the past, they are asked to recall things that this person has said or done in the past that they found disagreeable, and to refer to them during this conversation. It is stressed that the task is not simply to have a conversation, but to observe the impact of selected aspects of their own behavior on the person with whom they are conversing. I ask each of them to report their observations in our next meeting. (It is not uncommon for one or both marital partners to immediately voice opposition to the task. When this occurs I justify the task again by proposing that although such words, phrases, and interruptions may be unusual in their dealings with other people, it is their occurrence in a different relational context that may provide information of use in helping them escape the problem they are having in their marriage.)

Step 4: Task Review

In the next session each spouse is asked to describe what transpired in the meeting with their friends. (To date, all of the couples I have directed to perform this task have defied the prescription.)

Step 5: Task Prescription Revisited

This is a repeat of Step 3. (With reports that the task was not performed, I typically express concern that an opportunity may have been missed to learn something new about the problem. The prescription is made again, typically with reminders of the potential value of the task. Another meeting is arranged.)

Step 6: Task Review Revisited

This is a repeat of Step 4. (With the return of the couple to the next session, additional explanations are commonly provided as to why the task was not performed. I again express concern. Renewed and sometimes more intense opposition from the couple is not uncommon. It is at this stage that the marital partners often unite against me to explain either why they will not perform the task, or why they do not have to. Changes in the way they are treating one another—less frequent and intense arguments— are sometimes noted to justify their nonperformance of the task.)

Step 7: What If?

Commenting that it seems unlikely that I will be able to convince the couple to perform this potentially informative task, I ask each marital partner to speculate about how they think things might have gone had they actually followed the prescription. (It is during this step that marital partners commonly provide additional justification for their noncompliance. The comments offered are often variations on a common theme of the damage they presume would have occurred to the relationships they share with their friends had the task been performed.)

Step 8: Moving On

With continued opposition to performing the assigned task and continued comments suggesting that the couple has been fighting less (with in-session evidence of the same) the stage is set to begin the next phase of treatment, a discussion and resolution of key issues in their relationship.

CASE EXAMPLE

Tera and Steve had been married for almost four years. This was Tera's second marriage, Steve's third. All of the children from their former relationships resided with them. During the telephone intake interview, Tera indicated that things had been "bad" in their marriage for about a year and were rapidly getting worse. As she put it, "We can't agree on anything anymore. We seem to yell at each other nonstop." Tera confirmed that Steve agreed that their marriage was in trouble and that he was willing to participate in therapy. A conjoint meeting was arranged.

I went to the waiting room to meet them at the time of our appointment. Tera and Steve were sitting far away from each other. Once in the therapy room, they indicated that over the past few months, they had spent as little time together as possible. Their marriage had reportedly deteriorated to the point where even brief interchanges about seemingly benign topics could end disastrously. Since this had been happening with increasing regularity, if they could avoid one another, they did so. In fact, although both Tera and Steve had left home at the same time for our scheduled meeting, each had driven separately. Offering an explanation, Steve said, "We didn't want to take any chances." Despite their reported skittishness around one another, the initial phase of the session was quite relaxed. We briefly discussed their respective occupations—Tera's work in health care, Steve's job as a supervisor—and they talked about the children, who ranged in age from six to thirteen. I found each of them to be quite pleasant and humorous.

A different picture emerged, however, when I steered the conversation toward their relationship. With a general inquiry about what each of them hoped to accomplish in therapy, I was treated to an example of how quickly things could get out of hand, and how they could remain so. Tera reacted negatively to one of Steve's stated goals for therapy. She said that he was accusing her. Steve quickly denied this, but counterattacked by proposing that her comment once again proved his point that she was "thin-skinned" and that their relationship was "hopeless." The race was on. From that point forward, virtually every comment from either one of them was instantaneously and intensely negated by the other.

Within a matter of minutes, the tension in the room had risen to an alarming level. There was a tremendous amount of yelling, name calling, and blaming. Occasionally, one of them would angrily refer to something the other had done in the past. Tera and Steve could also masterfully broaden the purview of their attacks to include others, most notably their respective children, in-laws, and former spouses. I made recurrent efforts to interrupt Tera and Steve but my requests for order went largely unheeded. On those rare occasions when I was able to insert a comment or suggestion that I hoped would interrupt and redirect the conversation, the resulting calm was a temporary one. Soon they were at it again, often with renewed vigor and intensity. Growing increasingly frustrated and fatigued, with approximately half of the session remaining, I asked them to "PLEASE BE QUIET!" They stopped yelling, and except for one or two comparatively minor outbursts, things remained generally calm for the remainder of the session—calm enough that we could address the behavior that had characterized the previous thirty minutes.

The couple agreed that what I had witnessed was not unusual. In fact, they reported that their battles at home often lasted longer and were more intense. Neither of them could recall a day in recent memory that hadn't been filled with name calling and fighting. Tera and Steve expressed sadness that their relationship was in such disrepair. They said that they were tired of fighting over the same things and proposed that if only they could resolve a few key issues—divergent ideas about parenting, and the best ways to handle recurrently intrusive in-laws and former spouses—their relationship would be significantly improved. I inquired if they thought that the way they attempted to speak with each other about their respective concerns had become part of the problem. They seemed confused. Although Tera and Steve freely admitted to saying extreme and hurtful things, each blamed the other for having to do so; to paraphrase, "Things get our of control because he/she never listens."

Although their interest in resolving the topics mentioned above was commendable, I predicted that their chances of doing so would probably be minuscule if they continued to go at one another in the manner I had witnessed throughout most of the session. It concerned me that each of them assumed little responsibility for what transpired between them. Verbal abuse from either of them was consistently described either as the fault of the other (e.g., "I say these things because he never listens."), or as an artifact of their collective circumstance (e.g., "Once things get going, we can't control what we say."). Either way, Tera and Steve seemed quite disconnected from the idea that what spouses say to one another, and how they say it, actually matters. We talked about ground rules that hopefully would guide more productive discussions in upcoming sessions. Tera and Steve seemed intrigued at my suggestion that at least a portion of our work together should focus on mastering more appropriate "fair fighting" techniques (Bach and Wyden, 1969; Dayringer, 1976).

As a homework task, I proposed that we needed to get a clearer appreciation of how much control they actually had over the verbal battles that could erupt between them. I said that although there might be multiple opportunities for arguments over the next two weeks, I wanted them to work hard to avoid verbal confrontations. In the event that a fight could not be avoided, I directed Tera and Steve to confine their arguing to ten minutes or less. They agreed to try. Tera and Steve were my last clients of the evening. As I walked to my car, I could see and hear them in an adjoining parking lot; they were arguing intensely.

In the second session, Tera and Steve reported no success in terms of either avoiding arguments or containing the duration of those that had erupted. Characteristically, each blamed the other for the failure, and not unlike what had happened in the first session, the action quickly escalated. Although I was able to interrupt a few of their heated exchanges, my efforts had no lasting effect. Within minutes they would be going at each other again, and in the concluding minutes of yet another unproductive session, I implored them once again to "PLEASE BE QUIET!" Each apologized for their behavior and renewed their promise to make a more concerted effort to do the previously assigned homework tasks.

Tera and Steve looked exhausted when they came to the third session. They agreed that things had been difficult, and that they had failed to control their fights. At the first sign of the next potentially escalating interchange, I interrupted them and commented that we obviously needed to proceed differently than we had in this and the previous two meetings. Tera and Steve listened intently as I built a case for the intervention summarized above (Step 1).

With their permission to proceed, I asked each of them to identify someone they saw regularly whom they liked and respected (Step 2). Tera selected a former roommate from college and Steve, a supervisor at his place of work. They were asked to schedule face-to-face meetings with these people (Step 3), and to insert into the ensuing conversations behaviors that they routinely exchanged with one another during their arguments. Tera and Steve immediately said that they didn't think that they would be able to perform the task. The directive was justified once again, and I underscored the idea that by performing the task, they might learn something new that would help in the resolution of their marital problem. Tera and Steve sat silently. Another meeting was arranged.

At the beginning of the fourth session, I requested a task update from Tera and Steve (Step 4). Each timidly reported that the task had not been completed. Steve said that after thinking about the task, he had invited his supervisor out for a beer. However, instead of duplicating aspects of his verbal behavior toward Tera, he had taken this opportunity to tell his supervisor how much he valued his friendship. I expressed concern that neither of them had performed the task; it was prescribed again (Step 5), and another meeting was arranged.

When I went to the waiting room to meet Tera and Steve at the beginning of the fifth session, they were sitting next to each other reading the same magazine. In the therapy room, I again asked for a task update (Step 6). They each laughed and proclaimed in unison that they had not done it. They added, however, that they did not think it was necessary to do the task. Both of them agreed that things had improved between them. A few arguments had reportedly occurred over the past couple weeks, but they were described as being much less frequent and intense than before. Tera added that Steve had even asked her out to see a movie. This was their first outing without the children in almost a year. I indicated that I although I was pleased that things had changed, I was hard-pressed to offer an explanation that might account for the change. I said that despite its potential value, it seemed clear that I wasn't going to convince them to do the task. I asked each of them to speculate, however, about what they thought might have happened if the task had been performed (Step 7). Steve immediately commented that he feared that he might have "done some kind of damage" to the relationship he shared with his supervisor. Tera offered a more forceful denouncement of the task, stating, "Behaving that way would be mean and disrespectful to my friend. Why would I do that to someone I care about?" I indicated that although I respected their decision to not perform the task, I was concerned that without the information that could have been gained, the progress that had been reported in this session might only be temporary. I also expressed concern that things might be changing too quickly. Tera laughed and said, "I don't care what you say, David, we aren't doing that horrible task!" Cautiously, I proposed that we should move on to the next phase of our work (Step 8). Tera and Steve agreed.

Outcome

With significant decreases in the frequency and intensity of their arguments, work that was designed to address some of the more fundamental issues in their relationship could begin. This was a difficult and lengthy therapy; from start to finish, it took nearly eight months. We usually met twice monthly. Besides working to enhance their fair-fighting and problem-resolution skills, a number of other critical relational topics were addressed (e.g., intimacy, loyalty to extended family members, lingering resentments regarding a number of premarital matters, sexuality, and the blending of their respective families). Although the majority of the sessions involved Tera and Steve, the topics covered in several sessions necessitated the involvement of the children. Over the course of my work with Tera and Steve, several setbacks did occur. These episodes often seemed to coincide with stuck points in the negotiation of important relational issues. The arguing that did occur, however, was consistently less frequent and intense than that reported and witnessed at the beginning of therapy. With the progressive resolution of many issues in their marriage, Tera and Steve came to see the relationship as a source of strength and nurturance rather than anger and animosity. At both a one- and two-year follow-up, Tera and Steve reported continued satisfaction with their relationship.

CONCLUDING COMMENTS

The intervention described above essentially targets the individual behaviors of each marital partner. Although it lacks some of the target-system reflexivity that characterizes many defiance-based interventions (Papp, 1980), in my experience, this individual-level prescription can have a powerful impact on the marital system.

Given its indirect nature, this intervention is not recommended when working with couples who report either substance abuse or physical abuse. (See Straus, 1974, for a data-based discussion of the relationship between verbal abuse and physical abuse.) Similarly, it should be noted that I have never used this intervention in instances of unilateral verbal abuse. It has been employed when there is evidence that each spouse is verbally abusing the other. Although the intervention may be useful with cases involving unilateral abuse, my concern is that the spouse whose verbal behavior is prescribed might perceive this as evidence of an alliance against him or her. If this occurred, it could obviously cause the abusive spouse's premature departure from therapy. This intervention has not been evaluated empirically (see Schwartz and Perotta, 1985). And although I have found it to be useful when working with a number of couples, like most interventions, it has not proved to be universally effective. The particular mix of problem-couple-therapist characteristics that would reliably predict success is unknown at this time.

When the intervention works, however, I would propose that it does so in part because it capitalizes on some of the resistance that was inherent in the marital system. Its effectiveness may also be related to the fact that with their consideration of the assigned task—even if only long enough to oppose it—some spouses obviously start to contemplate the damage that the verbal abuse may be doing to their partner and to the marriage.

This intervention is clearly only a tiny part of a much lengthier therapy. When it is successful, it interrupts an abusive pattern of interaction that often has become a recurrent feature in the couple's relationship. A successful interruption by itself, however, rarely ensures a positive clinical outcome. This can occur only if the couple, with the assistance of the therapist, can successfully negotiate the previously unresolved issues in their marriage.

REFERENCES

Bach, G. and Wyden, P. (1969). *The intimate enemy: How to fight fair in love and marriage*. New York: William Morrow.

Dayringer, R. (1976). Fair-fight for change: A therapeutic use of aggressiveness in couple counseling. *Journal of Marriage and Family Counseling, 2,* 115-130.

Deutsch, M. (1973). *The resolution of conflict: Constructive and destructive processes*. New Haven, CT: Yale University Press.

Haley, J. (1988). *Problem-solving therapy* (Second edition). San Francisco: Jossey-Bass Publishers.

Papp, P. (1980). The Greek chorus and other techniques of paradoxical therapy. *Family Process, 19,* 45-57.

Schwartz, R. and Perotta, P. (1985). Let us sell no intervention before its time. *The Family Therapy Networker, 9,* 18-25.

Straus, M. (1974). Leveling, civility, and violence in the family. *Journal of Marriage and the Family, 36,* 13-29.

Vuchinich, S. (1987). Starting and stopping spontaneous family conflicts. *Journal of Marriage and the Family, 49,* 591-601.

Weeks, G. R. and L'Abate, L. (1982). *Paradoxical psychotherapy: Theory and practice with individuals, couples, and families*. New York: Brunner/Mazel.

73

Seeing the Child in You

Wendy Wen-Yi Shieh

I had a hard time relating to one couple. My supervisor told me, "Try to look at them as two wounded little children and see if it can change the way you perceive them." I tried this and it worked. I was able to have much more understanding and empathy for them and the therapeutic relationship improved significantly. It occurred to me that spouses could do this with their partners, too. I credit Imago Couples Therapy (Hendrix, 1988; Luquet, 1996) for giving me a practical and theoretical framework within which I use the intervention I present below.

THE INTERVENTION

I call this intervention "seeing the child in you," and have found it a powerful tool in creating empathy and nurturance between partners. It works best when both partners are committed to their relationship.

I usually do this exercise after going through both partners' genograms so they have some basic ideas what each partner had been through as a child. In this exercise, each partner gets a turn as a child or an adult. First, I ask one partner to close his/her eyes to go back to his/her childhood to reexperience some major feelings. The other person (the adult) sits across from his/her partner and imagines the partner as a child. I then ask the "child" to open his/her eyes and share with the other person all the feelings he/she had and what he/she would like to have. I then ask the "adult" partner to hold the "child's" hands and I help him/her to show empathy and to comfort the "child." After both partners get their turns as both a child and an adult, I ask them to look into each other's eyes while holding hands, and again to see the child within. Each sees the other as a vulnerable hurt child, and not as a hurtful adult. This experience can soften their reactions to each other and expand the ways they relate. They can be each other's nurturing parents, friends, or even playmates.

CASE EXAMPLE

Kevin and Cindy have been married for two years. They are both in their twenties and are both adult children of alcoholics. They both went through many struggles and pains in their childhoods. Their past histories played an important role in almost all their marital conflicts. When they first came in, they said that they loved each other very much but they wondered if their marriage would be able to continue due to all their hurtful conflicts.

After several sessions of a combination of emotion-focused therapy, communication skills teaching, and genogram, I decided it would be good to do this exercise with them. I asked Cindy to go back to her childhood.

> **Therapist:** Cindy, now I would like you to close your eyes and take several deep breaths. Relax all the tension in your muscles . . . OK, now I want you to go back to your childhood home and find that little Cindy there. Did you see her?
> **Cindy:** Yes, she is there.
> **Therapist:** What was it like for her to live in that family?
> **Cindy:** She is always in fear. She feels sad, afraid, controlled, and lonely.

After she experienced some of those childhood memories and feelings, I asked her to open her eyes and look at Kevin. I asked Kevin to take her hands to listen to what she wanted to express.

> **Cindy** [to Kevin]: I was always afraid that my dad would come home drunk and might yell at me or criticize me. He was so unpredictable and mean. Mommy sometimes would ask me to do something or say something to please him, but sometimes she would ask me to do the opposite. I felt powerless and confused [starts crying]. No one seemed to really love me.
> **Therapist:** Kevin, can you share with little Cindy how you feel, and can you comfort her?
> **Kevin** [to Cindy]: I felt *sad* for you and felt angry the way they treated you. I know how hard it must be for you. Don't be afraid, I am here with you and you are not with them anymore. I will take care of you.

Therapist [to Cindy]: What would you like Kevin to do for you at this time?

Cindy [to Kevin]: Please let me know that I am lovable and please be more patient with me. I know sometimes I make mistakes, but I am trying hard [sobbing].

Kevin: I do love you very much. I know you tried. I am sorry for being too hard on you sometimes. I understand how that must remind you of your dad.

Kevin leaned forward to give Cindy a big hug. I then asked Cindy to close her eyes again to come back as an adult and then Kevin had his turn to be the child.

Kevin talked about how he always had to have everything in control so his dad would not punish him or his mom and other brothers. He had to protect everyone in the family. Cindy also gave him a lot of understanding, comfort, and love. With tears in his eyes, he accepted the nurturance that he did not get when he was a child from Cindy.

Therapist: I would like you now to hold each other's hands and look into each other's eyes again. See that little wounded child inside your partner. They both need more love and acceptance. When you get into your power struggles [which was their usual pattern of conflict] again, remember this moment and try to see that child in your partner again. That may provide you with a different way of perceiving what happens. You both deserve a happier childhood and it is never too late to have that. You can be each other's parents who are nurturing rather than criticizing or manipulating. You can play with each other like two little kids. You both deserve that.

With tears and smiles, Kevin and Cindy went out of the therapy room hand in hand. Before they left, Kevin told me that was the most unforgettable moment in therapy. Cindy smiled at me and said, "Now I know my marriage will be all right."

A FINAL NOTE

I have used this exercise with several couples and they all responded well to it and found it to be helpful. However, I don't use it with all couples and I don't use it when there is not enough trust and safety. Before I use this exercise, I always have to make sure that both partners are committed, and both have enough trust and safety in the relationship.

As I write about this intervention, I remember some real turning points in therapy. It is heartwarming to see tears turn into smiles and pain turn into affection. Those are the moments when I know how lucky I am to be a therapist.

REFERENCES

Hendrix, H. (1988). *Getting the love you want: A guide for couples.* New York: Holt.

Luquet, W. (1996). *Short-term couples therapy: The imago model in action.* New York: Brunner/Mazel.

74

A Picture of Health: Using Guided Imagery to Facilitate Differentiation

Catherine E. Ford Sori
Fred P. Piercy
Carolyn Tubbs

BRIEF INTRODUCTION OF THEORETICAL FOUNDATION

Bowen Systems Theory

Bowen (1978) stated that the health of family members is determined by one's level of differentiation of self, or in being able to separate from the family's "undifferentiated family ego mass." Bowen also encouraged clients to develop one-on-one relationships with individual family members, and to avoid unhealthy family triangles and the emotional flooding that can cloud more rational decision making (Bowen, 1978; Piercy and Sprenkle, 1986).

This intervention is useful with individuals who want to differentiate from their families of origin, and with couples whose family-of-origin issues are interfering with their marital relationship. Bowen (1978) believed that helping individuals to define selves within their families of origin had a ripple effect that also improved their marital relationship and their relationships with their children.

Guided Imagery

According to Piercy and Tubbs (1996), guided imagery is simply an altered state of consciousness in which clients are more receptive to suggestions. Clients do not lose consciousness or control of their will, but rather choose to follow the therapist's suggestion to explore their inner world.

In guided imagery exercises, clients begin to explore untapped inner resources. Through this process of self-discovery, new and unique perspectives of problems often emerge. The intervention we present below was inspired and adapted from an imagery activity originally described by Stevens (1971).

Although the therapist is directive in leading the client through this exercise, the questions are open-ended. This approach reduces hierarchy and respects the client's worldview. In our imagery instructions, we encourage clients to call upon their own strengths and inner resources (Piercy and Tubbs, 1996). Philosophically, this approach is based on social constructionism, and offers a context within which a more collaborative effort can occur between the client and therapist, similar to the intent of other collaborative models of family therapy (Anderson and Goolishian, 1992; Hoffman, 1993). In our intervention, the therapist empowers clients to discover for themselves how to differentiate from their families of origin.

Indications for Use

This guided imagery exercise has three primary purposes, and is designed to be used in the early-to-middle stages of family-of-origin therapy. The first purpose is to help clients clarify their goals for therapy. Second, we use this intervention to motivate clients who are "stuck." Finally, we use this intervention to help clients explore what they must do to reach their goals. If clients can visualize a goal, and are motivated to reach it, what they must do often becomes quite obvious (Cameron-Bandler, 1985).

DESCRIPTION OF THE INTERVENTION

Initial Relaxation Instructions

Using a soft voice, read the following slowly to the client:

> I'd like for you to sit comfortably in a chair and close your eyes. Take some deep breaths and slowly exhale, focusing on your breathing. As you breathe in and out, you will gradually begin to feel your body relax. As you continue to exhale, you will feel the tension leave your head and neck . . . [. . . means wait five seconds] then your shoulders and arms . . . your stomach and hips . . . and finally your legs and feet. You are probably beginning to feel more peaceful.

Family-of-Origin Sculpture

Continue to read to the client:

> Now, picture yourself standing in a hallway in front of a door. As you open the door, you enter a dark room. Bright sunlight is flooding into the room from a skylight, illuminating a statue positioned directly below. The statue is a sculpture of your relationship with your father/mother as you are now. Pause a moment and experience the impact of that sculpture. Notice the position of your father/mother . . . of yourself. Now walk closer to the statue. Look into the face of your father/mother . . . what is he/she feeling? . . . what is he/she saying to you? For a moment, imagine that you are your father/mother in the sculpture. What is that like? Now look into your own face. What are you saying to your father/mother? Become you in the sculpture. What are you thinking? . . . feeling? . . . Now slowly walk around the sculpture . . . look at it from all angles . . . reach out and touch the sculpture. How does it feel to you? Walk back to the door and look again at the sculpture. Reflect on what you have learned from this sculpture about you and your father/mother.
>
> Now open the door and leave the room. Directly across the hall is another door. As you enter, you see it is an identical room, with sun streaming down on a different sculpture. This statue is of your ideal relationship with your father/mother—how you wish you and he/she were. Pause and allow yourself to experience the full impact of this new sculpture. Note the differences in this sculpture . . . how are you and your father/mother positioned? What are you doing? As you walk closer to this sculpture, look into the face of your father/mother. Experience what he/she is feeling . . . what he/she is thinking . . . and saying to you. Imagine, for a moment, that you are your father/mother in this statue. What does this feel like to you? Now look into your own face in the statue. What are you feeling . . . thinking . . . and saying to your father/mother? What does it feel like to be you in this sculpture? Now walk slowly around the outside of the sculpture, and examine it carefully from all angles. Reach out and touch it . . . how does it feel to you? Now stand back and reflect on how this sculpture is different from the first . . . on what you have learned from this new sculpture . . . and what you want to bring back with you.

Repeat this exercise for the other parent, and for any other significant family members or primary caregivers.

As I count backward from five to one, you will open the door and be back in the present. Five, four, three, two, one. Whenever you are ready, you may open your eyes and join me here in this room.

NOTE: If a client appears dazed or does not seem to be present at the conclusion of this exercise, you may ask the client to stand up, move about, or tell you the correct time. This will help the client reorient to the present (Piercy and Tubbs, 1996).

DISCUSSION

When discussing this experience with clients, be prepared for some startling descriptions of family sculptures. Be sure to thoroughly discuss the following for both the present and ideal sculptures for both parents (and any other primary caregivers):

- What was the position and appearance of the sculpture?
- How did the parent look?
- How was the parent positioned?
- What was the parent doing, saying, and feeling?
- How did the client look?
- How was the client positioned?
- What the client was doing, feeling, and saying?
- How does the client describe his/her relationship with each parent in both sculptures?
- What did the client learn from this experience?
- What does the client believe he/she can do in the present to move toward a more positive relationship with his/her parent(s)?

Be sure to repeat the above questions for both parents. Also, you may wish to encourage clients to write down their feelings and reactions to this exercise.

CASE EXAMPLE

Patsy and Jerry came in for marital therapy because of arguments they were having concerning Patsy's family. They had been married only a year, and had recently moved to the Midwest. He was a project engineer for a national construction firm, while Patsy was a lawyer specializing in tax law and probate. Both had been married before and were in their early thirties. This move marked a big step for Patsy, who was an only child. She felt she was emotionally leaving home for the first time. Both were passionately in love with each other. They were anticipating starting a new life together, while leaving behind the pain of their past relationships.

Patsy and Jerry both agreed that their main problem was Patsy's family, who called her too frequently and at inopportune times. One of her parents might call when they were in bed at night, or just as they were leaving the house to play golf. These conversations usually lasted about two hours, and revolved around her parents' recent divorce. As the minutes turned to hours, Jerry became increasingly angry and impatient. Patsy was aware of Jerry's growing frustration, and would become increasingly anxious about his potential reaction. Though she tried, she had difficulty limiting these conversations with her parents. Jerry's anger would build during the calls, and a major blow-up usually erupted when Patsy finally hung up the telephone.

In conjoint sessions, Patsy described how she longed to be more autonomous from her parents. She described their decision to move a thousand miles from home as an attempt to create some emotional distance from her family. Both agreed that her parents were intrusive, and intended to keep her emotionally involved in their very conflictual relationship and recent divorce. While both found the phone calls extremely annoying, somehow Patsy could never quite bring herself to ask her parents to change. We explored why it was difficult for Patsy to set firm limits on phone calls from her family. As Patsy described her childhood in an alcoholic home, Jerry began to understand her guilt, and how she had learned to protect her parents.

At this point, Patsy had an individual session. In this session we did the sculpture imagery exercise described above. The following is Patsy's description of this experience:

> In the present sculpture of my mom and me, we were so close we looked like a big blob. I was still a child, and Mom's arms were all entwined around me, holding me close—too close. I felt smothered, and couldn't breathe. Mom was desperately holding onto me. The statue felt all soft and mushy.
>
> Boy, was the ideal sculpture different! In this one, I was an adult. Mom and I were sitting on a park bench, about a foot apart, turned toward each other with our knees touching. We were talking, and really enjoying ourselves. I was explaining a letter I had written to her about the phone calls. She was really listening to me, and understanding what I was feeling. It felt so good—and I felt like we were

friends. This is what I want! I want my mom and me to be friends! Now I know what I need. I need her to let go of me, not to smother me, and to let me be an adult. Then we can really be friends. I never knew before exactly what it was that I needed from my mom.

Patsy described the imagery exercise with her dad in the following way:

> In the first sculpture, the one of our present relationship, Dad and I each held the opposite ends of a rope, and we were playing tug-of-war. He pulled one way, while I pulled another. I struggled to be heard, to be understood. Boy, does that ever describe our relationship! In fact, that's how I've always felt with Dad.
>
> The second sculpture was so different. I was sitting on Dad's lap. My dad was actually holding me—something he never did. Yet, I wasn't being smothered, but was free to come and go. It just felt so comfortable, and there was no struggle at all!

How Client Responded

I could sense Pasty's excitement as we discussed the above exercise. She felt she was finally able to picture exactly how she wanted to alter her relationship with her parents. Having a clear focus helped her get unstuck, and she was finally able to tell her parents in a firm, yet loving way, how she felt about their calls. She told them she loved them and wanted to stay in contact with them, but explained that she needed to set limits on the frequency and duration of telephone calls so that she could focus on building her new life with Jerry. She validated their feelings, and then firmly told each she did not want to be in the middle of their conflicts anymore.

Patsy was thrilled with her new inner strength and confidence, and Jerry was immensely pleased that Patsy had finally taken a stand. Their relationship rapidly began to improve. Patsy received a letter from her father, in which he told her that he had never guessed how she felt, and that he was happy that she had shared her feelings with him. As anticipated, her mother was a little less enthusiastic. However, Patsy continued to validate her mother's feelings, while maintaining a clear boundary around her relationship with Jerry. There was a gradual shift in Mom's attitude. Patsy had made it clear she didn't want to hear Mom complain about Dad anymore, and they began to find new things to talk about, such as Patsy's new home and job. Mom even came out for a visit, which went surprisingly well.

Jerry and Patsy stayed in therapy for several more sessions as we explored issues related to their divorces, and worked to improve their communication skills. As they neared termination, Patsy remarked to me that the single most helpful thing we had done in therapy was the sculpting imagery exercise. When I asked her why, she replied:

> This exercise really had an impact on me. Before, I knew something needed to change, but I didn't know what. I couldn't really put my finger on what didn't feel right about my relationship with my parents. This exercise helped me to see clearly what I didn't like, and what I wanted to change about these relationships. Once I saw what I wanted and needed from my parents, it was easy to ask for it! Because I understood how they were feeling, I was able to ask in a way that didn't hurt them. This was what I couldn't figure out—what I needed, and how to ask for it so I wouldn't hurt them.

CONTRAINDICATIONS

Guided imagery is generally not harmful to most clients. However, Piercy and Tubbs (1996) caution that this should not be used with schizophrenic or paranoid clients, or those who are psychotic, delusional, or hallucinatory. As is the case with all interventions, it is wise to use good clinical judgment and assess each client on an individual basis for the appropriateness of this and any other intervention.

CONCLUDING REMARKS

The main purpose of this exercise is to help clients working on family-of-origin issues begin the process of differentiation by discovering what it is they wish to change about their current relationships within their families. Therapists may repeat this exercise midway through therapy to assess the client's progress. How do the sculptures look at the midpoint of therapy? How has the statue changed from the original, and is it beginning to resemble the ideal sculpture?

REFERENCES

Anderson, H. and Goolishian, H. (1992). The client is the expert: A not-knowing approach to therapy. In S. McNamee and K. Gergen (Eds.), *Therapy as social construction* (pp. 25-39). Newbury Park, CA: Sage.

Bowen, M. (1978). *Family therapy in clinical practice.* New York: Jason Aronson.

Cameron-Bandler, L. (1985). *Solutions: Enhancing love, sex, and relationships.* Moab, UT: Real People Press.

Hoffman, L. (1993). *Exchanging voices: A collaborative approach to family therapy.* London: Karnac Books.

Piercy, F. and Sprenkle, D. (1986). *Family therapy sourcebook.* New York: Guilford Press.

Piercy, F. and Tubbs, C. (1996). Tapping internal resources: Guided imagery in couple therapy. *Journal of Systemic Therapies, 15,* 53-64.

Stevens, J. O. (1971). *Awareness: Exploring, experimenting, experiencing.* Moab, UT: Real People Press.

75

It's Never Too Late to Have a Good Childhood: Reworking at the Source

Beth M. Erickson

From time to time, even the best, most seasoned therapists feel stuck. Often with obstreperous clients and sometimes even with the most motivated, both therapists and clients sometimes trip again and again over a subtle but keenly felt barrier to change. These are the vexing times when both therapists and clients feel like Sisyphus pushing the rock up the hill, only to have it roll back down, each time generating an ordeal and diminishing hope for everyone involved.

One way to understand what caused this roadblock that impedes clients' growth and development, despite their fondest conscious wishes to the contrary, is the phenomenon of early decisions. That is, what initially may appear to be an elaborate game of "Stump the Therapist" probably is the intrusion of a relic from the client's past in the form of an early decision, made outside the client's conscious awareness. It is important that the therapist apprehend that this was an attempt to ensure their emotional—and sometimes literal—survival and reframe it in this way to clients as well. Then, once this barrier to change has been identified and clients can see it as an example of resourcefulness that is no longer resourceful, they likely will be much more willing and able to surrender it to an adult decision that they know they "should" make.

THEORETICAL KIN TO THIS APPROACH

This intervention taps the synergy between individuals' intrapsychic functioning and their interpersonal connections. It helps clients reconcile the dimensions of their inner, unconscious lives with their intellectual processes and with the multiple relationship systems in which they operate.

Whereas some current family theorists and therapists appear perennially to have difficulty in keeping the individual's place clearly in perspective when working systemically, many prominent voices in our field have not. Notably, the work of Bowen (1978), Framo (1982), Napier and Whitaker (1978), Paul and Paul (1986), Pinsof (1983, 1991), Schwartz (1987, 1988), and Nichols (1987) speaks to the need for a meaningful place in our systemic conceptualizations for a focus on individuals. Each of these theorists espouses the belief that the key to unlocking solutions to clients' problems lies in understanding and correcting early experiences, a view I heartily endorse.

ASSUMPTIONS ABOUT THE ETIOLOGY OF THIS TRAP

To change something responsibly, we first must know it in context. Little can be changed substantively if we fail to understand how dysfunctional responses develop. People do not behave in a vacuum; their behavior springs from somewhere. The primary source of fuel for their behavior is intrapsychic issues that develop from events variously described as early decisions (Goulding and Goulding, 1979), source experiences (Paul and Paul, 1986), or nuclear family scripts (Johnston, 1995; Johnston and Campbell, 1988). These are the indelible images that form a template for how individuals and families "should" be and provide the "logic" for people's illogical, unconstructive behavior.

When therapists can help clients articulate and examine these motifs and discharge the emotional fuel that they encapsulate, the power of these issues is markedly diminished, if not dissipated entirely. Not only does this allow people to bring these more primitive reactions and the dysfunction they generate under conscious control; but also doing so restructures the personality into more effective ways of being and perceiving.

How do these responses develop? People cope with any trauma, particularly that which is experienced in their early family life (e.g., parents' divorce, abuse, or death) by unconsciously developing a set of expectations about how interpersonal relationships work and, most particularly, about whom and how they have to be, in order to stay psychologically and physically safe. These conclusions become an emotional and perceptual prism through which all further experience is filtered. Then, both a worldview and a personality structure are shaped in accordance with it. These decisions, most often made unconsciously, were designed to satisfy the overt and covert instructions that were communicated to them by the powerful people in their lives, usually their parents. These decisions may have been helpful in that they guaranteed clients' survival in childhood, but they are archaic now. In fact, they likely compromise clients' functioning in adulthood because they were made when the child had only concrete reasoning ability, was highly egocentric, and had few adequate emotional defenses (Erickson, 1993). Moreover, until that script or early decision is made conscious, it cannot readily be either reality-tested or modified.

The family is the cradle for the development of the individuals in it. Therefore, if something disabling happened in the family, particularly to children, it is important for therapy to address that source experience, in order to modify and mollify its effects. For many people, simply making an intellectual decision to change will go for naught. Giving intellectual assent to the need for change and attaining the requisite flexibility to accomplish the actual change often are two different matters. That is, it is important to assess for and treat, if discovered, these early traumas, for their burial is their preservation. Otherwise, they will continue to shape people's worldviews, their personalities, their relationship choices, and thus every facet of their lives.

THE INTERVENTION

The intervention itself is easy to describe and simple to execute. However, the key to its usefulness is in the preparation. The therapist must take care not to promote yet another intellectual, logical decision that will be countered by the client's unconscious "illogical logic." This only wallpapers yet another layer of defenses over an already substantial self-protection racket. In fact, the primary diagnostic indicator for timing this intervention is when the therapist's reasonable suggestions and the client's earnest intentions do not yield the change that the client, on a conscious level, is actively seeking. Then, it is time to prowl around in the unconscious, to see what can be uncovered, and to enlist its aid. It is as though client and therapist must ask the permission of the unconscious mind to do something different by giving it another, more functional way to protect the individual.

Before describing the intervention itself, the author will describe several key diagnostic indicators that point to the client's readiness to do redecision work. Then the intervention will be described step by step.

Introducing the Intervention

The following markers provide cues that clients may be ready to make a new, more appropriate decision, thereby replacing the relic by which they have lived their lives. Clients:

1. have appeared resistant to multiple other interventions to change their behavior;

2. are able to articulate their early decision;
3. are able to identify what factors prompted them to choose this way of coping;
4. can see the wisdom in their now archaic decision and can develop empathy, rather than judgment, for themselves for making such a decision;
5. have demonstrated in multiple ways that they no longer want or need the protection that the early decision provided;
6. grasp that continuing to live by that early decision is interfering with their life and happiness now;
7. have incentives to make a different decision and acknowledge its benefits;
8. have experienced enough pain from living by that decision that any discomfort from learning how to live without that protection seems like a small price to pay;
9. recognize at both intellectual and visceral levels that they no longer desire the illusion of control they believed they experienced when living by that early decision;
10. recognize that they can make choices for their life now that are different from those that implicitly prompted the need for the early decision.

Usually, the preparatory work is more arduous and involved than the actual intervention itself. It typically centers around helping people apprehend the elegant paradox of gaining greater control of their lives by giving up the illusion of safety that their early decision provided.

Steps for the Therapist

Helping clients to make a new, more flexible decision as a guiding principle for their lives involves the following steps.

- Develop your own potential hypothesis about the nature and function of the client's early decision.
- Identify the source experience that likely prompted the now-antiquated decision to be made.
- Cultivate a healthy respect for the intuitive wisdom involved in making that survival-oriented decision, as dysfunctional as the decision now may seem to both of you.
- Resist your tendency to judge those whose conduct prompted the making of that decision, so that the client's unconscious does not

have to fight you to protect loved ones and thereby maintain the defense that decision provides.

Steps with the Client

- Explain the concept of early decisions to the client, taking care to commend the protective function of such "logic."
- Ask the client if s/he thinks an early decision may have been made.
- If yes, invite the client to brainstorm options for what that early decision may have been.
- After the client states possible candidates for early decisions, ask him/her to check for the accuracy of each at a feeling, not an intellectual, level.
- Once the client has settled on an early decision that has the greatest ring of truth, ask him/her to brainstorm possible new decisions that would be more helpful now. Ask the client to check for emotional congruence of each possible new decision.
- Suggest trying one on until the next appointment.
- After the new decision has been made and there has been time to live with the new decision, help the client practice behaving in ways that are consistent with this new perspective and decision.
- Help the client anticipate and plan for any homeostatic reactions in self or in others.

Following these simple steps that have their own intuitive logic makes it easy for most clients to make better decisions that tap their adult, abstract cognitive resources, rather than the concrete and usually defensive ones to which a child is naturally relegated.

This elegantly simple intervention can be done when treating individuals or couples. However, when implementing this technique in couples therapy, I recommend that only one person's early decision be focused on at a time. To try to do both simultaneously likely would wildly unbalance the system at worst, or be unnecessarily confusing at best.

CASE EXAMPLE

Jack (not his real name) is a forty-one-year-old computer programmer who almost died of spinal meningitis at age eleven. The sequellae of this illness were impaired memory, arrested physical and therefore sexual development for two years, and generally being puny and weak for much of his adolescence. Although this situation would be difficult for anyone, it would be particularly devastating to adolescents. This is because their particular kind of egocentrism causes them to believe that they are on stage for all to see and to criticize. In addition, the occurrence of this unfortunate illness at a time when fitting in and peer acceptance are everything also left its deep scars. Trying to keep up with his age mates while enduring their ridicule was deeply humiliating and frustrating just when a young boy's socialization dictates that he is to be tough.

He decided never to let anyone see any evidence of his weakness, lest he feel even more powerless and helpless than he already did. This was especially true with his mother, who he experienced as smothering him out of her understandable concern for him. He reasoned that if his weakness were exposed to anyone, especially to her, his neediness would generate the ultimate in humiliation. Thus began a long, lonely life of feeling not good enough and of never letting anyone close, which he, of course, continued with his wife, despite her protestations, demands, and pleadings to the contrary.

Not surprisingly, when he presented for treatment, his marriage was arid and in shambles, and his battered self-esteem was thinly veiled by a mask of irritating arrogance. His only attempts to experience closeness were in the relative safety of a string of extramarital affairs. His wife understandably was both furious and wary, and he was extremely confused about what he wanted and what he was doing.

A major piece of the therapeutic work that was required to enable him to reach for the closeness he said he had always craved in relationships turned on the early decision work described above. This was undertaken after the therapist could get no leverage to make any progress in the couples therapy by working with standard approaches aimed at shifting the couple's interaction patterns. However, once his early decision was discovered and understood, then couples therapy of a more systemic nature could take place. Furthermore, throughout the couples therapy, Jack's early decision became a touchstone for all subsequent work.

CONTRAINDICATIONS

Because of its psychodynamic foundation, it might be easy to disqualify this intervention when operating within the confines of the brief therapy that more and more is being prescribed by fiat of managed care. But this is not necessary. For example, I recently used this technique midway through an eight-session course of treatment with a fifty-four-year-old woman who remained stuck in the aftermath of childhood sexual abuse, despite many hours of psychotherapy with various providers. It was highly effective in dislodging a major stumbling block that would have rendered virtually any treatment, whether short- or long-term, ineffective.

However, there are three contraindications of which the reader may wish to be aware when contemplating the use of this typically extremely potent intervention. The first is that this is likely to be of questionable effectiveness with highly resistant or extremely rigid clients. However, in the author's experience, this usually will take care of itself. That is, they and their unconscious minds will render them impervious to this intervention, too. They either will humor the therapist who brings up the concept of early decisions, or will downright block any attempt to understand even this sliver of their unconscious. The second group for whom this intervention likely is contraindicated is children, with their inability to think abstractly, or adults whose intellectual development has been arrested such that they are able only to think concretely. These populations simply will be unable to grasp a concept this abstract. Although no harm is likely to come of this, one can expect little therapeutic efficacy, either. And the third group, one for which the use of this technique should be approached with extreme caution, is those with dissociative disorders. These clients can be expected either to have no access to important and traumatic data from their childhoods, or, if they do recall before they are ready to remember, this may prompt a major abreaction that could be damaging to them and to the therapy.

CONCLUSION

Recently, the female client discussed above asked me a very pointed question that speaks to the overall reason for taking people back to the source of their pain. She asked, "Why is it, when I start remembering back to my childhood, I only remember the bad times, and not the good times?" My answer was simple. "Because the bad times that you have never finished dealing with are in the way. Once we resolve them, they will be out of the way, and you will be able to claim the good parts of your childhood, along with the bad." That explanation seemed to satisfy her.

Truly, it is never too late to have a good childhood.

REFERENCES

Bowen, M. (1978). *Family therapy in clinical practice.* New York: Jason Aronson.
Erickson, B. (1993). *Helping men change: The role of the female therapist.* Newbury Park, CA: Sage Publications.

Framo, J. (1982). *Explorations in marital and family therapy: Selected papers of James L. Framo, PhD.* New York: Springer.

Goulding, M. and Goulding, R. (1979). *Changing lives through redecision therapy.* New York: Brunner/Mazel.

Johnston, J. (1995, October). No more fighting: Strategies for stabilizing conflict in the divided home. Seminar presentation for the Albuquerque Family and Child Guidance Center, Albuquerque, NM.

Johnston, J. and Campbell, L. (1988). *Impasses of divorce.* New York: The Free Press.

Napier, A. and Whitaker, C. (1978). *The family crucible.* New York: Harper & Row.

Nichols, M. (1987). The individual in the system. *Family Therapy Networker, 11*(2), 32-38; 85.

Paul, N. and Paul, B. (1986). *The marital puzzle: Transgenerational analysis of marriage counseling.* New York: Gardner.

Pinsof, W. (1983). Integrative problem-centered therapy: Toward the synthesis of family and individual psychotherapies. *Journal of Marital and Family Therapy, 9*(1), 19-34.

Pinsof, W. (1991, June). Rediscovering the individual: A step forward or back? Plenary presentation for the American Family Therapy Academy annual meeting, San Diego, CA.

Schwartz, R. (1987). Our multiple selves. *Family Therapy Networker, 11*(2), 24-31; 80-83.

Schwartz, R. (1988). Know thy selves. *Family Therapy Networker, 12* (November/December), 20-29.

76

The Typical Day Interview:
A Play Therapy Intervention

Geoffrey L. Smith

The typical day interview (Gil, 1994) is a play therapy technique that is usually used as an assessment tool. To do a typical day interview, the therapist provides the child with dollhouses and dolls. The therapist then encourages the child to explain his/her "normal" day and to use the dolls as props to tell the story.

Dr. Eliana Gil (1994) describes the Typical Day Interview in her book, *Play in Family Therapy*. While doing the interview, the therapist should pay close attention to the child's narrative and feel free to ask any questions that seem pertinent. Also, there are six areas of questioning that the therapist should not ignore. These areas are: television watching, eating habits, sleeping habits, hygiene, anger, and affection.

The amount of television that the family watches can tell a lot about their family interactions. Also, sometimes TV is used as a substitute baby-sitter for the children. Eating habits are important to consider because in some families children feed themselves and may not be receiving the appropriate nutritional requirements. Asking questions about sleeping habits will provide clues about what happens after the child goes to bed. This line of questioning might alert the therapist to any possible sexual abuse. Questions about hygiene are important for two reasons. First, in some families the children might be so dirty that other children or teachers treat them unfairly. Second, in some cases, parents might use the excuse of cleaning a child to sexually molest him/her.

Anger is another area that should be addressed. By asking questions about anger, the therapist can learn about any possible physical abuse in the home. The last area that Gil recommends as an important line of questioning is affection. Affection is an important part of family functioning and appropriate affection is good for the child's development and self-esteem. Also, questions along this line might lead to the therapist's learning about inappropriate affection in the family. In addition to these six lines of questioning, the therapist should take time to ask about school days and weekend days or about "Mommy's house" and "Daddy's house" if the parents are no longer living together. There is often more than one typical day to consider.

Clearly, by obtaining so much information, the Typical Day Interview can be an effective assessment tool. Although Gil primarily uses the Typical Day Interview in this manner, I have also had some success using the Typical Day Interview as an intervention that helps parents and children learn more about each other and increase empathy for each other's thoughts and feelings. A recent example of a case where I was able to use the Typical Day Interview as an intervention was with Charlene, a forty-two-year-old single mother, and Billie, her nine-year-old daughter.

Charlene brought her daughter into therapy because Billie was not doing well since her parents' recent divorce. In the time that I had been getting to know this family I could see that the mother and daughter cared about each other, but they seemed unable to communicate it in a way that was powerful enough to make the sentiment last. The Typical Day Interview seemed to be an appropriate intervention to use in this case.

One night after we had spent a few minutes coloring, I asked Billie to use the dolls to describe her typical day to me. She started out with getting up in the morning and getting ready for school. The only morning interactions she described with her mother were those of her mother nagging her to get ready for school and of Charlene being angry about having to do so much. Billie felt that Charlene was mad at her for "busying up" her life (having to get her up in the morning, make some breakfast for her, and drive her to school). Billie described her school day, which seemed to go well. After school Billie came home and was unsupervised for a couple of hours. She explained that she normally watched TV or played with friends in the neighborhood. At 5:30, Charlene arrived home from work and Billie felt that her mother was usually grumpy. Billie would then start whining and often ask her mother why the family could not live together anymore. Charlene would then withdraw and Billie would spend the rest of the evening playing video games in her room and then going to bed at 9:00 when Charlene would come to put her to bed (often Billie would act like she was sleeping to avoid a possible tirade by her mother). Most of the interactions with her mother that Billie described were negative.

After having Billie explain her typical day, I asked Charlene to share hers. At this point, she was feeling so guilty and sad that she really did not want to share her day. After some gentle persuasion, she decided to go ahead with her typical day narrative. Charlene would often be tired from the previous day when she got up early to have things ready for Billie. She explained that being tired from the previous day often made her irritable from the time she got up. Rushing around in the morning made her less pleasant than she would like to be. As she drove to work she would usually worry about the way that she had treated Billie in the morning. This would usually plague her thoughts for the rest of the day. She would often come home very repentant, but would become quickly angered whenever Billie mentioned the divorce or moving back in with her father. She would then spend the rest of the night caught up with her feelings about the recent divorce and thus not be emotionally available to her daughter. This vicious cycle would then repeat itself the next day. Throughout Charlene's story I paid attention to having Charlene share her thoughts and feelings, especially as they related to Billie. By following this line of questioning, Charlene was able to express to Billie how much she loved her.

By using the Typical Day Interview, Charlene and Billie were better able to understand each other. Charlene was not aware that Billie regarded so much of their relationship in a negative light. Charlene was able to get in touch with her daughter's feelings. This helped her realize that she was letting her anger and sadness regarding her divorce affect her relationship with Billie. Billie was able to see how much her mother cared for her and that a good portion of Charlene's actions were centered around trying to do what she felt was best for Billie. Billie did not realize that her mother thought and worried about her throughout the day.

In this case example, the Typical Day Interview intervention was a springboard for increased empathy in the mother-daughter relationship. The work that was accomplished in this session provided a nice base that allowed Charlene and Billie to improve their relationship. Charlene began controlling her anger regarding the divorce and not inadvertently having her emotions adversely affect her interactions with Billie.

The Typical Day Interview can be useful as an intervention and as an assessment tool; however, there are some factors that may contraindicate the use of this technique. First, if the therapist suspects that the parent in the interview may be neglectful or abusive toward the child, the therapist would be wise to interview the child without the parent's presence. Second, the Typical Day Interview may elicit intense emotion as it deals with potentially painful experiences that have happened in the child's home. The therapist should have built a trusting relationship with the child so that the child may be honest and feel comfortable with whatever he/she needs to talk about during the interview.

An intervention such as the Typical Day Interview, like many play therapy techniques, can facilitate open communication to the therapist because of the indirectness of the technique. The clients are actually telling the story through their dolls which may make it easier for them to share the story (Irwin and Malloy, 1975). However, using a play therapy technique does not decrease the intensity because it is clear who the dolls represent. This is what occurred in the above case example: Charlene and Billie were able to share their stories with each other in a less threatening way by using the dolls. By opening up to each other they were able to have increased empathy for each other. The Typical Day Interview, although often used as an assessment tool, can be a powerful intervention to help families understand one another at a deeper level and thus advance the therapeutic process.

REFERENCES

Gil, E. (1994). *Play in family therapy.* New York: Guilford.
Irwin, E. C. and Malloy, E. S. (1975). Family puppet interview. *Family Process, 14*, 170-191.

77

Peace at Any Price

Young Hee Chang

Couples often tire of arguing and develop ways "to keep the peace." However, these solutions often do not help the couple feel close or happy. Instead, the solutions themselves often become problems. In fact, by the time the couple reaches the therapist's office, they may have become stuck in a dance in which communication, intimacy, and connection are lost, and instead, many unspoken rules and assumptions guide what they do to avoid arguments. Through the use of "peace at any price diagrams" therapists can help couples explore how they have been keeping the peace in their relationship, and at what price to their relationship. In doing so, the therapist may then help the couple negotiate new ways to support each other.

THEORETICAL ORIENTATION

Harriet Lerner's (1985) work on peacemaking in couples and White and Epston's (1990) work on externalizing the problem have influenced the creation of this intervention. Lerner uses the phrase "peace at any price" when doing work with couples. She argues that women have been socialized to be peacemakers in relationships, and that many times women may not bring up problems in their relationships because they do not want to cause conflict. The price of being peacemakers, however, can be high, such as in cases where women develop depression or physical symptoms. The peace at any price diagram focuses not only on women's strategies for peacemaking but also on men's strategies, and can be used for both genders.

Michael White "externalizes" problems so that couples do not see their partners as the problem but instead see the "problem as the problem."

Therapists can also externalize a couple's problem using peace at any price diagrams.

Couples Best Suited for Intervention

This intervention can be used with couples with "communication problems." Oftentimes these couples have developed ways to keep the peace in relationship and avoid conflict.

THE INTERVENTION

Consider Harry and Sally. When Sally comes home from work feeling angry or frustrated from her hard day and in a bad mood, Harry tries to stay out of Sally's way. He tries to keep the peace by avoiding an argument and giving Sally her space. But when he does so, Sally feels neglected and abandoned, which puts her in an even worse mood. The angrier Sally feels, the more Harry tries to keep away, which in turn makes Sally angrier. They come in for therapy stating that they have communication problems.

The therapist can introduce the peace at any price intervention like this:

> Sometimes we have good intentions. We want to keep the peace in our relationship. However, the ways we try to do that can be stressful to us and may not help our partner feel any better. The end result is that both partners feel bad. On one hand, the person trying to keep the peace may end up feeling that "I'm trying so hard but still am not doing things right. I do not know what else to do to make him/her happy. I feel unappreciated for my efforts. What does he/she want?" Or, on the other hand, the partner may feel, "Why doesn't he/she understand me, why can't he/she support me, or understand the way I feel?" and might feel frustrated in the relationship. Let's take a look at how you try to keep the peace in your relationship, and see how that feels for you right now . . .

Then, the therapist asks: (1) "How do you currently try to keep the peace? For example, what is your strategy? What do you do? When do you find yourself using this strategy?" (2) "How do you feel when you are doing this?" (3) "What are you trying to achieve? That is, what do you want?"

The therapist writes the answers to these questions on the diagram using the following format. (The therapist can use a blackboard or pre-printed sheets the couple can take home.)

Harry's answers may be something like the following:

I try to keep the peace by . . .	because I feel . . .	and want . . .
not disturbing you when you are upset	scared we'll have an argument	to not get you more upset
leaving you alone when you come home from work looking angry or frustrated	nervous I'll say the wrong thing	to give you space to prevent an argument

The therapist then turns to the partner and charts the partner's response to the current peacekeeping strategy. Note that the therapist does not inquire about complaints about the other partner, but about the peacekeeping strategy. This way the therapist helps externalize the problem and helps the couple work together and band together against the strategy that is not working, rather than blaming each other or seeing the partner as the problem. Here is the example with Sally:

> **Therapist:** I'd like to see how you currently respond to this peacekeeping strategy.

The therapist asks: (1) "How do you interpret the current peacekeeping strategy?" (2) "How do you feel?" (3) "What would you prefer?"

However, I interpret that as . . .	and feel . . .	I would prefer if . . .
you avoiding me when I get upset	alone, abandoned	you let me know that you noticed I was upset
you not caring about me when I get upset	like I'm the bad guy for bringing home trouble	you could hold me when I'm upset

Harry may be surprised that Sally wants him to be supportive by giving her a hug and listening to her or acknowledging her feelings. Instead of giving her space, which Sally interprets as abandonment, the couple can then negotiate ways they can feel close and supported. It is not important that the partner agrees with all of the new requests, but that the couple can negotiate a new vision of how to support each other that feels satisfactory to both. Lastly, the therapist asks the couple to reflect upon the old peace-keeping strategy, the price of the old strategy for each individual, and on the relationship. The therapist then asks the couple to generate a new definition of peace and its benefits from the requests that the partner gives and the acceptance and negotiation of new ways to create peace.

The therapist asks: (1) "What was the peace like using the old peace-making strategy? Was it momentary or permanent, something you could believe in, or something that could fall apart at any time, something that felt real or fake, etc.?" (2) "What was the price of using the old peace-making strategy? What were the costs? to you? to your relationship?" (3) "What is the new peace that you achieve in your relationship by using the new peacemaking or peace generating (as opposed to peacekeeping) strategies?" (4) "What benefits do the new peacemaking strategies have?"

For Harry and Sally, they may answer the questions about their old and new peace as in the following:

Type of peace achieved using old strategy	Price of old strategy	Peace redefined with new strategies	Benefits of new peace
Peace is "momentary"—until the tension blows over Peace is not "real"—feel like we're walking on eggshells Peace means "no fighting" but does not mean really feeling relaxed with each other	Feels stressful Feels as if it could turn into a fight about no support No communication No real sense of support in the relationship Feel out of touch with how the other is feeling Feel inadequate to really help each other Builds up and could come up in next argument	Peace that is based on sharing our frustrations and supporting each other Peace that is based on feeling understood by the other Peace that is based on our relationship growing by learning about how to be there for each other even during hard days	Feeling connection Feeling supported and knowing how to be supportive Feeling understood Sharing our frustrations Being there for each other Learning new things about our partner Staying in touch Feeling safe and loved and loving

The diagram can then be turned around and Sally can answer these same questions for her peacekeeping strategies in the relationship. She may go on to answer that she tries to keep the peace by not talking about her bad day, or by trying to hide her anger, and so on. Harry can also make requests about what he would prefer Sally to do and offer new strategies. Thus, both partners can explore their own peacekeeping strategies, and both partners can make requests for alternative strategies.

CONTRAINDICATIONS

In an abusive relationship, a partner may try to keep the peace so that she/he will not be physically harmed or threatened. For instance, a woman might stay quiet when her partner is angry to prevent any physical retribution from her partner. Therapists should not use this intervention with couples who are physically violent, and should pay special attention to issues of power and control when carrying out this intervention. If power differences are identified, therapists should point out differences in power, and should pay close attention to safety in relationships.

REFERENCES

Lerner, H. (1985). *The dance of anger.* New York: Harper & Row.
White, M. and Epston, D. (1990). *Narrative means to therapeutic ends.* New York: W.W. Norton.

78

Teaching Metaphors

Betty Vos

I have developed two metaphors that I use often in therapy. The first helps my work with single parents; most frequently, single mothers. The single mother role is incredibly overburdened. So often, when a single mom truly cares about her children, she gives up too much of herself. Her energies focus almost entirely on work (extra hours, often, to secure barely enough financial support for her family), household, and children. If I try to tell her she needs to do something for herself, she is disdainful: there is no time for herself, I simply do not understand her situation.

Martha is such a mom. The mother of four children under ten, two of them preschoolers, she had just been deserted by her abusive husband, who left her for another woman. Devoutly religious, she believes she needs to sacrifice herself for her children. She takes in computer data entry work which she can do at home to supplement finances, but most of the time ends up having to stay up into the wee hours of the morning to finish because of being unable to work while the children are up during the day. This schedule wears her down so much that she is ill more often than not; the common colds to which she is so susceptible frequently develop into bronchitis. Moreover, she finds herself unable to ask her children to pitch in around the house, saying, "They have suffered so much already."

So I ask if she has ever flown in an airplane. Does she pay attention when the flight crew gives the safety lecture? What do they say when they start talking about oxygen masks? "If the cabin pressure drops, an oxygen mask will appear from the overhead compartment. Pull the mask toward your face, secure the strap, and breathe normally." If you are traveling with children, what are the instructions? Do you attend to the children first, before taking care of your own need for oxygen? No. Counterintuitive as it may seem, you can only be certain of saving your children if you put on your own mask first. If you start with the child's mask, you may run out of oxygen—out of consciousness—before you finish the task, and both you and the child will die. If you put on your own first, you will stay conscious, and even if your child has temporarily become unconscious from lack of oxygen, you will be alert and able to put the child's mask in place and restore the life-giving oxygen supply.

The literature is clear that children in single-parent families are better adjusted when the residential parent is healthy and well adjusted, not depressed. Taking sufficient care of her own valid needs is not a luxury for the single mother but a necessity. Working with Martha, the oxygen mask becomes a language we can use over the course of therapy to check in on self care, on the balance of meeting her own needs and meeting her children's needs. The metaphor contains both: she *must* put on her own mask first, but she must also secure the mask on her child. For this religious, self-sacrificing woman, the metaphor does not challenge her basic belief in being there for her children. Paradoxically, it points out how she can *only* be there for them if she attends to her own needs enough to survive. Using the metaphor, we attempt to weave together appropriate levels of self care and care for her children.

The second metaphor surfaces often in work with couples and adult individuals in the process of working through how early relationship experiences affect the present. Conceptually it is related to "inner child" work, though I do not always explicitly use that language. Frequently clients become frustrated as they begin to identify repetitive, destructive habits in their ways of relating which, in the early stages of therapy, they are unable to change. Over and over they return to the next session distressed because they have "done it again:" they have shut down when overwhelmed with a negative feeling, they have said things in anger they wish they had left unsaid, they have pushed someone away when they wanted to get close, and on and on. Usually by this time we have spent some energy identifying what they learned they had to do to survive as a child: how shutting down was functional, how exploding in anger might have been modeled for them, how intimacy and getting close might have been dangerous.

So at this point, I talk about "who is driving the bus." I offer the notion that most of the time, when the road is smooth, our adult self is driving the bus: we know how to steer, we know what to do with the brakes, how to respond to bumps in the road or steep hills. But sometimes a situation frightens the tiny child inside who knows that feelings are not safe, who knows that the only useful response to being hurt is rageful attack, who knows survival is not possible if relationships become too close. In that moment, it is as though the child takes over the driver's seat on the bus. The child who knows these things no longer trusts us to drive safely, and suddenly we are not in charge, and the bus is careening out of control.

There are two tasks for our adult self at this point: to wrench control back from the child, and simultaneously to convince the child that we can be trusted: we will keep the child safe, even if we break all the rules the child believes are necessary for survival.

In couples work, there is also a task for the partner: to learn to recognize those moments when the mate's child has taken over the bus, and to try to contact the adult about the problem of who is driving the bus. Asking this question is often less threatening than the more typical responses: "I'm sick of how you shut down"; "I don't deserve to be treated this way"; "I can't stand how you push me away." And, when it works, it enables the adult component of *both* partners to join together and help provide safety for the unruly "child" who has surfaced, rather than fight each other about what the child is doing.

Stan and Kayla began therapy because of marital problems that were causing disturbing levels of depression in both of them. History revealed that Stan had come from a family where emotions were repressed and his mother kept up the facade of happiness and perfection. Stan learned early that his own feelings did not count and, worse, that his awareness that something was wrong was in error; his reality was not validated. Kayla's family was opposite in many respects. Her father had an explosive temper, so she learned to be perfect in a vain effort to stave off her father's wrath. But the lesson learned was the same: hide or deny any negative or vulnerable feelings. In Kayla, this was accompanied by a profound sense of failure over mistakes of even the smallest, most inconsequential nature.

Each of them wanted empathy and understanding from the other, each of them craved the expression of real feelings, and each was painfully unable to give what they so desired. "If he could just learn how I need to hear that he loves me, to know that he's interested," was Kayla's lament. Stan's reciprocal was, "If she could just learn that I'm unable to give her what she wants, that I can't verbalize it, that I try to show her in other ways." These impasses led to long bouts of silent withdrawal, each hurt and angry that the other could not "be there" for them, each feeling punished and pushed away.

They were curious and vaguely interested when I introduced the bus metaphor. It is as though when Stan senses Kayla might be unhappy with something he has done or said, the little boy inside is convinced that any sharing of feelings is going to be extremely dangerous. So he takes over the wheel in spite of the grown-up Stan's intentions, and steers the bus toward "safety": toward shutting down, retreat, distancing. Kayla has the same mechanism, in response to a mistake she herself may have made, or a perception that Stan has fallen short, and the little girl inside takes her bus as far away from danger as she can manage. I suggested they begin to focus on the question of "who is driving the bus" at such moments.

It really does not matter who wakes up first once the concept is understood. Either partner can fruitfully identify his or her own bus driver problem, or that of the partner. The key is to open up the question and invite the possibility that someone in the scene can have empathy for at least one of the children driving the bus and can make contact. Once that transition has happened, the interaction that unfolds will be different. For Stan and Kayla, the next important development was the insight that each one was struggling just as hard, having just as much difficulty, and came from just as dysfunctional a history as the other. This insight rapidly transformed the moment of hurt and disappointment into a moment of empathy for the hurt and disappointed partner—which led to exactly the kind of sharing they had so despaired of.

79

Fostering Accountability: A Reconstructive Dialogue with a Couple with a History of Violence

Yvette G. Flores-Ortiz

According to some experts (e.g., Straus and Gelles, 1990), domestic violence affects hundreds of thousands of heterosexual couples in the United States. Increasingly, as family therapists we see couples and families in which the bonds of trust have been compromised by the injustice inherent in intrafamily violence. When couples want to stay together, often the therapy focus is on rebuilding the marriage after the physical violence has ended.

Although domestic violence can result in the death of a spouse, it is less likely to bring about the death of the dream (or fantasy) of marriage, particularly in women raised in highly familistic cultures. Latinas, for example, inherit the cultural mandate to marry and have children. Furthermore, the culture dictates that a woman's primary obligation is to her spouse and children, while her principal duty is to keep the family together, under any circumstances and regardless of the personal cost (Flores-Ortiz, 1993). Thus, very few battered Latinas leave their abusive spouses, even if they have the economic resources to do so (and most do not).

CONTEXTUAL THERAPY AS A MODEL FOR ACCOUNTABILITY

My work as a family therapist has been guided by the Contextual Intergenerational model of Ivan Boszormenyi-Nagy (Boszormenyi-Nagy and Spark, 1974; Boszormenyi-Nagy and Krasner, 1979; Boszormenyi-

Nagy, Grunnebaum, and Ulrich, 1991). Modified to address the particular circumstances of Latinos (Bernal and Rodriguez-Dragin, 1985; Bernal, Flores-Ortiz, and Rodriquez-Dragin, 1986; Bernal and Flores-Ortiz, 1982; Flores-Ortiz and Bernal, 1989; Flores-Ortiz, 1993; Flores-Ortiz, Esteban, and Carrillo, 1994), the Contextual model provides a useful framework for the treatment of domestic violence.

A number of facts shape the reality of Latinos, including their status as an ethnic minority and their higher rates of unemployment, economic instability, and poverty.[1] In addition to multiple migration-related and acculturative stressors, Latinos face the daily indignities of prejudice, stereotyping, and discrimination, which are legacies of racism. The psychological sequelae of such facts may exacerbate the normative pressures of marriage and family life, potentiating the development of unjust and violent behaviors against family members.

Moreover, social and intimate violence are deeply connected. Unjust family patterns, including domestic violence, can be traced to the history of conquest, invasion, war, continued political instability of the region, and the colonization and neocolonization of Latinos in the United States. Domestic violence also may be a manifestation of invisible legacies and loyalties to families of origin (Flores-Ortiz, 1993; Flores-Ortiz, Esteban, and Carrillo, 1994).

Thus, to help Latinos transform violent marriages into satisfying and just partnerships, contextual therapy aims to make visible the invisible multigenerational legacies of social injustice that can poison fairness and create abuse (Flores-Ortiz, 1993; Flores-Ortiz, Esteban, and Carrillo, 1994). By countering injustice and balancing accounts, violence can be prevented in future generations as well.

The contextual model posits that any experience of injustice earns destructive entitlement for the person victimized, who in turn may exploit others. This exploitation indebts the victimizer to his or her victim. In this way, vicious cycles of injustice and destructive entitlement are perpetuated (Boszormenyi-Nagy and Spark, 1974; Boszormenyi-Nagy and Krasner, 1979). To break these patterns, the abusive spouse must become accountable to his partner for the physical, psychological, emotional, and spiritual injuries he has caused. Otherwise, the abusive spouse will remain indebted to his wife, maintaining a relational imbalance that can foster the continuation of psychological and emotional abuse, even when the physical violence has ended.

Unless the victimizer accepts responsibility for his actions and begins a process of restitution, the marriage will stagnate and a genuine reconnecting will not happen. To promote accountability, restitution, and authentic reconnecting, a "reconstructive dialogue" is facilitated by the therapists' stance of multidirected partiality. Within this dialogue, each partner examines loyalty to family of origin, the degree of destructive entitlement earned in that family, and the ways in which victimization in the marriage may have been an attempt to exonerate an abusive parent or obtain retribution for social injustices perpetrated upon him or her.

The following excerpts demonstrate how accountability is fostered through a reconstructive dialogue in a couple with a twenty-year history of extreme physical, emotional, and psychological violence.

BRIEF FAMILY STORY

The Morales are a Spanish-speaking Nicaraguan couple with five children ranging in age from six to twenty-three.[2] Don Francisco is forty years old and his wife Rosa is thirty-eight.[3] Don Francisco served in the Nicaraguan military and suffers from post-traumatic stress disorder due to the war against the Sandinistas. He has a twenty-year history of alcohol abuse but has been sober for two years. He emigrated to the United States after the war ended and a major earthquake decimated the country. He did not tell his family he was leaving; he just disappeared. His wife came to the United States five years later and found him living with another woman. After beating his wife when she confronted him, the couple reconciled and were joined by the older children. The two youngest were born in the United States.

Family or couples therapy with the Morales was not indicated until he learned to control his violence. He frequently threatened to kill his wife, using weapons in his assaults. He beat the children regularly. Doña Rosa and the children lived in fear he would kill them all. She never sought assistance or received psychotherapy and she never felt she could leave him. He had participated in individual and group therapy for alcohol abuse and domestic violence for eighteen months prior to the family consultation. The couple was seen for ten sessions, five of them with their children.

The excerpts are presented bilingually for the benefit of Spanish-literate readers. The therapy was conducted in Spanish; although the English translation conveys information, it fails to transmit the cultural nuances inherent in language. In the first excerpt, the husband listens as his wife begins to link her childhood victimization to the violence in her marriage. The husband for the first time truly hears the suffering his wife has endured. The male cotherapist suggests that her tolerance of suffering and his violence were learned in the family of origin.

R.C.:[4] *Doña Rosa, cómo se sintió usted la primera vez que su esposo le pegó?*/How did you feel the first time your husband hit you?

D.R.: *Yo no lo podía creer, que después de sufrir tanto con los golpes y el maltrato de mi padre, me fuera a pasar lo mismo. Yo jamas había esperado eso de mi esposo, entonces pensé que bueno, todos los hombres pegan, esa es mi suerte. Pero fue un dolor tan grande, una desesperanza tan profunda. Porque yo nunca fui feliz en mi casa con mis padres, para nosotros una Nochebuena, un cumpleaños, eran como cualquier día. No había alegría, y eso todavía me duele, que en mi casa de niña, y en mi casa ahora, no ha habido paz o alegría, solo violencia y dolor.*/I couldn't believe it, after all the suffering, all the beatings and abuse from my father, the same thing would happen to me. I never expected that from my husband. Then I thought, well, all men hit, that was my luck. But the pain was so great, the hopelessness so deep. Because I was never happy at home with my parents, for us Christmas or a birthday was like any other day. There was no joy, and that still hurts, that as a kid, and now in my own home, there has been no peace or happiness, only violence and pain.

R.C.: *Entonces en su casa, señora, usted aprendió a aguantar, mientras que Don Francisco aprendió a golpear.*/Then in your family, you learned to tolerate suffering, while in his family your husband learned to hit.

In the second excerpt, the wife tells the husband how he can begin to earn her forgiveness. In the previous session, the husband disclosed that Doña Rosa had a tumor that prevented any physical intimacy. Doña Rosa, however, indicated that the tumor was only of tears.

Y.F.O.: *La semana pasada usted me contaba que su tumor de lágrimas, de toda esa tristeza acumulada por veinte años de maltrato, se podría decir, le impide a su esposo acercarse a usted. Que necesita hacer su esposo para balancear las cuentas? Me parece que sería muy injusto que usted tuviera ese tumor por otros veinte años.*/Last week you were telling me that the tumor of tears, all that accumulated sorrow after twenty years of mistreatment, one might say, does not allow your husband to get close to you. What does he need to do to pay his debt to you? It seems to me that it would be most unfair for you to have that tumor for another twenty years.

D.R.: *Lo único que yo le pido a el, es que no maltrate más a los niños./*The only thing I ask of him is not to abuse the children. [At this point she removes a photograph from her purse. This is a photo of her inebriated husband with their youngest son, who was about two years old at the time. Don Francisco is holding the son by the hair. The child is suspended in the air, crying.] *Esto no puede pasar nunca más. Por eso yo cargo esta foto siempre, para no olvidar o perdonar jamas. Yo para mi no quiero nada./*That can never happen again, that is why I always carry this photo with me, to never forget or forgive. I do not want anything for myself.

Y.F.O.: *Don Francisco, qué puede hacer usted para ganar la confianza de su esposa?/*What can you do to earn your wife's trust?

D.F.: *Bueno no sé, yo creo que mis palabras no valen, me causa mucho dolor ver esa foto, y darme cuanta de lo mucho que ella ha sufrido. Yo creo que necesito tomar clases o algo./*Well, I don't know, I don't think my word means much. It is very painful for me to see that photo and to realize how much she has suffered. I think I need to take classes or something. [Subsequently, he takes parenting classes from a local agency.]

Y.F.O.: *Doña Rosa, entiendo que para usted es muy importante proteger a sus hijos, pero hay algo que usted quisiera pedirle a él, para que él pueda empezar a pagar esa deuda tan grande que tiene con usted?/*I understand that it is very important for you to protect your children, but is there something you would like to ask of him, so he may begin to pay off that immense debt he owes you?

D.R.: [smiling and looking down, as if a bit embarrassed] *Pues yo nunca tuve novio, no más lo vi y me fui con el. El podría cortejarme, invitarme a salir, llevarme al cine. Pues así como las otras parejas. También quiero que me deje aprender a manejar./*Well, I never really had a boyfriend, I just saw him and went with him. He could court me, invite me out, take me to the movies, you know like other couples. I also want him to let me learn how to drive.

R.C.: [to Don Francisco in a friendly, half-joking way] *Que la dejes aprender a manejar!, que es eso? Ella es tu señora, mano, no tu esclava. O que no te tiene ella derechos propios?/*That you let her learn to drive? How is that, she is your wife, man, not your slave! Or is it that she doesn't have any rights?

D.F.: *Pues sí, claro que sí. Ella tiene derechos. Talvez en el grupo me den ideas de cómo conquistarla otra vez.*/Well sure, she has rights. Maybe the guys in the [therapy] group can give me some suggestions to win her over.

The session concluded with a ritual of divorce, because the old marriage has ended, and now the couple can think about what kind of marriage they might want to form. In the final excerpt, the husband tells other men in his group therapy what he has learned in couples therapy.

D.F.: *Ustedes no saben lo que les espera, uno piensa que con dejar de tomar y pegar ya basta. Yo no tenía ninguna idea que mi esposa tenía tanto dolor. Ahora tengo que aprender a ser buen hombre con ella, a mejorarle la vida, pues toda una niñez infeliz y veinte años de sufrimiento conmigo es suficiente.*/You guys have no idea what you have coming. One thinks that it is enough to stop drinking and hitting. I had no idea my wife felt so much pain. Now I need to learn how to be a good man for her, to make her life better, because such an unhappy childhood and twenty years of suffering with me are enough.

As he became more accountable, Don Francisco began the process of rebuilding trust. He successfully courted Doña Rosa, who agreed to eventually remarry him. Also he began to develop closer bonds with his children. In order to exonerate his violent actions, he became a padrino (sponsor) for other men who were at the beginning of their journey to accountability.

CONTRAINDICATIONS

While Contextual interventions foster accountability in all modalities of treatment, the first step toward accountability for an individual who has battered is to admit to the violence. Therefore, I will not treat couples who are actively violent unless the abusive spouse is engaged in group or individual treatment to unlearn the violence. Likewise, I demand sobriety among violent individuals and will not recommend family or couples work unless the substance abuser is engaged in twelve-step or other recovery programs.

NOTES

1. The contextual model proposes an examination of four levels of relational reality: (1) the dimension of facts, (2) the dimension of individual psychology, (3) the systemic or transactional dimension, and (4) the dimension of relational ethics (see Boszormenyi-Nagy and Spark, 1974; Boszormenyi-Nagy and Krasner, 1979; Boszormenyi-Nagy, Grunnebaum, and Ulrich, 1991). With Latino clients an analysis of the factual dimension is essential to understand the sociocultural and political factors that may have potentiated violent behaviors.

2. For a detailed description of contextual family therapy with this family see Y. Flores-Ortiz, M. Esteban, and R. Carrillo (1994). La Violencia en la Familia: Un Modelo Contextual de Terapia Intergeneracional. *Revista Interamericana de Psicología, 28*(2), 235-250.

3. We intentionally used the title "don," a Spanish signifier of respect, with the husband to convey our belief that, despite his cruel and violent behaviors, we considered him a person of inherent worth. Also as therapists, we wanted to model accountability and respect, particularly since Mr. Morales was a man treated quite disrespectfully by social agencies because of his past affiliation with the Somoza regime and his long history of domestic violence.

4. The therapists were Yvette Flores-Ortiz (Y.F.O.) and Ricardo Carrillo (R.C.). D.R. = Doña Rosa, D.F. = Don Francisco.

REFERENCES

Bernal, G. and Flores-Ortiz, Y. (1982). Latino families in therapy: Engagement and evaluation. *Journal of Marital and Family Therapy, 8,* 358-365.

Bernal, G., Flores-Ortiz, Y., and Rodriguez-Dragin, C. (1986). Terapia familiar intergeneracional con Chicanos y familias Mexicanas inmigrantes a los Estados Unidos. *Cuadernos de Psicología, 8,* 81-99.

Bernal, G. and Rodriguez-Dragin, C. (1985). Terapia familiar intergeneracional: Intervencion breve en una familia con problemas de alcoholismo y depresión. *Monografias EIRENE, 10.*

Boszormenyi-Nagy, I., Grunnebaum, J., and Ulrich, D. N. (1991). Contextual therapy. In A. S. Gurman and D. P. Kniskern (Eds.), *Handbook of family therapy,* volume II. New York: Brunner/Mazel.

Boszormenyi-Nagy, I. and Krasner, B. (1979). Trust-based therapy: A contextual approach. *American Journal of Psychiatry, 137,* 767-775.

Boszormenyi-Nagy, I. and Spark, G. (1974). *Invisible loyalties.* New York: Harper & Row.

Flores-Ortiz, Y. (1993). La mujer y la violencia: A culturally based model for the understanding and treatment of domestic violence in Chicana/Latina communities. In N. Alarcón (Ed.), *Chicana critical issues.* Berkeley, CA: Third Woman Press, 169-182.

Flores-Ortiz, Y. and Bernal, G. (1989). Contextual family therapy of addiction with Latinos. In G. W. Saba, B. M. Karrer, K. V. Hardy (Eds.), *Minorities in family therapy.* Binghamton, NY: The Haworth Press, 123-142.

Flores-Ortiz, Y., Esteban, M., and Carrillo, R. (1994). La violencia en la familia: Un modelo contextual de terapia intergeneracional. *Revista Interamericana de Psicología, 28*(2), 235-250.

Straus, M. and Gelles, R. (1990). *Physical violence in American families: Risk factors and adaptations to violence in 8,145 families.* New Brunswick, NJ: Transaction Publishers.

80

Carols in the Trenches

Gary C. Dumbrill

INTRODUCTION

Working with mandated clients can become like trench warfare, particularly in child protection work. It begins with social workers and parents taking opposing positions over an issue. Saber rattling occurs as each side uses argument and perhaps even coercion to try to make the other side change their position. Rather than change, each side digs in and becomes increasingly rigid. Trench warfare has begun.

Unfortunately, while parents and protection workers battle, children are often caught in the middle. In such warfare, children may be removed from home to ensure their safety while simple collaboration between workers and parents might enable children to live at home safely. It is crucial, therefore, to develop ways of breaking out of entrenchment. The intervention of "carols in the trenches" does just that: it provides a way social workers can break entrenchment and develop collaborative relationships with parents.

DESCRIPTION OF INTERVENTION

During the First World War, German and British troops were spending Christmas in the trenches. The English troops began singing carols and were surprised to find that the German troops started singing carols back. After a time of exchanging carols, one brave soldier stood and sang in full view of the enemy. Soon the English and German armies were singing together in the wasteland between the trenches. From that day on, the soldiers stopped fighting and spent their time playing soccer together.

Unfortunately, the generals did not like this turn of events. The generals made it a capital offense to play soccer or sing carols with the enemy. The frontline troops were replaced with new troops who had not gotten to know the enemy and war resumed.

If singing carols can briefly halt one of the most brutal wars in history, it has the potential to end deadlocks occurring between social workers and mandated clients. Using principles taken from what occurred in those muddy trenches to casework easily overcomes entrenchment.

Three sequential events occurred in the trenches. The first was the initiation of nonhostile communication between both sides. Singing carols allowed this nonhostile interaction to occur. Through this interaction, each side began recognizing the humanity of the other.

The second event was a gesture of faith from one side to the other. This occurred when a solder stood and sang in view of the enemy. The soldier was probably urged to do this by his newfound belief in the enemy's humanity. The soldier's act led the enemy to make a similar gesture and soon both armies were singing together in the land between the trenches.

The final event was both armies recognizing that they had things in common. This recognition developed as the soldiers got to know each other and realized that both armies were in similar cold trenches away from their families at Christmas.

The above three events had an almost inevitable result. After each side recognized the humanity of the other and the fact that they were in the same predicament, both sides worked together to make life more comfortable. The armies gave up fighting, refused to return to their damp trenches, and played soccer together.

CASE EXAMPLE

The three elements above can be successfully applied to entrenched cases. Consider the case of the B family. The B children, aged three years old and one year old, were apprehended by child protection services after being physically abused by both Mr. and Mrs. B. At the time of the abuse, the parents had been going through a period of extreme stress.

Within weeks of the apprehension Mr. and Mrs. B seemed to be overcoming their problems and dealing with their stressors in a more effective manner. However, they refused to cooperate with any assessment of their functioning and would not discuss the abuse of the children or how they intended to prevent similar abuse occurring again. Mr. and Mrs. B soon became entrenched and stated that there was only one way they were willing to show the authorities their problems were under control; the children should be returned and the authorities could then observe that the children were well cared for.

Unfortunately, as the children's injuries had been serious, it would have been irresponsible to return the children without firm evidence that Mr. and Mrs. B had overcome the problems that led to the abuse. With no option for negotiation, the protection worker became equally entrenched and said that returning the children would not even be discussed until a full assessment was completed showing that Mr. and Mrs. B no longer presented a risk to the children.

As the protection worker and parents argued to try to break their impasse, their respective positions became increasingly entrenched. Meetings between the social worker and parents became a time for posturing where no constructive work was undertaken. Each side became convinced their position would be vindicated by a judge after a full trial.

The trial could not be scheduled for six months. As the children were very young and needed to be bonded with their parents, it was crucial that a speedier resolution be found without compromising the children's safety. That resolution was found through the intervention of "carols in the trenches."

The first objective was to connect with Mr. and Mrs. B on a nonhostile level. This was done by the worker no longer trying to convince them to cooperate with an assessment. Instead, the worker actively avoided arguing with Mr. and Mrs. B and found aspects of what the parents were saying or doing that could be praised. Initially, they continued to posture with such comments as, "Don't ask us to undergo an assessment because we won't and after the trial the judge is going to tell you how we were right all along." The worker responded with comments such as, "I will not ask you to undergo an assessment anymore and I admire you taking a stand on what you believe is right."

It was not long before Mr. and Mrs. B began to respond to the worker on a nonhostile level and gave up much of their posturing. Although hostilities had ceased, both sides remained entrenched. The worker still needed an assessment and the parents were still unwilling to be assessed. At this point the worker applied the second element of "carols in the trenches" by making a gesture of goodwill toward the parents.

"I am really concerned and I don't know what to do," the worker confessed. "I really want to send the children home. I can see you have both made progress, but I am not sure how I can get them home."

"Just tell your boss to send the children home, your boss will listen to you," Mrs. B responded.

"I wish I could," the worker replied, "but my boss and the court expect me to give evidence that things are better. The judge will laugh at me and my boss will fire me if I try to send the children home unless I can say exactly why I believe things are better."

In taking this position, the worker also shared her vulnerability. She revealed her genuine inability to effect change as a result of constraints placed on her by the courts, her supervisor, and the demands of her role as a child protection worker. The worker was out of the trench and standing in full view of the other side.

The worker continued to apply this strategy, remaining careful not to argue with the parents. When the parents continued to tell the worker to "just send the children home," the worker would reiterate, "I wish I could, I just don't know what to do, I feel so stuck without concrete evidence for the courts." After several weeks of applying the intervention, the third element of "carols in the trenches" began to take effect. Mr. and Mrs. B began to realize that the worker was in a situation similar to their own. The worker wanted to see the children returned home yet, like them, did not have the power to achieve the objective in the present circumstances.

As the worker shared more of her frustration about being unable to return the children home without concrete evidence that they were safe, Mr. and Mrs. B began to consider how they might help the worker convince the court that their home was safe. It was then not long before Mr. and Mrs. B were collaborating with the social worker in successfully demonstrating that the children could be returned home safely.

CONCLUSION

The B case is not unique. Scenarios may be different, but the deadlock that comes from entrenched positions maintains many child welfare cases in stalemate positions. As shown above, "carols in the trenches" does not compromise the safety of children and is a powerful way of breaking entrenchment. Refusing to argue with clients and establishing nonhostile communication, making a gesture of goodwill and placing emphasis on what the clients and worker have in common (e.g., wanting to get the children home safely) is an effective way of making progress in many deadlocked situations.

The intervention does, however, use methods that might be considered controversial. The first issue that might cause concern is a worker showing vulnerability by expressing to his/her clients a genuine inability to effect change. It is usual to discuss inability to bring change with a supervisor, but not a client. Yet why not discuss such concerns with a client? After all, the client has more ability to change the situation than a supervisor. Also, if the worker is in a position where he/she cannot bring change, it important to be honest with clients about this because the inability to bring change will affect the client more than anyone else in the situation.

The second concern that might be raised about the intervention is that a worker might express a desire to trust and return children to parents who have been abusive. Just because a social worker expresses a desire to return children, however, does not mean that the worker should allow this desire to override a desire and duty to keep children safe. In the previous example, although the worker expressed a *real* desire to return the children to their home, she remained adamant that concrete evidence was needed to show that the children would be safe. Rather than being a problem, the attitude of this worker is what every parent of a child in short-term care should expect; a worker who has a genuine desire to see children returned home, but at the same time a worker who will not compromise the safety of children.

Balancing keeping children safe and maintaining a desire to return the children home is not easy. Balancing these roles with mandated protection clients often leads to workers and clients taking polarized positions. When such polarization produces trench warfare, the intervention of "carols in the trenches" provides a way entrenchment can be broken and progress made.

81

We Are Where We Live

Jan Nealer

Providing therapy to families in their homes has become reasonably common, especially for families who find transportation to a therapist's office difficult. Typically, the majority of families utilizing these services are considered high-risk and multiproblem and/or have low income. Home-based therapists, social workers, family specialists, and child protection workers are regular visitors to family homes, learning valuable information about how the family lives and interacts with each other, neighbors, and the community. A wealth of knowledge obtainable from visiting clients' homes is beneficial in exploring the presenting and obvious problems of the family, as well as providing insight to the processes and structure of the family.

Exploring and understanding the physical organization of a family home is not only useful with families that typically receive home-based services, but for all families. How families and/or individuals create their living situations, who they live with, their division of labor, sleeping arrangements, and even who gets to use particular equipment or appliances contributes valuable, often subtle information to the therapist. Therapists working with clients in the office may be missing advantageous details and families may not express these manifestations without direct questioning. Therefore, this intervention has been designed to assist therapists in how to inquire about the family home and use this knowledge in treatment strategies.

CASE EXAMPLE

The first time I understood the importance of how people live in their homes came about when I was supervising home-based services at a community counseling agency. The therapist was providing home-based therapy to a family that consisted of a single mom with a young son and an adolescent daughter. Therapy was focused on the mother/daughter relationship due to the daughter's acting-out behaviors and the arguments that followed when the mother tried to discipline the daughter. Although therapy had been going well, it seemed impossible for the mom, daughter, and son to coexist without help from outside the family. The family continually returned to a point of violating each other's boundaries and getting in each other's way. The therapist came to me asking for supervision with this family. We tried several interventions that seemed to work initially, but then the family would digress and become entangled in their old habits. Finally, after discussing this case on several occasions and trying many interventions and techniques, I asked the therapist if I could come with her to visit this family. As a consultant to the case, I thought I might be more objective and able to view the family from a fresh perspective.

The appointment was made with the family, and the therapist and I discussed what we would do when we arrived at the clients' home. We met outside the house and both went in together. The therapist introduced me and we all chatted for a little while. I finally asked the mom for a tour of her tiny home. She showed me around, and as we proceeded I noticed something rather surprising—there were no interior doors in the entire house. No bedroom doors, no doors leading into the living room or kitchen, and no doors on the bathroom. I asked the mom if they had taken the doors down, and she told me they had never had doors and that the landlord refused to supply them. With this new information, all of us including the children sat down and discussed privacy issues and how difficult it must be to have some space to themselves. This had been a long-standing issue between the mom and the children, especially the daughter who was now an adolescent and needing more privacy. There was nowhere to go to talk privately on the phone, nowhere to spend time alone, and furthermore, no one could take a bath or brush teeth without everyone watching. With one teenager and another child approaching adolescence, this seemed like a particularly important requirement. We were able to purchase doors for the family and get permission from the landlord to install them. Once this had occurred, the family was able to draw more appropriate boundaries and the therapist was able to successfully close the case.

THE "WE ARE WHERE WE LIVE" TECHNIQUE

Since the experience of the case example, I have used the "we are where we live" technique with many therapy clients, and have also used it in teaching marriage and family therapy students. I typically use this technique when I feel stuck with a family and/or need more information to guide the therapeutic process. Families are very comfortable participating in this very simple, straightforward procedure. In fact, most families actually enjoy sharing the description of their home and the routines of their everyday life. The following is the format for the "we are where we live" technique.

First, start with broad, engaging questions about where the family lives and what their neighborhood is like. Let the family ramble some, to hear everyone's input while also noticing the process. Families rarely tire of talking about themselves, and therefore information about the physical layout of their home is usually easy to elicit and nonthreatening. Follow up their descriptions of space with more specific questions about who uses the space and what happens in it. The more details about the space the better. Again, watch for disagreement and agreement about how the space is used and/or how it is described. Depending on where this questioning leads, more investigation may be done on other areas of the house, neighborhood, school, and/or community.

Other areas of questioning that may be helpful include:

- asking each member of the family to describe bedrooms, the living room, kitchen, den, family room, garage, bathrooms, private and nonprivate spaces, etc.;
- asking how people divide and/or use space when they are sharing various rooms;
- asking each member of the family where most least favorite spaces are and why it is a favorite or least favorite space;
- asking each member of the family where each has privacy and if each feels there is enough solitude;
- asking each member where and how space is shared and with whom;
- asking about doors, windows, size, lighting, noise, smell, comfort levels, colors, furniture, and other accoutrements that might be accessible (e.g., TVs, VCRs, telephones, games, stereos, food, books, plants, animals/pets);
- asking about the neighborhood and outside space that might be available;
- asking who visits and who does not visit;
- asking what they would change and what they would never want to change.

All of these questions will give insight into family members' lives and how they live together as individuals and as a family. Take note of the concrete explanations, as well as the more abstract descriptions, and the process by which the information is given.

Keeping the conversation light and informative will assist the family in remaining on task and open to sharing their experiences. Guided visualizations of the home may be used to relax clients and to acquire further information and intricate details. Drawing floor plans and/or pictures of rooms, the house, yard, or neighborhood can assist in visually understanding the home environment. Supplemental techniques such as genograms and ecomaps may also further help the family members describe their homes, families, and circumstances. Using several of these techniques together can provide the therapist with an abundance of contextual and process information that may otherwise stay hidden away.

CONTRAINDICATIONS

This direct, unpretentious technique has no specific contraindications nor directly introduces significant risk to client families. As previously stated, families typically enjoy talking about their homes and appreciate sharing details of their living situations. Yet caution should be considered. This technique should be used for gathering information and as a format for investigating how families organize and live individually, as a system, and within their community. Consequently, it is important not to overinterpret the meaning of particular features within the family environment, nor to read significance into distinctive or unusual situations. Whereas this information may provide valuable insight into family interactions and processes, discretion should always be used when summarizing. Specifically, biases of the therapist should be scrutinized, especially when personal judgment and/or understanding of the family's living situation is suspect. When used as an exploratory tool, this technique can enhance the therapeutic process by illuminating circumstances within the family's living situation and increase the likelihood of growth and potential clinical success.

82

Creating a Safe Space in Therapy

Volker Thomas

INTRODUCTION

As family therapists we work with people whose personal spaces have been severely violated. In order to create safe spaces for our clients we have to analyze how personal space is created, violated, and restored. Creating a safe space for clients is a necessary condition for successful therapy. Before I describe an intervention that has the goal of helping clients create a safe space in therapy and transferring that into their lives, I will briefly discuss how personal space is created, violated, and how it can be restored.

Drawing from the work of von Bertalanffy (1968), Bronfenbrenner (1979), and Wiener (1948), I use an interactional approach to looking at personal space. Although a person defines his/her personal space according to internal emotional and cultural norms, safety becomes an issue when interacting with others. Our space is surrounded by invisible boundaries which, when violated, solicit a protective response. We have physiological and psychological "red flags" telling us when the boundaries of our personal space are violated.

People's personal ecologies have different layers of boundaries that determine their level of safety. The innermost layer or core of our personal space is absolute and has nonnegotiable boundaries. This layer includes a person's physical and emotional integrity and entitlements for meeting basic needs such as food, shelter, clothing, and so forth. Any boundary violation of this inner layer compromises the person's safety in a serious way, constituting some form of violence. This safety issue arises at the interface between personal spaces, when one person violates and penetrates the core of another's personal space.

People also have outer layers of personal space designed to protect the core. They are more or less negotiable and vary over time. Safety becomes more important, the more layers are violated and the closer the perpetrator gets to the core of one's personal space. Most people have more leverage and freedom to negotiate the boundaries of their outer layers than in the core. The outer layers operate as a protective shield for the core. Although all people have a core of personal space, there is invariably a great number of outer layers available to secure the safety of the core. Building outer layers is part of the socialization process. For example, babies have only fragments of outer layers and need their parents to protect the core of their personal space. An important developmental task across the life span is to develop and maintain outer layers of personal space. Mastering those tasks includes the ability to negotiate boundaries according to one's safety needs.

INDICATIONS FOR USING THE INTERVENTION

Not all people have had the opportunity to develop a sufficient number and quality of outer layers. Some are more vulnerable than others, which means that the core of their personal space is violated much more easily and personal safety and boundary violations are a much greater issue for them than for those who have sufficient outer layers. Many of these vulnerable people are victims of various forms of childhood abuse that kept them from developing protective outer layers. For them even as adults, boundary violations mean penetrating the core of their personal space, which often takes the form of repeating the violence and abuse they experienced during childhood. These people are rarely safe when interacting with others. The only safe space they have available necessitates some kind of withdrawal from others. This is where the intervention of creating safe space originated. I did not come up with it, but learned it from many clients with whom I have worked. Most of them were childhood abuse survivors who created safe spaces for themselves to escape the abuse. These clients taught me to pass on this survival skill to other clients who could benefit from it in therapy and their lives.

DESCRIPTION OF INTERVENTION

When safety becomes an issue in therapy I ask clients what they did when they did not feel safe at any time in the past. This invitation has two goals: (1) It acknowledges and validates the issue of safety for the client. At the same time the invitation implies that clients had resources in the past that they used to feel safe. (2) Cognitively finding this safe place, imagining it, makes clients feel safe in the here and now of the therapy session.

When a client has identified a safe place in the past, I suggest a guided imagery to visit the place (see also Intervention 74). Visually and emotionally reexperiencing this safe place is very powerful for most clients. After the guided imagery, clients process the value the place had in the past. The emphasis is not on the abuse from which the client needed protection, but on the value the place provided. Questions to ask include: What was it about the place that made you feel safe? What did the place look like? What effects did being in that place have on you? How did you choose the place? How did you feel being in the safe place (in addition to being safe)? What was it about the place that made you feel safe? Again, the purpose of this exercise is not to find out and focus on what caused the safety issue in the past, but on what resources the client had to feel safe. (When abuse has been talked about in previous sessions, I acknowledge that, but still focus on the safe place—having agreed that this is what the client needs at this time. If the client has not reported any abuse, I do not ask about it at this time, because this could worsen the client's current safety concerns.)

Once the client has visited the safe place of the past in his/her imagination and processed its value for the present, I invite the client to think about possibilities to transfer the safe place to the future and have it available when needed. Usually the literal place does not exist anymore or is too far away. Some clients would not want to go there, even if it was available (because it is too closely related to past abuse). However, most clients are very creative in transferring the metaphor and making it concrete in some way so that it can provide the safety they need. We explore together how the transfer can happen and how this new/old safe place may look. Some clients come up with a totally different place that gives them the same feeling of safety as the place in the past. Others find a place that resembles the old place very closely and actually go there when in need. Many clients only use the image of the past safe place by retreating inward and recalling the place when they feel unsafe. There are many ways to recreate and transfer the safe place from the past. The important part is that the recall or revisit is associated with the feelings of safety that helped the client survive.

When the client has found a way to transfer the safe place, we talk about ways when and how he/she can take advantage of this rediscovered resource. I invite the client to go to her/his place whenever she/he does not feel safe during our sessions. Usually we agree on some clue the client gives me before she/he "leaves" (e.g., verbally telling me, waving a hand, closing eyes). Clients rarely need to do this during sessions, because the opportunity and the permission provides enough safety for future sessions. It is equally important to talk in detail about how the client may use the safe place between sessions in the future. We spend time identifying situations in which the client may need to retreat and talk about how to communicate that to other people without losing the possibility of feeling safe. I invite the client to try the exercise at least once in a situation when his/her safety is only mildly threatened, in order to have a positive experience he/she can build on when it is needed even more.

CASE EXAMPLE

A few years ago, I worked with a client, Sue, who had been sexually abused by her stepfather during childhood. She had come to see me not because of the childhood abuse (she had worked through that with another therapist several years before), but because she had recently separated from her husband (who refused marital therapy) and wanted to find out whether or not to get back together with him. After a few sessions Sue and I were stuck in our work. When I brought up the fact that I was a man working with her on how she wanted her relationship with her husband to be, the client admitted that at times she did not feel safe with me and that this was also a big issue in her relationship with her husband.

I asked Sue what she had done in the past when she did not feel safe and whether she ever had had a place where she did feel safe. Hesitantly, Sue recalled and shared the following story with me: "During the time my stepdad abused me, we lived out in the country. Whenever I heard his car driving up the road, I ran behind the house into the woods. There was a bush that had an 'entrance' at the back side, a hole too small for an adult to get in. I crawled through the hole and sat there for hours knowing that I was safe. I created my own little world there imagining I was big and strong to protect myself, traveling wonderful places." I was very moved by Sue's story and thanked her for her courage to share it with me. Then I invited her to go there in a guided imagery, but she declined because it sounded too scary. Instead she suggested thinking about it for a week or two.

When she returned to the next session, Sue was much more relaxed and ready to visit her childhood bush. We discussed ways to use the exercise as described above. Sue designated a chair in her living room as her "bush." Whenever she felt unsafe, she would sit on the chair and imagine crawling through the little hole in the bush to be safe. The women's bathroom became her bush at work. A few weeks later, she told some of her co-workers and her husband, who respected her need, about her "bush." Occasionally, Sue went there when she needed to. During our subsequent sessions, Sue would tell me about it and we processed her experience. Eventually, her husband agreed to come in for conjoint sessions. By then,

Sue felt safe enough to address the safety issue with her husband directly. He responded positively after some initial defensiveness. In time, Sue needed the bush less and less and was able to deal with safety issues more openly. When we concluded therapy, Sue told me that she would keep her bush and take it with her, just in case she needed it in the future.

CONTRAINDICATIONS

Generally, I have found this intervention to be very respectful of even very vulnerable clients. Therefore, I see very few contraindications. Clients who present as acutely psychotic, having hallucinations especially of paranoid content should not be exposed to this intervention. Clients who are unable to use visual images and process them, do not benefit from the exercise. Finally, there may be a few clients whose severe childhood abuse has never surfaced, who may get in touch with the abuse while exploring their safe places. Then the abuse may have to become the therapy focus before the client can benefit from the safe place. If the client does not want to deal with the abuse at that time, the intervention is contraindicated.

REFERENCES

Bertalanffy, L. von (1968). *General systems theory: Foundations, development, applications*. New York: Braziller.

Bronfenbrenner, U. (1979). *The ecology of human development*. Cambridge, MA: Harvard University Press.

Wiener, N. (1948). Cybernetics. *Scientific American, 179*(5), 14-18.

83

Family Assessment
Using Subjective Genograms

Daniel J. Wiener

The genogram is a mapping and organizing tool used widely by family therapists to explore numerous patterns in their clients' families of origin. As McGoldrick and Gerson (1985) note, "Genograms are appealing to clinicians because they are tangible and graphic representations of a family" (p. 1). While continuing to make extensive use of conventional genograms in my clinical practice, I have developed another, related tool that supplements this "objective" graphical representation of family information—the Subjective Genogram (SG).

The SG is constructed by each client on a large sheet of paper using crayons (or colored markers if no small children are participating). It is advantageous to have at least two sets of crayons or markers so that colors are not monopolized. Clients are instructed to represent their family (or relationship network) impressionistically, using shapes, sizes, relative positions, and colors. Upon its completion I have the client explain the drawing to me, usually in the presence of other family members, asking follow-up questions about unexplained features, including persons omitted, and eliciting emotional reactions to the material described. In family therapy, members may be offered the option of displaying and explaining their subjective genograms to one another.

I usually offer the family the SG construction experience early in therapy, but after I have sketched out a preliminary conventional genogram (for my own orientation to the family and the clients' orientation to relational diagraming). The drawing process can take from ten to thirty minutes; there is often great variability in detail and time expended among family members. Younger children tend to make representational rather than abstract SGs; I restrain parents or older siblings from "helping." Obviously, doing the conventional genogram first influences clients to employ similar notational features, yet in my instructions I emphasize that they are free to depict their family in any way they wish.

Once the SGs are constructed I invite family members to show and describe their SGs, a process that can (but need not) take another whole session. I ask permission to label the figures (and sometimes relationship lines) in pencil on the SG for future reference. Once all SGs offered have been explored in more obvious ways, I next inquire about such themes and family patterns as status (i.e., ways of displaying relative importance of self and others), temperament, and emotional expressiveness. My twelve-year experience with hundreds of SGs has taught me to be very tentative regarding interpretation. A larger-than-average figure may represent a person important to the maker—or the person represented might be physically large. Colors may represent emotional qualities other than those the therapist associates to—or may be used because they are that person's favorite.

The chief advantages of the SG over a conventional genogram are: (1) clients can represent and express family information in a way that is consistent with their own experience; (2) therapists can access emotive and intersubjective aspects of family relationships more fully; (3) clients take a more active, invested role in the construction and interpretation of their SGs; (4) through comparing their SGs clients can grasp and appreciate similarities and differences in the ways that they and other family members experience the family; (5) family interaction that results from comparing SGs is more likely to result in a focus on relational issues; (6) members who are less verbally facile (particularly children) may participate in the assessment process on a footing equal to those who are more skilled or comfortable with speaking; and (7) SGs may be redone at intervals throughout treatment, or at the resumption of treatment, permitting therapist and clients to assess attitudinal and emotive shifts.

CASE EXAMPLE

Paula, twenty-three, lived at home with her fifty-five-year-old mother, Irene. They entered therapy to improve their relationship, which had deteriorated since the death, eight months earlier, of Paula's father, Robert. Paula felt burdened and irritated by the constraint of having to "walk on eggshells" to avoid upsetting Irene, whom she characterized as still in mourning for Robert. What distressed Irene were Paula's angry moods and vehement way of expressing herself, which she contrasted with the behavior and temperament of her elder married daughter, Janice. When Irene stated that Paula displayed anger "just like her father," Paula started crying. For as long as she could remember, Paula had received feedback from others that she was "hot-tempered," a description that did not fit her sense of self.

Having explored the content described above and sketched out a conventional genogram during the first session, I began the second session by having both Paula and Irene draw their SGs. Paula had placed herself (a medium-sized, blue and grey oblong shape with a purple border) in the lower right corner; her father Robert (a larger red and yellow teardrop with a thick orange border) was surrounded by some of his relatives (drawn as small yellow circles) in the lower left quadrant; her mother Irene was rendered as a large, jagged green and orange mass just above center; and her sister Janice was a smaller, less jagged blob, yellow crosshatched with orange stripes, just under Irene's figure and connected to her by tangled red filaments. Paula's deceased maternal grandmother, the only figure included from that generation, was drawn at the top right corner of the page as a swirling, loose blue cloud with diffuse boundaries.

Irene had placed her own figure (a small brown and orange triangle with curved sides) at center left, almost touching her husband Robert's red-with-brown-spots diamond shape. Robert's figure had a dotted black border; both figures were surrounded by an orange "aura" that touched (but did not encompass) the figures of Paula and Janice. Janice was rendered as a medium-size yellow globular figure with brown filaments directly beneath and almost touching Irene's figure; Paula's figure was a medium-sized spiky ball, red and orange inside with a thick, black border, located alongside Robert's figure so that his was directly between Irene's and Paula's.

When each had taken a turn explaining her SG, I asked Irene to comment on what similarities and differences stood out for her. She expressed surprise that Paula saw herself as so different from the rest of their nuclear family and at her grandmother's inclusion. Paula was curious about the orange aura which Irene had not mentioned initially; Irene described it as a warm, affectionate spirit that she and Robert had shared (later in therapy, Irene acknowledged that it represented sexual passion). Paula also drew attention to their contrasting views both of Janice's role and of any temperamental similarity between herself and her father. When I asked Paula what she saw her grandmother and herself having in common she replied that the light blue color represented a spiritual and ethical sensitivity, something lacking in others of her nuclear family. She added that she sometimes saw grandmother "looking down at her" approvingly. Numerous other features of their SGs received attention over that session and the following ones, including Irene's placement of Robert between herself and

Paula, the meaning of color and thickness of borders, and the relative sizes and shapes of figures.

The SG is a versatile tool without significant contraindication except where the narrowest goal focus and briefest treatment is required. There are numerous useful ways to adapt the SG to the therapist's purpose, mostly after the unrestricted SG has been drawn: (1) to narrow the session's focus to specific relationships by instructing clients to depict only one subset of their extended family, such as their present nuclear family household, members of their nuclear family of origin, or only those family members present in the session; (2) to shift the client's perspective to considering self in a different context, such as by instructing clients to depict only the self and the spouse's extended family, placing a specified person's representation first at the center of the SG, or applying the SG to work systems; and (3) to explore attitudinal and relationship changes over time by redrawing the SG from the perspective of childhood. By far the most fruitful variation I have found is for the *therapist* to construct an SG of the family between sessions, a practice that both helps make assumptions explicit and aids in formulating further lines of inquiry.

REFERENCE

McGoldrick, M. and Gerson, R. (1985). *Genograms in family assessment*. New York: W.W. Norton.

84

The Marital Conference

Peter E. Maynard
Jerome F. Adams

INTRODUCTION

A common complaint of couples beginning marital therapy is lack of communication. Yet spouses often have trouble describing clearly what the communication problem is. When asked, they are only aware that they frequently argue or they have difficulty agreeing, even on the most trivial topics. The therapist is left with a vague notion of the systemic dynamics of the problem, little information on the spouses' motivation for treatment, and no clear treatment goals. Because these couples are also typically distressed and discouraged about their ability to resolve difficulties on their own, they are looking for some immediate relief and signs that the situation is not hopeless. An intervention that comforts clients, improves their morale, and enables the therapist to assess the problem more thoroughly would be beneficial in these beginning sessions.

The marital conference was discussed by Dinkmeyer, Pew, and Dinkmeyer (1979). Our version is adopted from their model but has been greatly revised for use in our clinical practice of marriage therapy. The marital conference exercise is assigned at the end of the first or second session, after the therapist has given the couple adequate time to air their complaints. The therapist writes out the instruction for the exercise, hands it to the couple, and asks for a report in one week. Drawing on Adlerian theory, the original intent of the assignment was to enhance communications and create a climate of mutual respect. It served to revitalize couples because it created the feeling that each spouse mattered or had significance in the marriage. It was also encouraging for spouses to carry something out of the office akin to a medical doctor's prescription for a lab test. The doctor may need more information, but we have already started to do something to get to the bottom of the problem.

The task as we have adapted it can also have a more strategic theoretical application. For example, the couple's ability to carry out the task provides feedback to the therapist about their level of motivation for treatment. Couples who are unable to complete the task may be ambivalent about their stated goals or preoccupied with other marital or personal issues. Reassignment of the conference for such couples has the effect of raising the intensity of interaction. Undisclosed problems such as drinking, affairs, or loss of marital commitment are often brought out in the open. As a result, more immediate goals become clearer to the therapist.

DESCRIPTION OF INTERVENTION

The instructions given to the couple are as follows:

During the next week you are to schedule two marital conferences. Each of these is to be one half hour in duration. Pick a time and a place where you will not be interrupted, for instance, in the family room after the children go to bed. Turn off the television, turn off the ringer on the telephone or unplug it or let it go to the answering machine or voice mail. One of you will speak first and the other person will just listen. There will be no interaction or verbal or nonverbal communication between you. In fact, the listener will face away from the speaker or sit at the opposite end of the sofa and not look at the speaker. This ensures that the speaker will not be influenced by the listener's frowns, smiles, smirks, or hand or eye movements. At the end of the fifteen minutes the other person will speak, using the same rules. At the end of your first session, you are not to discuss what was said in the session. The topic to be explored in this conference is: Who am I?

The second session is scheduled two or three days after the first session. The person who went first in the last session will go second this time. Again in this session you will position yourselves to avoid nonverbal feedback influencing the speaker. You may choose some alternative places for the conferences. A long walk together could be used as a method of holding the conference and avoiding interruptions. Again at the conclusion of the conference you are not to discuss the material that was brought up; rather, you are to bring that material into the next therapy session. The topic to be explored in this conference is: Who am I in this marriage?

Response of the Couple

Couples respond in a variety of ways to the intervention. One group consists of highly motivated couples who comply fully with the prescription and come to the next therapy session eager to discuss their experience with the exercise. In our experience, this happens with about 30 percent of couples. They report they enjoyed most aspects of the exercise, learned new things about their partner, or listened to information they had known but needed to hear again.

Case Example #1

Bill and Eleanor requested marital therapy, on the recommendation of their physician, to discuss having another child. They had two boys and both wanted to have a daughter. Eleanor had experienced a recent miscarriage and there were some health concerns regarding a new pregnancy. They completed both conferences and found the structured format helped them converse in a way they had not been able to previously. Eleanor, a shy person, was reluctant to introduce her own opinions into their conversations. Bill, a corporate executive, had been trained to jump in, ask questions, and challenge ideas. Doing this at home, however, was intimidating to his wife. The conferences allowed Eleanor to have uninterrupted time to explore and express her ideas and feelings. It also required Bill to listen before trying to solve problems.

A second group of couples completes only the first conference. Many of these couples say they enjoyed the conference or learned something from the experience, but offer reasons such as busy schedules or the interference of children for not doing both exercises.

Case Example #2

David and Susan had the second conference scheduled but discovered their daughter had a late soccer practice and one of them had to drive her. Upon further questioning they admitted they were frightened by the level of intimacy the conference created. They were uncomfortable, and didn't really try to find the time to reschedule the task.

A third group consists of those who fail to complete or do not attempt either conference. This may be a sign that the couple is reluctant to discuss especially sensitive issues or there is ambivalent commitment to the relationship.

Case Example #3

Peter and Beth, married two years, have no children. Peter complained about his wife's increasing distance in the marriage. They did not do either conference even when assigned a second time. Following a very tense period of silence in the fourth session Beth suddenly confessed she was having an affair and was considering ending the marriage.

REASSIGNMENT

The therapist carefully evaluates the response of the couple to determine the course of treatment. Compliance with the task is a cue for the therapist to work in a direct fashion, even if the couple has modified the assignment in some minor ways. The couple's efforts can be complimented and further assignments given with an increased assurance that future tasks will be carried out as well. Some couples who enjoy the task decide to incorporate it into their regular routine. Others learn to use it more sparingly when important issues come up. For example, one couple who successfully completed the assignment was at an impasse about how to resolve their credit card debt. The therapist modified the conference format and asked them to discuss the question, "How would I solve our financial difficulties?" The couple used the marital conference format with some innovations of their own and were able to begin a plan of action to handle their finances better.

Sometimes the assignment is not completed for legitimate reasons (e.g., urgent family business). It is important that the therapist ask enough follow-up questions to make this determination. In this case the conference can be reassigned and once again evaluated for compliance.

Repeated noncompliance or partial compliance is a cue for the therapist to consider working more indirectly or strategically. Here the therapist needs to probe carefully for covert or other agendas. If the topic "who am I in this marriage" is not done, it may be due to a lack of assertiveness in one of the partners. The therapist can then slow down and coach the couple on how to improve this skill. In other instances the self-examination triggered by the topic "who am I" can prove so distressing, a partner may need to address this agenda before proceeding to the declared marital issues. If the couple does not do the task at all, even after reassignment, the therapist can inquire about the inconsistency between their stated goals and their behavior. In one case when the therapist wondered aloud if there was something preventing them from doing the conference that he was not aware of, the wife blurted out that it was an impossibility when her husband was drunk every night.

Utilizing the conference task in this way places the therapist in a win/win situation. The therapist gains valuable information whether or not the couple complies with the intervention.

CONTRAINDICATIONS

Couples occasionally present with a concurrent crisis such as sudden unemployment, the death of a child, or judicial indictment. In such situations it is advisable to first attend to the crisis and introduce the conference assignment once the family has restabilized. In cases where the power imbalance of the couple is so acute that retaliation or imminent harm is likely to result, the conference is not only ill advised but may be unethical. Couples with a history of physical or emotional abuse as a marital pattern should not be given the assignment in the early stages of treatment. It may be considered later in treatment if safety issues have been adequately addressed. Lastly, because the intervention solicits intense self-examination, the therapist needs to be attentive to the psychological resources of the participants. A history of significant psychopathology in either spouse would be considered a risk factor to be carefully evaluated before the assignment of the intervention.

REFERENCE

Dinkmeyer, D. C., Pew, W. L., and Dinkmeyer, D. (1979). *Adlerian counseling and psychotherapy.* Pacific Grove, CA: Brooks/Cole.

85

Policymaking *Within* Families: A Clinical Example of Family Process and Governance

Kyle N. Weir

Social science researchers have commonly used the structure of families to create typologies of families (Zimmerman, 1947; Popenoe, 1993). Although therapists include structure in the assessment of any family, the field of marriage and family therapy encourages the inclusion of yet another measure—one of process. There has been an enormous amount of research on family process, but the most notable contributions of Kantor and Lehr (1975) and Broderick (1993) represent some of the typologies of families that utilize process and consider the "modes of operation" within a family as a central component of their typology.

Carlfred B. Broderick's *Understanding Family Process: Basics of Family Systems Theory* (1993) is generally recognized as a thorough review of literature and concepts in the study of family systems and family process theory. An aspect of his work that is often overlooked is the unique contribution of his family typology. Broderick (1993, pp. 164-171) describes a new typology based on "family governance" and the "overall styles of interaction" within a family. His typology is based on his clinical experience and an abridgment of Kohlberg's model of "cognitive moral development" (Kohlberg, 1969; Kohlberg and Turiel, 1973). Broderick depicts the following typology of families as paradigms of interaction: the Competitive paradigm, the Policy-Governed Cooperative paradigm, and the Principled Interaction paradigm. For the purposes of brevity these types of families will simply be termed competitive-oriented, policy-oriented, and principle-oriented families. Common features of competitive-oriented families are zero-sum struggles, mixed motives, and a general sense of "looking out for one's own self." Policy-oriented families tend to be governed by rules. These families have cooperation as a central goal of family governance, and thus there is generally a fairly open (though not always egalitarian) process for the establishment of governing policies in the family. A rarer form of family is the principle-oriented family, where a sense of personal maturity is achieved by all members and principles of mutual respect, empathy, and equity govern instead of specific policies.

Having done my undergraduate studies in public policy and management in the School of Public Administration at USC, this typology of families based on styles of family governance intrigued me. It occurred to me that there is much rhetoric and discussion concerning policymaking *about* families from a governmental level, but very little has been written about policymaking *within* families. I began developing a model that could utilize tools of policy analysis to be applied to policy-oriented families and explore the internal processes of families who seem to "make policy" within a therapeutic context. The outcome of this line of thinking can be seen in the model policymaking *within* families.

POLICYMAKING WITHIN *FAMILIES:*
POLICYMAKING STAGES

Although there is some dissension in the matter (Lindblom and Woodhouse, 1993, pp. 10-11), policymaking can be viewed as occurring in a series of five stages: agenda setting, policy formation, decision making, implementation, and evaluation (Anderson, 1990, pp. 35-37).

Agenda Setting

Each family can only allocate its emotional, temporal, and financial resources to a limited point. Families can only attend to a finite number of problems. Agenda setting is the selection process by which the family determines which issues will be addressed and which ones will not receive the family's attention. At this stage, clinicians could be asking questions such as: "Who commonly gets the attention and resources of the family? How is the appeal made? How does the family determine what issues are important to deal with? What is the family's common response?" Knowing what gets selected and what is dismissed from the family agenda is revealing, even diagnostic, of both the mode and structural patterns of family governance.

Policy Formation

As issues become fixed within the family agenda, families start to form ideas and maneuver concepts into a way that a policy will form around the issue at hand. Coordination of time schedules, the inclusion (and exclusion) of various members and subsystems of the family, and the format of discussion are pertinent aspects of this stage of policymaking. Important questions to ask in this stage are: "Do you have a set time to discuss issues as a family? Are household rules formed in a family planning meeting or do the parents formulate policies on their own and then present them to the remainder of the family? Is the process and format of forming policies fairly open or closed?" This stage is crucial to the whole policymaking process because it is also concerned with the sources of information. The use and reliability of information in policy formation affect the outcome of the entire policymaking process. Questions such as "Where does the family get information from? Does the family consult with friends, other family members, ecclesiastical leaders, therapists or other professionals, books, magazines, or other media? How reliable are these sources? What roles do the various social networks play?"

Decision Making

Decision making is the process by which the family adopts a policy and determines a course of action. Therapists should consider whether the process is democratic or authoritative and hierarchical. Is a policy within the family a result of a vote from the "family legislature," a judicial decision based on past precedent, or does it come in the form of an "executive order?"

Implementation

Often families create policies that seem appropriate, but the implementation is problematic. Policies are often created with an eye toward certain ideals, without proper consideration for the realistic accomplishment of such goals. Therapists should work toward refining the policy formation stage in a family such that consideration for realistic implementation of policies is built into the policies themselves. Also, the rules and policies of a family may be acceptable, but the enforcement (or the lack of enforcement) of such policies creates difficulties in the family system.

Evaluation

Policies need to be evaluated to determine if they are on course for accomplishing the proposed goals, if they have become obsolete due to subsequent developments, or if the task has been completed. Appropriate questions at this point in the process might be: "How are family policies evaluated? Are there methods whereby parents and children can evaluate what works and what does not work in a family policy? What aspects of policies are renegotiable and what parts are not renegotiable." Are there periodic checkpoints where the family might say, "In six months we will check to see how this policy is working?"

CLINICAL EXAMPLE

Sean and Jenny MacDonald came into the therapy seeking assistance in communicating as a couple. Both were well-educated professionals. Sean was finishing his dissertation and teaching part-time at local colleges, while Jenny was working as a manager in a local manufacturing firm. They each complained that the other was not behaving in expected ways, and that when they tried to communicate those expectations, the discussions turned to arguments. It became clear that each had a set of rules they expected the other to live by, but coordinating those rules and expectations was difficult. On top of this they were expecting a baby and wanted to have some order in the home so that the child would know what to expect and that as parents they would have ways to negotiate differences in parenting styles and beliefs.

I began to use policymaking *within* families with this couple as a diagnostic. When questioned about how issues were brought up at home, they both agreed that bringing up issues to the attention of the other was not a difficulty, but finding time to talk about them or having an open discussion was problematic. I noted that policy formation and decision making were areas to work on.

I also used policymaking *within* families as an intervention that we openly discussed in session. The model became a framework that they readily adopted and seemed to provide language for a familiar process already occurring in their relationship. It seemed to both of them that they would set the agenda about what were the issues at hand, but then expect the other spouse to jump right into the implementation. We began to develop weekly routines that protected time for communication such as "date night" and "family planning meetings" to plan for the upcoming family needs, finances, and schedules. The focus of these planned communications was to help them slow down the process and focus on forming policies through discussion. There was an emphasis on providing each other with sufficient information so that the policies would include input from both parties. The family planning meetings were compared to a lunch meeting between two policymakers seeking to find common ground. This work led to a more open and egalitarian decision-making process. With both parties sufficiently informed through these family planning meetings and other discussions, they could then make decisions about implementation. Questions such as the who, what, and when of implementation became much more clear due to an informed policy formation procedure. To a great degree, as earlier stages of the process are adjusted, the later stages of policymaking tend to become more flexible and healthy.

In the MacDonald case, policymaking *within* families was used as a diagnostic for the use of the clinician and as an intervention or model given to the clients for their own use. Policymaking *within* families can also be used without actually discussing the framework with the clients. For example, if it becomes clear in a family that the rules or policies parents give to the children are acceptable, and the process by which these policies are formed is open, but the lack of implementation or enforcement of these policies causes difficulties, then the therapist may choose simply to focus on the hierarchical position of the parental dyad without revealing the entire framework. If the diagnosis can be isolated to one particular stage of the process, then it may not be useful to try to teach an entire new framework, model, or language.

CONCLUSION

Policymaking *within* families is a powerful tool for working with families that are policy oriented, but require some direction in their family system toward clarification of the process. It tends to promote language and implies a framework that fosters an open process for family members. One of the limitations of this model is that it is specific to only a certain type of family—policy-oriented families—and does not adequately address the competitive and principle-oriented families. These policy-oriented families tend to be cerebral and cognitively oriented; thus a cognitive model resonates with them. Unfortunately, this may lead the therapist away from important affective needs and approaches. With this caveat in mind, clinicians can use policymaking *within* families as part of a larger treatment approach. In the MacDonald case, once progress had been made using policymaking *within* families, the family stabilized its patterns of interaction, and the presented symptoms had been attenuated, the focus of therapy shifted to address deeper, affective needs that newly arose in the course of therapy. Didactic material was also prepared, using a psychoeducational approach, for the parenting issues.

Policymaking *within* families is beneficial to clinicians of policy-oriented families due to its clear focus on the stages of the policymaking process in families. Although this linear format is merely a construct of an often circular and complex process, it possesses a certain level of utility in the room when applied in this step-by-step manner. To the extent that the policymaking process is an adequate representation of the processes described in Broderick's (1993) typology of policy-governed cooperative families, policymaking *within* families can be a successful clinical tool in the practice of marriage and family therapy.

REFERENCES

Anderson, J. (1990). *Public policymaking: An introduction.* Boston: Houghton Mifflin.

Broderick, C. B. (1993). *Understanding family process: Basics of family systems theory.* Newbury Park, CA: Sage Publications.

Kantor, D. and Lehr, W. (1975). *Inside the family.* San Francisco: Jossey-Bass.

Kohlberg, L. (1969). Stage and sequence: The cognitive-developmental approach to socialization. In D. A. Goslin (Ed.), *Handbook of socialization* (pp. 347-480). Chicago: Rand McNally.

Kohlberg, L. and Turiel, E. (1973). Overview: Cultural universals in morality. In L. Kohlberg and E. Turiel (Eds.), *Recent research in moral development.* New York: Holt, Rinehart and Winston.

Lindblom, C. E. and Woodhouse, E. J. (1993). *The policy-making process,* Third Edition. Englewood Cliffs, NJ: Prentice-Hall.

Popenoe, D. (1993, August). American family decline, 1960-1990: A review and appraisal, *Journal of Marriage and the Family, 55*: 527-555.

Zimmerman, C. C. (1947). *Family and civilization.* New York: Harper and Brothers.

86

Mapping Multiplicity: An Application of the Internal Family Systems Model

Katherine J. Michelson

Many clients respond positively when therapy takes a form that is different from typical talk-oriented therapy. Therapists facilitate that "ah-ha" experience for clients when they attempt to reach them in ways other than solely through language. In addition, clients often speak of themselves in "parts." A typical example is the individual who thinks of leaving a relationship who says, "Part of me wants to stay, but part of me wants to go!" This intervention takes into account both of these ideas in a way that has been very useful for clients.

INTERNAL FAMILY SYSTEMS MODEL

This intervention arose from my work with a model developed by Richard Schwartz (1995) called the Internal Family Systems (IFS) model. IFS assumes that individuals have an innate desire to know themselves completely, and assumes that they are willing to seek that knowledge (Schwartz, 1995). The IFS model provides a hopeful framework that hinges on individuals' resources and strengths (Breunlin, Schwartz, and MacKune-Karrer, 1992). This model has as its central tenets the idea of multiplicity of personality, the Self, categories of parts, and systemic interactions between these parts.

Key to the model is an understanding of multiplicity. This means that everyone has subpersonalities or aspects of his/her personality that interact internally, which the model calls "parts" (Schwartz, 1995). IFS states that it is appropriate to have multiple subpersonalities, not pathological. Also, all parts are valuable and have positive intentions for the individual. The parts were formed throughout a person's life to help that individual negotiate different situations. Difficulties arise when parts become polarized, which contradicts the client's desired way of being.

A therapist using the IFS model has to listen to parts' intentions for the client so that they can be released from their polarized roles and can resume their preferred, less extreme roles. It is also the therapist's job to facilitate clients' sensitivity to the voices of their own parts in this same way. Furthermore, it is desirable that the client's compassionate Self be the confident leader of the internal family system of parts. It is a higher being than the parts, able to facilitate relationships among the parts and override decisions of the parts (Schwartz, 1995). It is from the Self that clients get to know and describe their own parts. The parts take over when they do not trust the Self to keep their intentions in mind (Goulding and Schwartz, 1995). The therapist has the goal to facilitate part-informed Self–leadership in the client.

A strength of this model is its nonpathologizing orientation. It is much easier for clients to take control and responsibility over a part of themselves that is acting inappropriately for the situation rather than believing that all of them are "defective." Another strength of this model is its assumption is that changes in the internal system will affect the external system and vice versa, thus illustrating the systemic underpinnings and applicability to couples and families.

Schwartz (1995) uses the metaphor of an orchestra to convey how the parts and the Self operate. He describes a system in which the conductor knows the value of each instrument, and the importance of the crescendo of different sections at different times within a concert. It is also vital that each instrument (part) has respect for the conductor's ability to lead. Therapy utilizing the IFS model can be described as collaborative, normalizing, and empowering when done effectively (Breunlin, Schwartz, and MacKune-Karer, 1992).

SITUATIONS IN WHICH PARTS MAPPING IS MOST USEFUL

This intervention can be used with both individuals and couples. For individuals, mapping parts is useful when (1) therapy is in the initial stages of using the IFS model, (2) the client is particularly visual in the way he/she processes information, (3) the client has specific behaviors that he/she would like to change, and/or (4) the client describes him/herself in terms of parts that are in conflict with each other. These individuals flourish when given the opportunity to see and understand their parts in a user-friendly way.

Parts mapping can be useful for couples when they have a pattern of conflict that they are having trouble breaking. It can be useful for them to map out each of their particular parts and see how they are polarizing and protecting certain parts in relation to each other. This can be best explained through the common example of a couple in which one partner withdraws and the other pursues in times of conflict. Using this model and intervention, the partners would describe how their parts feel like withdrawing or pursuing. The clients can investigate the dynamics between their own intricate parts in relationship with the partner's parts. They also might each explore other situations in their lives where they have the same feelings so they can then focus on listening to that part so it can become less polarized.

Multiplicity Mapping

As clients describe themselves in a such a way that they can identify certain parts of their personalities, the therapist suggests that they try a visual way of understanding these parts. At the outset, it is important to explain that this exercise can help them to become "unstuck." In the case of a client who says "part of me wants to stay and part of me wants to leave," I ask him/her to talk about a specific part of him/herself. I might explore by asking, "Can you tell me more about the part of you that wants to stay with your spouse?" This assessment of parts continues until the client has some sense of several parts of him/herself.

Simultaneously, using a dry erase board or chalkboard, I ask the client to list the parts. The first part the client describes is drawn on the board at the location that he/she wants it. Every part from then on is drawn in relation to that part and questioned about with the original part as a frame of reference. Each part gets a name, description, size, and possibly a picture on the board. Common questions include "So do these parts ever go together?" and "Are there times when you feel needy so you explode in anger?" among others, which seek to describe these parts in more detail. Clients who are interested in drawing the map themselves can be encouraged to do that with a little guidance from the therapist.

Clients are the masters of this map. They conceptualize their parts working together at this point in time, with the realization that the map will change in different sessions, on different days, at different life stages. At this point I explain to the clients that individuals all have a Self that is wise and compassionate. The final project is to place their Self. They might say, "I can't see my Self right now," indicating that it could be blocked by one of the parts. They also might say that the Self is on the outer edge, or right in the middle of the parts. This is usually the most difficult task for clients. If clients struggle with positioning the Self, I return to talking about parts. Clients may take some time for their parts to be trustful enough to place the Self on the map.

Using this process of mapping their own multiplicity of parts can provide insight for the clients to triggers and patterns that keep them stuck. The next step is then to facilitate clients' listening to the parts so that they can become less polarized and resume a different position on the map.

EXAMPLE OF HOW CLIENTS RESPOND

Clients have responded very positively to this intervention. A client who was familiar with IFS work said that it had been very useful to see how his parts interact and respond to situations. He found it particularly useful to see these parts written up on the board in relation to each other. It seemed to make them more real to him. This mapping procedure used along with visualization exercises was very helpful in allowing this client to examine past trauma and to see how he was remaining stuck in that trauma. Upon completion of therapy, he had insight into how these parts, originated in hurt, were getting in the way of his Self. He was then able to put into place cognitive and behavioral plans in order to continue to listen to those parts and to be Self-led.

A couple with whom I worked were able to understand more clearly and change their pattern of over- and underresponsibility using the mapping techniques. At one point in therapy, when both members had mapped parts that either took responsibility or rejected it, both seemed to reach an "ah-ha" of understanding and compassion for the other's position. After graphically showing a few of each member's parts on the board and how they systemically "gang up" on other parts or react to certain situations, the couple were able to move from this pattern that had been plaguing them.

CONTRAINDICATIONS

It is a potential danger to map old, wounded parts with clients and then get stuck at that point with them. It is important that the therapist be able to facilitate understanding of parts using multiplicity mapping, and also be able to facilitate growth and change in areas where the person is not effectively managing his parts. It also could be contraindicated in couples work if the therapist senses that it is not safe for the clients to explore parts of themselves in the presence of the partner. There can be a treacherous minefield between couples in which parts could become ammunition if the climate is not right. If therapists are asking clients to explore parts of themselves that they see as less than desirable, the therapy atmosphere must be ripe for acceptance and compassion, not just for each other, but for themselves and all of their parts as well.

REFERENCES

Breunlin, D. C., Schwartz, R. C., and MacKune-Karrer, B. (1992). Of mind and self: The internal family systems metaframework. In *Metaframeworks: Transcending the models of family therapy.* San Francisco: Jossey-Bass.

Goulding, R. A. and Schwartz, R. C. (1995). *The mosaic mind: Empowering the tormented selves of child abuse survivors.* New York: W.W. Norton.

Schwartz, R. C. (1995). *Internal family systems therapy.* New York: Guilford Press.

87

Opening Space and the Two-Story Technique

Adam L. Hill
Catherine R. Scanlon

"Postmodernism" is a term heard with increasing frequency in the family therapy field today. The term relates to a range of theories and approaches that share common assumptions about the nature of reality (that it is socially constructed), the nature of language (that it is fundamentally political), and the nature of problems (that they are understood within relationships). While much has been discussed and written about the philosophy of postmodern approaches in family therapy, many family therapists have found it a difficult set of concepts to put into practice. Here we offer a simplified presentation of a postmodern technique that might be readily incorporated into other counseling approaches. We hope it will serve as an invitation for the reader to become further involved in postmodern perspectives of clinical practice.

WHAT IS "OPENING SPACE," AND WHY IS IT IMPORTANT?

Postmodern therapies posit that there are many ways of understanding and describing reality. First, what each of our clients describe as reality is actually his or her *experience* of reality. With regard to clients' realities, this idea is held in common with many other therapeutic approaches, such as the cognitive and psychodynamic orientations. Second, what each of us describes as reality is actually our *experience* of reality. While postmodern therapies are similar to some other therapies in that they distinguish

Author Note: Thanks to Elisabeth Anne Leonard, who helped with the editing of this chapter.

between reality and the client's *experience* of reality, postmodern therapies are dissimilar to other therapies in that they take the concept of reality two steps further. Postmodernists point out that not only is the client's reality a perspective of reality, but the counselor's reality is also nothing more or less than a perspective of reality as well. Therefore, further, postmodernists posit that there exists no valid and reliable way to determine the truth or accuracy of "realness" of one person's descriptions of reality over another's. Helping clients see their experience of reality ("how it is") as one of many possible experiences opens space for clients to generate alternative descriptions of reality, and to choose among them. When we help clients to understand that their description of events is not the only possible description that might be given, the possibility for other, more preferred, descriptions becomes a powerful source of hopefulness for creating descriptions of the future that do not include the problem. This, then, is what some postmodern family therapists call "opening space."

Further discussion of the "realness" of various descriptions of reality is beyond the scope of this chapter, but postmodernists often refer to clients' descriptions of their realities ("how it is") as "stories." Thus, we have come to find it useful to understand "how it is" as one of many possible stories that the client or family member might want to use to make sense of the experiences they have. Further, postmodern therapists often help clients discuss their stories by giving them names.

OPENING SPACE BY NAMING STORIES

Naming client experiences as stories takes some planning and care. Of primary importance is that story naming occur within a context of client-counselor rapport. We find that if we have not connected with "our experience of our clients' experience," as Michael White defined empathy (Epston and White, 1992), we are in danger of imposing a technique without regard to its context. This can be humiliating and harmful to clients. So we spend a good bit of time paraphrasing, restating, and reflecting content and feeling before we ask clients to help us to name story titles.

Once rapport and some trust have been established, we usually ask the client to work with us to make up a couple (or more) descriptive titles for "how it is" in their lives. There is a rich body of literature on how to elicit these descriptive titles (Epston, 1989; White and Epston, 1990), but often simply asking does the trick. As introduced by Michael White (1988), postmodern therapists usually ask for story titles depicting "before" and "after" (that is, old story and new story). For example, one family we worked with named their old story "Cold War" and their new story "The

Wall Is Down." The narrative style of postmodern therapy then goes on to employ a comparative questioning technique to encourage choice and movement from the old story to the new.

Another Way to Open Space by Naming Stories

Recently it has occurred to us that "before and after" narratives may be less than entirely helpful when we want to open space for more varied client descriptions. It has further occurred to us that while the old and new story technique (before and after) opens more space than does the "reality" perspective, it opens less space than allowing for two more ambiguous stories that do not necessarily represent before and after. For example, if the two stories chosen are "Brian Doesn't Do What He Is Told" (old title), and "Brian Does What He Is Told" (new title), family members will be less likely to have to struggle a little for unexamined possibilities. An example of more ambiguous story titles that we would prefer to endorse might be, "Brian Does What He's Told Except for Homework," and "Brian Has a Free Spirit." Ambiguous titles make room for what Anderson and Goolishian (1988) call the not-yet-said. Naming stories and discussing them afterward has the potential to unearth very surprising and unexpected client descriptions that we like to look for, and we have found that when one story title is clearly preferred over another, clients and family members don't look into the possibilities as fully as they do when the titles are ambiguous.

CASE EXAMPLE: THE TWO-STORY TECHNIQUE

I (A.H.) recently worked with a young man (who I will call Steve), who had a hard time describing why he was coming to therapy at all. The best he was able to come up with was, "I want to feel better about myself." Yet he even had trouble affirming whether this was what he wanted to work on. In keeping with the theme of opening space, I asked him to help me give descriptive names to some of the ways he was living. He came up with "Gregarious Me" and "Artist Me." I also suggested that there might be another description out there that didn't fit either of these, and I asked if it might be called "Door Number Three" for the time being. As we talked, it came out that when Steve was more like Gregarious Me, he had the ability to talk to women, and had the ability to gather together a large number of acquaintances. Steve also found that Gregarious Me had him " . . . planning sixty things and accomplishing three, and feeling guilty and angry at myself." When Steve was more like Artist Me, he was able to look at a tree shedding its leaves in the fall and compose a poem. Artist Me had Steve enjoying experiments with language, and made him more contemplative and reflective. Artist Me also had him believing he was somehow separate from other people and essentially alone.

As we talked about these different descriptions of his life, space was opened for other issues to emerge. As we talked, it became clear that the Gregarious Me/Artist Me descriptions were not accurate enough to describe the entirety of his experiences. Indeed, Steve told me that he didn't like being described as having different parts. And yet the descriptions were accurate enough to serve as a common language between us to discuss what appeared to be some pretty tough issues for Steve. In its simplicity, the process of naming and discussing his stories gave him room to say, "Wait a minute. It's not that simple. It's more like this." From that point on we began working collaboratively to clarify the subtleties of his experience and the meanings he wanted to ascribe to them. His willingness at that point to take a stand on how his life looked to him represented a contradiction to his inability to clarify what he wanted out of counseling at the outset. It seems to us (A.H. and C.S.) that this moment was an example of a "not-yet-said" aspect of his life that I could not have predicted for him before it came about. I could only make space for the possibility.

His willingness to take a stand on the Gregarious Me/Artist Me descriptions yielded further results. As we worked to further clarify some of the ways he lived, he described how a friend of his sometimes called Steve "Iron Guy" for shutting down emotionally when his life got stressful. The conversation appeared to give him space for considering how much he wanted to have Iron Guy as a description of his life. Another benefit that arose from the opening space conversation was that he did not like the idea of describing himself as being composed of polar opposites. This allowed me to raise the question of whether he was finding his life to have more extremes than he wanted it to, which led to a treatment goal of inviting more "shades of gray" into his life. And while such a treatment goal was still vague, it was arrived at collaboratively, and it seemed to us (A.H. and C.S.) that it was far more concrete than "I want to feel better about myself."

CONTRAINDICATIONS

Our purpose for opening space is to create just enough difference that the family member can begin to explore his/her own experiences in a new light. Opening space by way of the two-story technique seems to us to have greatest clinical utility when family members either are not certain of what they want to accomplish in counseling or when they are so certain of what they want to accomplish that they have closed off ways of thinking that we might consider valuable for them. After listening carefully, if we feel that clients have already given careful and reflective consideration to the issues that have brought them to counseling, we tend to prefer to use other techniques that would allow them to continue or hone this process. At such a point, we believe that opening space further would not be helpful.

Postmodern thinking is, by nature, ambiguous, and the technique described here encourages further ambiguity as the client struggles with the "not-yet-said" in order to understand him- or herself better. For that reason, clients and counselors who have a low tolerance for ambiguity (higher rigidity) should approach postmodern styles with caution. Similarly, clients experiencing difficulties with reality testing also need to be worked with carefully. The opening space techniques can become extremely helpful when a very experienced postmodern therapist works with these types of clients. However, a beginner should not initially attempt this level of sophistication.

SUMMARY

The foregoing has been offered as both a useful clinical technique and an invitation to family therapists to further pursue their involvement with postmodern thinking. While the therapist behavior described here will, we believe, have excellent clinical utility when applied as a technique, postmodern approaches are essentially and fundamentally perspectives and worldviews, and are most useful in working with individuals and families when applied that way. Clinicians who are interested in further exploring postmodern therapies and issues are encouraged to refer to Freedman and Combs (1996), McNamee and Gergen (1992), and Gilligan and Price (1993) for an understanding of the issues that underlie postmodern therapies.

REFERENCES

Anderson, H. and Goolishian, H. A. (19°° . Human systems as linguistic systems: Preliminary and evolving ideas   t the implications for clinical theory. *Family Process, 27*(4), 371-393.

Epston, D. (1989). *Collected papers.* Adelaide, South Australia: Dulwich Centre Publications.

Epston, D. and White, M. (1992). Family therapy training and supervision in a world of experience and narrative. In D. Epston and M. White (Eds.), *Experience, contradiction, narrative, and imagination* (pp. 75-95). Adelaide, South Australia: Dulwich Centre Publications.

Freedman, J. and Combs, G. (1996). *Narrative therapy: The social construction of preferred realities.* New York: W. W. Norton.

Gilligan, S. and Price, R. (Eds.). (1993). *Therapeutic conversations.* New York: W. W. Norton.

McNamee, S. and Gergen, K. J. (Eds.). (1992). *Therapy as social construction.* London: Sage Publications.

White, M. (1988). The process of questioning: A therapy of literary merit? *Dulwich Centre Newsletter,* Winter, 8-14.

White, M. and Epston, D. (1990). *Narrative means to therapeutic ends.* New York: W. W. Norton.

88

Using Art to Externalize and Tame Tempers

Rudy Buckman

Michael White and David Epston (1990) use the text analogy to conceptualize human problems. They believe that humans give meaning to their lives by storying their experiences and that a person comes to therapy oppressed by a dominant problem-saturated narrative. Consequently, therapy focuses on the generation of alternative stories that enable a person to experience a sense of agency in his/her life. One way of generating alternative stories is through what White and Epston (1990) refer to as "externalizing." They describes externalizing as "an approach that encourages persons to objectify and, at times to personify the problems that they experience as oppressive. In this process, the problem becomes a separate entity and thus external to the person or relationship that was ascribed as the problem" (White and Epston, 1990, p. 38). White's original work with externalizing was predominantly with families that identified the problem to be with a child. For example, in a case involving encopresis, White (1984) and a family of three generate an alternative story by externalizing the child's encopresis as "sneaky poo." As the family came to understand how "sneaky poo" had affected each of them and their relationships with each other, they could begin to explore stories of standing up to the influence of "sneaky poo."

After reading White (1984), Michael Durrant (1989) began to explore the usefulness of externalizing with children's temper problems, which are much more common. Both White (1984) and Durrant (1989) rely extensively, if not entirely, upon the use of questions to externalize problems. For example, Durrant (1989) uses questions such as, "So when the temper rears its ugly head and shows itself, how does it manage to get everybody so cranky? What tricks does it have for getting Mum and you shouting at each other?" (p. 6). Although externalizing has been very useful in my work with families, the overreliance upon cognitively demanding questions has made the process of externalizing very difficult and cumbersome for many children. Consequently, I've developed several ways to engage children in the process of externalizing that are more attuned to their natural affinity for play and their concrete stage of cognitive development.

Many of the children I have worked with seem to engage their imaginations more actively in the process of externalizing by artistically creating the externalized temper. Once the child has a concrete image of his/her temper, he/she seems much more able to respond to externalizing questions. For example, on a page divided equally in half by a line, the child can draw a picture of the temper on one side and a picture of him/herself on the other. Once this is done the therapist has an artistic personification of the temper and of self that can be used to explore the child's narratives about the temper and self.

While exploring problem-saturated narratives the therapist can ask the child: "How come the temper is bigger (or smaller) than you?, How does the temper use its big eyes against you? How come you colored the temper _____? What feeds the temper so it gets bigger and bigger? Who is most afraid of the temper? When is the best time for the temper to attack you? Your family?" Of course, other family members can also be asked to participate in these questions and the child can modify the picture to take into account different aspects of the narrative. For example, one child, in response to "What feeds the temper so that it gets bigger and bigger?," drew his mother yelling at him. In exploring the person's influence over the temper, the therapist can ask, "You drew the temper bigger than you, is that okay with you? Have you ever thought of growing yourself bigger than the temper? What would help grow you bigger? You drew your head bigger than the temper's head, is that because you're smarter? You're colored blue like water—have you ever used your blue water to cool the temper down?"

The picture can be taken home so the family can practice temper taming at home. One family took the picture home and put it on the refrigerator door and made a chart that depicted how often the mom was able to resist yelling at her son and how often he was able to grow himself larger than the temper. This picture and chart were brought to our weekly sessions so alternative stories of competence could be developed and extended into the future.

Clay is another medium that children enjoy playing with and can be used to invite the child to model his/her temper. The advantage clay has over drawing is that clay can be easily remolded into other things. For example, once the child has fashioned his/her temper in clay, the therapist can invite the child to change the clay temper into a ball that he can use in a game of toss with the therapist or roll it out of his life. Other ways to transform the clay temper are: break it into pieces while taking a deep breath for each piece; turn it into a musical instrument that can be played while singing along (e.g., Old MacDonald had some music e-i-e-i-o and he used the music to calm a mad pig e-i-e-i-o, and so on); or, fashion letters out of the temper that spell out an alternative to having a tantrum, like t-a-l-k for talking about feelings with someone the child trusts. Again, family members are encouraged to take this activity home so temper taming can be practiced outside of the weekly sessions.

A variation on this theme is for the therapist to become knowledgeable about current superheroes from clients, his/her own children, or by watching Saturday morning cartoons. The therapist can then use this knowledge to explore temper narratives. For example, in one family in which the two youngest children fought each other quite often, I found that they were collectors of Teenage Mutant Ninja Turtle characters. Since my son, Jonathan, had taught me more than I ever wanted to know about these characters, I felt comfortable in asking questions such as, "If your temper was one of these characters, who would it be? If you were one of these characters, who would you be? Is it easier to fight against the temper alone or as a team? What super powers do you possess that could help you in throwing the temper out of your lives?" In this case the boys identified the temper as Shredder, who they described as "settling everything by fighting" and identified themselves as Michelangelo and Donatello, who are Teenage Mutant Ninja Turtles. In their alternative narrative they were able to team up and learn how to use their powers to defeat Shredder.

In conclusion, the use of artistic representations and/or cartoon heroes has enabled me to playfully engage children in the concrete stage of cognitive development in temper taming. Their families have also seemed to enjoy an alternative way of working on temper tantrums within the context of their family. This approach has been most effective with children who have expressed some dislike for the temper being bigger or stronger than they are and for families who are willing to engage in the temper-taming activities at home. This approach has been less effective with children who are motivated by revenge on a world they feel has treated them unjustly.

REFERENCES

Durrant, M. (1989). Temper taming: An approach to children's temper problems—revisited. *Dulwich Centre Newsletter*, Autumn, 3-11.

White, M. (1984). Pseudo-encopresis: From avalanche to victory, from vicious to virtuous cycles. *Family System Medicine*, 2:2.

White, M. and Epston, D. (1990). *Narrative means to therapeutic ends*. New York: W.W. Norton.

89

Authoring Success Through Competency-Immersed Therapy

Peter A. Kahle
John M. Robbins

Michael White (1991) has suggested that the process of therapy from a narrative perspective is viewed as a means by which the clients and therapist work collaboratively to deconstruct old stories and construct new, more useful, stories. Through a "redescription" process, families become aware of the existence of alternative stories and begin the process of "re-authoring their lives" (White, 1989). Part of this re-authoring process is externalizing the problem, a linguistic method used to separate the problem from the symptom bearer. Based on the idea that the problem is the problem, rather than the person being the problem, White (1989) suggested that by externalizing the problem, family members can mobilize themselves against the problem, thus freeing individuals from blame and blaming. During an externalizing discourse, conversational and perceptual space opens, allowing the family to enter new dialogue around the problem. Since all clients are assumed to have a wealth of resources and strengths, individuals are expected to be able to acknowledge their unique strengths and to take responsibility for victories over the problem (Kowalski and Durrant, 1990).

What has not been addressed is an individual or family who finds it extremely difficult to ascribe strengths, competencies, and successes to himself or herself. There seems to be a continuum of willingness for individuals and families to internalize their own competencies and acknowledge their own stories of success. Questions that explore an individual's personal agency are sometimes met with uncomfortable feelings, anger, or denial of personal strengths. Therefore, we would like to demonstrate how the use of a competency-immersed approach can be used to open space for conversation around competencies. Through externalizing the success, competencies are used as a means of increasing the influence of success in the life of a family. This differs from White's ideas of using competencies and unique outcomes to decrease the influence of a problem (White and Epston, 1990).

To gain an accurate portrait of a client's life story, it is incumbent upon the therapist to elicit the client's reality about the problem and/or the success. When clients are able to "push" the problem away, they often want something positive to take the place of the problem. Yet clients who are unwilling or not yet ready to take the credit for the successful arrival of a desired goal at a particular point in time may feel rushed and/or unheard if they are working with an overzealous therapist. We refer to times in the re-authoring process when we have found ourselves being overzealous about searching for successes at the expense of the client's story as "writer's block." Writer's block influences both the therapist and the family because it refers to times when therapy ceases to be a collaborative process and instead becomes a process whereby the therapist directs the tempo and course of therapy. When this occurs, the therapist is requiring the client to possess ideas of personal agency. Thus, it is important to ensure that the new, dominant story is not a therapist-imposed narrative. When writer's block occurs, it may be helpful for the therapist to externalize the block and identify ways of pushing it out of the therapeutic process.

In our practice, we have strived to find additional ways to enter dialogues with families that free us from the limitation of viewing success only in relation to the problem. To open space for some families to reach a point where they are able and/or willing to internalize personal agency, we have found externalizing the success to be quite effective.

Externalizing the success is a process that uses and links the concepts of externalization and competency focus. We have used this idea in therapy for many of the same reasons White (1989) cited for externalizing the problem. Externalizing the success in therapy allows distance from an idea, thus providing a family with a new way of looking at their situation that promotes cooperation. Externalizing the success is employed in the hope that space can be opened for a different perspective, new dialogue can take place, and the re-authoring process can progress in a manner that facilitates the authoring of new, client-desired and client-driven life chapters.

Instead of conversations about pushing, kicking, or fighting the problem away from them, the family is now working together to pull, lure, or attract the success to stay with them. Also, this concept allows a therapist to maintain the posture of a cowriter of the therapeutic conversation by avoiding the temptation to drive the conversation toward a desired goal. Therefore, we refer to externalizing the success as a competency-immersed approach because of the focus on increasing the influence of success in the life of a family.

When asked questions designed to elicit the meaning that they have made about these victories, some families respond by providing explanations that negate their own involvement in these unique outcomes. In other words, the reasons a family provides for these unique outcomes are often externalized and, thus, depersonalized. Therefore, we are not necessarily introducing the concept of externalizing to the family. We are simply following the tendency of some families to externalize their victories and strengths. By focusing on the success in a manner that provides a client with a new way of looking at the success, we are attempting to open space that will allow a family to internalize strengths at their own pace.

UNPACKING MARGINALIZED NARRATIVES OF COMPETENCE

We assume that it is beneficial for some families to externalize their successes and be in conversations about increasing the influence of the success. This assumption has led us to the concept of "unpacking" marginalized narratives of competence. Unpacking is simply defined as a collaborative process of eliciting a client's meaning of a concept through the exploration of additional pathways of meaning. Unlike the traditional psychoanalytic metaphor of peeling the layers of an onion, unpacking meaning does not assume there is a core reality to be discovered. Like a suitcase in which each packed item is significant and important to the traveler, client meanings that are unpacked are all given the same weight, thus adding to the richness of a concept. As defined, unpacking can take the form of the following two questioning processes: (1) asking multiple versions of the same basic question, or (2) asking follow-up questions designed to elicit additional meaning based on some meaning that a client has already espoused. For instance, if a client does not seem to respond well to a unique redescription question (White, 1989), unpacking the client's marginalized narrativescan be extremely useful to the re-authoring process. The rich description of a family's marginalized narrative of success serves as a pathway for them to value their own competencies. Thus, as space is opened through externalizing the success, part of that space can be filled with the unpacking of a narrative of competence.

Through unpacking the therapist is not asking multiple versions of the same question in an attempt to impose his or her own hypothesis of the problem on the client. Instead, the therapist is simply employing a subtle, meaning-eliciting method in a manner that is respectful and reassuring to a family and allows them to highlight their narratives of success and competence.

Although we offer this competency-immersed approach as a way of expanding the ideas of Michael White, we advise therapists that this approach remains limited in how problems and solutions are conceptualized. As with any other model of therapy, the assumptions of this approach can restrict the types of questions asked of a family. We suggest that therapists be mindful of the language of the family to avoid writer's block, thus not allowing these competency-immersed ideas to become a therapist-imposed view of how a family sees problems and solutions. We have found in our practice that when used thoughtfully, a competency-immersed approach has been useful with families presenting a variety of difficulties.

A THERAPEUTIC NARRATIVE

Mary Jones contacted us and requested our help because she reported that she was having problems with her sixteen-year-old son, Mark. Mary, a sole parent, reported that Mark was not respecting her parental authority. We invited her to meet with us along with Mark and her twelve-year-old son, Larry. Her infant daughter, Courtney, did not participate in therapy.

After several sessions with the family in which we attempted to map the influence of the problem, which was "anger" and "criticism," and ask questions that would solicit stories of unique outcomes, we sensed the arrival of the family's tendency to externalize and depersonalize their victories over the problem. Therefore, we thought it was an opportune time to invite them to entertain ideas of personal agency. After reinforcing their hard work and commending them for being modest individuals, we asked them how they thought the hard work that we had heard about and witnessed in therapy was affecting "anger." Larry responded by stating, "It's helped because we've been being cool."

Instead of assuming that we knew what "being cool" entailed, we asked the following questions in an attempt to unpack their meaning of this concept: (1) What is going on when you are being cool? (2) How are you able to be cool? (3) Is being cool something that you have to think about or does it come naturally? (4) If we were able to see you being cool, what would we see? (5) How does being cool affect "anger?" (6) What's your understanding of why you have been being cool lately? By asking several questions about the concept of "being cool," we were able to unpack it and gain a better understanding about the family's meaning of "coolness."

Mary proceeded to relate a story about a family who was inviting "coolness" to visit by listening and talking more openly than they had in the past. Mark and Larry reported that when they were being cool, they were "doing things quicker" and "doing things without being asked." Larry further reported that when "coolness" was around, his mother and brother were laughing, joking around, and everybody was having fun together. It was apparent that "coolness" was not simply the absence of "anger." A new story about a unified team working together to entice "coolness" to come around was unfolding. These explanations no longer suggested that they were simply passive recipients of good luck. At the conclusion of this session, Larry reported that his new goal was to "stay cool."

At the following session, Mary reported that Mark had other plans and happily noted that she no longer got upset when Mark wanted time off from therapy. To track the influence of the family in the life of the success, we asked Mary, "What's your understanding of why 'coolness' is coming around more often?" Mary stated, "I think it's us! You know 'anger' hasn't come around as much either." This example demonstrates that the exceptions were now meaningful to Mary. She was now ready and willing to take some of the responsibility (internalizing personal agency) for the day-to-day victories over "anger." We then worked to reinforce this emerging narrative of success by recruiting an audience for change. We asked Larry, "What's different with your mom when 'coolness' is around?" He stated, "My mom just relaxes now and she's not angry."

Over the next few sessions, the new alternative story was progressively becoming the dominant story. When confronted with difficult situations that could easily have tripped the family up, they were consistently working together to keep "anger" away. Our last session began by tracking the influence of the success in the life of the family. Mary and Larry reported that lately "coolness" had been around quite a bit. When asked, "What are you doing to invite 'coolness' to visit your family?" Larry reported that doing things in the house before his mother asked helped to bring "coolness" around. When asked about her meaning as to why "coolness" was around more often, Mary attributed a large part of her explanation to her increased confidence about being a good parent. Furthermore, she reported that she had recently developed the ability to stop certain behaviors that used to help bring "anger" around, and thus, was also helping to push "anger" away from her children. Mary's report verified that she was continuing to internalize personal agency for the newly evolving, dominant narrative of competence. The family decided to discontinue therapy because they were going to be out of town for the majority of the summer and we agreed that they had reached a point where a break from therapy might prove to be beneficial. As we walked down the hall with Mary, Mark, and Larry after the completion of our session, Larry mentioned that their apartment had flooded and some personal belongings had been destroyed. We asked Larry how the flood had affected the family, and he reported with a smile, " 'Anger' didn't even think about messing with us." When thinking about possible therapeutic narratives, we could not have scripted a better "The End." However, the Joneses' new dominant life story of competence was simply entering a new chapter.

REFERENCES

Kowalski, K. and Durrant, M. (1990, October). *Exceptions, externalising and self-perception: A clinical map.* Workshop presented at the 48th Annual American Association for Marriage and Family Therapy, Washington, DC.

White, M. (1989, Summer). The externalizing of the problem and the reauthoring of lives and relationships. *Dulwich Centre Newsletter, Special Edition,* 3-21.

White, M. (1991). Deconstruction and therapy. *Dulwich Centre Newsletter, 3:* 21-40.

White, M. and Epston, D. (1990). *Narrative means to therapeutic ends.* New York: W.W. Norton.

90

Finding the Horseshoe Nail

Thorana S. Nelson

I learned this intervention from Art, one of my first supervisors in marriage and family therapy. He had learned it from his supervisor of supervision, Bruce, and it seems to be one of those things that sticks with both of us. I recently talked with Art about this intervention, to verify my recollection of its origin. We had a good chuckle over several stories each of us had about the intervention and different ways we each had modified it.

The power of the intervention lies, I believe, in its metaphorical connections and association to learning experiences, particularly meaningful and enjoyable ones. I like to fantasize that it also has power in relation to my effectiveness as a therapist. I am not so sure about the latter, but it's always fun to fantasize.

THE INTERVENTION

The intervention is very simple. It requires that the therapist keep on hand several small items, do-dads, if you will. Bruce's story included horseshoe nails. His story went like this: a couple he had been working with lived a long distance from his office. He met with them for several months and their ability to communicate with each other improved significantly. Like many couples, they were ready to terminate therapy before they thought they were. Bruce approached the idea with them, and they were reluctant. They knew they were doing much better, but were afraid of what would happen during times of disagreement if Bruce were not available to help them. On the other hand, the long drives had ceased to be productive and they often had other ideas of how to spend that time and expense. So, Bruce gave them a horseshoe nail that had been sitting on his desk in a prominent spot.

Bruce solemnly told the couple a story about the horseshoe nail: how he had found it in a field one day when he was particularly troubled, confused, and unsure of himself, how he had taken it home and cleaned it up, and how he had placed it on his desk as a reminder of long walks in farmland as a way of clearing his mind and reassuring himself of his worth and his abilities. He told the couple that he would miss the nail, but would feel very good, knowing that they had it and were putting it to good use.

The couple were instructed to take the nail home and put it in a place of honor, perhaps in the kitchen, dining room, or bedroom. Whenever they needed to discuss something that one or both thought might be difficult, they were to place the nail on the table or couch between them as a reminder of Bruce and all that he had taught them, and as a reminder of what they had learned and how well they worked together. Should they ever decide they no longer needed the nail, they were to send it back to him or give it to another couple who needed it along with the story of its origin and importance.

The Reaction

The couple looked at the horseshoe nail with awe and the wife placed it in her purse with reverence. Bruce smiled as they left the office and shook their hands warmly. The couple reassured him (and themselves?) that they would be fine, especially with the nail to remind them of Bruce's influence and their relationship with him in therapy. They chatted with the receptionist as they left the waiting room.

Bruce grinned and whistled a little tune to himself as he returned to his office. He walked to a closet lined with shelves, reached into a box, pulled a horseshoe nail from it, and tossed it jauntily into the air before placing it on his desk.

The Aftermath

Art and I have both modified the intervention over time and for particular situations. I especially like to give little wooden eggs to my female clients who need to move on from therapy but are reluctant to give up our relationship. The egg is a symbol of their ability to decide for themselves when and how they are going to "hatch." As a gift from me, it symbolizes our relationship and my regard for them and their abilities. I often tell my clients that they should be judicious in following advice from others, especially me; the egg reminds them that advice is fragile and should be treated with care. No one has ever commented on the paradox of my gift in the context of the advice.

Art likes to give things to people to remind them of the importance of their heritage. He told me a story of one couple that was presented with a carefully wrapped copy of their genogram as a memento of what they had learned about where they came from, its importance, and their hard work in therapy. Art had placed himself on the genogram to one side.

With clients who have had difficulty making decisions and for whom the main goal of therapy has been to learn decision-making skills, I have a stash of wooden nickels. I find it very useful, for myself as well as for advising others, to flip a coin when faced with dilemmas. Heads, I will do "A" and tails, I will do "B." After flipping the coin, I check my feelings about its advice. If I like the feeling, I go for it; if I do not, I either do the other or flip the coin again, sometimes with different choices. This trick is especially useful when it appears there are only two options; somehow, it helps force people into not giving up on the process of generating more solutions. Giving clients a coin often symbolizes the capriciousness of chance, especially with the logo-stamped ones I have bought in tourist traps in the West. Using wooden coins can also help inject a bit of humor into a serious situation in which people may need to be taken outside of themselves to get unstuck.

Keepsakes serve to keep us in the minds and hearts of our clients; they also, at least for me, have kept many clients in my mind and heart. Sometimes, I tell a story of a client when I give a little gift. Often, I think about particular clients when I find the gew-gaws. Always, I have a little lift of humor or heart and hope when I think I have something that will be useful in a tangential way.

CONTRAINDICATIONS

Generally, I might hesitate to give such symbols to clients who have developed an overly dependent relationship with me. However, they can be extremely useful as transition objects, allowing clients to find their own strengths as the immediacy of our relationship fades. I am cautious about giving these gifts to clients with whom I am uncomfortable and fear they may misuse the meaning or relationship inherent in the gift—we sometimes have clients that we *hope* will not remember us.

91

Reconnecting Through Touch

Volker Thomas

INTRODUCTION

Touch has always been a controversial issue in psychotherapy as well as marriage and family therapy (MFT) for clinical as well as ethical reasons. Within the humanistic tradition of psychotherapy, therapeutic touch has been a legitimate therapeutic technique for many years. For example, Gestalt therapy (Pearls, 1973) and Psychodrama (Blatner, 1973; Moreno, 1964) have utilized physical contact between client and therapist as a therapeutic tool to encourage the client's emotional catharsis. In the field of family therapy, some schools of thought consider touch more or less as a boundary violation and unethical (e.g., MRI, Milan, Strategic, Solution-Focused, Psychodynamic, Behavioral, Intergenerational), while a few others embrace therapeutic touch in their clinical repertoire (e.g., Experiential, Communication), as long as it is done for the client's benefit within the professional code of ethics. Carl Whitaker (Whitaker and Bumberry, 1988) and Virginia Satir (1983, 1988) are two of the most prominent proponents favoring physical contact between therapist and client as a therapeutic means that can be helpful to clients.

The intervention below describes how physical touch between therapist and clients can facilitate the emotional reconnection between partners in couples therapy. Derived from the humanistic tradition of psychotherapy and closely related to Whitaker's and Satir's work, the intervention allows therapists to help couples reconnect on a nonverbal level, when their verbal attempts have failed. The intervention is based on the belief that effective couples therapy can, even must, include physical contact, since couples relate to each other not only verbally, but physically. Touching clients in appropriate ways enables the therapist to model ways of relating from which the couple may have been excluded for a long time. Thus, it may facilitate a process that shows clients how they can reconnect not only on a physical, but even more so on an emotional level. A second premise underlying this intervention is that physical touch actually enables clients to reconnect emotionally and cognitively. As will be described in more detail below, the physical reconnection can break down emotional barriers that have kept couples from communicating effectively, rebuilds trust to open up new interactional space, and to be more vulnerable with each other. Touch can facilitate this process with the help of the therapist. The third premise of this intervention, fully in the tradition of Satir's work (Simon, 1992; Winter and Parker, 1991), is that couples have the emotional resources within themselves to be emotionally connected with each other, and that breaking down the barriers of fear and distrust helps clients to reconnect emotionally and stay connected using their inner resources.

INDICATIONS FOR USING THE INTERVENTION

In my clinical experience, I have found the intervention particularly helpful for couples who exhibit a very high level of emotional reactivity that is mainly expressed through repeated and very intense arguments. Frequently, these couples complain about a lack of communication. Each feels rejected by the partner, leaving both with the sense of "I can't do anything right in the relationship." There is high tension within the relationship, and attempts to resolve conflict end up in endless and fruitless arguments.

A pursuer-distancer pattern often develops. Attempts to solve problems escalate into a spiral of anger and fear during which one partner (more often the male) withdraws from the relationship as a means of stopping the fruitless arguments, feeling discounted and rejected. Simultaneously, the other partner (more often the female) pursues for the same reasons in an attempt to continue the argument until the conflict is resolved and the fear and rejection have subsided. This recursive pattern keeps the couple connected in anger and pain, and, at the same time, disconnects them from their vulnerabilities and real selves. The couple is caught in a destructive connection that keeps them emotionally protected from more pain, while suffering a great deal, yet not sharing that pain with the partner openly.

Another relationship pattern between couples that warrants the intervention is characterized by fears of emotional connection that have been brought into the relationship from previous experiences in other couple relationships and/or the families of origin. While couples of the first pattern frequently have been together for a long time in conflictual but stable relationships, the relationships of the second pattern are much shorter. The partners have not developed the necessary trust yet to openly deal with emotionally charged issues. They have tried unsuccessfully to avoid them. Abuse in previous relationships is quite common in this pattern. The intervention can be quite helpful for these couples, but can also be contraindicated as discussed below.

What both couple patterns have in common is the fact that the partners want to be emotionally connected, but their attempts to reach the desired connection have failed and the fear of rejection and abandonment have prevailed. The intervention provides couples with an alternate means to reach the desired connection. Thus, the intervention assumes that couples want to be connected and have the means within the relationship to do so. All they need is a different way to open the door to meet in a safe place for each other and the relationship. The main objective of the intervention is to create a temporary safe place within the therapeutic relationship and then help the couple to transfer this newfound emotional space outside the therapeutic setting.

DESCRIPTION OF INTERVENTION

The intervention has three goals: (1) to interrupt destructive recursive communication spirals that keep couples from emotionally connecting or reconnecting; (2) to create new emotional space through an experiential exercise; and (3) to cognitively process the experience and thus to establish or reestablish a more constructive communication pattern between the couple.

When couples present with the conflictual pattern of destructive argument, they frequently display this pattern during the session spontaneously. I stop them and thank them for having the courage and trust in me to show me their unsuccessful attempts to get unstuck and resolve their conflicts. Then we talk about what keeps them from getting their needs met in the relationship and identify the experience they have in common (but have not shared with each other) that they have tried so hard to do the right thing and please the partner, but that they have felt rejected and abandoned, and that they both hide behind an emotional wall that protects them from getting hurt even more. I often use the metaphor of a rowboat. The couple sits in the same boat, back to back, each rowing on one side. This way they keep going in circles, without ever moving forward, despite working as hard as they can. The metaphor provides them with a frame for the notion of being connected in pain, rather than in joy. When the couple agrees with this assessment, I ask them whether they would like to try a different way of reconnecting. Most couples agree, when they feel safe enough with the therapist and trust him/her to protect them from getting hurt.

Upon receiving both partners' approval, I move my chair closer to one partner, usually the "withdrawer" in the pursuer-distancer pattern. Since this is usually the man and I am a male therapist, starting with the man minimizes potential jealousy by the male partner when I touch his female partner, when I work with a heterosexual couple. The other reason to start with the withdrawer is that it decreases the chance of withdrawal as a reaction to me working closely with the partner. ("She is getting from the therapist what I have been longing for, now I am shutting down.") I invite the person to put her/his hand into my hand. Making eye contact, I ask the client to describe how it feels to have skin contact. I carefully monitor the nonverbal and verbal reactions, telling the client to let me know when things get too close. For about five minutes I work with the client exploring the experience of the physical contact of me holding his/her hand. Thus, I help the client to verbalize the experience. Most clients find this experience very warm and comforting. The partner witnesses this process and listens to the conversation. Then I thank the client for his/her courage to be physically connected with me and tell her/him that I will repeat the exercise with the partner, inviting him/her to carefully observe the partner's experience.

Thanking the other partner for his/her patience and openness to witness me touching his/her partner, I move to him/her and ask for permission to repeat the exercise. I take great care to put as much effort into connecting with the second partner as the first and help him/her to have a positive experience. At this point both partners are usually much more relaxed and far away from their destructive arguing spirals. They have built some trust in me so that holding hands opens up some emotional space that has not been available to them within their relationship before.

As the third step of the intervention, I invite both partners to turn to each other and sit within physical reach. Then I gently ask the first partner again to hold my hand and simultaneously ask the second partner to do the same. Now I am holding one partner's hand with my right hand and the other's with my left hand. Making eye contact with both of them, I ask how it feels to be connected with me again. Then I turn their attention to the fact that I am connected with both of them and state my intention to function as a connector between the two. I encourage them to imagine that the emotional energy from one partner flows through me to the other, and vice versa. We process how that feels. When the couple continues to have a positive experience (most clients are very soft and open at this point), I take their hands and lead them together. They end up touching their hands, with one of my hands holding theirs from underneath and the other on the top. This way the three of us are connected through two of their and both of my hands. I take time to process the body sensations they have making physical contact with each other, still being "attached" to me. For most couples this is a very powerful experience. They feel what they have yearned for and not received for a long time. If they appear comfortable enough I ask the couple to make eye contact and verbalize to one another how it feels to hold and to be held. Finally, I tell the couple that I will slowly withdraw my hands and leave theirs connected as long as they feel safe and comfortable enough. I encourage them, again, to verbalize how it feels to be connected or reconnected physically and to tell each other. After a while, I ask the couple to slowly let go of each other's hands and take a deep breath.

At the conclusion of the exercise we process the experience, putting it into the context of their attempts to be connected and to resolve conflict. The exercise is seen as physically connecting or reconnecting and symbolically as a metaphor to create emotional space that overcomes their mutual fear of rejection and abandonment. The exercise and the couple's experience serve as a springboard to discuss how the couple can find new and creative ways to repeat the experience of reconnection during the intervention. It becomes a building block for creating safe space that gets the relationship unstuck and prevents them from slipping back into the destructive spirals described above.

Most couples have a cathartic experience at the end of the exercise, crying while letting down their protective walls. As important as this experience is, it is equally important to take time—frequently several sessions—to process the exercise and help couples to cognitively understand their needs and the needs of the partner, and think creatively about ways to get these needs meet without reengaging in destructive interactions.

CASE EXAMPLE

John and Julie were in their late thirties when they came to see me. Both were professionals who had invested all their energy in their careers and thus decided not to have children. When I first saw them, they reported destructive arguments that centered around John's use of alcohol and his angry outbursts when drunk. He justified his drinking and anger with Julie's "bitching" about everything he did or did not do, and her invading his space, even when he told her to leave him alone. When John was on one of his frequent business trips, they would miss each other greatly. But when John would come home, the couple would regularly start arguing about unimportant details, which would set off the spiral of John withdrawing in drinking, Julie "bitching" about it, and so on. They agreed to missing each other and wanting to be connected, yet both were to afraid to be rejected in their attempts to reconnect.

I began the exercise with John, who expressed his discomfort with being gently touched by a man, but felt the warmth of my hand. As we continued the process he relaxed more and more. He began tearing up, admitting that he had longed for this feeling of connection with Julie for a long time. As she observed the process, Julie also began crying. She felt very trusting and comfortable when I repeated the exercise with her, being encouraged by John's positive response. When I connected their hands and held them for a few seconds they both made spontaneous eye contact and cried together for several minutes. When I let go of their hands, they spontaneously hugged each other sobbing, comforting each other and being comforted at the same time.

During the following processing, which lasted three sessions, the couple reported that Julie had grown up with an alcoholic father who physically abused her when he was drunk. John, on the other hand, was raised on a farm where he mainly worked by himself in the fields as an adolescent, being a loner and not accountable to anybody, until the farm went bankrupt when he was in his early twenties. While solitude was a common way for John to deal with his feelings, it was very threatening to Julie, because her father would become very quiet before he would get drunk and hit her. Conversely, Julie survived her abusive adolescence by frequently talking with her younger sisters and trying to anticipate when their father would become violent again. Thus, her attempts to verbally process her fears with John threatened him and justified his withdrawal into alcohol.

The intervention helped the couple to identify this destructive pattern and to develop alternative ways to express and process their fears and needs. The exercise did not establish a new way of relating constructively for Julie and John, but created a new and safe space to explore these ways.

CONTRAINDICATIONS

There are three contraindications to using the intervention. The first lies within the therapist. Therapists who feel uncomfortable in dealing with high levels of emotional intensity and/or physical touch, if they do not believe in the power of catharsis, should not (and probably will not) attempt to use this intervention. I agree with Bowen (1978) and Whitaker (Whitaker and Bumberry, 1988) that clients cannot exceed the therapist's level of differentiation and that their threshold for anxiety and tension in therapy is limited to the therapist's threshold.

Two more contraindications depend on the therapist's gender. If the therapist is male and one of the presenting problems is extremely high jealousy by the male partner in heterosexual relationships, he can become so jealous when the male therapist touches the female partner that no healing catharsis can occur. Instead, the male partner may withdraw from therapy and become quite resistant to any further treatment.

A third contraindication relates to female survivors of abuse. If a male therapist touches a female client without having established enough safety, the client may have flashbacks from her abuse that could have the opposite effects of those intended by the intervention. Instead of helping the client and her partner to reconnect emotionally, the intervention would reabuse the female client and prevent her and the relationship from healing. This contraindication is not only true for female clients who suffered abuse in a previous relationship, but also for couples who present with abuse and violence. The therapist has to be extremely cautious not to recreate an abusive experience for the victim through the intervention.

In summary, I have used the intervention with many couples successfully. If the therapist monitors very closely and through open interaction with the couple their level of comfort and discomfort, respectively, stopping the process at any time, and if the level of discomfort of anybody involved reaches that person's threshold, this is a very powerful intervention. Not only is it very effective in interrupting destructive spirals, it also opens or reopens safe space for couples to explore the level of emotional connection they want and need. In general, I would only recommend the intervention for more experienced therapists who feel comfortable using experiential exercises in their work with clients and who trust the healing process of human relationships.

REFERENCES

Blatner, A. (1973). *Acting-in: Practical applications of psychodramatic methods.* New York: Springer.

Bowen, M. (1978). *Family therapy in clinical practice.* Northgate, NJ: Jason Aronson.

Moreno, J. (1964). *Psychodrama: Vol. 1* (Third edition). New York: Beacon House.

Pearls, F. (1973). *The Gestalt approach and eye witness to therapy.* Palo Alto, CA: Science and Behavior Books.

Satir, V. (1983). *Conjoint family therapy* (Third edition). Palo Alto, CA: Science and Behavior Books.

Satir, V. (1988). *The new peoplemaking.* Palo Alto, CA: Science and Behavior Books.

Simon, R. (1992). *One on one: Conversations with the shakers of family therapy.* New York: Guilford.

Whitaker, C. A. and Bumberry, W. M. (1988). *Dancing with the family: A symbolic-experiential approach.* New York: Brunner/Mazel.

Winter, J. R. and Parker, L. R. E. (1991). Enhancing the marital relationship: Virginia Satir's parts party. In B. J. Brothers (Ed.), *Virginia Satir: Foundational ideas.* Binghamton, NY: The Haworth Press.

92

The Parents' Closet: A Family Therapy Approach for "Coming to Acceptance" of Gay/Lesbian/Bisexual Children

Özlem Çamli
Laura M. I. Saunders

INTRODUCTION

Families provide support and nurturance while enhancing the social and emotional growth of their members. They play an especially crucial role in the lives of gay/lesbian/bisexual youth who, in particular, need acceptance, love and affirmation to cope with a homophobic society. Approximately seven million Americans under age twenty identify themselves as gay or lesbian (Singer and Decamp, 1994). Even though most gays and lesbians are aware of their sexual orientation from their early teenage years, they typically come out to their parents during their mid- to late twenties (Çamli and Saunders, 1995; Durby, 1994; Savin-Williams, 1996). Nearly half of gay/lesbian/bisexual individuals experience rejection by their family members once they come out (Bass and Kaufman, 1996; Çamli and Saunders, 1995; Mallon, 1994). It is quite common that parents need to experience a process of coming to understanding and acceptance similar to their child's coming out, as they deal with the child's homosexuality.

THE COMING TO ACCEPTANCE PROCESS

"My child came out of the closet and I went in" sums up the experience of many families. Parents report undergoing shock, guilt about the "cause" of their child's sexual orientation, and embarrassment in relation

457

to reactions of friends and family (Bass and Kaufman, 1996; Çamli and Saunders, 1996). Parents' initial feelings in response to finding out about their child's sexual orientation tend to include a significant amount of anxiety and fear for the child's well-being and physical safety, some level of relief and grief, and disappointment over "lost" dreams for the child (Çamli and Saunders, 1996; Savin-Williams, 1996). As stated by numerous parents, these vacillating emotions and the parents' experiences parallel Kübler-Ross's five stages of grief and loss (Çamli and Saunders, 1996; Morris, 1993). We conducted some preliminary research investigating the reaction parents experience after finding out about their child's homosexuality. One parent described her son's coming out to her as being like the time she found out her husband had cancer. Another parent stated that when her daughter came out to her, her response was, "I have not had a headache like this since my father died."

The first stage of the grieving process is denial. Approximately a third of all parents, when their children come out to them, think and hope that their child is going through a phase. They are willing to take all the necessary steps to change the situation and help their child move through "this stage." Some parents choose to simply do nothing with the information about their child's sexual orientation; they neither talk about it nor acknowledge it. As one parent pointed out, this tends to be easier when the child lives away from home. This mother stated that her daughter had come out to her two years ago. However, since they lived miles apart, she did not "deal with the situation" until her daughter recently invited her to a commitment ceremony.

The experience of anger was one of the most intense stages parents tend to face. Some parents express a significant amount of discontent, blame their child for "making such a choice" and thus overburdening the family; some parents go as far as disowning their children (Bass and Kaufman, 1996; Durby, 1994; Mallon, 1994). Parents may also turn this anger inward and blame themselves or their spouses for their parenting styles as the "cause" of their child's sexual orientation.

As parents try to change the situation, they engage in bargaining. They are willing to give their children more chances to gain more experience in dating the opposite sex. When a teenager "comes out," parents may suggest going to therapy as a family or taking their child to see a therapist as a means of "fixing" or changing the situation.

As parents struggle with the above emotions, depression frequently catches up with them. Parents often cry for the dreams they had for their children, and the grandchildren they may not have. Another tremendous source of sadness is feeling different and isolated from other families and having a secret they are not able to share. Parents often express that once their child came out of the closet, they went into it. Shame tends to prevent parents from coming out to others around them, making it even more difficult to obtain crucial emotional and social support. The level of anxiety experienced by parents intensifies as they find themselves sad, lonely, and embarrassed about their children's sexual orientation.

It is not until a period of struggle with these emotions that parents can arrive at the stage of acceptance. Most parents indicate that they would like to see their children happy and successful and that they would not want to lose their children over this issue. Parents indicated that meeting their gay/lesbian/bisexual child's friends and partner frequently helped them accept their child's orientation more easily. Once parents reach this stage and feel comfortable with their child's sexual orientation, they express strong pride and love for their child.

Even though these five stages were discussed in a particular order, parents do not typically experience them in a set sequence. Instead, they vacillate among the stages, and may stagnate for long periods of time.

INITIAL FAMILY ASSESSMENT

As with any family therapy case, a number of factors may directly affect the level of success in therapy with parents of gay/lesbian/bisexual individuals. A family's overall level of functioning, including their communication style, emotional connectedness and cohesion, and problem-solving skills, is very likely to determine how the family members will respond to the child's sexual orientation. Assessing the family's coping skills, communication patterns, and emotional resources as well as their potential difficulties and conflicts will help the therapist guide the family through the revelation of their child's homosexual orientation. In families who already experience a high level of conflict and lack cohesion, the therapist may focus on helping the family develop more effective communication skills and enhance their understanding of the nature of the relations among family members before the family can work productively on the issues raised by the child's sexual orientation.

The therapist needs to assess the family's anticipated amount of involvement in therapy. For those families who may come in for a single session at the time of a crisis, that is, the child's coming out to the parents, the family therapy session may need to consolidate all three major components of the intervention including validation, psychoeducation, and community referral. These components will be discussed in further detail. For families who may stay in therapy for a short time, the therapist may have more time to explore parents' reactions and feelings and follow the family's evolution in coming to acceptance. When the child's sexual orientation emerges within therapy, the therapist should take the time to address the issue utilizing the three components outlined below, while continuing to provide support and guidance to the family throughout the course of treatment.

INTERVENTION

The three major components of family intervention with parents of gay/lesbian/bisexual individuals involves therapeutic support, education, and community involvement. When parents and their children seek therapy after their children's coming out, the therapist's initial responsibility (i.e., the first level of intervention) is normalizing the range of emotions expressed. It is important to remember that gay/lesbian/bisexual children dealt with their own feelings over a long period of time before they came out to their parents. Consequently, their parents will also need time to go though their own "coming out" process. This may be difficult as children fear rejection, and need a significant amount of support themselves. It is then the therapist's responsibility to facilitate communication among family members and clarify the needs and expectations so everyone feels acknowledged and understood. Family members, especially parents, should be informed of the stages of the coming-to-acceptance process, and encouraged to discuss how these stages may be experienced in their families.

The second component involves psychoeducation of family members. Most parents have numerous questions concerning the origins of homosexuality and the social and emotional issues their children will face in society. As stated above, parents typically experience a significant amount of guilt and shame. Many parents reported that factual information delivered in a straightforward manner relieved the significant anxiety and guilt (Çamli and Saunders, 1996). An updated bibliography for additional reading on gay/lesbian issues and how other parents deal with this topic is invaluable.

The third component of the family intervention involves referral to sources of community support for the parents and the entire family. This is crucial given that therapy tends to be short term and that most effective therapeutic work after the initial phase of therapy takes place within a supportive peer group. Parents and families will return to their communities and thus need a supportive system that will help them cope with the myriad of emotions to, hopefully, reach the stage of acceptance. Numerous parents stated that community-based support groups such as the national organization PFLAG (Parents and Friends of Gays and Lesbians) were "their lifesavers." It allowed parents and families to hear from others who have been through the same experiences, share new information, compare coping strategies, participate in supportive events, and feel validated and empowered. Community-based support groups may include parent support groups as well as youth groups and school-based gay/straight alliances. Parents who are not ready to attend groups may be put in contact with parents of gay/lesbian/bisexual individuals within their communities through the local support groups.

CONTRAINDICATIONS

It is important for the therapist to understand that this volatile issue may increase parental discord and/or family conflict. Finding that parents are in markedly different phases of the coming-to-acceptance process is not uncommon. One parent may be more prone to sadness and depression over lost dreams while the other is angry and displacing blame onto others. Their child's revelation of a homosexual orientation may intensify unresolved past conflicts, thereby deflecting the source of pain from the present issue.

As stated earlier, it is essential to assess the family members' ability to effectively cope with the child's coming out at this time. In case of severe discord and rising conflict during therapy, the therapist needs to utilize conflict management strategies and reduce the amount of emotional tension so that all family members feel stable and can benefit from the components of the proposed intervention. The therapist may also need to address the different stages that the family members may be experiencing and help them understand each other more clearly. Should parents find themselves in intense conflict with each other, it may be best to focus on the marital dyad to address the possible underlying sources of disagreement. At times it may also be useful to work with a parent-child dyad to resolve long-standing issues which may hinder the coming-to-acceptance process. Apart from the issues listed above, the intervention does not have any other potential contraindications.

CONCLUSION

It is essential that therapists recognize the stages of a family's coming-out process in order to intervene appropriately. Once they start coping with the myriad of emotions, family members will embark on a remarkable journey, full of struggles as well as joyful moments. Family therapy provides a supportive environment to facilitate this process, ease the journey, and allow the family to reach acceptance. Along with therapy, psychoeducation enables parents to attain some perspective on the issue at their own pace, utilizing factual information and testimonials. Community support provides the family with a peer group, which allows for tremendous growth once the parents are ready to reach out and establish connections. The model of "coming to acceptance" may thus be utilized by the therapist to facilitate change and direct the family through the stages of denial, bargaining, anger, and depression to reach acceptance.

REFERENCES

Bass, E. and Kaufman, R. (1996). *Free your mind: The book for gay, lesbian and bisexual youth and their allies.* New York: Harper Perennial.

Çamli, O. and Saunders, L. M. I. (1995, November). Issues of gay youth: Risk factors and implications. Paper presented at the Annual Meeting of American Association of Marriage and Family Therapy, Baltimore, MD.

Çamli, O. and Saunders, L. M. I. (1996, October). "Coming-to-acceptance" by parents of gays and lesbians. Paper presented at the Annual Meeting of American Association of Marriage and Family Therapy, Toronto, Canada.

Durby, D. (1994). Gay, lesbian and bisexual youth. In DeCrescenzo, T. (Ed.), *Helping gay and lesbian youth: New policies, new programs, new practice* (pp. 1-37). Binghamton, NY: Harrington Park Press.

Mallon, G. (1994). Counseling strategies with gay and lesbian youth. In DeCrescenzo, T. (Ed.), *Helping gay and lesbian youth: New policies, new programs, new practice* (pp. 75-91). Binghamton, NY: Harrington Park Press.

Morris, C. (1993). *Psychology: An introduction*, New Jersey: Prentice-Hall.

Savin-Williams, R. (1996). Self-labeling and disclosure among gay, lesbian and bisexual youths. In Laird, J. and Green, R. (Eds.), *Lesbians and gays in couples and families* (pp.153-182). San Francisco: Jossey-Bass Publishers.

Singer, B. L. and Decamp, D. (Eds.) (1994). *Gay and lesbian stats: A pocket guide of facts and figures*. New York: The New Press.

93

Respecting the Purpose of the Old Pattern and the New Pattern

Joseph L. Wetchler

There exists an inherent bias in the family therapy literature that there is something wrong with the old pattern that must be corrected with a new one. It is maintained across all theories, no matter how much they may diverge on other issues. For example, strategic therapy believes that problems are maintained by repetitive first-order change strategies, and are resolved by the use of second-order change that creates new patterns (Watzlawick, Weakland, and Fisch, 1974). Transgenerational therapists state that low levels of differentiation and high levels of anxiety lead to rigid interactions that maintain problems, while raising differentiation and lessening anxiety yields new transgenerational patterns which, in turn, resolves problems (Bowen, 1978; Kerr and Bowen, 1988). Further, White and Epston (1990) believe that problems are maintained due to the oppression of a dominant story that must be overthrown through the recognition of alternative stories. Finally, Minuchin (1974; Minuchin and Fishman, 1981) states that problems are best solved through creating a new family structure. No matter the theoretical orientation, and no matter the wording, there is a belief that old patterns are bad and new patterns are good.

Postmodern ideas promote leveling the playing field between therapist and client (e.g., Anderson and Goolishian, 1988; de Shazer, 1991; White and Epston, 1990). They oppose the notion that therapists have greater knowledge about what is necessary for change than their clients. However, by promoting client exceptions (de Shazer, 1991) or alternative stories (White and Epston, 1990) as the royal road to problem resolution, they inadvertently claim a dominance of therapist knowledge over client knowledge. Specifically, that new patterns or beliefs are better than old ones at resolving problems.

Not only does this belief promote therapist knowledge over client knowledge, it is not always the best way to resolve problems. For example, Watzlawick, Weakland, and Fisch (1974) caution against therapists inappropriately recommending second-order change strategies when first-order change is needed. Further, as no pattern is perfect, all patterns have the potential to be ineffective with various problems. Milton Erickson was one of the few therapists to respect the influence of the old pattern on a client's life (Haley, 1973). After clients had begun to make changes in their lives, he would ask them to view their initial problem as a friend and decide what aspect of that friend they would wish to keep with them for the rest of their lives. This would enable them to take what was important from their old pattern and not have to relapse when they needed it again.

This chapter proposes that different patterns are effective with different problems, and occasionally with similar ones. Having clients identify both the old pattern and its function, and some alternative new patterns may be a more efficacious approach than simply siding with the new pattern. The choice of which pattern to use lies with the client.

To respect both the old pattern and the new one, therapists are advised to be knowledgeable in transgenerational (e.g., Kerr and Bowen, 1988), strategic (e.g., Haley, 1987; Watzlawick, Weakland, and Fisch, 1974), and solution-focused (de Shazer, 1991) or narrative (White and Epston, 1990) approaches. The first step is to overtly discuss the old problem-maintaining pattern. This can be either a present-centered or transgenerational exploration. Then, the therapist and client discuss possible helpful meanings for that pattern. Third, the client is asked to explore specific behaviors that led to times the problem was successfully resolved. If the client is unable to identify any exceptions, either the therapist can provide directives for behaving differently, or the client can generate possibilities on how to break the pattern. Finally, the client is asked to choose which pattern would be *the best way to solve the problem this time.*

CASE EXAMPLE

Tom was a biology premed student who began to experience anxiety attacks the semester before he was to take his MCATs (the medical school admissions test). He reported that he was unable to do his coursework and described the sensation as "freezing up." In response to the therapist's query if he had ever experienced this freezing up in the past, he stated that he had had a similar experience as a child. His late father had been extremely abusive with his brother and him and would often come home drunk and beat the boys. Tom explained that when his father began to hit him, he would freeze up while his brother would run away. Further exploration revealed that his father would only hit him a few times and then chase his brother, whom he would severely beat when he caught him. In discussing the past meaning of his behavior, Tom realized that it served a protective mechanism for him. By freezing up, he avoided the beatings his brother got. Tom also identified that the classes in which he had the most trouble were ones taught by authoritarian professors.

When asked if he had ever had a situation in a class in which he was able to fight through his anxiety, he reported that the past semester he had become anxious over an exam from an authoritarian teacher, yet was able to pass the test. When asked how he had done this, he responded that he imagined himself talking to the professor and kept repeating, "You won't beat me, I will pass this test!" This provided an important alternative story to his dominant one of freezing up.

Because of his science background, the therapist stated that perhaps he was experiencing a "fight or flight" reaction. He explained that animals experience a rush of adrenaline when they are placed in a stressful situation and the way they interpret it leads to whether they use the adrenaline to avoid the situation or to fight back. Both responses serve to protect the animal. The therapist then said that Tom's freezing up was a flight response that protected him from receiving the severe beatings his brother got while his self-talk about "his professor not beating him with the exam" was a fight response that enabled him to pass his test. In the frame of the fight or flight response, Tom was now asked to make decisions about which was the best way to deal with specific anxious situations.

The following week, he reported that he had been able to successfully take an exam in a class in which he had been freezing up by telling himself that he would not let the professor beat him. He said that he decided to use his fight response to get through the test. When asked why he chose fight instead of flight, he responded that it was the best way to handle this situation. Several weeks later he reported that he had used the flight response by refusing to challenge an authoritarian professor who had made an unkind remark to him. When asked why he had done this, he responded that the professor was known for being vindictive when confronted and Tom did not wish to incur his wrath. He stated that he did not feel anxious in this class anymore because he felt in control of the situation. The therapist responded that he had learned an important lesson. Sometimes, "He who fights and runs away, lives to fight another day." Needless to say, Tom terminated therapy shortly afterward, feeling less anxious and much more in control of his life.

DISCUSSION

It is important to note how both the old and new patterns served an important function in Tom's life. In fact, his recognition of this, and his ability to use his own wisdom in deciding how to proceed provided sufficient self-efficacy to gain control of his anxiety. Siding with either pattern against the other would have denied the importance of both patterns in his life. Perhaps a sense of one's strength comes from having the flexibility to choose among a series of behaviors rather than viewing one as superior to another.

REFERENCES

Anderson, H. and Goolishian, H. (1988). Human systems as linguistic systems: Preliminary and evolving ideas about the implications for clinical theory. *Family Process, 27,* 371-393.

Bowen, M. (1978). *Family therapy in clinical practice.* New York: Jason Aronson.

de Shazer, S. (1991). *Putting difference to work.* New York: W.W. Norton.

Haley, J. (1973). *Uncommon therapy: The psychiatric techniques of Milton H. Erickson, MD.* New York: W.W. Norton.

Haley, J. (1987). *Problem-solving therapy* (Third edition). San Francisco: Jossey-Bass.

Kerr, M. E. and Bowen, M. (1988). *Family evaluation.* New York: W.W. Norton.

Minuchin, S. (1974). *Families and family therapy.* Cambridge, MA: Harvard University Press.

Minuchin, S. and Fishman, H. C. (1981). *Family therapy techniques.* Cambridge, MA: Harvard.

Watzlawick, P., Weakland, J. H., and Fisch, R. (1974). *Change.* New York: W.W. Norton.

White, M. and Epston, D. (1990). *Narrative means to therapeutic ends.* New York: W.W. Norton.

94

Notice the Difference

Victor H. Nelson

Solution-focused therapies (SFT) offer a wide range of resources for therapists. Many of these resources empower clients to be more active in the therapy process and subsequently more in charge of the changes that occur in their life situations. For example, scaling questions (de Shazer, 1994) can help clients assess the severity of a problem in order to recognize changes as they occur. The Miracle Question (Berg, 1993) encourages clients to imagine a reality that is already in the process of becoming and into which the client can move. I have learned that the "notice the difference" directive (de Shazer, 1991) is a particularly effective intervention that has evolved in SFT. Because of its simplicity, I suspect that therapists tend to underrate its effectiveness and therefore underutilize this intervention.

Using this intervention is very simple: therapists instruct clients to notice differences. The directive may be applied to people, objects, activities, place, and time (who, what, where, and when). As clients focus their attention on differences in any of these areas, they can identify even small changes and improvements as they occur. By identifying small changes, the therapist can help the client focus on what contributed to the improvement, how such improvement can be duplicated by the client, and what it will take for the client to make additional improvements that bring about greater change. As Milton Erickson taught, small changes inevitably lead to large changes (Haley, 1993).

Noticing differences can be particularly helpful in therapy with anxious clients. My working assumption is that anxiety is fluid, not static. It fluctuates in intensity rather than maintaining a constant, impenetrable barrier to change. However, the persistence and recalcitrance of anxiety symptoms can overwhelm clients. Symptoms can be easily exacerbated by some unforseen event. Clients can also regress quickly in the face of a stimulus that they believe they had already mastered. The anxiety seems to control the client; the same anxiety often can control the therapist as well. Solution-focused interventions empower anxious clients (and therapists!) to assume more authority and control over the symptoms of anxiety.

"Notice the difference" is a simple directive that instructs clients to notice differences in the symptom's level of intensity. Clients can notice the difference in their anxiety around the people *with whom* it occurs, around which *objects or activities* it occurs, *where* the anxiety occurs, and *when* it occurs. Clients are instructed to notice the difference in the level of anxiety as they make changes in any of these areas. When they find situations in which the anxiety diminishes, clients notice the differences and build on those differences to make changes.

On one occasion, I used this intervention with a highly anxious woman who was pregnant with her first baby. She had an extensive history of severe anxiety symptoms including panic attacks, social phobias, and pro-longed generalized anxiety. After nearly three months of therapy, her symptoms had virtually disappeared and she seemed to have mastered her anxiety. However, just three weeks before her due date, she came to therapy in a highly anxious state. She had just discovered that she could not enter the baby's nursery. Her anxiety had flared up so strongly that she was afraid to even set foot inside the door. I gave her the following instructions:

> Go back home and stand in the doorway of the nursery. I know you'll probably find this uncomfortable, but I want you to prepare yourself to walk into the nursery. Have your husband help you if you need his support. Enter the nursery and find the one spot in the nursery where you are least anxious. *Notice the differences in your anxiety as you move around the room.* Walk around the room. Sit in various places in the room. Face in different directions, sitting and standing, to discover the one place in the room where you are least anxious. Even though your anxiety may feel constant to you, you can be sure that there will be some places in the nursery where your anxiety will feel different to you than in other places. *Notice these differences.* When you find that spot where you are least anxious, become aware of what it's like for you to enjoy that reduced anxiety, that sense of calm and relaxation you've come to know and appreci-ate. Enjoy that spot, mark that spot, remember that spot so that you know you'll always be able to find a place in the nursery that is a calm place for you.

When she came to her next appointment, she appeared very different from the previous session. She was calm. She conveyed a sense of self-confidence. She even joked and laughed. She described what had happened.

She had stood at the door of the nursery and, despite her high anxiety, she entered the room, without her husband's help. She walked around the room. She stood in various places throughout the room. She looked at the new pictures she and her husband had hung on the wall. She said that, after about fifteen or twenty minutes in the room, she had become aware that the nursery was not complete. There was no rocking chair. She quickly had her husband move the rocking chair from the living room into the nursery and she found the exact place where it belonged, the place where she was least anxious. And then she sat in the rocking chair, learning again to enjoy the sense of relaxation and confidence that she had learned to acknowledge and appreciate. And she described that her anxiety "just seemed to melt away." Noticing the differences had helped her access her own resources and regain mastery over her anxiety.

Noticing the difference can be a very effective addition to the therapist's resources, since the range of application is so diverse. This is not to say that the intervention can or should be used indiscriminately or universally. The "who, what, where, and when" factors must be assessed when implementing the intervention. In the case I used to demonstrate the intervention, I had to assess the "where and when" application of the intervention. I had to weigh the risk of triggering a panic attack in my client against the benefit of the intervention. If time had not been such a critical issue, I would have returned to a less intense intervention process that had already proven effective in her therapy. The intervention should also be used judiciously for clients with impulse-control problems. The factors "with whom and in what situation" must be carefully assessed. For example, with domestic violence offenders I would use the intervention only after I was confident that the client had developed effective self-management skills. Relying on the intervention early in the treatment of such clients runs the risk that the client may have limited abilities for self-awareness or self-control in a moment of emotional intensity. The intervention can certainly be used as part of the treatment approach, but should not be viewed as a behavior management intervention.

Noticing differences empowers clients and helps them access their own resources for change. The intervention can be used with young children, adolescents, and adults alike. It is particularly useful when working with family groups because each person in the family is likely to notice different differences, a scenario that can promote better communication and understanding between family members. Use the intervention and notice the difference it can make in your therapy.

REFERENCES

Berg, I. (1993). "Pretend a miracle happened": A brief therapy task. In T. Nelson and T. Trepper (Eds.), *101 interventions in family therapy* (pp. 278-282). Binghamton, NY: The Haworth Press.

de Shazer, S. (1991). *Putting difference to work.* New York: W. W. Norton.

de Shazer, S. (1994). *Words were originally magic.* New York: W. W. Norton.

Haley, J. (1993). *Jay Haley on Milton Erickson.* New York: Brunner/Mazel.

95

Mad About You

Richard B. Smith

Due to two runaway attempts, Kelly, a fifteen-year-old girl, was living with her older sister and brother-in-law. In session one, the following argument occurred. "You don't know how I feel about him!" screamed Kelly to her sister, Kate, when told that she couldn't see her boyfriend. "First of all," replied Kate, "he smokes pot, drinks, has no job, and is a high school dropout. Second of all, you have told so many lies and have snuck out of the house twice such that my husband and I can't trust you. We have zero trust right now and that's our problem!"

THEORETICAL CONTEXT

As the family therapist in a hospital adolescent psychiatric unit, I have seen many family members become angry while recounting the adolescent's history of violent or inappropriate behaviors, suicide attempts or suicide gestures, or feeling stymied by their inability to compromise over issues leading to the child's hospitalization. However, I have found that by using the anger model I will detail next, clients have been able to punctuate the unsatisfying response sequence (Fisch, Weakland, and Segal, 1982), address core emotions in more emotionally satisfying enactments (Minuchin, 1974), illuminate "exceptions" to their patterns of hostility (Walter and Peller, 1992), and practice "I-messages" (Gordon, 1970), which helps them to accept responsibility for their feelings.

The purpose of this model is twofold. First, it helps hostile clients understand their anger. More specifically, it has been my experience that clients who do not understand the origins of their anger, the speed of their reactivity (i.e., why they become angry so quickly), or the sequence of cognitive and emotional processes previous to their angry reactions tend to benefit from this approach. Second, it serves as a primer in punctuating conflictual communication patterns by addressing both the cognitive and affective components of those patterns.

THE INTERVENTION

I start off by suggesting to clients that anger is a secondary emotion and I write that at the top of the paper or white board. Then I explain to them that for every event in life, we have a corresponding expectation (some greater than others) and proceed to cite several examples after writing "Events = Expectations." Depending on the age of the client, I will note, for instance, that our daily expectations may include the alarm clock going off in the morning, being able to eat breakfast and start the car, meeting our friends at school, being on time for important meetings, appropriate relationships with co-workers, and so on. In addition, I note that we also have expectations for our families.

Next, I pose the question, "How do you feel when your expectations are not met?" Often the response is "Angry." I then proceed to challenge them by saying, "Eventually, yes, but there's some emotion that happens beforehand. Can you think of what it is?" After giving them the opportunity to guess, I then draw an arrow from expectations to disappointment. Almost without fail, my clients have agreed that this occurs.

My next question is, "What is at the root of disappointment?" Again, the frequent reply is "Anger." "Not yet," I say, "but we're getting closer. Actually, sadness is at the core of disappointment." I draw an arrow from disappointment to sadness. This is followed by the question, "What emotion is going on in between the disappointment and sadness? Well, we feel hurt." I then write the word *hurt* between the words *disappointment* and *sadness*. The next question is, "What's building up in between this sadness and the anger?" Frequently, the words *tension, anxiety,* and *frustration* are noted, and I write them accordingly. Then, I draw an arrow from the word *anger* to the word *reaction* and then to the word *events*. Often my clients can relate to this process and the model has helped them visualize it.

The next step includes drawing a line from just before the word *disappointment* to the word *anger* and writing the words *learned response* on that line. I explain to my clients that anger is a wonderful motivator. We learn, for example, that we can use this anger-driven motivation to help control our circumstances and those with whom we have contact (e.g., spouse, children, or subordinates at work). In essence, we find out that we can manipulate others using our anger (and I write the word *control* under the word *anger*). Furthermore, I explain to them that because we habitually choose this route to address our frustrations, we wind up ignoring the core emotions. I add that facing some core emotions (for example, disappointment, hurt, and sadness) seems particularly challenging for males in this society. However, regardless of gender, if we do not address them, we become emotionally handicapped (and I shade in that portion of the model to indicate that those emotions have been ignored). This is unfortunate, I reason, because healthy people can experience the full range of emotions.

I then call my clients' attention to the word *anxiety* with special emphasis on how anxiety impedes moral decision making. The definition of morality that I prefer is "knowing what is helpful and harmful to oneself and others in a given context and acting in accordance with that which is most helpful to all involved" (Scoresby, 1994). Examples of moral people given by past clients include Ghandi, Martin Luther King Jr., and Jesus Christ. In any case, it is pointed out that these people knew what was helpful and harmful to those with whom they associated. Pointing to the word *anxiety,* I suggest that anxious people cannot concentrate fully on what is helpful and harmful to themselves and others in a given context, because they only know how the circumstances are affecting them. Thus, the likelihood of appropriate decision making decreases as anxiety increases—leaving the therapist a wide-open opportunity for discussing how to reduce anxiety in the home.

This model has been useful for several reasons. First of all, using this illustration slows the pace of emotionally heated sessions. Second, many clients have become so habitually angry that they cannot discern the root causes of their anger, much less be able to begin punctuating the cycle. When I describe this pattern to them, most clients agree that they need to be aware of their expectations and then discuss them in detail. Third, this model appeals to clients who may be both more cognitive or more affective in their response patterns. Specifically, the more cognitive clients can understand the rationale behind the anger, while the more affective clients appreciate being understood in terms of their emotionality. In addition, when a relationship includes one partner who is more affective and one who is more cognitive, the model provides the therapist with an opportunity to help each partner to understand his/her counterpart as each gains this insight about the response patterns. However, I believe that insight is not enough for change.

For example, the clients can decide where (along the cycle) and how they would like to address the core emotions. It is suggested that in the next session following the illustration of the model, the therapist can briefly review the model and then promote the use of "I-messages" and reflective listening skills while emphasizing that the clients discuss the core emotions (i.e., when and how each has felt disappointed, hurt, and sad) and take ownership for those feelings. It has been my experience that when the clients are able to communicate clearly about their core emotions and compromise about their expectations, anger is alleviated.

INDICATIONS AND CONTRAINDICATIONS

This model can best be used with clients ages twelve and older whose attention span and intellectual capacity are sufficient to follow the step-by-step procedure. In addition, this approach tends to appeal to more verbal clients. Thus, it has been noted that younger children tend to lack the patience or level of cognition necessary to process this procedure. However, it is an excellent vehicle for joining with hostile clients who really want to be understood and want their partners and other family members to understand them.

REFERENCES

Fisch, R., Weakland, J. H., and Segal, L. (1982). *The tactics of change: Doing therapy briefly*. San Francisco: Jossey-Bass.

Gordon, T. (1970). *Parent-effectiveness training: The no-lose program for raising responsible children*. New York: P. H. Wyden.

Minuchin, S. (1974). *Families and family therapy*. Cambridge, MA: Harvard University Press.

Scoresby, L. (1994). Moral development lecture series. Provo, UT: Brigham Young University.

Walter, J. L. and Peller, J. E. (1992). *Becoming solution-focused in brief therapy*. New York: Brunner/Mazel.

96

Increasing Homework Compliance: The SEA Method or Effective Use of the 167 "Nontherapy" Hours of the Week

D. Kim Openshaw

Historically, homework has been touted as a critical, adjunctive component to psychotherapy (e.g., Shelton and Ackerman, 1982). Two premises have evolved and form the foundation of our current thinking regarding the use of homework in the context of psychotherapy. The first suggests that systematic use of homework permits therapy to become a twenty-four-hour-a-day experience. The second recognizes that assigned tasks outside of the therapy hour promote transfer from the therapy session, and generalization into day-to-day living. Homework assignments encourage clients to integrate relevant concepts which repattern rules and meta-rules regarding themselves, their interaction styles, and/or coping methodologies (Burns and Auerbach, 1992).

Research suggests that homework increases the likelihood of producing desired therapeutic outcomes (e.g., Burns and Nolen-Hoeksema, 1992). Taylor (1996; see also Neimeyer and Feixas, 1990) suggests that in-session interventions, when combined with homework assignments, are more effective in facilitating change than other experimental conditions employed in their study (e.g., placebo conditions, cognitive restructuring without exposure exercises, social skills training, control waiting list, and homework exposure alone).

HOMEWORK COMPLIANCE

In reviewing various strategies, one key component continues to manifest itself as a critical dimension of homework effectiveness, namely,

475

compliance. Homework compliance refers to the willingness of a client to engage the homework assignment on an active and continuous basis outside of the therapy hour (Burns and Nolen-Hoeksema, 1992; Forgatch and Ramsey, 1994). Startup and Edmonds (1994) encourage therapists to identify strategies that enhance early compliance.

THE SEA (SUMMARIZATION, EMPOWERMENT, AND ACTIVE INVOLVEMENT) METHODOLOGY

Attempting to devise a method of introducing homework that is amenable to compliance, and that can be initiated early in therapy, led to the conclusion that the oft-used technique of, "Well, for homework this week I would like you to . . ." is an inefficient strategy as well as an ineffective method of enhancing homework compliance. Three therapeutic techniques appear to be related to enhancing homework compliance, namely, summarization, empowerment, and active involvement. While these techniques are often used throughout therapy in a variety of contexts, they are not often incorporated into the formulation of homework.

Summarization

Summarization statements are a frequent part of the therapeutic hour, used to demonstrate understanding, clarify direction, and maintain focus. Used with homework, summarization involves reiterating, in an abridged fashion, key patterns and foci elucidated during the session.

> **Therapist:** Kerry and Annette, as the two of you have reflected with (1) each other your perception of the past seven years of marriage, you have pointed out a number of meaningful strengths and separate concerns. Your discussion suggests that although there are (2) differing opinions regarding various aspects of your relationship, you are (3) united in your perception about several areas, which when strengthened, would enhance your relationship. (4) Is seeking the opportunity to enhance these areas of your relationship an accurate representation of why you have come to therapy at this time?

Commentary

The above example of summarization reflects a bias (1) toward having the couple share with each other their dynamic relationship history and perception of the events that led them to therapy. The therapist points out this unity through commonly reported strengths (3), while at the same time normalizes differentiation (2). Finally, (4) a question is asked that reframes the chief complaints into an opportunity, and sets out the expectation of a positive outcome.

Empowerment

While summarization leads naturally into empowerment, it is also appropriate, as illustrated above, to interweave statements of empowerment within the summarization statement. Empowerment is a technique by which the therapist facilitates the strengthening of the client's ego (self-esteem). An empowerment intervention emphasizes how the client's unique talents, perspectives, and coping strategies have effectively worked, and/or reframes the situation in a manner that instills hope and encourages internal motivation.

> **Therapist:** What is (1) intriguing to me is that the two of you have not only been able to (2) unite in your understanding of what it is you want to (3) enhance, but you have also been (4) actively involved in seeking out resources—(5) even to the point of coming to therapy. (6) I am wondering how you have been able to be so united.

Commentary

Making an expression of "amazement," (1) while pointing out that the couple has united (2) in their understanding of what they want to (3) enhance, suggests that the couple has initiated a problem-solving process critical to resolving and enhancing the area of concern. Including the statement (5) "even to the point of coming to therapy" normalizes their presence in therapy, points out their courage, and suggests that they have an open mind in the examination of alternative solutions. Pointing out that they have actively been involved (6) in the problem-solving process sets out the expectation that they have the ability to examine resources as a team. This decreases dependency on the therapist, and encourages the therapist to stay out of the counseling role. Finally, the therapist underscores the amazement, and empowers the couple by having them "discover" (6) their unique method of acquiring a sense of unity and focus.

Active Involvement

Active involvement indicates that the client has become an active participant in the creative endeavor of formulating a homework assignment that they believe they can successfully accomplish.

Annette: It has not been easy. There have been many difficult times and even talk of separating.

Kerry: Annette is absolutely right, it has not been easy. We have sought out many different resources as we shared with you. Each has offered something, but we have not been able to put it together. For me, I have just decided not to give up.

Therapist: You have shared with me three vital problem-solving techniques you (1) may not even know that you know you are using. First, you have indicated that you have used these difficult times as (2) catalysts. What I mean by this, is that you have taken the energy which has been created from combining your past positive experiences and present frustrations, and used the reaction to move you from complacency and toleration, to motivation and change. Second, you have (3) not neglected to recreate positive memories of the past, in particular times when there were exceptions to how it is now. Third, you have given yourselves (4) permission to maintain open minds to possible solutions, including (5) separation. Finally, you have (6) unified your efforts toward seeking out resources for the purpose of enhancing personal and interpersonal satisfaction.

Commentary

Each element of this statement is designed to empower the couple while recognizing their personal efforts to initiate change. Using an Ericksonian technique, (1) "you may not know that you know," reinforces the unique and inherent capacity of the couple in applying problem-solving strategies. The metaphor of a (2) catalyst is purposely employed, with emphasis on the constructive use of the energy produced from the catalytic reaction. This metaphor can be introduced in different sessions and serve as a therapeutic anchor when situations become tense. Recalling (3) exceptions, presented during the session, helps the couple remember that there were times when they were doing things that brought personal and interpersonal satisfaction. Suggesting that the couple has given themselves (4) "permission to maintain open minds," a solution-based orientation in which the client is an active participant, discourages reliance on the "all-knowing therapist." Next, the term (5) "separation" provides a metalevel message. At one level, it suggests the ability of the client to engage in an acceptance of and receptiveness to extreme alternatives. At another level the term exposes the couple to the present dichotomy being addressed—stay together or separate. Finally, at a subconscious level, the term continues to encourage differentiation, a vital aspect of intimacy. By disclosing the couples' (6) unity and effort toward enhancement of personal and interpersonal satisfaction, the therapist empowers the couple's joint efforts towards resolution, but within the context of interdependence.

> **Kerry:** Well, I never thought of it that way, but now that I think about it, we have done that.
>
> **Annette:** I never thought of separation as a way of keeping an open mind. I guess it is an alternative.
>
> **Therapist:** As we wrap this session up, I am (1) curious as to what it is you believe will be a first step (2) you will want to initiate this week, which would bring you closer to enhancing one of these three areas? In the next (3) five minutes could you (4) demonstrate how you have been able to unify yourselves toward a common goal by selecting something you (5) agree on that will increase your chances of bringing satisfaction to (6) one or more of the three areas you have presented to me today?

At this point, the clients are encouraged to formulate an intervention they will utilize between sessions. Approaching the situation with (1) "I am curious as to what it is you believe . . ." takes the therapist out of the "all-knowing" role, but more important, shifts the responsibility of creating an intervention for the week to the client. There is a higher probability that the couple will actively involve themselves in outside therapy assignments when they have been empowered with the opportunity to formulate what they believe will be most beneficial to them at this point in time.

The insertion (2) of the statement "you will want to initiate" is an embedded message suggesting the positive expectation that the couple will want to involve themselves in whatever it is they have decided would be advantageous to them.

A (3) time frame is provided and the couple is asked to (4) demonstrate their ability to work together in defining the area they would be willing to actively involve themselves with between sessions. The time frame encourages focusing of efforts. Asking the couple to demonstrate enhances the aspect of curiosity, and generates the expectation that they will be able to select an area of focus. Finally, having the couple (4) agree that their (5) selection will "bring satisfaction to one or more of the three areas" indicates not only that their choice can bring satisfaction, but that fulfillment may be experienced in more than one of the three areas (isomorphic effect).

CONTRAINDICATIONS

Contraindications in the use of this intervention are rare. However, there are two obvious ones; one with regard to clientele, and the other relating to the therapist. In terms of clients, there are those who initially require considerable structure and direction (e.g., the extremely depressed client, the psychotic client, or the marital couple where one of the two does not want the relationship to work, or when there is violence in the relationship that needs containing before interactive endeavors begin) before entering a collaborative homework process.

Perhaps the most significant contraindication lies with the novice therapist. While summarization, empowerment, and active involvement are the principle intervention strategies in and of themselves, embedded within each are a variety of interventions designed to enhance the effectiveness of encouraging clients to become responsible for their own therapeutic outcome. Novice therapists should take care to avoid moving too quickly through the steps.

CONCLUSION

Summarizing the key points for coming to therapy and empowering clients to make changes sets the foundation for their active involvement in formulating the homework intervention. Prochaska, DiClemente and Norcross (1992) note that moving the client into active involvement necessitates that they have already decided that change is beneficial at both the personal and interpersonal levels (i.e., clients have made the transition from precontemplation to contemplation, and are now preparing for action). The SEA method encourages clients to make the transition to action in an efficient and effective manner, thus increasing the probability that homework assignments will be effectively implemented. In so doing, the SEA method discourages dependency, and when utilized effectively has isomorphic properties.

REFERENCES

Burns, D. D. and Auerbach, A. H. (1992). Does homework compliance enhance recovery from depression? *Psychiatric-Annals, 22*(9), 464-469.

Burns, D. D. and Nolen-Hoeksema, S. (1992). Coping styles, homework compliance, and the effectiveness of cognitive-behavioral therapy. *Journal of Consulting and Clinical Psychology, 59*(2), 305-311.

Forgatch, M. S. and Ramsey, E. (1994). Boosting homework: A videotape link between families and schools. *School Psychology Review, 23*(3), 472-484.

Neimeyer, R. A. and Feixas, G. (1990). The role of homework and skill acquisition in the outcome of group cognitive therapy for depression. *Behavior Therapy, 21*(3), 281-292.

Prochaska, J. O., DiClemente, C. C., and Norcross, J. C. (1992). In search of how people change: Applications to addictive behaviors. *American Psychologist, 47*(9), 1102-1114.

Shelton, J. L. and Ackerman, J. M. (1982). *Homework in counseling and psychotherapy.* Springfield, IL: Charles C. Thomas.

Startup, M. and Edmonds, J. (1994). Compliance with homework assignments in cognitive-behavioral psychotherapy for depression: Relation to outcome and methods of enhancement. *Cognitive Therapy and Research, 18*(6), 567-579.

Taylor, S. (1996). Meta-analysis of cognitive behavioral treatment for social phobia. *Journal of Behavior Therapy and Experimental Psychiatry, 27*(1), 1-9.

97

A Solution-Focused Approach to Physical Abuse

Jacqueline Corcoran
Cynthia Franklin

Solution-focused therapy by its very name implies that solutions, not problems, are the focus of the work that is done in treatment (e.g., Berg, 1994; O'Hanlon and Weiner-Davis, 1989). The main assumption of the model is that clients possess the strengths and capacities that are needed to solve the problems that plague them. The task of the therapist is to identify strengths and amplify them so that clients can apply these solutions. To this end, therapists assist clients in identifying "exceptions," times when the problem is either not a problem, or it is lessened in intensity or frequency (O'Hanlon and Weiner-Davis, 1989). The assumption is that the construction of solutions from exceptions is easier and more successful than stopping or changing existing problem behavior.

The therapist gains cooperation of the client in finding solutions by "joining" with the client as the initial phase of engagement. Joining is the clinician's task of establishing a positive, mutually cooperative relationship (Berg, 1994). But how to join when clients are not amenable to treatment? One way *not* to do so is through confronting, arguing, or debating with the client why change should happen (Cade and O'Hanlon, 1993). These approaches are generally seen as counterproductive in that defensive clients are less amenable to working with the therapist and to change. In the solution-focused model, cooperative work can still be fostered between client and therapist even if clients are in treatment involuntarily. This departs from traditional psychotherapeutic models that assume clients come to treatment willing to make changes in their lives.

The following case study illustrates the principles of joining with a nonvoluntary, physically abusive mother, and how strengths and exceptions can be amplified and applied toward solutions. It will also illustrate the short-term focus of the solution-focused model reflecting the assumption that clients already possess the knowledge and skills needed to provide their own solutions (O'Hanlon and Weiner-Davis, 1989).

CASE EXAMPLE

This case example is drawn from the first author's work as a therapist at a community intensive supervision program for juvenile offenders. Juveniles were mandated to be part of this program either as an alternative to detention until their court hearings or for a trial period on probation. As a result of these conditions, program attendance tended to be short-term; therefore, the therapist's contacts were brief in nature, limited to an average of one or two sessions. The case example involves a thirteen-year-old Hispanic male, Gilbert Martinez, who was involved with the juvenile justice system for possession of marijuana. The caseworker at the community program had referred Gilbert, stating that his mother (who did not want to be involved with therapy) had mentioned to her that Gilbert had talked about committing suicide.

During the first individual session, Gilbert admitted to feelings of suicidality but was unable to explain the events leading up to these feelings. The therapist probed for an understanding of the various aspects of his life. Gilbert described that he lived in a public housing development with his single-parent mother, his older sister (age fifteen), and brother (age seventeen). When asked about his relationship to his mother, Gilbert began to relate numerous episodes of her physically abusing him, such as repeatedly hitting him with her fist and slapping him in the face and head. However, he said that he currently did not have any marks or bruises on his body from the physical punishment.

During this account, Gilbert became very emotional. This emotional reaction was striking due to the usual inhibition against its expression in this population (mainly Hispanic, male adolescent youth). When the therapist first suggested that she intervene with his mother to talk with her about the abuse, Gilbert said he considered the situation at home "hopeless." He also confessed to feeling "scared" that his mother would become even angrier with him for telling about the physical abuse. It was finally negotiated between therapist and client that the therapist would schedule a home visit with his mother at a time when he would still be in school.

Since Gilbert's mother, Connie Valdez, was not amenable to participation in counseling, her cooperation was gained by phrasing it as a meeting with the therapist to discuss concerns about her son. Ms. Valdez said she could not come to the therapist's office due to transportation problems so the therapist agreed to a home visit.

The session with the mother began with the therapist bringing up Ms. Valdez's concerns about her son's suicidality, and how the therapist was sure if the mother could do something about the way he felt, she would. Ms. Valdez agreed this was so. The therapist then suggested that perhaps it was something about his home life, and it might relate to the way he was being punished. Ms. Valdez was asked about the discipline methods she used and freely admitted that she hit her children. She also volunteered that she had been investigated by Children's Protective Services for a previous incident of physical abuse of her daughter. Ms. Valdez related that she had told the caseworker at that time, "If you think you can do better, you can take my children."

Ms. Valdez said that of her three children, Gilbert gave her the most trouble, and therefore he was the most likely to be physically punished. The therapist validated Ms. Valdez's frustrations with Gilbert as she relayed accounts of his behavior. It also became apparent as Ms. Valdez related how she had handled his misbehavior that in addition to physical punishment, she relied on many other discipline methods as well. Examples included grounding, withholding allowance, and making the purchase of expensive items, such as tennis shoes or jewelry, contingent upon appropriate behavior (e.g., helping around the house without arguing). One of her more creative methods, developed in response to her son's sneaking out of the house at night, was to have him sleep with her. The therapist continually reinforced Ms. Valdez for her flexibility and creativity in disciplining her children.

The session ended with Ms. Valdez agreeing that physically punishing her son was not helping her achieve the effect she wanted, and she had many more skills and an array of more effective methods from which to choose. She also agreed that her son might be most assisted to change his inappropriate, and sometimes even illegal, behavior if he continued being open and honest in future sessions with the therapist. To this end, she stated she would not punish him or be angry toward him for revealing the physical discipline at home.

A subsequent session with Gilbert and further contacts with the caseworker revealed that his mother was no longer physically abusive toward him and that his suicidal feelings had been eradicated. Shortly after, Gilbert's involvement with the program ended due to the terms of his probation.

SOLUTION-FOCUSED APPLICATIONS

Ms. Valdez's openness to the therapist, her honesty in describing her frustrations with the children, and her acceptance of feedback from the therapist was a result of three solution-oriented techniques used by the therapist. The first technique was joining with the client. Joining was established by identifying an initial common ground of interest, to help her son so that he no longer felt suicidal, and then to validate her frustrations regarding his misbehavior. Joining became the goal of the engagement process rather than confronting the client about her physically abusive behavior. The latter approach might have caused Ms. Valdez to respond defensively, further entrenching her behavior and views as a way of maintaining control of her own life. Ms. Valdez's defensiveness was evident when she described a previous confrontation with a Children's Protective Services investigator, and was in marked contrast to her attitude and behavior with the current therapist.

Application of the solution-oriented approach was primarily illustrated by the focus on positive parenting practices, the solutions and exceptions to the problem rather than the problem itself (Berg, 1994). The therapist avoided soliciting details about the problem, such as when Ms. Valdez began hitting her children, how often she hit them, where she had learned this method, how it might have played a role in her own childhood, and so on. Rather, the focus was on the many times Ms. Valdez *did not* rely on physical punishment when faced with her children's misbehavior. In response to the therapist's orientation to these exceptions, the client, too, began to adopt this focus, and she proceeded to relay more and more incidents of appropriate parenting behavior. Finally, the therapist developed an agreement with the mother to amplify these positive parenting practices based on the client's existing behavioral resources. The solution-oriented approach in this case also demonstrated the effectiveness of brief treatment. For instance, in this case, Ms. Valdez did not agree to treatment; however, she did agree to a single meeting with her son's therapist and change was enacted during this intervention.

CONCLUSION

The success of this intervention demonstrates a solution-focused approach to working with even the most challenging clients, those who are coerced into treatment by community agencies that want to influence clients to adopt the goals, beliefs, and values of the dominant culture. Therapists often feel overwhelmed and hopeless when faced with such difficult problem situations; however, even the most serious situations are seen to contain the seeds of solutions. Exceptions to problems, the solutions, are identified and amplified, with clients demonstrating strengths and the capacity for their own change.

REFERENCES

Berg, I. K. (1994). *Family-based services: A solution-focused approach.* New York: W.W. Norton.

Cade, B. and O'Hanlon, W. H. (1993). *A brief guide to brief therapy.* New York: W.W. Norton.

O'Hanlon, W. H. and Weiner-Davis, M. (1989). *In search of solutions: A new direction in psychotherapy.* New York: W.W. Norton.

98

An Older Child or a Young Adult?
An Intervention Based
on the Integrated Model

Victor H. Nelson

The following intervention is based on an integrated model of family therapy (Ault-Riché and Rosenthal, 1986) which incorporates the assumptions, tenets, and techniques of three family therapy models: structural, strategic, and intergenerational family therapy. This model is particularly effective for therapy with adolescents and their families.

The "older child or young adult?" intervention emphasizes the structural (Minuchin, 1974) importance of clearly defined boundaries between the parent-child subsystems that keep parents in charge of parenting. It punctuates key interactions to change a behavioral sequence in the parent-child interaction, a strategy utilized by strategic therapists (Watzlawick, Weakland, and Fisch, 1974). It also draws from the intergenerational concept of differentiation (Bowen, 1978) to engage the thinking processes of both the parents and the adolescent so each can learn to avoid simply reacting to the emotionality of the interactions in the relationship. The elegance of this intervention lies in its simplicity and in the immediate effect it has on both parents and adolescents. The content of the issues that initially organized the interactions between the parents and the adolescent becomes secondary to the process of how they are attempting to manage their relationship differences or disagreements.

The very first family with whom I used this intervention included a fourteen-year-old girl and both of her parents, so I will refer to "the daughter" or "her" when speaking of the adolescent and "the parents," or "they" when referring to her parents. The intervention applies equally well to families with both male and female adolescents, as well as to two-parent, stepparent, or single-parent families.

I begin the intervention by asking the parents, "Would you rather parent your daughter more like a child who is just getting older or like a young adult?" We then explore how they distinguish between the two parenting approaches, particularly regarding their expectations and whether their own specific parenting behaviors are consistent with their expectations. I underline the basic distinctions between the two approaches: protecting and nurturing form the foundation for parenting the older child; launching and letting go form the foundation for parenting a young adult. The intervention is effective regardless of the parents' response, so long as the parents are able to distinguish between the two parenting styles. Usually, parents *desire to* launch a young adult, but *act out* the more familiar approaches of protecting an older child. There are times when parents state that they still see their child as an older child and intend to parent her accordingly. If this is the case, I ask what they will be doing differently when they decide their daughter is ready to be parented as a young adult and how they will know when that time comes. This initial set of questions provides an organizing framework that helps parents make conscious determinations about the consistency between their parenting aims and approaches. Parents tend to emphasize the responsibilities they expect of their daughter and de-emphasize their daughter's desire for independence at this stage of the intervention.

I next ask the adolescent, "Do you prefer being parented as though you are an older child or a young adult?" I have never heard an adolescent opt for the former; adolescents energetically press toward adulthood. I ask her what she sees as the distinctions between the two. This, too, involves some basic teaching that helps her become more self-aware and categorize her specific behaviors. Adolescents tend to emphasize the independence they seek from their parents and de-emphasize their responsibilities at this stage of the intervention.

By this point in the intervention, conflict between the parents and the daughter has diminished or has been redirected to their respective views about which expectations and behaviors fall into which of the two categories. Energy levels actually can go up as the parents and daughter experience a higher level of intensity in their relationship, but one that is also less threatening to their relationship.

In cases where the level of intensity is so great that the parents and their child have difficulty talking about these differences or agreeing about them, a homework assignment (strategic) can allow them to separate from each other without separating from the issue. I tell the parents and the adolescent, "Make a list of all the possible behaviors and their consequences that you think apply to young adults and all those which you think apply to an older child. Don't compare your lists with each other until our next session." Usually, however, the intervention can proceed in one session.

I then suggest that the parents pay more attention to what their daughter does than what she says; her *behavior,* not her words, is how she will indicate the kind of parenting she needs. If she says she wants to be treated like a young adult (launching) but acts in ways that tell her parents she needs closer supervision (protection), the parents are instructed to respond to the behavior and provide protection. The parents might say something like, "I understand what you said about wanting to be treated like a young adult, and I want to parent you as a young adult, but your behavior indicates you still want us parents to take charge of your behavior and take care of you." Such a comment may evoke responses ranging from denial to explosive outburst to (miraculously!) cooperation on the part of the adolescent. It does not take long for most adolescents to catch on that their parents will relinquish control and extend limits only when they are certain that their child can manage self-control, accept consequences, and align her behavior with her parents' expectations.

The family can demonstrate how well they understand these two categories by enacting (structural) a minor issue that they have dealt with, such as curfew times. I act as a coach to help each of them assess their intentions and behavior, and whether or not these intentions and behavior fit the older child category or the young adult category. The degree to which she is able to make her case by acting out of the young adult framework, the more likely it is that her parents will respond to her like a young adult.

Parents quickly learn to ask a simple question that enables the adolescent to shift quickly to a more productive approach: "I'm confused. Are you telling me you want to be treated as a young adult right now or like an older child?" If the adolescent falls into familiar patterns and begins a tantrum, withdraws, or explodes, the parents need not react to the behavior, but simply say, "Oh, now I understand. You want to be an older child right now and have us take care of you." Two or three of these responses are usually sufficient to engage the young adult behavior of the adolescent rather than the older child behavior.

REFERENCES

Ault-Riché, M. and Rosenthal, D. M. (1986). Family therapy with symptomatic adolescents: An integrated model. In G. Leigh and G. Peterson (Eds.), *Adolescents,* pp. 474-504. Cincinnati, OH: South-Western Publishing.

Bowen, M. (1978). *Family therapy in clinical practice.* New York: Jason Aronson.

Minuchin, S. (1974). *Families and family therapy.* Cambridge, MA: Harvard University Press.

Watzlawick, P., Weakland, J., and Fisch, R. (1974). *Change: Principles of problem formation and problem resolution.* New York: W.W. Norton.

99

Balloon Bouquets

Evan F. Hanson

A favorite intervention of mine which is useful with families that are highly conflictual (usually with adolescents) can be both enjoyable and nonthreatening. I call it the "balloon bouquet." This intervention creates an opportunity for the family to see and experience anger while also providing an opportunity to explore and create new options for anger. The family must be at a point where they see anger as something that is negative and harmful to the family.

This intervention is especially useful when anger has become the catalyst for relationships within the family. In a sense, anger has become a form of intimacy that the family uses to "get together" emotionally. As the family drifts apart, the homeostatic mechanism (anger) is activated to restore balance. The family must be willing to try new things, and genuinely must want to try something new other than continually using various forms of anger to relate. It is my experience that the therapist must be well-joined with the family and have a fair amount of emotional "money in the bank" to draw upon. The family must also see the therapist as an ally rather than a manipulator.

GOAL OF THE INTERVENTION

The goal of this intervention is to externalize the problem (White and Epston, 1990). The intervention provides a safe context for the entire family to relate differently in new and nonthreatening ways. This technique also encourages the family to explore new alternatives for relationship other than anger. Finally, when families experience change in session rather than just talking about it, they are more likely to take their experience home and try it.

INTERVENTION

For this intervention, it is important to have the family seated in a circle to avoid overt positions of power. By reducing the inherent power structure, the family generally is more willing to venture into unknown territory. The family is then provided with a package of medium-sized balloons and asked to each select a balloon of a color that best represents anger for them. Once the balloons have been selected, the family is asked to choose a recent family argument that involved lots of anger. Using the balloons as a measuring device, each member is asked to inflate the balloon to a size representing their own anger level during the last argument. Once this has been accomplished, each family member has his or her balloon size evaluated by the remainder of the family. If the family feels the amount of air in the balloon does not accurately reflect that person's anger level, more air can be added under the direction of the therapist. This procedure allows the family to interact around the process of anger rather than the content.

The therapist encourages interactions in the family about anger as opening the way for further dialogue and exploration. After each person has had his or her anger balloon adjusted and pinched off, the balloons of anger are held in the center to form the bouquet of anger. At this point the therapist asks, "How does this family deal with all this anger?" Each family member is encouraged to answer the question. Ideas such as letting the air out or letting go of the balloon become metaphors for reducing the anger in families.

The value of this intervention is that it allows the family to experience the problem of anger in nonthreatening and often humorous ways and to consider new options that may be less destructive. On one occasion I was using this intervention with a family that had several adolescents. When I asked the question of how the family deals with all this anger, the youngest boy quickly grabbed his pencil from his pocket and popped everyone's balloons. The family's immediate response was extreme anger, which eventually opened the way for the entire family to interact differently and to see it in ways never considered before.

The therapist can drive home the point of how anger creates pressure in relationships by taking a balloon and blowing it up until it is very full and about to burst. The therapist should then talk about the tension present in the circle as everyone wonders when the balloon will pop. The therapist then asks, "If one balloon could be blown up to represent the collective anger in this family, how large would it be?"

CONTRAINDICATIONS

This intervention does not work well with rigid or extremely dependent families. Rigid families generally are unwilling to attempt anything where the outcome is unknown or the power structure could be threatened, whereas dependent families tend to be unwilling to individuate with balloons of different colors or with different levels of anger. In these families everyone tends to end up with the same color and size balloon, thereby maintaining family enmeshment. This intervention is generally not useful when only one member, such as an adolescent, is the primary member using anger to relate. Isolating and focusing on one family member should be avoided as it tends to galvanize the process rather than creating new options for rotating roles in the family.

REFERENCE

White, M. and Epston, D. (1990). *Narrative means to therapeutic ends.* New York: W.W. Norton.

100

Community Service Intervention

Jon L. Winek

According to the AAMFT code of ethics, version 6.5, "Marriage and Family Therapists participate in activities that contribute to a better community and society, including devoting a portion of their professional activities to services for which there is no financial return" (AAMFT, 1991, p. 8). In most instances, this involves seeing some reduced-fee or pro bono clients. A problem in fulfilling this ethical mandate is that free or reduced-fee therapy can be treated like free advice, which tends to be ignored and results in little therapeutic change. The community service intervention is designed to minimize this effect. In exchange for the therapy they receive at a reduced fee, clients agree to perform community services. The community service intervention allows clients to feel entitled to their treatment and to take more responsibility for therapeutic change.

Finances are the last taboo in the therapy field. A review of the family therapy literature is barren of material on finances for psychotherapy. We all know that money and sex are what couples most frequently fight about, but we do not really address the issue of finances between therapist and clients. Since Freud (1958), analytically minded therapists have seen payment of fees and requests for reduced fees as transference issues. While fees are sometimes a transference issue, there are times when clients simply do not have financial resources or insurance coverage to pay full fee for therapy. The community service intervention allows clients the opportunity to invest in their therapy in another way. By spending their time, energy, and caring doing some form of community service, clients can invest emotionally in their therapy. I have found that it is often the clients' emotional investment, not how much they pay for therapy, that is related to their success.

The community service intervention developed out of frustration that I experienced as an intern. I was building my practice by agreeing to see reduced-fee clients. However, many of my clients were not motivated and seemed to miss appointments and/or drop out of treatment with a frequency with which I was uncomfortable. My supervisor, Michael Drouilhet, first suggested the idea of asking my reduced-fee clients to do something in return for their fee reduction. After some thought about this idea, I put it into practice and refined it. I currently devote a portion of my practice to this work and find it rewarding.

This intervention is consistent with ideas generated in social psychology. Walster, Walster, and Berscheid (1978) developed a theory of social interaction based on what they called equity theory. Their third proposition clearly states:

> When individuals find themselves participating in inequitable relationships, they will become distressed. The more inequitable the relationship, the more distressed individuals will feel. (p. 6)

In instances where clients are being seen for a reduced fee, the distress of the inequitable client-therapist relationship will be added to distress they are already experiencing in their lives. In addition, the therapist can be distressed by the inequity of the relationship. The community service intervention is a mechanism that makes the financial aspects of the client-therapist relationship more equitable.

This intervention can be utilized with individual clients or with entire families. In instances where families come in for therapy, the identified patient and all family members except very young children are asked to engage in community service. There are only a few instances where use of this intervention would be contraindicated. Individuals with character disorders or severe difficulties may not be able to perform the community service. Also, family systems that are already overburdened may not be good candidates for this intervention. In some families, time is as scarce a resource as money and asking them to engage in community service would be an undue hardship. However, in most instances, the key issue is not if they should perform some community service but what service they should perform.

Several different systems at various levels are affected by the community service intervention. First, the clients and their families benefit by feeling entitled as well as motivated to work during their therapy. The intervention is designed to frame the therapy so that it is likely to be more successful. Second, the intervention benefits the community at large. In several instances, clients have terminated therapy successfully, but have continued to perform their community service. Finally, the therapist benefits from the intervention by fulfilling the ethical mandate with more motivated and successful clients. The therapist also develops relationships with the organizations in which their clients volunteer.

The intervention is framed by stating that by seeing clients for a reduced fee, the therapist is performing a community service and is contributing to the good of the community. Therefore, the therapist is asking them to perform some community service in return for the fee reduction so they may feel entitled to treatment. In many therapeutic situations, entitlement is a key therapeutic issue. For example, a depressed client may not feet entitled to a good mood, or a neglected person may not feel entitled to love. By having clients pay their communities for their therapy through service, they are given the opportunity to claim entitlement in a healthy way. Specifically, the intervention allows clients to become entitled to good and successful therapy. The intervention is not meant to be a barter arrangement. It is incorporated into therapy as any homework assignment would be.

The client who contacts you requesting reduced-fee therapy is informed of the community service intervention. It is best to tell the client during the intake that you will be asking them to volunteer somewhere in the community. I also ask clients to think about the type of work they could do and where they would like to volunteer. This helps clients prepare to work in therapy. As Napier and Whitaker (1978) would say, it helps the therapist win the battle for initiative. When a client requests help and you respond with a request that they give help to someone else, you are giving them the initiative. Clients come to know that therapeutic success is their responsibility and that you will act as a consultant, not a caretaker.

During the intake session, a site is selected. It is important that the clients be involved in the selection of the site where they will be performing their community service. Clients are encouraged to provide services in locations that might produce positive therapeutic experiences for them. This is accomplished by carefully considering the clients' presenting problems when suggesting placement. Through exposure to different contexts, clients may experience shifts in their interpretations of their own contexts. Examples include depressed clients working at nursing homes or physical abuse survivors who are further along in their recovery volunteering at domestic violence shelters. Other placement site examples include hospitals, homeless shelters, day care centers, schools, drug rehabilitation clinics, and animal shelters.

After a site is agreed upon, a contract is drawn up between the therapist and client. Clients should do enough community service that they can incorporate the experience into their growth. Some clients take on so much community responsibility that it distracts from their treatment. My experience has shown that two to four hours a week is a good range of involvement to promote growth. Contracts should be written. I like the contract to be simple and open such as the sample that follows:

SAMPLE CONTRACT

I, _____, agree to perform _____

hours of community service at _____

in exchange for each hour of family therapy that I receive at a reduced

fee. I understand that if the community service becomes emotionally

overwhelming, I can renegotiate the contract at any time.

As therapy progresses, I periodically ask clients about their experiences. Clients are encouraged to discuss how their experiences are affecting their self-concepts. Placements often suggest natural reframes of the clients' contexts. For example, a depressed woman who was volunteering at a nursing home started to think differently about her depression. She said that the nursing home was full of people who were depressed because they could not get out. She became angry at herself because she had the physical strength to get out of her house but not the emotional strength. She further reported that she just started to get out and do things. This activity helped her feel less depressed. When asked about her depressed feelings, she stated that she is saving them until she is old and unable to get out. Once this shift occurs, therapy simply supports the change that has occurred and gives witness to the differences in the client.

Even if such a dramatic shift does not occur, the intervention improves clients' motivation. The idea of doing something to be entitled to the therapy moves therapy from a passive to an active part of the clients' lives. If the client is having difficulty performing the service or becomes overwhelmed, the contract is renegotiated. In most instances, this is unnecessary and the client is able to perform the community service, which becomes an integral part of treatment.

REFERENCES

American Association for Marriage and Family Therapy. (1991). *American Association for Marriage and Family Therapy code of ethics.* Washington, DC: Author.

Freud, S. (1958). Further recommendations in the technique of psychoanalysis: On beginning the treatment. In J. Strachey (Ed. and Trans.), *The standard edition of the complete psychological works of Sigmund Freud.* London: Hogarth Press.

Napier, A. and Whitaker, C. (1978). *The family crucible.* New York: Harper & Row.

Walster, E., Walster, G., and Berscheid, E. (1978). *Equity: Theory and research.* Boston: Allyn and Bacon.

101

Training in Family Therapy

Shannon B. Dermer

Family therapists work with a range of family configurations and types of clients. One of the most delightful types of client is the teenager. As we all know, teenagers are predisposed to being cooperative, verbal, realistic creatures that obey their parents and relish attending sessions. However, once in a blue moon a family therapist will meet an obstinate, rebellious adolescent, the type of youth that thinks s/he knows it all and if only the family would do what the teenager requests, then all would be right with the world.

Although one would conclude, based on this last sentence, that the latter type of adolescent bears no resemblance to a therapist, some teenagers behave as if they are family therapists. Family therapy literature has referred to the parentified child, but after entering the teenage years, s/he may covertly act as the "family therapist." S/he tries to take care of the family relationships, mediate between members, and often tries to emotionally support parents. Making this job position overt by teaching the teenager therapy basics along with the ethical guidelines that constrain therapist behavior is an effective way to reach therapeutic goals without engaging in power struggles.

Training consists of acknowledging the teenager's intelligence, interest in the workings of his or her family, and making overt many of the practices of therapy—not signing the teenager up in the nearest marriage and family therapy program. Training the client in the ways of family therapists is especially helpful in cases where the teenager has previously been in therapy and acts like he or she knows all the "tricks" of therapy. Teaching the teenager about family therapy alters the relationship from expert and client to an apprentice-type relationship in which the therapist shares with the client the secrets of the trade. The advantages of creating a more collaborative relationship include engaging the teenager in the therapy process and diffusing power struggles.

The following is a case example in which the teenager's attempt at being a family therapist was made overt. The "hired therapist" accepted the teenager's tendency to act like a therapist and reinforced it as long as she agreed to follow a "code of ethics."

CASE EXAMPLE

Chris was a sixteen-year-old female referred to therapy after being released from an inpatient hospital setting. The mother, Chris, and two younger brothers were being seen in family therapy and Chris also attended individual therapy. Chris had been in the inpatient setting for thirty days after physically assaulting her two younger brothers.

Before Chris entered the inpatient setting she experienced extreme mood swings, but improved after taking medication. After her release she continued medication and utilized some of the anger management and communication skills she learned while hospitalized. When I started meeting with Chris she had been home two weeks and was interacting with her family without violence.

In many ways Chris was a typical teenager. She focused on her friends, rebelled against authority, maintained average grades, and loved her family but fought with them constantly. She had an overresponsible role in the family in which she often took care of the house and her younger siblings, and was the mother's confidante. However, she did not possess the skills to parent her siblings effectively and sometimes hit them when she was frustrated.

The major point one noticed when talking with Chris was her grandiosity. Chris assumed she knew more than anyone else in her family and had a special "power" over people. She believed that she could read people very well and then use this knowledge to manipulate them. In the past, she had used this power to harm people, but decided she wanted to start using it for more constructive purposes. In fact, she expressed interest in someday assisting teenagers by entering the mental health field.

I acknowledged Chris's intelligence, ability to scrutinize people, the progress she had made thus far, and her attempts at using her power for good instead of bad. In fact, I was so impressed by her mental capabilities and her interest in becoming a therapist that I offered to teach her the basics of therapy. However, there was one hitch: she had to agree to follow a code of ethics.

Two statements made up the basic code of ethics: (1) The knowledge she gained about therapy could not be used to harm others and; (2) Chris could not have any dual relationships. Chris was to utilize the information she gained to understand relationships better and to learn a little about how to do therapy. In addition, the rule about dual relationships meant that she could not be a family therapist within her own family or with friends. She agreed to the ground rules and part of each session was set aside for teaching Chris about family therapy.

We discussed such topics as systems theory, boundaries, patterns, triangles, and basic professional issues. The topics for lessons emerged from Chris's questions, or related to the content or process during session. For example, after discussing the fact that Chris did not like it when her mother revealed to Chris details about her love life we talked about boundaries and the basics of structural theory. Afterward we discussed how Chris could maintain her boundaries while still respecting her mother's position in the family. In addition, when looking at patterns of behavior that Chris shared with her mother we discussed the basics of transgenerational theory. Subsequently we addressed what she would like to do differently than her family. In addition, Chris would sometimes ask questions such as how therapists decide who to see in therapy, what questions to ask, and how therapists know if people are telling the truth. Each question was answered and related to issues in Chris's life or the therapy process.

SUMMARY

Chris was an intelligent young woman who enjoyed using her intellectual and observational abilities to place herself in a one-up position with her family, friends, and teachers. In particular, she enjoyed trying to beat therapists at their own game by out-therapizing them. Instead of engaging Chris in this covert power struggle, the patterns were made overt and reframed within a positive context. There was nothing wrong with many of the things she was doing as long as there were limitations to their use.

Not only did the agreement to teach Chris about family therapy reframe and set limits on many of her behaviors, it also allowed for a deeper level of processing within sessions. For example, one day Chris asked a personal question in therapy and I used that question as a training moment and as a way to set boundaries. I stopped the session and explained to her that therapists have to weigh how answering personal questions will benefit or take away from therapy. I processed my thoughts about answering her question aloud and decided to answer it. At a later point in the session she asked another personal question and then stopped me before I could say anything because she decided, based on our previous conversation, that it was not an appropriate line of inquiry. She began utilizing her knowledge not only to analyze relationships, but also to monitor herself.

Training Chris in the ways of a family therapist set boundaries with her role in her family, tapped into her strengths, appealed to something that motivated her, and allowed us to have conversations around therapeutic issues that therapists often find difficult to discuss. I was able to address these issues and ask her to practice them within the realm of warning about family therapy. Chris learned new concepts and readily practiced them within sessions.

CONTRAINDICATIONS

Chris and I met in individual sessions, which meant that I did not have to worry about usurping parental power or about balancing the needs of other people in the family during session. Teaching a teenager about family therapy other than in individual sessions may not be practical. In addition, although the client did tend to get into quite a bit of trouble, she had a basic sense of fairness and of what is right or wrong. Therefore, I trusted her when she stated that she would abide by the code of ethics. Without this . trust, training could easily become one more way to try to one-up the therapist. However, as long as the therapist keeps tying the training back to the issues that happen in and out of session, this should not be a problem.

CONCLUSION

The intervention described was a combination of solution-focused and structural/strategic therapy. We focused on her strengths and reframed many of her problems as strengths taken to an extreme. In addition, we focused on her current and future goals. It was pointed out that her current behavior was not congruent with reaching her goals. Chris's behaviors did not necessarily need to be eradicated, but she did need to alter some of the patterns of how, when, and why she used them. Unfortunately, pointing out this incongruence is usually not enough in itself. Because power was very important to Chris, a way had to be found for her to reach her goals without feeling like she was giving in. This task was accomplished under the umbrella of teaching her about being a therapist. Learning about family therapy was contingent upon her adherence to a basic code of ethics that all therapists have to follow.

Making her attempts at being the family therapist overt, teaching her about therapy basics, and having her follow the ethical guidelines for a therapist was an effective means, in this case, to reach therapeutic goals without getting into power struggles. This process is not meant to train clients to become therapists. Rather, it is meant to demystify therapy, bypass power struggles, and create an alliance between therapist and teenager.

Topical Index

Entries are listed by volume and intervention number. "Vol. 1" refers to *101 Interventions in Family Therapy* (1993); "Vol. 2" refers to *101 More Interventions in Family Therapy* (1998).

Order Your Own Copy of
This Important Book for Your Personal Library!

101 MORE INTERVENTIONS IN FAMILY THERAPY

_____ in hardbound at $69.95 (ISBN: 0-7890-0058-X)

_____ in softbound at $39.95 (ISBN: 0-7890-0570-0)

COST OF BOOKS_____

OUTSIDE USA/CANADA/
MEXICO: ADD 20%_____

POSTAGE & HANDLING_____
(US: $3.00 for first book & $1.25
for each additional book)
Outside US: $4.75 for first book
& $1.75 for each additional book)

SUBTOTAL_____

IN CANADA: ADD 7% GST_____

STATE TAX_____
(NY, OH & MN residents, please
add appropriate local sales tax)

FINAL TOTAL_____
(If paying in Canadian funds,
convert using the current
exchange rate. UNESCO
coupons welcome.)

☐ **BILL ME LATER:** (\$5 service charge will be added)
(Bill-me option is good on US/Canada/Mexico orders only;
not good to jobbers, wholesalers, or subscription agencies.)

☐ Check here if billing address is different from
shipping address and attach purchase order and
billing address information.

Signature_____

☐ **PAYMENT ENCLOSED: $**_____

☐ **PLEASE CHARGE TO MY CREDIT CARD.**

☐ Visa   ☐ MasterCard   ☐ AmEx   ☐ Discover
☐ Diner's Club
Account # _____

Exp. Date _____

Signature _____

Prices in US dollars and subject to change without notice.

NAME _____

INSTITUTION _____

ADDRESS _____

CITY _____

STATE/ZIP _____

COUNTRY _____ COUNTY (NY residents only) _____

TEL _____ FAX _____

E-MAIL_____
May we use your e-mail address for confirmations and other types of information? ☐ Yes   ☐ No

Order From Your Local Bookstore or Directly From
The Haworth Press, Inc.
10 Alice Street, Binghamton, New York 13904-1580 • USA
TELEPHONE: 1-800-HAWORTH (1-800-429-6784) / Outside US/Canada: (607) 722-5857
FAX: 1-800-895-0582 / Outside US/Canada: (607) 772-6362
E-mail: getinfo@haworthpressinc.com
PLEASE PHOTOCOPY THIS FORM FOR YOUR PERSONAL USE.

BOF96